MW00476966

THE
ESOTERIC WORLD
OF
Madame
Blavatsky

THE
ESOTERIC WORLD
OF
Madame
Blavatsky

INSIGHTS INTO THE LIFE
OF A MODERN SPHINX

COLLECTED BY
DANIEL H. CALDWELL

Quest Books
Theosophical Publishing House

Wheaton, Illinois ◆ Chennai (Madras), India

The Theosophical Society in America and
The Theosophical Publishing House
gratefully acknowledge the support of the
Kern Foundationin the publication of this book.

Originally published as *The Occult World of Madame Blavatsky*
© 1991 by Daniel H. Caldwell

First Quest Edition 2000
© 2000 by the Theosophical Society in America.
All rights reserved. No part of this book may be
reproduced in any manner without written permission
except for quotations embodied in critical articles or reviews.
For additional information write to

Quest Books
Theosophical Publishing House
P. O. Box 270
Wheaton, IL 60189–0270

Library of Congress Cataloging-in-Publication Data

Occult world of Madame Blavatsky
  The esoteric world of Madame Blavatsky : insights into the life of a
modern sphinx / collected by Daniel Caldwell.
      p. cm.
  Originally published: The occult world of Madame Blavatsky. 1st ed.
Tucson, Ariz. : Impossible Dream Publications, 1991.
  Includes bibliographical references and index.
  ISBN 0-8356-0794-1
  1. Blavatsky, H. P. (Helena Petrovna), 1831–1891. 2. Theosophists—
Biography. I. Caldwell, Daniel H. II. Title.

BP585.B6 O23 2000
299'.934'092—dc21
[B]
                                                              00-058959

         10 09 08 07 06 05 04 03 02 01 00   5 4 3 2 1

Cover and interior design by Dan Doolin
Index by Michelle Graye

Printed in the United States of America

Contents

List of Illustrations

Preface

*H*ere for the first time is the story of H. P. Blavatsky's life in the words of her contemporaries. Although not a biography per se, this book tells the story of Madame Blavatsky's eventful life with a special look at the "Esoteric World" in which she lived. These reminiscences by her relatives, acquaintances, friends, co-workers, and enemies give a vivid portrayal of Madame Blavatsky's personality and allow the reader to enter into the historical milieu of her time.

The narratives, which are arranged in chronological order, include

- striking word portraits of HPB;
- reminiscences giving insight into HPB's enigmatic character;
- incidents that are sometimes humorous and witty;
- accounts of HPB's psychic phenomena; and
- descriptions of encounters with HPB's Masters.

Each chapter begins with a brief sketch of HPB's life during the period it covers. Each narrative starts with an identification of its author, time period, and location. Biographical information about the authors is in the section titled "Biographical Sketches" at the back of the book. The narratives have been transcribed from the original sources with spelling and punctuation modernized. For people's names, the spelling used in HPB's *Collected Writings* (vols. 1 and 15) has been adopted. Material not relevant to the immediate narrative has been silently deleted. The original texts, however, can be found from the bibliographical references. Explanatory notes added by the editor are enclosed within square brackets.

I should like to dedicate this book to Walter A. Carrithers, Jr. (1924–1994), author of *Obituary: The "Hodgson Report" on Madame Blavatsky* and *The Truth about Madame Blavatsky*. Walter always gave me encouragement in my Theosophical and Blavatsky studies.

Special thanks and appreciation to John Algeo, Mary Lessie Caldwell, David M. Dunkle, and Michelle B. Graye for their help and support on this book.

I would also like to express my gratitude and appreciation to the following individuals who have helped me in my research on the life of Madame Blavatsky: Dorothy Abbenhouse, Anita Atkins, Geoffrey A. Barborka, John Cooper, Ted G. Davy, Boris de Zirkoff, Dara Eklund, Caren M. Elin, Victor A. Endersby, Michael Freeman, Michael Gomes, Virginia G. Hanson, Jerry Hejka-Ekins, Grace F. Knoche, Mary J. Schneider Kokochak, George E. Linton, Joy Mills, Lakshmi Narayan, Ernest Pelletier, Rogelle Pelletier, David Pratt, Leslie Price, David Reigle, Nancy Reigle, Richard Robb, Carmen Small, W. Emmett Small, H. J. Spierenburg, Leona Sterba, Joan Sutcliffe, Dallas TenBroeck, Will Thackara, Gregory Tillett, Elisabeth Trumpler, John Van Mater, Kirby Van Mater, Henry Van Thiel, and Maikka Van Thiel.

If readers have any questions or comments concerning the subject matter covered in this book, they may address inquiries to me:

Daniel H. Caldwell
P. O. Box 1844
Tucson, Arizona 85702
U.S.A.

Helena de Fadeyev (HPB's mother)

Chapter 1

RUSSIA
1831–1849

HELENA PETROVNA VON HAHN was born at Ekaterinoslav, a town on the river Dnieper, in Southern Russia, on August 12, 1831. She was the daughter of Colonel Peter von Hahn and Helena de Fadeyev, a renowned novelist. On her mother's side, she was the granddaughter of the gifted Princess Helena Dolgorukov, a noted botanist and writer. After the early death of her mother in 1842, Helena was brought up in her maternal grandparents' house at Saratov, where her grandfather was Civil Governor.

Helena was an exceptional child, who at an early age was aware of being different from those around her. Her possession of certain psychic powers puzzled her family and friends. At once impatient of all authority, yet deeply sensitive, she was gifted in many ways. A clever linguist, a talented pianist, and a fine artist, she was yet a fearless rider of half-broken horses, and always in close touch with nature. At a very early age she sensed that she was in some way dedicated to a life of service and was aware of a special guidance and protection.

When almost eighteen, in a mood of rebellious independence and possibly with a plan to become free of her surroundings,

she married the middle-aged Nikifor V. Blavatsky, Vice-Governor
of the Province of Yerivan. The marriage, as such, meant nothing
to her and was never consummated.

1a. The Birth of Helena Petrovna von Hahn
August 12, 1831, Ekaterinoslav, Southern Russia

[Sinnett 1886, 18–20]

The baby [Helena Petrovna] was born on the night between
[August 11 and 12, 1831]—weak, and apparently no denizen of
this world. A hurried baptism had to be resorted to, therefore, lest
the child died with the burden of original sin on her soul. The
ceremony of baptism in orthodox Russia is attended with all the
paraphernalia of lighted tapers, and pairs of godmothers and god-
fathers, every one of the spectators and actors being furnished
with consecrated wax candles during the whole proceedings.
Moreover, everyone has to stand during the baptismal rite, no one
being allowed to sit in the Greek religion, as they do in Roman
Catholic and Protestant churches, during the church and religious
service. The room selected for the ceremony in the family mansion was large, but the crowd of devotees eager to witness it was
still larger. Behind the priest officiating in the center of the room,
with his assistants, in their golden robes and long hair, stood the
three pairs of sponsors and the whole household of vassals and
serfs. The child-aunt of the baby—only a few years older than her
niece, aged twenty-four hours—placed as "proxy" for an absent
relative, was in the first row. Feeling nervous and tired of standing
still for nearly an hour, the child settled on the floor unperceived
by the elders, and became probably drowsy in the over-crowded
room on that hot day. The ceremony was nearing its close. The
sponsors were just in the act of renouncing the Evil One and his
deeds, a renunciation emphasized in the Greek Church by thrice

spitting upon the invisible enemy, when the little lady, toying with her lighted taper at the feet of the crowd, inadvertently set fire to the long flowing robes of the priest. The result was an immediate conflagration, during which several persons—chiefly the old priest—were severely burnt. That was [a] bad omen, according to the superstitious beliefs of orthodox Russia; and the innocent cause of it—the future Mme. Blavatsky—was doomed from that day in the eyes of all the town to an eventful life, full of trouble.

1B. VERA P. DE ZHELIHOVSKY (HPB'S SISTER) 1842–1846, SARATOV, RUSSIA (WHERE HPB'S MATERNAL GRANDPARENTS LIVED)

[Collated from Zhelihovsky 1894–5, 203, 204, 203; and Sinnett 1886, 30–5, 37–9]

Helena was a precocious child, and from her earliest youth attracted the attention of all with whom she came in contact. Her nature was quite intractable to the routine demanded by her instructors; she rebelled against all discipline, recognized no master but her own good will and her personal tastes. She was exclusive, original, and at times bold even to roughness.

When her mother was dying, although her eldest daughter was only eleven years old, she was filled with well-founded apprehensions for her future, and said: "Ah well! perhaps it is best that I am dying, so at least I shall be spared seeing what befalls Helena! Of one thing I am certain, her life will not be as that of other women, and that she will have much to suffer!!"

At the death of our mother, we went to live with her parents. The great country mansion occupied by us at Saratov, was an old and vast building, full of subterranean galleries, long abandoned passages, turrets, and most weird nooks and corners. It looked more like a medieval ruined castle than a building of the past century. The man who took care of the estate for the proprietors had been known for his cruelty and tyranny. The legends told of his ferocious and despotic temper, of unfortunate serfs beaten by him to death, and imprisoned for months in dark subterranean dungeons, were many and thrilling. Our heads were full of stories about the ghosts of the martyred serfs, seen promenading in chains during nocturnal hours and other stories that left us children and girls in an agony of fear whenever we had to cross a dark room or passage. We had been permitted to explore, under the protection of half a dozen male servants and a quantity of torches and lanterns, those awe-inspiring "catacombs." Still Helena would not remain satisfied with one solitary visit, nor with a second either. She had selected the uncanny region as a safe refuge where she could avoid her lessons. A long time passed before her secret was found out, and whenever she was found missing, a deputation of strong-bodied servant men was dispatched in search of her. She had erected for herself a tower out of old broken chairs and tables in a corner under an iron-barred window, high up in the ceiling of the vault, and there she would hide for hours, reading a book known as "Solomon's Wisdom," in which every kind of popular legend was taught. Once or twice she could hardly be found in those damp subterranean corridors, having—in her endeavors to escape detection—lost her way in the labyrinth. For all this she was not in the least daunted or repentant, for, as she assured us, she was never there alone, but in the company of "beings" she used to call her little "hunch-backs" and playmates.

Intensely nervous and sensitive, speaking loud, and often walking in her sleep, she used to be found at nights in the most out-of-way places, and to be carried back to her bed profoundly asleep. Thus she was missed from her room one night when she was hardly twelve, and the alarm having been given, she was searched for and found pacing one of the long subterranean corridors, evidently in deep conversation with someone invisible for all but herself. She was the strangest girl one has ever seen, one with a distinct dual nature in her, that made one think there were two

Vera P. de Zhelihovsky (HPB's sister)

beings in one and the same body; one mischievous, combative, and obstinate—every way graceless; the other mystical and meta-physically inclined. No schoolboy was ever more uncontrollable or full of the most unimaginable and daring pranks as she was. At the same time, when the paroxysm of mischief-making had run its course, no old scholar could be more assiduous in his study, and she could not be prevailed to give up her books, which she would devour night and day as long as the impulse lasted. The enormous library of her grandparents seemed then hardly large enough to satisfy her cravings.

Fancy, or that which we all regarded in these days as fancy, was developed in the most extraordinary way, and from her earli-est childhood, in my sister Helena. For hours at times she used to

5

narrate to us younger children, and even to her seniors in years, the most incredible stories with the cool assurance and conviction of an eyewitness and one who knew what she was talking about. When a child, daring and fearless in everything else, she got often scared into fits through her own hallucinations. She felt certain of being persecuted by what she called "the terrible glaring eyes" invisible to everyone else and often attributed by her to the most inoffensive inanimate objects; an idea that appeared quite ridiculous to the bystanders. As to herself, she would shut her eyes tight during such visions, and run away to hide from the ghostly glances thrown on her by pieces of furniture or articles of dress, screaming desperately, and frightening the whole household. At other times she would be seized with fits of laughter, explaining them by the amusing pranks of her invisible companions. Every locked door notwithstanding, Helena was found several times during the night hours in those dark apartments in a half-conscious state, sometimes fast asleep, and unable to say how she got there from our common bedroom on the top story. She disappeared in the same mysterious manner in daytime also. Searched for, called and hunted after, she would be often discovered, with great pains, in the most unfrequented localities; once it was in the dark loft, under the very roof, to which she was traced, amid pigeons' nests, and surrounded by hundreds of those birds. She was "putting them to sleep" (according to the rules taught in "Solomon's Wisdom"), as she explained. And, indeed, pigeons were found, if not asleep, still unable to move, and as though stunned, in her lap at such times.

For her all nature seemed animated with a mysterious life of its own. She heard the voice of every object and form, whether organic or inorganic; and claimed consciousness and being, not only for some mysterious powers visible and audible for herself alone in what was to every one else empty space, but even for visible but inanimate things such as pebbles, mounds, and pieces of decaying phosphorescent timber.

At about [6.6 miles] from the Governor's villa there was a field, an extensive sandy tract of land, evidently once upon a time the bottom of a sea or a great lake, as its soil yielded petrified relics of fishes, shells, and teeth of some (to us) unknown monsters. Most of these relics were broken and mangled by time, but one could often find whole stones of various sizes on which were imprinted figures of fishes and plants and animals of kinds now wholly extinct, but which proved their undeniable antediluvian origin. The marvelous and sensational stories that we, children and schoolgirls, heard from Helena were countless. I well remember when stretched at full length on the ground, her chin reclining on her two palms, and her two elbows buried deep in the soft sand, she used to dream aloud, and tell us of her visions, evidently clear, vivid, and palpable as life to her! How vividly she described their past fights and battles on the spot where she lay, assuring us she saw it all; and how minutely she drew on the sand with her finger the fantastic forms of the long dead sea monsters, and made us almost see the very colors of the fauna and flora of those dead regions. While listening eagerly to her descriptions of the lovely azure waves reflecting the sunbeams playing in the rainbow lights on the golden sands of the sea bottom, of the coral reefs and stalactite caves, of the sea-green grass mixed with the delicate shining anemones, our imagination galloped off with her fancy to a full oblivion of the present reality. She never spoke in later years as she used to speak in her childhood and early girlhood. The stream of her eloquence has dried up, and the very source of her inspiration is now seeming lost! She had a strong power of carrying away her audiences with her, of making them see actually, if even vaguely, that which she herself saw. Once she frightened all of us youngsters very nearly into fits. We had just been transported into a fairy world, when suddenly she changed her narrative from the past to the present tense, and began to ask us to imagine that all that which she had told us of the cool blue waves with their dense populations, was around us, only invisible and intangible, so far. "Just fancy! A miracle!" she said; "the earth suddenly opening, the air condensing around us and rebecoming sea waves. Look, look . . . there, they begin already appearing and moving. We are surrounded with water amid the mysteries and the wonders of a submarine world!"

She had started from the sand, and was speaking with such conviction, her voice had such a ring of real amazement, horror, and her childish face wore such a look of a wild joy and terror at the same time, that when, suddenly covering her eyes with both hands, as she used to do in her excited moments, she fell down on the sand, screaming at the top of her voice, "There's the wave . . . it has come! . . . The sea, the sea, we are drowning!" Everyone of us fell down on our faces, as desperately screaming and as fully convinced that the sea had engulfed us, and that we were no more!

Nadyezhda A. de Fadeyev (HPB's aunt)

1c. Nadyezhda A. de Fadeyev (HPB's aunt) 1831–1849, Russia

[Sinnett 1886, 26–8]

From her earliest childhood she was unlike any other person. Very lively and highly gifted, full of humor and of most remarkable daring, she struck everyone with astonishment by her self-willed and determined actions. Thus in her earliest youth and hardly married, she disposed of herself in an angry mood, abandoning her country, without the knowledge of her relatives or husband, who, unfortunately was a man in every way unsuited to her and more than thrice her age. Her restless and very nervous temperament, one that led her into the most unheard of, ungirlish mischief; her unaccountable—especially in those days—attraction to, and at the same time fear of, the dead; her passionate love and curiosity for everything unknown and mysterious, weird, and fantastical; and, foremost of all, her craving for independence and freedom of action—a craving that nothing and nobody could control—all this, combined with an exuberance of imagination and wonderful sensitiveness, ought to have warned her friends that she was an exceptional creature, to be dealt with and controlled by means as exceptional. The slightest contradiction brought on an outburst of passion, often a fit of convulsion. Left alone with no one near her to impede her liberty of action, no hand to chain her down or stop her natural impulses, and thus arouse to fury her inherent combativeness, she would spend hours and days quietly whispering, as people thought, to herself, and narrating, with no one near her, in some dark corner, marvelous tales of travels in bright stars and other worlds, which her governess described as "profane gibberish"; but no sooner would the governess give her a distinct order to do this or the other thing than her first impulse was to disobey. It was enough to forbid her doing a thing to make her do it, come what would. Her nurse, as indeed other members of the family, sincerely believed the child

9

possessed "the seven spirits of rebellion." Her governesses were martyrs to their task, and never succeeded in bending her resolute will, or influencing by anything but kindness her indomitable, obstinate, and fearless nature.

Spoilt in her childhood by the adulation of dependents and the devoted affection of relatives, who forgave all to "the poor, motherless child"—later on, in her girlhood, her self-willed temper made her rebel openly against the exigencies of society. She would submit to no sham respect for or fear of the public opinion. She *would* ride at fifteen, as she had at ten, any Cossack horse on a man's saddle! She would bow to no one, as she would recede before no prejudice or established conventionality. She defied all and everyone. As in her childhood, all her sympathies and attractions went out towards people of the lower class. She had always preferred to play with her servants' children rather than with her equals, and as a child had to be constantly watched for fear she should escape from the house to make friends with ragged street boys. So, later on in life, she continued to be drawn in sympathy towards those who were in a humbler station of life than herself, and showed as pronounced indifference to the "nobility" to which by birth she belonged.

1D. NADYEZHDA A. DE FADEYEV
SPRING AND SUMMER 1849, RUSSIA

[Sinnett 1886, 54–5]

[Helena] cared not whether she should get married or not. She had been simply defied one day by her governess to find any man who would be her husband, in view of her temper and disposition. The governess, to emphasize the taunt, said that even the old man [Nikifor V. Blavatsky] she had found so ugly, and had laughed at so much, calling him "a plumeless raven"—that even he would decline her for a wife! That was enough: three days after she made him propose, and then, frightened at what she had done, sought to escape from her joking acceptance of his offer. But it was too late. Hence the fatal step. All she knew and understood was— when *too late*—that she had been accepting, and was now forced to accept—a *master* she cared nothing for, nay, that she hated, that she was *tied* to him by the law of the country, hand and foot. A "great horror" crept upon her, as she explained it later; one desire, ardent, unceasing, irresistible, got hold of her entire being, led her on, so to say, by the hand, forcing her to act instinctively, as she would have done if, in the act of saving her life, she had been running away from a mortal danger. There had been a distinct attempt to impress her with the solemnity of marriage, with her future obligations and her duties to her *husband*, and married life. A few hours later, at the altar, she heard the priest saying to her, "Thou shalt honor and obey thy husband," and at this hated word, "shalt," her young face was seen to flush angrily, then to become deadly pale. She was overheard to mutter in response, through her set teeth, "Surely, I *shall* not."

And surely she has not. Forthwith she determined to take the law and her future life into her own hands, and she left her "husband" for ever, without giving him any opportunity to ever even think of her as *his wife*.

Thus Mme. Blavatsky abandoned her country at seventeen, and passed ten long years in strange and out-of-the-way places, in Central Asia, India, South America, Africa, and Eastern Europe.

H. P. Blavatsky in her youth

Chapter 2

TRAVELS AROUND THE WORLD AND HOME TO RUSSIA
1849–1865

A FEW MONTHS after her marriage, Helena escaped from Russia and traveled widely in Turkey, Egypt, and Greece with money supplied by her father.

On her twentieth birthday, in 1851, being then in London, she met the individual whom she had known in her psycho-spiritual visions from childhood—an Eastern Initiate of Rajput birth, the Mahatma Morya or M, as he became known in later years among Theosophists. He told her something of the work that was in store for her, and from that moment she accepted fully his guidance.

Later the same year, Helena embarked for Canada, and after adventurous travels in various parts of the United States, Mexico, South America, and the West Indies, went via the Cape and Sri Lanka to India in 1852. Her first attempt to enter Tibet failed. She returned to England via Java in 1853. In the Summer of 1854, she went to America again, crossing the Rockies with a caravan of emigrants, probably in a covered wagon.

In late 1855, she left for India via Japan and the Straits. On this trip she succeeded in entering Tibet through Kashmir and Ladakh, undergoing part of her esoteric training with her Master. In 1858 she was in France and Germany, returning to Russia in the late fall of the same year to stay a short time with her sister Vera at Pskov. From 1860 to 1865, she lived in and traveled through the Caucasus, experiencing a severe physical and psychic crisis that placed her in complete control over her occult powers.

2A. COUNTESS CONSTANCE WACHTMEISTER
1851, LONDON

[Wachtmeister 1893, 56–7]

During her childhood [Madame Blavatsky] had often seen near her an Astral form, that always seemed to come in any moment of danger, and save her just at the critical point. HPB had learnt to look upon this Astral form as a guardian angel, and felt that she was under His care and guidance.

In London, in 1851, she was one day out walking when, to her astonishment, she saw a tall Hindu in the street with some Indian princes. She immediately recognized him as the same person that she had seen in the Astral. Her first impulse was to rush forward to speak to him, but he made her a sign not to move, and she stood as if spellbound while he passed on. The next day she went into Hyde Park for a stroll, that she might be alone and free

Countess Constance Wachtmeister

to think over her extraordinary adventure. Looking up, she saw the same form approaching her, and then her Master told her that he had come to London with the Indian princes on an important mission, and he was desirous of meeting her personally, as he required her cooperation in a work which he was about to undertake. He then told her how the Theosophical Society was to be formed, and that he wished her to be the founder. He gave her a slight sketch of all the troubles she would have to undergo, and also told her that she would have to spend three years in Tibet to prepare her for the important task. HPB decided to accept the offer made to her and shortly afterwards left London for India.

2B. VERA P. DE ZHELIHOVSKY
CHRISTMAS DAY 1858 – SPRING 1859, PSKOV, RUSSIA

[Collated from Zhelihovsky 1894–5, 205–6;
and Sinnett 1886, 86, 87–91]

Madame Blavatsky returned to Russia [in 1858]. After her
return, she first came and settled herself in Pskov, where I was living. We were not expecting her to arrive for some weeks to come,
but, curiously enough, no sooner did I hear her ring at the doorbell than I jumped up, knowing that she had arrived. As it happened there was a party going on that evening in my father-in-
law's house, in which I was living. His daughter was to be married
that very evening, the guests were seated at table, and the ringing
of the doorbell was incessant. Nevertheless I was so sure it was she
who had arrived that, to the astonishment of everyone, I hurriedly rose from the wedding feast and ran to open the door, not wishing the servants to do so.

We embraced each other, overcome with joy, forgetting for
the moment the strangeness of the event. I took her at once to my
room, and that very evening I was convinced that my sister had
acquired strange powers. She was constantly surrounded, awake or
asleep, with mysterious movements, strange sounds, little taps
which came from all sides—from the furniture, from the windowpanes, from the ceiling, from the floor, and from the walls. They
were very distinct and seemed intelligent into the bargain; they
tapped once and three times for "yes," twice for "no."

My sister asked me to ask them a mental question. This I did,
selecting a question as to a fact only known to myself. I recited the
alphabet, and the reply I received was so true and so precise that I
was positively astounded. I had often heard talk of spirit-rapping, but
never before had I had an opportunity of testing their knowledge.

Before long the whole town was talking of the "miracles"
which surrounded Madame Blavatsky. The not only intelligent,
but even clairvoyant, answers given by these invisible forces,
which operated night and day, without any apparent intervention

on her part, all round her, struck more astonishment and wonder into the minds of the curious than even the movement of inanimate objects, which apparently gained or lost their weight, which phenomena she directly produced by merely fixing her eyes on the object selected.

It is impossible to give in detail even a portion of what was produced in the way of such phenomena during the stay of Mme. Blavatsky amongst us in the town of Pskov.

The following took place in the presence of many eyewitnesses.

As usual, those nearest and dearest to her were, at the same time, the most skeptical as to her occult powers. Her brother Leonid and her father stood out longer than all against evidence, until at last the doubts of the former were greatly shaken by the following fact.

The drawing room was full of visitors. Some were occupied with music, others with cards, but most of us, as usual, with phenomena. Leonid did not concern himself with anything in particular, but was leisurely walking about, watching everybody and everything. He stopped behind the back of his sister's chair, and was listening to her narratives of how some persons, who called themselves mediums, made light objects become so heavy that it was impossible to lift them, and others which were naturally heavy became again remarkably light.

"And you mean to say that you can do it?" ironically asked the young man of his sister.

"Mediums can, and I have done it occasionally; though I cannot always answer for its success," coolly replied Mme. Blavatsky.

"But would you try?" asked somebody in the room; and immediately all joined in requesting her to do so.

"I will try," she said, "but I beg of you to remember that I promise nothing. I will simply fix this chess table, and try. He who wants to make the experiment, let him lift it now, and then try *again* after I shall have fixed it."

"After you shall have fixed it?" said a voice, "and what then? Do you mean to say that you will not touch the table at all?"

"Why should I touch it?" answered Mme. Blavatsky, with a quiet smile.

Upon hearing the extraordinary assertion, one of the young men went determinedly to the small chess table, and lifted it up as though it were a feather.

"All right," she said. "Now kindly leave it alone, and stand back!"

The order was at once obeyed, and a great silence fell upon the company. All, holding their breath, anxiously watched for what Mme. Blavatsky would do next. She apparently, however, did nothing at all. She merely fixed her large blue eyes upon the chess table, and kept looking at it with an intense gaze. Then, without removing her gaze, she silently, with a motion of her hand, invited the same young man to remove it. He approached, and grasped the table by its leg with great assurance. The table *could not be moved!*

He then seized it with both his hands. The table stood as though screwed to the floor.

Then the young man, crouching down, took hold of it with both hands, exerting all his strength to lift it by the additional means of his broad shoulders. He grew red with the effort, but all in vain! The table seemed rooted to the carpet, and would not be moved. There was a loud burst of applause. The young man, looking very much confused, abandoned his task and stood aside.

Folding his arms in quite a Napoleonic way, he only slowly said, "Well, this is a good joke!"

"Indeed, it is a good one!" echoed Leonid.

A suspicion had crossed his mind that the young visitor was acting in secret confederacy with his sister, and was fooling them.

"May I also try?" he suddenly asked her.

"Please do, my dear," was the laughing response.

Her brother upon this approached, smiling, and seized, in his turn, the diminutive table by its leg with his strong muscular arm. But the smile instantly vanished, to give place to an expression of mute amazement. He stepped back a little and examined again very carefully the, to him, well-known chess table.

Then he gave it a tremendous kick, but the little table did not even budge.

Suddenly applying to its surface his powerful chest he enclosed it within his arms, trying to shake it. The wood cracked, but would yield to no effort. Its three feet seemed screwed to the floor. Then Leonid Hahn lost all hope, and abandoning the ungrateful task, stepped aside, and frowning, exclaimed but these two words, "How strange!" his eyes turning meanwhile with a wild expression of astonishment from the table to his sister.

The loud debate had meanwhile drawn the attention of several visitors, and they came pouring in from the drawing room into where we were. Many of them, old and young, tried to lift up, or even to impart some slight motion to, the obstinate little chess table. They failed, like the rest of us.

Upon seeing her brother's astonishment, and perchance desiring finally to destroy his doubts, Mme. Blavatsky, addressing him with her usual careless laugh, said, "Try to lift the table now, once more!"

Leonid approached the little thing very irresolutely, grasped it again by the leg, and, pulling it upwards, came very nearly to dislocating his arm owing to the useless effort: the table was lifted like a feather this time!

2C. VERA P. DE ZHELIHOVSKY
SPRING 1859, ST. PETERSBURG, RUSSIA

[Sinnett 1886, 91–7]

Mme. Blavatsky left Pskov with her father and sister. Living in a hotel, they had come to St. Petersburg. All their forenoons were occupied with business, their afternoons and evenings with making and receiving visits, and there was no time for, or even mention of, phenomena.

One night they received a visit from two old friends of their father; both were old gentlemen, one of them Baron M———, the other the well-known K———w. Both were much interested in recent spiritualism and were, of course, anxious to see something.

After a few successful phenomena, the visitors declared themselves positively delighted, amazed and quite at a loss what to make of Mme. Blavatsky's powers. They could neither understand nor account, they said, for her father's indifference in presence of such manifestations. There he was, coolly laying out his "*grande patience*" [a solitaire game] with cards, while phenomena of such a wonderful nature were occurring around him. The old gentleman, thus taken to task, answered that it was all bosh and that he would not hear of such nonsense, such occupation being hardly worthy of serious people, he added. The rebuke left the two old gentlemen unconcerned. They began, on the contrary, to insist that Col. Hahn should, for old friendship's sake, make an experiment, before denying the importance or even the possibility of his daughter's phenomena. They offered him to test the *intelligences* and their power by writing a word in another room, secretly from all of them, and then asking the raps to repeat it. The old gentleman, more probably in the hope of a failure that would afford him the opportunity of laughing at his two old friends, than out of a desire to humor them, finally consented. He left his cards, and proceeding into an adjoining room, wrote a word on a bit of paper, after which conveying it to his pocket, he returned to his *patience*, and waited silently, laughing behind his gray moustache.

"Well, our dispute will now be settled in a few moments," said K———w. "What shall you say, however, old friend, if the word written by you is correctly repeated? Will you not feel compelled to believe in such a case?"

"What I might say, *if* the word were correctly guessed, I could not tell at present," he skeptically replied. "One thing I could answer, however, from the time I can be made to believe your alleged spiritism and its phenomena, I shall be ready to believe in the existence of the devil, sorcerers, and witches—

in the whole paraphernalia, in short, of old women's superstitions; and you may prepare to offer me as an inmate of a lunatic asylum."

Upon delivering himself thus, he went on with his *patience*, and paid no further attention to the proceedings. He was an old "Voltarian," as the positivists who believed in nothing, are called in Russia. But we, who felt deeply interested in the experiment, began to listen to the loud and unceasing raps coming from a plate brought there for the purpose.

The younger sister was repeating the alphabet; the old general marked the letters down, while Mme. Blavatsky did nothing at all—apparently.

By the means of raps and alphabet we got *one word*, but it proved such a strange one, so grotesquely absurd, as having no evident relation to anything that might be supposed to have been written by her father, that all of us who had been in the expectation of some complicated sentence looked at each other, dubious whether we ought to read it aloud. To our question, whether it was all, the raps became more energetic in the affirmative. We had several *triple raps*, which meant in our code—Yes! yes, yes, yes!!!

Remarking our agitation and whispering, Madame B.'s father looked at us over his spectacles, and asked—

"Well! Have you any answer? It must be something very elaborate and profound indeed!"

He arose and, laughing in his moustache, approached us.

"We only got *one* word."

"And what is it?"

"*Zaitchik!*"

It was a sight indeed to witness the extraordinary change that came over the old man's face at this one word! He became deadly pale. Adjusting his spectacles with a trembling hand, he stretched it out while hurriedly saying "Let me see it! Hand it over. Is it really so?"

He took the slips of paper, and read in a very agitated voice,—"Zaitchik. Yes, Zaitchik; so it is. How very strange!"

Taking out of his pocket the paper he had written upon in

the adjoining room, he handed it in silence to his daughter and guests.

They found on it both the question offered and the answer that was anticipated. The words read thus—

"What was the name of my favorite warhorse, which I rode during my first Turkish campaign?" And lower down, in parenthesis: ("Zaitchik").

This solitary word, *Zaitchik*, had an enormous effect upon the old gentleman. As it often happens with inveterate skeptics, once that he had found out that there was indeed *something* in his eldest daughter's claims, and that it had nothing to do whatever with deceit or juggling, having been convinced of this one fact, he rushed into the region of phenomena with all the zeal of an ardent investigator. As a matter of course, once he believed he felt no more inclined to doubt his own reason.

Having received from Mme. Blavatsky one correct answer, her father became passionately fond of experimenting with his daughter's powers.

2D. VERA P. DE ZHELIHOVSKY
1859–1865, RUGODEVO, TIFLIS, AND OTHER
PARTS OF THE CAUCASUS, RUSSIA

[Sinnett 1886, 115–6, 134–5, 143, 146–51, 150, 152]

In the early part of 1859 Mme. Blavatsky went to live with her father and sister in a country house at Rugodevo.

[But] the quiet life of the sisters at Rugodevo was brought to an end by a terrible illness which befell Mme. Blavatsky. Years before, perhaps during her solitary travels in the steppes of Asia, she had received a remarkable wound. We could never learn how she had met with it. Suffice to say that the profound wound reopened occasionally, and during that time she suffered intense agony, often bringing on convulsions and a deathlike trance. The sickness used to last from three to four days, and then the wound would heal as suddenly as it had reopened, as though an invisible hand had closed it, and there would remain no trace of her illness. But the affrighted family was ignorant at first of this strange peculiarity, and their despair and fear were great indeed. A physician was sent for; but he proved of little use, not so much indeed through his ignorance of surgery, as owing to a remarkable phenomenon which left him almost powerless to act through sheer terror at what he had witnessed. He had hardly examined the wound of the patient prostrated before him in complete unconsciousness, when suddenly he saw a large, dark hand between his own and the wound he was going to anoint. The gaping wound was near the heart, and the hand kept slowly moving at several intervals from the neck down to the waist. To make his terror worse, there began suddenly in the room such a terrific noise, such a chaos of noises and sounds from the ceiling, the floor, windowpanes, and every bit of furniture in the apartment, that he begged he might not be left alone in the room with the insensible patient.

In the spring of 1860 both sisters left Rugodevo for the Caucasus, on a visit to their grandparents, whom they had not seen for long years. The three weeks' journey to Tiflis [was taken] in a coach with post horses. Mme. Blavatsky resided at Tiflis less than two years, and not more than three in the Caucasus. The last year she passed roaming about in Imeretia, Georgia, and Mingreliya and along the coasts of the Black Sea.

Her occult powers, all this while, instead of weakening, became every day stronger, and she seemed finally to subject to her direct will every kind of manifestation. The whole country was talking of her. The superstitious nobility began very soon to regard her as a magician, and people came from afar off to consult her about their private affairs. She had long since given up communication through raps, and preferred—what was a far more rapid and satisfactory method—to answer people either verbally or by means of direct writing. At times, during such process, Mme. Blavatsky seemed to fall into a kind of coma, or magnetic sleep, with eyes wide open, though even then her hand never ceased to move, and continued this writing. When thus answering to mental questions, the answers were rarely unsatisfactory. Generally they astonished the querists—friends and enemies.

Meanwhile sporadic phenomena were gradually dying away in her presence. They still occurred, but very rarely, though they were always very remarkable. We give one.

It must, however, be explained, that some months previous to that event, Mme. Blavatsky was taken very ill. No doctor could understand her illness. Soon after the commencement of that illness, she began—as she repeatedly told her friends—"to lead a double life." This is how she herself describes that state:

"Whenever I was called by name, I opened my eyes upon hearing it, and was myself, my own personality in every particular. As soon as I was left alone, however, I relapsed into my usual, half-dreamy condition, and became *somebody else*. I had simply a mild fever that consumed me slowly but surely, day after day, with entire loss of appetite, and finally of hunger, as I would feel none for days, and often went a week without touching any food whatever, except a little water, so that in four months I was reduced to a living skeleton. In cases when I was interrupted, when in my other *self*, by the sound of my present name being pronounced, and while I was conversing in my dream life— say at half a sentence either spoken by me or those who were with my second *me* at the time—and opened my eyes to answer the call, I used to answer very rationally, and understood all, for I was never delirious. But no sooner had I closed my eyes again than the sentence which had been interrupted was completed by my other self, continued from the word, or even half the word, it had stopped at. When awake, and *myself*, I remembered well who I was in my second capacity, and what I had been and was doing. When *somebody else*, *i.e.* the personage I had become, I know I had no idea of who was H. P. Blavatsky! I was in another far-off country, a totally different individuality from myself, and had no connection at all with my actual life."

Such is Mme. Blavatsky's analysis of her state at that time. She was residing then at Ozurgety, a military settlement in Mingreliya, where she had bought a house. It is a little town, lost among the old forests and woods, which, in those days, had neither roads nor conveyances, save of the most primitive kind. The only physician of the place, the army surgeon, could make nothing of her symptoms; but as she was visibly and rapidly declining, he packed her off to Tiflis to her friends. Unable to go on horseback, owing to her great weakness, and a journey in a cart being deemed dangerous, she was sent off in a large native boat along the river—a journey of four days to Kutais—with four native servants only to take care of her.

In that solitary boat, on a narrow river, hedged on both sides by centenarian forests, her position must have been precarious.

The little stream they were sailing along was, though navigable, rarely, if ever, used as a means of transit. As they were gliding slowly along the narrow stream, cutting its way between two steep and woody banks, the servants were several times during three consecutive nights frightened out of their senses by seeing, *what they swore was their mistress*, gliding off from the boat, and across the water in the direction of the forests, while the body of that same mistress was lying prostrate on her bed at the bottom of the boat. Twice the men who towed the canoe, upon seeing the "form," ran away shrieking and in great terror. Had it not been for a faithful old servant who was taking care of her, the boat and the patient would have been abandoned in the middle of the stream. On the last evening, the servant swore he saw two figures, while the third— his mistress, in flesh and bone—was sleeping before his eyes. No sooner had they arrived at Kutais, where Mme. Blavatsky had a distant relative residing at that place, than all the servants, with the exception of the old butler, left her, and returned no more.

It was with great difficulty that she was transported to Tiflis. A carriage and a friend of the family were sent to meet her; and she was brought into the house of her friends apparently dying.

One afternoon, very weak and delicate still, after the illness just described, Mme. Blavatsky came in to her aunt's,

N. A. de Fadeyev's, room. After a few words of conversation, remarking that she felt tired and sleepy, she was offered to rest upon a sofa. Hardly had her head touched her cushion when she fell into a profound sleep. Her aunt had quietly resumed some writing she had interrupted to talk with her niece, when suddenly soft but quite audible steps in the room behind her chair made her rapidly turn her head to see who was the intruder, as she was anxious that Mme. Blavatsky should not be disturbed. The room was empty! There was no other living person in it but herself and her sleeping niece, yet the steps continued, audibly, as though of a heavy person treading softly, the floor creaking all the while. They approached the sofa, and suddenly ceased. Then she heard stronger sounds, as though someone was whispering near Mme. Blavatsky, and presently a book placed on a table near the sofa was seen by N. A. de Fadeyev to open, and its pages kept turning to and fro, as if an invisible hand were busy at it. Another book was snatched from the library shelves, and flew in that same direction.

More astonished than frightened—for everyone in the house had been trained in and become quite familiar with such manifestations—N. A. de Fadeyev arose from her armchair to awaken her niece, hoping thereby to put a stop to the phenomena; but at the same moment a heavy armchair moved at the other end of the room, and rattling on the floor, glided toward the sofa. The noise it made awoke Mme. Blavatsky, who, upon opening her eyes, enquired of the invisible presence what was the matter. A few more whisperings, and all relapsed into quietness and silence, and there was nothing more of the sort during the rest of the evening.

As soon as she was restored to life and health, she left the Caucasus, and went to Italy. Yet it was before her departure from the country in [1865] that the nature of her powers seems to have entirely changed. At what time this complete change in her occult powers was wrought we are unable to say, as she was far away from our observation, and spoke of it but rarely—never unless distinctly asked in our correspondence to answer the question. And we believe her statements with regard to her powers to have been entirely true when she wrote to tell us, "Now [in 1865]

I shall never be subjected to external influences." *It is not HPB who was from that time forth victim to "influences" which would have without doubt triumphed over a less strong nature than was hers; but, on the contrary, it is she who subjected these influences—whatever they may be—to her will.*

H. P. Blavatsky about 1875

Chapter 3

MORE
WORLD TRAVELS
1865–1873

HELENA BLAVATSKY left Russia again in the fall of 1865 and traveled extensively through the Balkans, Greece, Egypt, Syria, Italy, and various other places. In 1868 she went via India to Tibet. On this trip HPB met the Master Koot Hoomi (KH) for the first time and stayed in his house in Little Tibet. In late 1870 she was back in Cyprus and Greece. Embarking for Egypt, she was shipwrecked near the island of Spetsai on July 4, 1871; saved from drowning, she went to Cairo where she tried to form a *Société Spirite*, which soon failed. After further travels through the Middle East, she returned for a short time to her relatives at Odessa, Russia, in July 1872. In the Spring of 1873, Helena was instructed by her Teacher to go to Paris, and on further direct orders from him, left for New York City.

3a. Nadyezhda A. de Fadeyev
November 11, 1870,
Odessa, Russia

[Theosophical Society 1885, 94–5]

[The letter from Master Koot Hoomi referred to in the following passage is preserved in the archives of the Theosophical Society, Adyar, Madras, India. A facsimile of it with background information is in C. Jinarajadasa's *Letters from the Masters of the Wisdom*, Second Series, 3–5. —DHC]

I [will] narrate what happened to me in connection with a certain note, received by me phenomenally when my niece was at the other side of the world, and not a soul knew where she was— which grieved us greatly. All our researches had ended in nothing. We were ready to believe her dead, when—I think it was about the year 1870—I received a letter from him whom I believe you call Kouth-humi [Koot Hoomi]—which was brought to me in the most incomprehensible and mysterious manner, by a messenger of Asiatic appearance, *who then disappeared before my very eyes.* This letter begged me not to fear anything, and announced that she was in safety.

My niece spoke of [these Mahatmas] to me, and at great length, years ago. She wrote me that she had again met and renewed her relations with several of them, even before she wrote her *Isis [Unveiled].* If I who have ever been, and hope ever to continue, to be a fervent Christian, believe in the existence of these men—although I may refuse to credit all the miracles they attribute to them—why should not others believe in them? For the existence of at least one of them, *I can certify.* Who, then, could have written me this letter to reassure me at the moment when I had the greatest need for such comfort, unless it had been one of those adepts mentioned? *It is true that the handwriting is not known to me;* but the manner in which it was delivered to me was phenomenal, that none other than an adept in occult science

could have effected it. It promised me the return of my niece—
and the promise was duly fulfilled.

The 1870 letter from KH to Nadyezhda de Fadeyev

TRANSLATION

To the Honorable,
   Most Honorable Lady,
      Nadyéjda Andréewna Fadeew,
         Odessa.

The noble relations of Mme H. Blavatsky have no cause whatsoever for grief. Their daughter and niece has not left this world. She lives, and desires to make known to those whom she loves that she is well and very happy in the distant and unknown retreat which she has selected for herself. She has been very ill, but is so no longer; for under the protection of the Lord Sangyas she has found devoted friends who take care of her physically and spiritually. The ladies of her house should therefore make themselves easy. Before 18 new moons shall have risen, she will return to her family.

3B. VERA P. DE ZHELIHOVSKY
OCTOBER 1871 – APRIL 1872, EGYPT

[Sinnett 1886, 158–63, 167–8, with additions and corrections from the original English translation of Vera's account in the Adyar Archives.]

In 1871 Mme. Blavatsky wrote from Cairo to tell her friends that she had just returned from India, and had been wrecked near [Spetsai, an island in the Gulf of Nauplia, Greece]. She had determined to establish a *Société Spirite* for the investigation of mediums and phenomena according to Allan Kardec's theories and philosophy,* since there was no other way to give people a chance to see for themselves how mistaken they were. She would first give free play to an already established and accepted teaching and then, when the public would see that nothing was coming out of it, she would offer her own explanations. To accomplish this object, she said, she was ready to go to any amount of trouble— even to allowing herself to be regarded for a time as a helpless medium. "They know no better, and it does me no harm—for I will very soon show them the difference between a passive medium and an active doer," she explains.

A few weeks later a new letter was received. In this one she showed herself full of disgust for the enterprise, which had proved a perfect failure. She had written, it seems, to England and France for a medium, but without success. *En desespoir de cause*, she had surrounded herself with amateur mediums—French female spiritists.

"They steal the society's money," she wrote, "they drink like sponges, and I now caught them cheating most shamefully our members, who come to investigate the phenomena, by bogus manifestations. I had very disagreeable scenes with several persons who held me alone responsible for all this. So I gave orders that their fees of membership should be returned to them, and I will bear myself the costs and moneys laid out for hire of the premises and the furniture used. My famous *Société Spirite* has not lasted a fortnight—it is a heap of ruins—majestic, but as suggestive as those of the Pharaoh's tombs. To wind up the comedy with a drama, I got nearly shot by a madman—a Greek clerk who had been present at the only two public seances we held and got possessed, I suppose, by some vile spook."

She broke all connection with the "mediums," shut up her *Société* and went to live in Boulak near the Museum. The sceptics who had, moved by idle curiosity, visited the *Société* and witnessed the whole failure made capital of the thing; ridiculing the idea of phenomena, they had as a natural result declared such claims to be fraud and charlatanry all round. Conveniently mixing up the whole truth, they even went the length of maintaining that instead of paying the mediums and the expenses of the Society, it was Mme. Blavatsky who had herself been paid, and had attempted to palm off juggler tricks as genuine phenomena. The groundless inventions and rumors thus set on foot by her enemies did not prevent Mme. Blavatsky from pursuing her studies and proving to every honest investigator that her extraordinary powers of clairvoyance and clairaudience were *facts* and independent of mere physical manifestations, over which she possessed an undeniable control.

A gentleman, Mr. G. Yakovlef, who happened to visit Egypt at that time, wrote to his friends the most enthusiastic letters about Madame Blavatsky. Thus he wrote in a letter we have in our possession: "She is a marvel, an unfathomable mystery. That which she produces is simply phenomenal. Once I showed her a closed medallion containing the portrait of one person and the hair of another, an object which I had had in my possession but a few months, which was made at Moscow and of which very few know, and she told me without touching it, 'Oh! it is your god-mother's portrait and your cousin's hair. Both are dead,' and she proceeded forthwith to describe them, as though she had both before her eyes. How *could* she know!"

Further on he speaks of visiting [Madame Blavatsky] in a hotel of Alexandria. They remained sitting on a sofa and having a chat together. Before the sofa there stood a little teapoy, on which the waiter had placed for Mr. Yakovlef a bottle of liqueur, some wine, a small wineglass, and a tumbler. As he was carrying the [wineglass] with its contents to his mouth, without any visible cause, the glass broke in his hand into many pieces. She laughed, appearing overjoyed, and made the remark that she hated liqueurs and wine, and could hardly tolerate those who used them too freely.

"You do not mean to infer that it is you who broke my wineglass? It is simply an accident. The glass is very thin; it was perhaps cracked, and I squeezed it too strongly!" I lied purposely, for I had just made the mental remark that it seemed very strange and incomprehensible, the glass being very thick and strong. But I wanted to draw her out.

She looked at me very seriously, and her eyes flashed. "What will you bet," she asked, "that I do it again?"

"Well, we will try on the spot. If you do, I will be the first to proclaim you a true magician. If not, we will have a good laugh at you or your spirits tomorrow at the Consulate." And saying so, I half filled the tumbler with wine and prepared to drink it. But no

34

sooner had the glass touched my lips than I felt it shattered between my fingers, and my hand bled, wounded by a broken piece in my instinctive act at grasping the tumbler together when I felt myself losing hold of it.

Disgusted with the failure of her spiritist society, Mme. Blavatsky soon went home via Palestine, and lingered for some months longer, making a voyage to Palmyra [an ancient city of Syria] and other ruins, whither she went with Russian friends. At the end of 1872, she returned in her usual way without warning, and surprised her family at Odessa.

*[Allan Kardec (1804–1869), the father of Spiritism (Spiritualism) in France. His most famous work, *Le Livre des Esprits* (The Spirits' Book), first published in 1856, expounded a theory of human life and destiny in which the doctrine of "reincarnation" was a prominent feature. —DHC]

3c. EMMA COULOMB
1872, CAIRO, EGYPT

[Coulomb 1884, 3–4]

In the year 1872 one day as I was walking through the street called "Sekke el Ghamma el harmar"—"the street of the red mosque"—in Cairo, Egypt, I was roused from my pensive mood by something that brushed by me very swiftly. I looked up and saw a lady. "Who is that lady?" I asked a passer-by. "She is that Russian Spiritist who calls the dead and makes them answer your questions." This news was to me tidings of great joy, as I was just mourning for the death of my dear and only brother, whom I had recently lost. The idea of being able to hear his voice was for me heavenly delight. I was told that if I asked the Secretary of her Spiritualistic Society to introduce me toher he would do so (he was a Greek gentleman of my acquaintance). I was introduced, and found her very interesting and very clever. My first essay at the spirits was not successful; I neither saw nor heard anything but a few raps. Having shown my disappointment to the Secretary of the Society, I was told that the spirits did not like to appear in a room which had not been purified and not exclusively used for the purpose, but if I would return in a few days I would see wonders, as they were preparing a closet where nothing else but seances was to be done. I went to see the closet, and saw that it was lined with red cloth, all over the four sides and also the ceiling, with a space between the wall and the cloth of about three inches. I was so ignorant of these things at the time that I formed no malicious idea of it. I called again when the closet was ready, but what was my surprise when, instead of finding the kind spirits there to answer our questions, I found a room full of people, *all alive*, and using most offensive language towards the founder of the Society, saying that she had taken their money and had left them only with this, pointing at the space between the wall and the cloth, where several pieces of twine were still hanging which had served to pull through the ceiling a long glove stuffed with cotton, which was to represent the materialized hand and arm of some spirit. I went away, leaving the crowd as red as fire, ready to knock her down when she came back. Later on I met her again, and I asked her how she came to do such a thing; to which she answered that it was Madame Sebire's doings (this was a lady who lived with Madame Blavatsky), so I let this matter drop. I saw that she looked very unhappy. I called on her the next day. Our acquaintance continued all the while she remained in the country.

To my knowledge Madame Blavatsky while in Cairo never lived in an hotel. I have known her in three different apartments. The first was in "Sekke el Ghamma el harmar," the second at "Abdeen," and the third at "Kantara el dick." In "Abdeen" she had opened her apartment to the public, who went there to consult her spirits, and where the fiasco of the materialized hand and arm took place.

She [then] left Cairo for Russia.

3D. COUNTESS LYDIA A. DE PASHKOV
SPRING 1872, LEBANON

[Pashkov 1878]

I was once traveling between Baalbek and the river Orontes, and in the desert I saw a caravan. It was Mme. Blavatsky's. We camped together. There was a great monument standing there near the village of Dair Mar Maroon. It was between Lebanon and the Anti-Lebanon [Mountains]. On the monument were inscriptions that no one could ever read. Mme. Blavatsky could do strange things with the spirits, as I knew, and I asked her to find out what the monument was.

We waited until night. She drew a circle and we went in it. We built a fire and put much incense on it. Then she said many spells. Then we put on more incense. Then she pointed with her wand at the monument and we saw a great ball of white flame on it. There was a sycamore tree near by; we saw many little flames on it. The jackals came and howled in the darkness a little way off. We put on more incense. Then Mme. Blavatsky commanded the spirit to appear of the person to whom the monument was reared. Soon a cloud of vapor arose and obscured the little moonlight there was. We put on more incense. The cloud took the indistinct shape of an old man with a beard, and a voice came, as it seemed, from a great distance, through the image. He said the monument was once the altar of a temple that had long disappeared. It was reared to a god that had long since gone to another world. "Who are you?" asked Mme. Blavatsky, "I am Hiero, one of the priests of the temple," said the voice. Then Mme Blavatsky commanded him to show us the place as it was when the temple stood. He bowed, and for one instant we had a glimpse of the temple and of a vast city filling the plain as far as the eye could reach. Then it was gone, and the image faded away. Then we built up big fires to keep off the jackals and went to sleep.

H. P. Blavatsky, 1875

Chapter 4

NEW YORK AND CHITTENDEN
1873 – April 1875

*H*P. BLAVATSKY was forty-two years old and in controlled possession of her many and most unusual spiritual and occult powers when she arrived in New York City. In the opinion of the Mahatmas, she was the best available instrument for the work they had in mind, namely to offer to the world a new presentation, though only in brief outline of the age-old *Theosophia*, "The accumulated Wisdom of the ages, tested and verified by generations of Seers," that body of Truth, of which religions, great and small, are but as branches of the parent tree. Her task was to challenge on the one hand the entrenched beliefs and dogmas of Christian theology and on the other the equally dogmatic materialistic view of the science of her day. A crack, however, had recently appeared in this twofold set of mental fortifications. It was caused by Spiritualism, then sweeping America. To quote Helena's own words: "I was sent to prove the phenomena and their reality, and to show the fallacy of the spiritualistic theory of spirits."

In October, 1874, HPB was put in touch by her Teachers with Colonel Henry Steel Olcott, a man of sterling worth who had acquired considerable renown during the Civil War, had served the U.S. Government with distinction, and was at the time practicing law in New York. They became firm friends, and through HPB, his view of Spiritualism and his knowledge of Eastern esotericism underwent a revolutionary change.

4A. ANNA BALLARD
JULY 1873, NEW YORK CITY

[Olcott 1895, 1:21–2]

My acquaintanceship with Mme. Blavatsky dates back [to] July 1873, at New York, not more than a week after she landed. I was then a reporter on the staff of the *New York Sun*, and had been detailed to write an article upon a Russian subject. In the course of my search after facts, the arrival of this Russian lady was reported to me by a friend, and I called upon her, thus beginning an acquaintance that lasted several years. At our first interview she told me she had had no idea of leaving Paris for America until the very evening before she sailed, but why she came or who hurried her off she did not say. I remember perfectly well her saying with an air of exultation, "I have been in Tibet." Why she should think that a great matter, more remarkable than any other of the travels in Egypt, India, and other countries she told me about, I could not make out, but she said it with special emphasis and animation.

4B. ELIZABETH G. K. HOLT
AUGUST 1873 – JUNE 1874, NEW YORK CITY

[Holt 1931]

It was hard for respectable women workers of small means to find a fitting place in which to live; so it happened that some forty of them launched a small experiment in co-operative living. They rented a new tenement house, 222 Madison Street. It was a street of small two-story houses occupied by their owners, who were proud of their shade trees, and kept their front and back yards in order.

My mother and I had spent the summer of 1873 at Saratoga. In order to be ready for school when it opened, I was sent home in August to the Madison Street house, where we had a friend who would take me under her protection; and there I found Mme. Blavatsky. She had a room on the second floor, and my friend had a duplicate room next to her, so that they became very friendly neighbors. Being a co-operative family, we all knew one another familiarly, and kept a room next the street door as a common sitting room or office, a meeting place for members, and a place where mail and messages were cared for.

Mme. Blavatsky sat in the office a large part of her time, but she seldom sat alone; she was like a magnet, powerful enough to draw round her everyone who could possibly come. I saw her, day by day, sitting there rolling her cigarettes and smoking incessantly. She had a conspicuous tobacco pouch, the head of some fur-bearing animal, which she wore round the neck. She was certainly an unusual figure. I think she must have been taller than she looked, she was so broad; she had a broad face and broad shoulders; her hair was a lightish brown and crinkled like that of some Negroes. Her whole appearance conveyed the idea of power.

Madame referred often to her life in Paris. Later she gave practical demonstration that she had ability in the arts. I had a piano, and Madame sometimes played, usually because somebody pressed her to do so.

41

She described their past life to the people who asked her to do so, and these accounts must have been accurate, they made such a profound impression. I never heard that she told them their future. She was considered to be a Spiritualist, though I never heard her say she was one. When my friend, Miss Parker, asked Madame to put her in communication with her dead mother, Madame said it was impossible, as her mother was absorbed in higher things and had progressed beyond reach. The spirits she spoke about continually were the *diaki*, tricksy little beings, evidently counterparts of the fairies of Irish folklore, and certainly nonhuman from her description of them.

I never looked upon Madame as an ethical teacher. For one thing, she was too excitable; when things went wrong with her, she could express her opinion about them with a vigor which was very disturbing.

In mental or physical dilemma, you would instinctively appeal to her, for you felt her fearlessness, her unconventionality, her great wisdom and wide experience and hearty good will—her sympathy with the underdog.

An instance of this kind comes to mind. Undesirable people were beginning to move into the street, and the neighborhood was changing rapidly. One evening one of our young girls, coming home late from work, was followed and greatly frightened; she flung herself breathless into a chair in the office. Madame interested herself at once, expressed her indignation in most vigorous terms, and finally drew from some fold in her dress a knife (I think she used it to cut her tobacco, but it was sufficiently large to be a formidable weapon of defense) and said she had *that* for any man who molested her.

At this time Madame was greatly troubled about money; the income she had received regularly from her father in Russia had stopped, and she was almost penniless. Some of the more conservative people in our house suggested that she was, after all, an adventuress, and the want of money was only what might be expected; but my friend, Miss Parker, whom she took with her to the Russian Consul, assured me that she was really a Russian

Countess, that the Consul knew of her family, and had promised to do all he could to get in touch with them and find out what was the difficulty. I may say here that the holding up of her income was caused by the death of her father and the consequent time required to settle up his affairs.

She had a long table in her private room and I saw her for days, perhaps weeks, steadily writing page after page of manuscript.

Shortly after this and while Madame was still without income, she met and became intimate with a French lady, a widow, whose name I have forgotten.

At this time she lived a short distance away in Henry Street. She offered to share her home with HPB until the latter's money difficulties had passed. This offer was accepted, and Madame left our house. Many of our people, however, and notably Miss Parker, kept in close touch with her.

Shortly after this Madame received money from Russia, and moved to the northeast corner of 14th Street and Fourth Avenue. The house was very unpretentious, with a liquor saloon on the street floor, and the two upper floors let as furnished rooms. To this house Miss Parker took me. There I found Madame in a poorly furnished top-floor room; her bed was an iron cot, and beside her bed on a table was a small cabinet with three drawers.

Madame was in a state of great excitement. Earlier in the day her room had been on fire; she said it had been purposely set on fire to rob her. After the fire was out, and the firemen and curious strangers had gone, she found that her valuable watch and chain had been stolen. When she complained to the proprietor of the saloon, who was her landlord, he intimated that she had never had a watch to lose. She told us that she asked "Them" to give her some proof which she could show her landlord and convince him that she really had lost her property; immediately there appeared before her a sheet of paper all gray with smoke except for white spots, the size and shape of a watch and chain, indicating that after the fire had darkened the paper, the watch and chain had been lifted from it, revealing the white spots which they had covered.

I had always heard the "They" and "Them" explained by the people who were round her, as referring to her "Spirit Guides"; naturally I thought she spoke of them. I knew nothing of Occultism.

My visit to HPB was the last time I saw her.

4C. HANNAH M. WOLFF
1874, NEW YORK CITY

[Wolff 1891]

There is such a diversity of opinion in regard to this remarkable and notorious woman and the combined result of the articles published concerning her is of such an oddly kaleidoscopic character that I am tempted to add my bit of color to the mass of evidence which will eventually determine the verdict regarding her.

That she was a woman of strong intellectual ability and great diversity of talent cannot be denied. She had been solidly educated, had traveled extensively, was almost insanely fond of adventure, had no physical or moral fear, was a close observer of whatever scenes she passed through and of whatever circumstances surrounded her. She had marvelous readiness of adaptability to her environment and knew "how to abound and how to suffer need." She delighted in gaining any kind of intellectual ascendancy over those about her, and particularly in dominating men of known strong mental caliber. She would go any length to dupe them and scorn and mentally deride them when duped.

I first saw her in the early part of 1874 at the Working Woman's Home in Elizabeth Street, New York, where I called on business for the newspaper upon the staff of which I was then engaged. On entering the room of the lady [Miss M] whom I was to interview (the room was shared with four other inmates) I saw, half sitting, half reclining on the carpetless floor, a scantly clad, and, as I then thought, very stupid and unprepossessing woman who was introduced as Madame Blavatsky. She was at that time quite stout, though not as unwieldy as she subsequently became. Her complexion, which must in her youth have been fair, was torpid, pasty, and grimy; her eyes were magnetic and peculiar, with a strange compelling fascination in their blue-gray depths, but were in no sense beautiful, as some have described them. Her nose was a catastrophe, like Petrea's, an appendage for use and not for ornament, and her mouth lacked power and was animalistic. The shape of her head was finely intellectual, and her hair was the most peculiar I have ever seen. It was very thick, and not long, gathered into a knot at the back of her head. Its peculiarity consisted in that, while it was blonde in color, its texture was like that of the Negro's. It was soft and fine and light-colored, but woolly.

When my interview with Miss M was concluded, Madame Blavatsky, who retained her position and extremely careless attitude upon the floor and had, while attentively listening to our conversation, rolled and smoked cigarettes with a most marvelous rapidity, entered into conversation with me. She appeared desirous of informing herself concerning the position of women of the press in this country, and my role of interviewer was changed to that of the interviewed in the colloquy that ensued between us. I gave her all the information I could; but I left that room with the new sensation of having met an educated, intellectual woman with marvelous conversational powers, who had no more sense of propriety or feeling of natural modesty than the cat or the dog that sprawls about the floor at will.

During this conversation, she informed me that she was stopping at the Working Woman's Home for economical reasons. A month or six weeks after this I met her in the anteroom at one of the women's conventions. She then told me that she had received a large sum of money from Russia and was staying at an expensive hotel on Fourth Avenue, near Twenty-Third Street. On this occasion she invited half a dozen ladies to lunch with her and subsequently told me that her bill footed up at the rate of $5 each. I think that this lavishness of expenditure was habitual to her when she had means. When her purse was collapsed, she retired to humble quarters and contented herself with frugal fare. She was prodigal, but not generous; lavish, but not benevolent. She had at no time any need to be cramped for the means of comfort, for she had a ready pencil and could, whenever the incentive presented itself, dash off most graphic and salable sketches of Russian or other life, with which she was familiar. It was no uncommon occurrence for her to receive $30, $40, or $50 for sketches limned in a few minutes when the mood was upon her.

Two or three months after I first met her, she expressed the wish to a near friend of mine, who was an ardent Spiritualist, to attend some of the Spiritualist lectures and to study its phenomena and philosophy, of which she professed herself ignorant. Mr. W took her to a lecture, given by E. V. Wilson, a noted trance speaker and test medium. At the close of the lecture, she received from him what she declared was a very remarkable test and told Mr. W that it was the first experience of that sort she had ever had. Since that time she has claimed, and others have for her, that years previous to this she had not only investigated spiritualistic phenomena, but had attempted to establish some sort of spiritualistic organization in Constantinople. I do not know which of her statements was true. I know only what she told us. She told us, however, that she had for many years been conscious of strange and peculiar psychic gifts and experiences which probably could be best accounted for on the spiritualistic hypothesis of mediumship.

At this time she fell into the habit of dropping in at my rooms and conversing with me about her travels, occult phenomena, etc. She spoke of having been with Garibaldi in his struggle, but I was never able to hold her to the subject so as to get any succinct or lucid account of her adventures as a soldier. She showed me the scar of what she claimed was a saber wound. A Russian acquaintance of hers told me it was the mark of the knout, one of the many that scarred her body, received for complicity with the Nihilists. If this were true, I cannot imagine why she should not have told me so, for she knew that I was in hearty sympathy with this class in Russia, although disapproving of some of the methods. In relating her experiences in the East, she never touched once upon having made any study of Buddhism.

It was evident from the first that she smoked tobacco to great excess, frequently, as she told me, using a pound a day. I soon learned also that she was addicted to the use of hashish. She several times endeavored to persuade me to try the effect upon myself. She said she had smoked opium, seen its visions and dreamed its dreams, but that the beatitudes enjoyed in the use of hashish were as heaven to its hell. She said she found nothing to compare with its effects in arousing and stimulating the imagination.

In all the interviews I had with her, and they were many, during the four or more months of my intercourse with her, she never mentioned Theosophy. I always believed it was an afterthought sprung from some seed sown in her fertile brain by some of her experiences in Spiritualism and her dabblings in an at least semispurious mediumship. Very soon after her attendance at the lecture of E. V. Wilson above alluded to, she professed to Mr. W to have had a new and singular development of occult power. She claimed that photographs left in her possession and shut up in a box or drawer would without aid of human instrumentality become colored as by watercolor pigments. She asked Mr. W to go to her lodgings and see some of these specimens of spirit art and invited me also. We went.

At this time she had spent the large sum of money received from Russia and had moved into cheap quarters downtown. The apartment she occupied was shared on the cooperative plan with a party of journalists of rather Bohemian tendencies, two gentlemen and a lady. There was a good-sized room that served as a sort of *salle a manger* into which the bedrooms opened. The furniture of the room consisted of a small dining table, a few chairs, and an old-fashioned chest of drawers, which also served as a sideboard. This bureau was just opposite the door of a small bedroom occupied by Madame Blavatsky. The pictures were in one of the three little drawers at the top of the bureau. She showed them to us and explained that the coloring seemed chiefly to be done in the night when nature was in her negative mood.

Subsequently I made acquaintance with the three young journalists who occupied the other three rooms of the apartment and was told by them that they, being skeptical as to the Madame's occult powers, had laid wait for the spirit who worked in the night watches and had discovered it materialized in the form of Madame Blavatsky, dressed in *saque de nuit*, had seen it glide softly across the room, armed with lamp, colors, and brushes, take the pictures from the drawers, and rapidly work upon them one after another until they were as nearly completed as could be at one sitting.

About this time she called at my rooms and told me that she was doing some literary work in English and, not being sufficiently conversant with the language to write it with grammatical correctness, she wished to secure my services as editor. In reply to my inquiry as to the nature of the work, she said it was a humorously satirical criticism on the government of the United States. I ventured to suggest that it might be thought an impertinence for a person who had been so short a time in the country as herself, who had so little insight into its institutions, to attempt such a stricture, but she cried me down and declared that I must examine before I condemned it. She left, engaged to bring manuscripts in a few days.

In the meantime I met Mrs. Y., the lady who shared the apartment with her, and told her of the proposition. She looked quizzical and said, "When you get that manuscript, let me know, and I shall have something to propose to you. Do not engage to attempt the work until I have seen you."

In a few days the unfinished manuscript was left at my rooms. I dropped a line to Mrs. Y., and she promptly responded by coming to see me.

"Now," she said, "I want you to go to Brooklyn with me to the house where this thing was written, while Madame was the guest of the people, who are Russians."

We went, and I found Mr. ——— and wife very cultured and charming people. Mrs. Y. told our host that Madame B. asked me to edit her work on our government.

"Did she tell you it was original?" he asked.

"Certainly," I replied. "She claimed that it was an expression of her own views of our government in satire."

"Well," said he, "the portion of it that you have, she translated from this volume," taking a book from the case near by. "The second volume she borrowed when she left here and has not yet returned."

The book was the work of a celebrated Russian humorist whose name has escaped me. Mr. ———— said, "If you will follow me on the pages you have, I will translate a few paragraphs from the print."

This he did. The manuscript was an almost verbatim translation of the book, "United States" being substituted for "Russia," "President" for "Czar," and certain other needful changes and adaptations being introduced. The Madame's pretended original work was a complete theft.

When I returned the manuscript with a note explaining my reasons for not accepting the commission, she made no reply, but later, when I accidentally met her and brought up the matter, she sneering said that as Americans were almost entirely ignorant of Russian literature she saw no harm in what she had attempted. This closed my personal acquaintance with the founder and high priest of Theosophy.

4D. HENRY S. OLCOTT
OCTOBER 1874, CHITTENDEN, VERMONT

[Olcott 1895, 1:1–10]

One day, in the month of July 1874, I was sitting in my law office thinking over a heavy case in which I had been retained by the Corporation of the City of New York, when it occurred to me that for years I had paid no attention to the Spiritualist movement. I went around the corner to a dealer's and bought a copy of the

Banner of Light. In it I read an account of certain incredible phenomena, viz. the solidification of phantom forms, which were said to be occurring at a farmhouse in the township of Chittenden, in the State of Vermont, several hundred miles distant from New York. I saw at once that, if it were true that visitors could see, even touch and converse with, deceased relatives who had found means to reconstruct their bodies and clothing so as to be temporarily solid, visible, and tangible, this was the most important fact in modern physical science. I determined to go and see for myself. I did so, found the story true, stopped three or four days, and then returned to New York. I wrote an account of my observations to the *New York Sun,* which was copied pretty much throughout the whole world. A proposal was then made to me by the Editor of the *New York Daily Graphic* to return to Chittenden in its interest, accompanied by an artist to sketch under my orders, and to make a thorough investigation of the affair. The matter so deeply interested me that I made the necessary disposition of office engagements, and on September 17th was back at the "Eddy Homestead," as it was called from the name of the family who owned and occupied it. I stopped in that house of mystery, surrounded by phantoms and having daily experiences of a most extraordinary character, for about twelve weeks. Meanwhile, twice a week there appeared in the *Daily Graphic* my letters about the "Eddy ghosts," each one illustrated with sketches of specters actually seen by the artist, Mr. Kappes, and myself, as well as by every one of the persons—sometimes as many as forty—present in the "seance-room." It was the publication of these letters which drew Madame Blavatsky to Chittenden, and so brought us together.

I remember our first day's acquaintance as if it were yesterday. It was a sunny day and even the gloomy old farmhouse looked cheerful. It stands amid a lovely landscape, in a valley bounded by grassy slopes that rise into mountains covered to their very crests with leafy groves. This was the time of the "Indian Summer," when the whole country is covered with a faint bluish haze and the foliage of the beeches, elms, and maples, touched by early frosts, has been turned from green into a mottling of gold and crimson that gives the landscape the appearance of being hung all over with royal tapestries.

The dinner hour at Eddy's was noon, and it was from the entrance door of the bare and comfortless dining room that Kappes and I first saw HPB. She had arrived shortly before noon with a French Canadian lady, and they were at table as we entered. My eye was first attracted by a scarlet Garibaldian shirt the former wore, as in vivid contrast with the dull colors around. Her hair was then a thick blond mop, worn shorter than the shoulders, and it stood out from her head, silken-soft and crinkled to the roots, like the fleece of a Cotswold ewe. This and the red shirt were what struck my attention before I took in the picture of her features. It was a massive Calmuck face, contrasting in its suggestion of power, culture, and imperiousness as strangely with the commonplace visages about the room as her red garment did with the gray and white tones of the walls and woodwork and the dull costumes of the rest of the guests.

All sorts of cranky people were continually coming and going at Eddy's to see the mediumistic phenomena, and it only struck me on seeing this eccentric lady that this was but one more of the sort. Pausing on the doorsill, I whispered to Kappes, "Good gracious! look at *that* specimen, will you." I went straight across and took a seat opposite her to indulge my favorite habit of character study. The two ladies conversed in French, making remarks of no consequence. Dinner over, the two went outside the house and Madame Blavatsky rolled herself a cigarette, for which I gave her a light as a pretext to enter into conversation. My remark having been made in French, we fell at once into talk in that language.

She asked me how long I had been there and what I thought of the phenomena, saying that she herself was greatly interested in such things and had been drawn to Chittenden by reading the letters in the *Daily Graphic*: the public were growing so interested in these that it was sometimes impossible to find a copy of the paper on the bookstalls an hour after publication, and she had paid a dollar for a copy of the last issue. "I hesitated before coming here," she said, "because I was afraid of meeting that Colonel Olcott."

"Why should you be afraid of him, Madame?" I rejoined. "Oh! because I fear he might write about me in his paper." I told her that she might make herself perfectly easy on that score, for I felt quite sure Col. Olcott would not mention her in his letters unless she wished it. And I introduced myself.

We became friends at once. Each of us felt as if we were of the same social world, cosmopolitans, freethinkers, and in closer touch than with the rest of the company. It was the voice of common sympathy with the higher occult side of man and nature, the attraction of soul to soul, not that of sex to sex.

Strolling along with my new acquaintance, we talked together about the Eddy phenomena and those of other lands. I found she had been a great traveler and seen many occult things and adepts in occult science, but at first she did not give me any hint as to the existence of the Himalayan Sages or of her own powers. She spoke of the materialistic tendency of American Spiritualism, which was a sort of debauch of phenomena accompanied by comparative indifference to philosophy. Her manner was gracious and captivating, her criticisms upon men and things original and witty. She was particularly interested in drawing me out as to my own ideas about spiritual things and expressed pleasure in finding that I had instinctively thought along the occult lines which she herself had pursued. It was not as an Eastern mystic, but rather as a refined Spiritualist that she talked. For my part I knew nothing then, or next to nothing, about Eastern philosophy, and at first she kept silent on that subject.

The seances of William Eddy, the chief medium of the family, were held every evening in a large upstairs hall, in a wing of the house, over the dining room and kitchen. At the farther end of the séance hall was a narrow closet in which William Eddy would seat himself to wait for the phenomena. He had no seeming control over them, but merely sat and waited for them to sporadically occur. A blanket being hung across the doorway, the closet would be in perfect darkness. Shortly after William had entered the cabinet, the blanket would be pulled aside and forth would step some figure of a dead man, woman or child temporarily solid and substantial, but the next minute resolved back into nothingness or invisibility. They would occasionally dissolve away while in full view of the spectators.

Up to the time of HPB's appearance on the scene, the figures which had shown themselves were either Red Indians, or Americans or Europeans akin to the visitors. But on the first evening of her stay, spooks of other nationalities came before us. There was a Georgian servant boy from the Caucasus, a Mussulman merchant from Tiflis, a Russian peasant girl, and others. The advent of such figures in the séance room of those poor, almost illiterate Vermont farmers, who had neither the money to buy theatrical properties, the experience to employ such if they had had them, nor the room where they could have availed of them, was to every eyewitness a convincing proof that the apparitions were genuine. At the same time they show that a strange attraction to call out these images from what Asiatics call the Kamaloka attended Madame Blavatsky. It was long afterwards that I was informed that she had evoked them by her own developed and masterful power.

HPB tried her best to make me suspect the value of William Eddy's phenomena as proofs of the intelligent control of a medium by spirits, telling me that, if genuine, they must be the double of the medium escaping from his body and clothing itself with other appearances; but I did not believe her. I contended that the forms were of too great diversities of height, bulk, and appearance to be a masquerade of William Eddy; they must be what they seemed, viz., the spirits of the dead. Our disputes were quite warm on occasions, for at that time I had not gone deep enough into the question of the plastic nature of the human double to see the force of her hints, while of the Eastern theory of Maya I did not know its least iota. The result, however, was, as she told me, to convince her of my disposition to accept nothing on trust and to cling pertinaciously to such facts as I had, or thought I had acquired. We became greater friends day by day, and by the time she was ready to leave Chittenden, she had accepted from me the nickname "Jack," and so signed herself in her letters to me from New York. When we parted it was as good friends likely to continue the acquaintance thus pleasantly begun.

CHAPTER 4

4E. HENRY S. OLCOTT
NOVEMBER 1874 – APRIL 1875,
NEW YORK CITY AND PHILADELPHIA,
PENNSYLVANIA

[Olcott 1895, 1:10–1, 40–2, 17]

In November 1874, when my researches were finished [at Chittenden, Vermont], I returned to New York and called upon [HPB] at her lodgings at 16 Irving Place, where she gave me some seances of table-tipping and rapping, spelling out messages of sorts, principally from an invisible intelligence calling itself "John King." I thought it a veritable John King then, for its personality had been as convincingly proved to me, I fancied, as anybody could have asked. But now, after seeing what HPB could do in the way of producing *mayavic* (i.e., hypnotic) illusions and in the control of elementals, I am persuaded that "John King" was a humbugging elemental, worked by her like a marionette and used as a help towards my education. Understand me, the phenomena were real, but they were done by no disincarnate *human* spirit. She kept up the illusion for months, and I saw numbers of phenomena done as alleged by John King.

An experiment [was] made by HPB, with myself as a passive agent after my coming to her house in Philadelphia. She was tipping tables for me, with and without the contact between her hands and the table, making loud and tiny raps—sometimes while holding her hand six inches above the wood and sometimes while resting her hand upon mine as it lay flat upon the table—and spelling out messages to me from the pretended John King, which, as rapped out by the alphabet, I recorded on scraps of paper. At last some of these messages relating to third parties seemed worth keeping, so one day, on my way home, I bought a reporter's notebook, and, on getting to the house, showed it to her and explained its intended use. She was seated at the time and I standing. Without touching the book or making any mystical pass or sign, she told me to put it in my bosom. I did so, and after a moment's pause she bade me take it out and look within. This is what I found inside the first cover, written and drawn on the white lining paper in lead pencil:

JOHN KING,
HENRY DE MORGAN,

his book.

4th of the Fourth month in A.D. 1875.

Underneath this, the drawing of a Rosicrucian jewel; over the arch of the jeweled crown, the word FATE; beneath which is her name, "Helen," followed by what looks like 99, something smudged out, and then a simple + [etc.]. I have the book on my table as I write, and my description is taken from the drawing itself. One striking feature of this example of psycho-dynamics is the fact that no one but myself had touched the book after it was purchased; I had had it in my pocket until it was shown to HPB, from the distance of two or three feet, had myself held it in my bosom, removed it a moment later when bidden, and the precipitation of the lead-pencil writing and drawing had been done while the book was inside my waistcoat. Now the writing inside the cover of the book is very peculiar. It is a quaint and quite individual handwriting, not like HPB's, but identical with that in all the written messages I had from first to last from "John King." HPB having, then, the power of precipitation, must have transferred from her mind to the paper the images of words traced in this special style of script; or, if not she, but some other expert in this art did it, then that other person must have done it in that same way—i.e., have first pictured to himself mentally the images of those words and that drawing, and then precipitated, that is, made them visible on the paper, as though written with a lead pencil.

Little by little, HPB let me know of the existence of Eastern adepts and their powers, and gave me by a multitude of phenomena the proofs of her own control over the occult forces of nature.

H. P. Blavatsky about 1876 or 1877

Chapter 5

NEW YORK AND ITHACA: WRITING *ISIS UNVEILED*

August–October 1875

*T*HE GENERAL REACTION to HPB was an interest in the "wonders" she could perform and a thirst for marvelous phenomena. She began to gather around her a circle of persons curious about spiritualism and the paranormal. Among the latter was Hiram Corson, a distinguished professor at Cornell University, at whose home HPB spent some weeks in the fall of 1875, working on *Isis Unveiled*.

Corson was a spiritualist and hoped through HPB to contact his daughter, who had died as a teenager. He was surprised by HPB's opposition to any such efforts, but his interest in the marvelous was served by observing her work on *Isis*, which involved long quotations from books not in his library or, he thought, in America. He wrote that she told him she could see the original works "on another plane of objective existence" and simply recorded what appeared before her. Corson's son, Eugene, later published a volume of correspondence from HPB.

William Quan Judge

5A. WILLIAM Q. JUDGE
AUGUST 1875–1878, NEW YORK CITY

[Sinnett 1886, 186–99]

My first acquaintance with H. P. Blavatsky began [when] she was living in apartments in Irving Place, New York City. She had several rooms en suite. The front rooms looked out on Irving Place, and the back upon the garden. My first visit was made in the evening, and I saw her there among a large number of persons who were always attracted to her presence. Several languages were to be heard among them, and Mme. Blavatsky, while conversing volubly in Russian, apparently quite absorbed, would suddenly turn round and interject an observation in English into a discussion between other persons upon a different topic to the one she was engaged with. This never disturbed her, for she at once returned to her Russian talk, taking it up much where it had been dropped.

Very much was said on the first evening that arrested my attention and enchained my imagination. I found my secret thoughts read, my private affairs known to her. Unasked, and certainly without any possibility of her having inquired about me, she referred to several private and peculiar circumstances in a way that showed at once that she had a perfect knowledge of my family, my history, my surroundings, and my idiosyncrasies.

The next day I thought I would try an experiment with Mme. Blavatsky. I took an ancient scarabaeus that she had never seen, had it wrapped up and sent to her through the mails by a clerk in the employment of a friend. My hand did not touch the package, nor did I know when it was posted. But when I called on her at the end of the week the second time, she greeted me with thanks for the scarabaeus. I pretended ignorance. But she said it was useless to pretend, and then informed me how I had sent it, and where the clerk had posted it. During the time that elapsed between my seeing her and the sending of the package no one had heard from me a word about the matter.

Very soon after I met her, she moved to 34th Street, and while there I visited her very often. In those rooms I used to hear the raps in furniture, in glasses, mirrors, windows, and walls, which are usually the accompaniment of dark "spiritist" seances. But with her they occurred in the light, and never except when ordered by her. Nor could they be induced to continue once that she ordered them to stop. They exhibited intelligence also, and would at her request change from weak to strong, or from many to few at a time.

She remained in 34th Street only a few months, and then removed to 47th Street.

After she had comfortably settled herself in 47th Street, where, as usual, she was from morning till night surrounded by all sorts of visitors, mysterious events—extraordinary sights and sounds—continued to occur. I have sat there many an evening, and seen in broad gaslight, large luminous balls creeping over the furniture, or playfully jumping from point to point, while the most beautiful liquid bell sounds now and again burst out from the air of the room. These sounds often imitated either the piano or a gamut of sounds whistled by either myself or some other person. While all this was going, H. P. Blavatsky sat unconcernedly reading or writing at "Isis Unveiled."

Precipitation of messages or sentences occurred very frequently, and I will relate one which took place under my own hand and eyes, in such a way as to be unimpeachable for me.

I was one day, about four o'clock, reading a book that had just been brought in by a friend of Colonel Olcott. I was sitting some six feet distance from H. P. Blavatsky, who was busy writing. I had carefully read the title page of the book, but had forgotten the exact title. But I knew that there was not one word of writing upon it. As I began to read the first paragraph, I heard a bell sound in the air and, looking, saw that Mme. Blavatsky was intently regarding me.

"What book do you read?" said she.

Turning back to the title page, I was about to read aloud the name, when my eye was arrested by a message written in ink across the top of the page, which, a few minutes before, I had looked at and found clean. It was a message in about seven lines, and the fluid had not yet quite dried on the page—its contents were a warning about the book. I am positive that when I took the volume in my hand not one word was written in it.

About any object that might be transported mysteriously around her room, or that came into it through the air by supermundane means, there always lingered for a greater or less space of time a very peculiar though pleasant odor. It was not always the same. At one time it was sandalwood mixed with what I thought was attar of roses, at another time some unknown Eastern perfume, and again it came like the incense burnt in temples.

One day she asked me if I would care to smell again the perfume. Upon my replying affirmatively, she took my handkerchief in her hand, held it for a few moments, and when she gave it back to me it was heavy with the well-known odor. Then in order to show me that her hand was not covered with something that would come off upon the handkerchief, she permitted me to examine both hands. They were without perfume. But after I had convinced myself that there was no perfumery or odoriferous objects concealed in her hands, I found from one hand beginning to exhale one peculiar strong perfume, while from the other there rolled out strong waves of incense.

One evening I was in a hurry to copy a drawing I had made, and looked about on the table for a paper cutter with which to rub the back of the drawing so as to transfer the surplus carbon to a clean sheet.

As I searched, it was suggested by someone that the round smooth back of a spoon bowl would be the best means, and I arose to go to the kitchen at the end of the hall for a spoon. But Mme. Blavatsky said, "Stop, you need not go there; wait a moment." I stopped at the door, and she, sitting in her chair, held up her left hand. At that instant a large tablespoon flew through the air across the room from out of the opposite wall and into her hand. No one was there to throw it to her, and the dining room from which it had been transported was about thirty feet distant, two brick walls separating it from the front room.

My office was at least three miles away from her rooms. One day, at about 2 P.M., I was sitting in my office engaged in reading a legal document, my mind intent on the subject of the paper. No one else was in the office, and in fact the nearest room was separated from me by a wide opening, or well, in the building, made to let light into the inner chambers. Suddenly I felt on my hand a peculiar tingling sensation that always preceded any strange thing to happen in the presence of HPB, and at that moment there fell from the ceiling upon the edge of my desk, and from there to the floor, a triangularly folded note from Madame to myself. The message was in her handwriting and was addressed to me in her writing across the printed face.

5B. THE REV. JAMES H. WIGGIN
LATE AUGUST 1875, NEW YORK CITY

[Wiggin 1875]

Rosicrucianism claims that a brotherhood of occultists has existed and still exists, reaching perfection in the far East, that in the fraternity's archives are preserved grand records of truths about men and nature, that Rosicrucians can work what are false-ly called miracles, by their knowledge of the true essence of things, that human bodies can disappear and reappear at will, that they can float in the air, that all nature is subject to their decrees through their knowledge of divine laws.

It is a little startling to find oneself associating with those who possess, or claim to possess, such powers. Of late Rosicru-cianism has been brought to the front by the advent in the [United] States of a Russian baroness, Madame H. P. De Blavatsky. I was kindly bidden by my friend Mr. [Charles] Sotheran, of the *American Bibliopolist*, to meet both Madame and Colonel [Olcott] the following evening in [46] Irving Place.

Col. Olcott is well known as the author of *People from Another World*. His experience as a lawyer and a war detective might be supposed to guard him against deception.

Judge M., of New Jersey, represented the judicial mind, and his poetic wife graces any gathering.

There was present also a Boston gentleman.

The center of the group was Madame De Blavatsky, who is certainly a most original and interesting woman to meet. The journals have complained of her cigarettes. Madame speaks English with a strong accent, but with remarkable fluency and

accuracy, distinguishing nicely its delicacies and quickly understanding its allusions. Her fantastic Rosicrucian jewel she wore
about her neck. She is perhaps forty years old, strong-built,
brusque, and generous appearing. Interesting were the stories she
had to relate about her residence in Asia and Africa. Marvelous
were her narratives of her attempts at commerce, selling a cargo
for coconuts, which the unseaworthy ship could not bring away.
Strange sights had she seen among the tribes of sorcerers in
Africa. The phallic element in religions, the souls of flowers,
recent wonders among the mediums, Nature's duality, Romanism,
gravitation, the Carbonari, jugglery, the literature of magic—were
among the topics of animated discussion lasting till after midnight.

If Madame Blavatsky can indeed bring order out of the chaos
of modern spiritism she will do the world a service. Col. Olcott
declares that till he met her he had no philosophy which could
adequately explain the contradictory phenomena he witnessed.

5c. Eugene Rollin Corson
September–October 1875, Ithaca, New York

[Collated from E. Corson 1929, 45–6, 24–6,
118, 26–8, 33, 35, 36–7, 47, 118]

My father's [Hiram Corson's] acquaintance and correspondence with Mme. Blavatsky came about in this way. On July 15th,
1874, my sister died, my father's only daughter, and the blow to
him was very great. In the religion of the churches he found no
comfort, and he turned to spiritualism for some sign and assurance
of the continued existence of his child. In the end he believed
that this sign had come to him, and the assurance of his daughter's
continued life became very strong.

HPB's appearance in this country first became generally
known after her visit to the Eddy brothers in Chittenden,

Vermont, when she published her experiences at the seances of these mediums. My father [then] wrote to her.

Her letters had so increased his interest in her, that he and my mother invited her to be their guest at their home in Ithaca. My father at that time was professor of Anglo-Saxon and English literature at Cornell University, and had been there since 1870. He was a fine scholar, of wide interests, and had become a great authority and teacher, and especially on English poetry. My mother, who was French, herself a fine scholar of the most varied interests, became interested in spiritualism in a moderate way only; it never possessed her as it did my father. She had accepted the loss of her daughter with great composure and resignation, and her interest in HPB was more in the woman herself than in her doctrines and mission. My mother, however, was not interested in occultism; on the contrary, she was greatly opposed to it.

HPB arrived in Ithaca about September 17th, 1875. At that time my father had a cottage known as the Richardson Cottage, on Heustis Street. At the time when HPB visited Ithaca, the weather is usually fine. In October there is the Indian summer; the trees have put on their autumn tints, the mornings and nights are crisp and frosty, with a pleasant warmth in the middle of the day, with the distant hills and lake bathed in the late summer haze. Ithaca proper is in the valley at the foot of Cayuga Lake, and is built up on the east, west, and south hills, with the outskirts heavily wooded. My father's home was on the east hill. On this hill the University stands, an imposing array of noble buildings.

My father in a letter dated October 2nd, 1875 [writes]: "Mme. B. is still with us. She gives us a good deal of trouble, and we get very little from her in return, for she is occupied wholly with her own work. I had expected we should have some [spiritualistic] 'sittings' together; but she is not only not disposed, but is decidedly opposed to anything of the kind. She is a smart woman, but ignorant of all the graces and amenities of life. She is a great Russian bear."

One day my father said to her, "It is a pity, Madame, for you not to see the beauties around you. I want to give you a carriage drive that you may see the University buildings and the lovely country." She finally consented to go, but my father begged her not to smoke in the carriage because the people were not used to it, and it would give them a bad impression and might cause comment, especially with a staid university professor. To this she also reluctantly consented. But before the drive was over, Madame said she would have to smoke a cigarette, she could not stand it a minute longer, and begged that she might get out of the carriage and sit on a stone on a side of the road and smoke in comfort. If the country people took her for a gypsy, why not, what harm would it do? So there sat the author of *Isis Unveiled* and the *Secret Doctrine*, satisfied with her own thoughts and oblivious of everything around her, even the waiting horses and coachman and the carriage with its occupants. Perhaps it was less the tobacco she wanted than the desire to be alone with herself and her own thoughts. When the cigarettes were finished she returned to the carriage and they continued on their drive.

My father dwelt especially on this incident as showing the woman's preoccupation. As he repeatedly said to me: "Never have I seen such an intense creature, intense in her purpose, intense in her endeavor; nothing around her mattered; though the heavens fall she would keep on her way."

It has always been a regret of my life that I did not meet her at that time. I was in Philadelphia studying medicine, [so] I have to rely on what my father and mother told me subsequently.

In her dress she wore mostly a loose wrapper with a sort of embroidered jacket, as my mother described it to me, with the cigarette papers in one pocket and the tobacco in the other. My father, who was a great smoker himself and a judge of tobacco, thought her brand a cheap kind; perhaps her lack of money accounted for it. The cigarettes were countless, and the flowerpots were full of the stubs.

She spent her time at her desk, writing, writing, writing most of the day and way into the night, carrying on a huge correspondence by long letters. Here she started *Isis Unveiled*, writing about twenty-five closely written foolscap pages a day.

On one occasion she asked [my father] for a Greek word on some text in the New Testament, and when [he] said he could not remember it but would look it up for her at once, she said to him, half irritated and half joking: "You school-boy! Why, don't you know it?" My father got the Greek for her, and she went on with her writing.

My mother described to me how HPB would sit down at the piano and improvise with great skill, showing a remarkable efficiency for one who played but at odd times as the spirit might move her.

HPB's phenomena with a few exceptions were not a feature of her visit. She showed the raps as produced by her willpower sometimes through a stack of hands, and again on different parts of the room. My father was familiar with this phenomenon in the seance room through the ordinary medium, but was much more impressed when produced by conscious willpower. On another occasion he had asked if she could place me and tell what I was doing, then a student of medicine in Philadelphia, and she gave him an accurate account of where I was and what was taking place. It happened to be that I was visiting my preceptor on Green Street. She said I was much under his influence, which was true. On another occasion she caused a heavy table to rise up in the air without touching it, and she repeatedly said that this was all due to her willpower, and was not to be classed with the ordinary mediumistic phenomena.

HPB left our home for New York after a visit of a month. [In] a letter from my father, he writes: "Mme. B. has gone. Though there were many things unpleasant in her stay with us, altogether we enjoyed her visit. She is a very remarkable woman, a woman of a frantic intensity. I never knew such a worker. She would write from morning until midnight often without stopping longer than to take dinner and make a cigarette. She smoked two hundred cigarettes in a day. Beardsley has taken some magnificent pictures of her. I shall send you one as soon as they are ready."

5D. Hiram Corson
September–October 1875,
Ithaca, New York

[Lazenby 1910, 9]

She wrote a considerable part of "Isis Unveiled" in my house at Ithaca, and living constantly with her for these weeks, she continually filled me with amazement and curiosity as to what was coming next. She had a profound knowledge of everything apparently, and her method of work was most unusual.

She would write in bed, from nine o'clock in the morning till two o'clock the following morning, smoking innumerable cigarettes, quoting long verbatim paragraphs from dozens of books of which I am perfectly certain there were no copies at that time in America, translating easily from several languages, and occasionally calling out to me, in my study, to know how to turn some old-world idiom into literary English, for at that time she had not attained the fluency of diction which distinguished the "Secret Doctrine."

She herself told me that she wrote down [quotations from books] as they appeared in her eyes on another plane of objective existence, that she clearly saw the page of the book and the quotation she needed, and simply translated what she actually saw into English.

The woman was so marvelous and had such mysterious funds of definite knowledge, that I find it much easier to believe her statement than to account for her quotations by any ordinary explanation of memory.

The hundreds of books she quoted were certainly not in my library, many of them not in America, some of them very rare and difficult to get in Europe, and if her quotations were from memory, then it was an even more startling feat than writing them from the ether. The facts are marvelous, and the explanation must necessarily bewilder those whose consciousness is of a more ordinary type.

Henry Steel Olcott

Chapter 6

THE FOUNDING OF THE THEOSOPHICAL SOCIETY AND THE WRITING OF *ISIS UNVEILED*
September 1875 – September 1877

O N SEPTEMBER 7, 1875, Blavatsky, Olcott, and Judge, together with several others, founded a society that they chose to call "The Theosophical Society," as promulgating the ancient teachings of Theosophy, or the Wisdom concerning the Divine which had been the spiritual basis of other great movements of the past, such as Neo-Platonism, Gnosticism, and the Mystery Schools of the Classical world. The Inaugural Address by the President-Founder, Colonel Olcott, was delivered on November 17, 1875, which is therefore considered to be the official date of the founding of the Society. Starting from a generalized statement of objectives, namely, "to collect and diffuse a knowledge of the laws which govern the Universe," the Founders soon expressed them more specifically. After several minor changes in wording, the Objects stand today as follows:

1. To form a nucleus of the universal brotherhood of humanity, without distinction of race, creed, sex, caste, or color.
2. To encourage the comparative study of religion, philosophy, and science.
3. To investigate unexplained laws of nature, and the powers latent in humanity.

CHAPTER 6

6A. HENRY S. OLCOTT
SEPTEMBER–NOVEMBER 1875, NEW YORK CITY

[Collated from Olcott 1890, 65–66,
67–70, and Olcott 1896, 2–3]

[On September 7, 1875,] a group of ladies and gentlemen agreed, upon my motion, to form a body, which became in due course the Theosophical Society. The meeting was an informal gathering of friends and acquaintances in Madame Blavatsky's parlour [at 46, Irving Place], to listen to Mr. George H. Felt's explanation of a certain alleged discovery by him of the Lost Canon of Proportion [of the Egyptians] by use of which the peerless architects of [Egypt and] Greece had built their temples and forums. His lecture, illustrated by a set of very fine colored drawings, was tenfold heightened in interest by his assertion that he had not only found, on reading the hieroglyphs, that the elemental spirits were largely used in the [Egyptian] temple mysteries, but he had even deciphered the *mantrams* by which they were subjugated, had practically tested them, and found them efficacious. In the company present were several old Spiritualists, myself included, of open mind, who were ready and willing to investigate this subject. As for myself, I had acquired a full conviction of [the] existence [of elemental spirits] and of the power of man to subjugate them, from seeing many phenomena produced by Madame Blavatsky. I had also come to know of the existence of initiated magical adepts in Egypt, India, and certain other parts of the world. The chance, therefore, of being able, with Mr. Felt's help and without dragging in the names of either of my Teachers, to throw such a flood of light upon the problem of psychical phenomena at once suggested itself to my mind; so I wrote on a slip of paper a line or two asking HPB if she thought it a good idea to propose the formation of such a Society, got Mr. Judge to pass it over to her to the opposite side of the room, and, upon her nodding assent, rose and, after making some remarks about the lecture and lecturer, asked if the company present would join me in orga-

70

nizing a society of research in the department covered by Mr. Felt's alleged discovery. I dwelt upon the materialistic tendencies of the age and the desire of mankind to get absolute proof of immortality; pointing to the enormous spread of the spiritualistic movement as the best evidence of the fact, and hinting at the possibility of our being helped in our philanthropic work by the Teachers, from whom HPB had learned what she knew, if we seriously and unselfishly set ourselves to study.

My views as to the necessity of such a society receiving general assent, a motion was made by Mr. Judge and adopted that I be elected chairman of the meeting, and on my motion Mr. Judge was elected secretary. A committee to frame Bye-laws was chosen. An adjourned meeting was held on the [8th] and another on the [13th of] September following, at which latter, the Bye-laws Committee reported progress, and the name of "The Theosophical Society" was adopted. Other meetings were held on the 16th and 30th October, at which the Bye-Laws were considered and adopted, subject of final revision: at a final meeting, on the 17th November, they were formally adopted as revised, the President delivered his Inaugural Address, and the Society was launched as a perfected organization. The officers had been elected at the meeting of October 30th, and were

> *President*, H. S. Olcott;
> *Vice-Presidents*, Dr. S. Pancoast and G. H. Felt;
> *Corresponding Secretary*, H. P. Blavatsky;
> *Recording Secretary*, John Storer Cobb;
> *Treasurer*, H. J. Newton;
> *Librarian*, Charles Sotheran;
> *Councillors*, Rev. J. H. Wiggin, R. B. Westbrook, Emma
>   Hardinge Britten, Dr. C. E. Simmons, Herbert D.
>   Monachesi;
> *Counsel to the Society*: W. Q. Judge.

The originally declared objects of the Theosophical Society were the study of occult science and esoteric philosophy, in theory and practice, and the popularization of the facts throughout the world. The original Preamble says: "(the Founders) hope that by going deeper than modern science has hitherto done into the Esoteric philosophies of ancient times, they may be enabled to attain for themselves and other investigators proof of the existence of an 'Unseen Universe,' the nature of its inhabitants, if such there be, and the laws which govern them and their relations with mankind." In a word, our hope was to acquire this occult knowledge with the aid of Mr. Felt and HPB. That our ideas were eclectic and nonsectarian is clearly shown in the second paragraph of our Preamble:

> Whatever may be the private opinions of its members, *the Society has no dogmas to enforce, no creed to disseminate.* It is formed neither as a Spiritualistic schism, nor to serve as the foe or friend of any sectarian or philosophic body. Its only axiom is the omnipotence of truth, its only creed a profession of unqualified devotion to its discovery and propagation. In considering the qualifications of applicants for membership, it knows neither race, sex, color, country, nor creed.

Our first bitter disappointment was the failure of Mr. Felt to fulfil his promises. With difficulty I got him to give one or two more lectures, but he never showed us so much as the wag of the tail of a vanishing elemental. HPB, then working night and day upon her first book, *Isis Unveiled*, soon refused to even attend our meetings, let alone do so much at them as make the smallest phenomenon—though she was continually astounding her visitors with them at her own house.

The above is a plain, unvarnished narrative of the beginnings of the Theosophical Society as it appears from the outside. I got no "order" to make the Society. The provocation of the suggestion lay in my long-felt and practical interest in psychical science, now fanned into a hot flame by HPB's phenomena, my fresh contact with Eastern adepts, and the apparently easy means of contributing enormously, with Mr. Felt's help and HPB's participation, to the current knowledge of the astral world and its races. The idea sprang up in my mind as naturally and spontaneously as possible, as such ideas do usually occur in one's every-day experience. But a deeper problem lies back of this mental fact. Did the thought of forming the Theosophical Society, really spring from my own brain, or was it put there *ab extra,* by some master of thought transference?

[In a note dated July, 1875, in her scrapbook HPB writes: "Orders received from India direct to establish a philosophico-religious Society and choose a name for it—also to choose Olcott." And in another note from the same scrapbook HPB specifically states: "M[orya] brings orders to form a Society—a secret Society like the Rosicrucian Lodge. He promises to help" (Blavatsky, *Collected Writings* 1:94, 73). —DHC]

6B. HENRY S. OLCOTT
CA. FEBRUARY 1876, NEW YORK CITY

[Olcott 1876]

Wonder treads upon wonder. I wrote an account of my [first] interview with the Brother I took for a Hindoo Brahmin, and was sorry enough afterwards I had said a word about it, either in letter or lecture. [Then] I began to doubt my own senses and fancy the scene had all been an objective hallucination, but I have seen him again yesterday and another man was with him.

Other persons have seen this man in New York. He is not a Brahmin, but a swarthy Cypriote. I did not ask him before of what country he was.

I was reading in my room yesterday (Sunday) when there came a tap at the door. I said, "come in," and then entered the Brother with another dark skinned gentleman of about fifty with a bushy gray beard and eyebrows.

We took cigars and chatted for a while. I asked him if he knew Madam B[lavatsky]. He turned the subject, thus giving me to understand that the first duty of a neophyte is to ask no questions of a personal nature, but take what comes.

He said he would show me the production of flowers as the adepts do it. At the same time pointing to the air, fancy—the shadowy outlines of flower after flower and leaf after leaf grew out of nothing. The room was perfectly light; in fact the sun was shining in. The flowers grew solid. A beautiful perfume saturated the air. They were suspended as the down of a thistle in the air, each separate from the other. Then they formed themselves into bouquets; and a splendid large one of roses, lilies of the valley, camellias, jasmine, and carnations floated down and placed itself in my hand. Then the others separated again and fell in a shower to the floor. I was stupefied with the manifestation.

He asked me if I recollected an instance last summer when I unintentionally left a stuffed armchair out on the balcony, of my being awakened in the night by a heavy thundershower, and of my amazement in the morning to find that the chair was as dry as paper while everything around it was soaking wet. I recalled the circumstances. He said that was a phenomenon made to sharpen up my intuitions, to set me to realize some of the powers that could be exercised by man.

As he spoke, raindrops began pattering around us in the room, and positively a drenching shower was falling about us. The carpet was soaked, and so were my clothes, the books on the table, and the bronzes, and clock, and photos on the mantelpiece. But neither of the Brothers received a drop.

They sat there and quietly smoked their cigars, while mine became too wet to burn. I just sat and looked at them in a sort of stupid daze. They seemed to enjoy my surprise but smoked on and said nothing. Finally the younger of the two (who gave me his name as Ooton Liatto) said I need not worry. Nothing would be damaged.

The shower ceased as suddenly as it had begun. Then the elder man took out of his pocket a painted lacquered case. Upon opening the case, a round flat concave crystal was displayed to view. He told me to look in it. Holding it a few inches from my eye and shading my eye from the light so that there might be no reflected rays cast upon the glass, the box exhaled a strong spicy aromatic odor much like sandalwood but still not just that. Whatever I wished to see, he said, I need simply think of, only taking care to think of but one thing at a time. I did as directed.

I thought of my dead mother as she used to sit with me twenty years ago. I saw, as it were, a door in the far distance. It came nearer and nearer, and grew plainer until I lost consciousness of external objects and seemed to be in the very room I had in mind. Details long forgotten, pictures, furniture, &c came into view. My mother sat there, and the conversation of twenty years ago was renewed.

I thought of a landscape—lo! I stood upon the spot and mountain, valley, river, and buildings lay smiling before me. I was there—not in my room on 34th Street. So for more than an hour, the thing went on. I seemed able to flit from one clime to another with the speed of thought, and to call up any spirit I wished to talk with. Things too that had occurred to me when out of the body (all recollection of which had been obliterated upon the return of my spirit to flesh) were shown me. But these were only a few and unimportant, for when I seemed to be growing inquisitive, some power prevented my seeing anything.

Was I hallucinated? No sir, I was not. At least I can't imagine a person being hallucinated and still be in such a state of mental activity as I was in. I have never been psychologized. I am like cast iron so far as sensitiveness to mesmeric influence, while I used to be a strong mesmerizer myself.

When I saw Liatto before, I tried to pump Madam B. about him. The infernally tantalizing woman would not tell me a word but just looked blank.

The seance being over, as I supposed, I asked Liatto if he knew Madam B. He stared too. But as I thought he ought to know her, since her flat was in the same house, I went on to descant upon her character, her virtues, her intellectuality, &c &c. The elder Brother asked me to present their compliments to Madam and say that with her permission they would call upon her.

I ran down stairs, rushed into Madam's parlor, and there sat these two identical men smoking with her and chatting as quietly as if they had been old friends. Madam motioned to me as if I had better not come in, as if they had private business to talk over. I stood transfixed looking from one to another in dumb amazement. I glanced [at] the ceiling (my rooms are over Madame B.'s), but they had not tumbled through.

Madam said, "What the Devil are you staring at Olcott? What's the matter? You must be crazy." I said nothing but rushed upstairs again, tore open my door, and the men were not there. I ran down again; they had disappeared. I heard the front door close, looked out of the window, and saw them just turning the corner. Madam said they had been with her for more than an hour. And that is all she would tell me about them.

When I showed her my wet clothes and the bouquet of flowers that remained in evidence that I had not been hallucinated, she only said, "That's nothing remarkable. Ask me no questions for I shall tell you nothing. Let the Brothers do what they please for you, I shan't have my name put out again as a medium."

In a half hour from the time the two men left, there was not a drop of moisture in the room nor a shade of dampness to indicate that there had been a shower. But my clothes stayed wet and had to be dried before the fire.

6c. HENRY S. OLCOTT
SUMMER 1875 – SEPTEMBER 1877, NEW YORK CITY

[Olcott 1895, 1: 202–4, 205,
208–12, 236–7, 243–7]

One day in the summer of 1875, HPB showed me some sheets of manuscript which she had written, and said: "I wrote this last night 'by order,' but what the deuce it is to be I don't know. Perhaps it is for a newspaper article, perhaps for a book, perhaps for nothing: anyhow, I did as I was ordered." And she put it away in a drawer, and nothing more was said about it for some time. But in the month of September she went on a visit to her new friends, Professor and Mrs. Corson, of Cornell University, and the work went on. She wrote me that it was to be a book on the history and philosophy of the Eastern Schools and their relations with those of our times. She said she was writing about things she had never studied and making quotations from books she had never read in all her life: that, to test her accuracy, Prof. Corson had compared her quotations with classical works in the University Library, and had found her to be right. Upon her return to town, she was not very industrious in this affair, but wrote only spasmodically, but a month or two after the formation of the Theosophical Society, she and I took two suites of rooms at 433 West 34th St., she on the first and I on the second floor, and henceforward the writing of Isis went on without break or interruption until its completion in the year 1877.

In her whole life she had not done a tithe of such literary labor, yet I never knew even a managing daily journalist who could be compared with her for dogged endurance or tireless working capacity. From morning till night she would be at her desk, and it was seldom that either of us got to bed before 2 o'clock A.M. During the daytime I had my professional duties to attend to, but always after an early dinner we would settle down together to our big writing table and work, as if for dear life, until bodily fatigue would compel us to stop. What an experience!

She worked on no fixed plan, but ideas came streaming through her mind like a perennial spring which is ever overflowing its brim. Higgledy-piggledy it came, in a ceaseless rivulet, each paragraph complete in itself and capable of being excised without harm to its predecessor or successor.

Her own manuscript was often a sight to behold: cut and patched, re-cut and re-pasted, until if one held a page of it to the light, it would be seen to consist of, perhaps, six, or eight, or ten slips cut from other pages, pasted together, and the text joined by interlined words or sentences.

I corrected every page of her manuscript several times, and every page of the proofs; wrote many paragraphs for her, often merely embodying her ideas that she could not then frame to her liking in English; helped her to find out quotations, and did other purely auxiliary work: the book is hers alone, so far as personalities on this plane of manifestation are concerned, and she must take all the praise and the blame that it deserves. Then, whence did HPB draw the materials which compose *Isis*, and which cannot be traced to accessible literary sources of quotation? *From the Astral Light*, and by her soul-senses, from her Teachers—the "Brothers," "Adepts," "Sages," "Masters," as they have been variously called. How do I know it? By working two years with her on *Isis* and many more years on other literary work.

To watch her at work was a rare and never-to-be-forgotten experience. We sat at opposite sides of one big table usually, and I could see her every movement. Her pen would be flying over the page, when she would suddenly stop, look out into space with the vacant eye of the clairvoyant seer, shorten her vision as though to look at something held invisible in the air before her, and begin copying on her paper what she saw. The quotation finished, her eyes would resume their natural expression, and she would go on writing until again stopped by a similar interruption. I remember well two instances when I, also, was able to see and even handle books from whose astral duplicates she copied quotations into her manuscript, and which she was obliged to "materialize" for me, to refer to when reading the proofs, as I refused to pass the pages for the "strike-off" unless my doubts as to the accuracy of her copy were satisfactory. It was when we were living at 302 West 47th Street—the once-famous "Lamasery," and the executive headquarters of the Theosophical Society. I said: "I cannot pass this quotation, for I am sure it cannot read as you have it." She said: "Oh don't bother; it's right; let it pass." I refused, until finally she said: "Well, keep still a minute and I'll try to get it." The far-away look came into her eyes, and presently she pointed to a far corner of the room, to an etagere on which were kept some curios, and in a hollow voice said: "There!" and then came to herself again. "There, there; go look for it over there!" I went, and found the two volumes wanted, which, to my knowledge, had not been in the house until that very moment. I compared the text with HPB's quotation, showed her that I was right in my suspicions as to the error, made the proof correction and then, at her request, returned the two volumes to the place on the etagere from which I had taken them. I resumed my seat and work, and when, after awhile, I looked again in that direction, the books had disappeared! After my telling this (absolutely true) story, ignorant skeptics are free to doubt my sanity; I hope it may do them good. The same thing happened in the case of the apport of the other book, but this one remained, and is in our possession at the present time.

The "copy" turned off by HPB presented the most marked dissemblances at different times. While the handwriting bore one peculiar character throughout, so that one familiar with her writing would always be able to detect any given page as HPB's, yet, when examined carefully, one discovered at least three or four variations of the one style, and each of these persistent for pages together, when it would give place to some other of the calligraphic variants. The style which had been running through the work of, perhaps, a whole evening or half an evening would suddenly give place to one of the other styles which would, in its turn, run through the rest of an evening. One of these HPB handwritings was very small, but plain; one bold and free; another plain, of medium size, and very legible; and one scratchy and hard to read, with its queer, foreign-shaped *a*'s and *x*'s and *e*'s. There was also the greatest possible difference in the English of these various styles. Sometimes I would have to make several corrections in each line, while at others I could pass many pages with scarcely a fault of idiom or spelling to correct. Most perfect of all were the manuscripts which were written for her while she was sleeping. The beginning of the chapter on the civilization of Ancient Egypt [ch. 14 of vol. 1] is an illustration. We had stopped work the evening before at about 2 A.M. as usual, both too tired to stop for our usual smoke and chat before parting; she almost fell asleep in her chair while I was bidding her good-night, so I hurried off to my bedroom. The next morning, when I came down after my breakfast, she showed me a pile of at least thirty or forty pages of beautifully written HPB manuscript, which, she said, she had had written for her by—well, a Master, whose name has never yet been degraded like some others. It was perfect in every respect, and went to the printers without revision.

Now it was a curious fact that each change in the HPB manuscript would be preceded, either by her leaving the room for a moment or two, or by her going off into the trance or abstract-ed state, when her lifeless eyes would be looking beyond me into space, as it were, and returning to the normal state almost imme-diately. And there would also be a distinct change of personality, or rather personal peculiarities, in gait, vocal expression, vivacity of manner, and, above all, in temper.

HPB would leave the room one person and return to it another. Not another as to visible change of physical body, but another as to tricks of motion, speech, and manners; with differ-ent mental brightness, different views of things, different com-mand of English orthography, idiom, and grammar, and differ-ent—very, *very* different command over her temper, which, at its sunniest, was almost angelic, at its worst, the opposite.

Did she write *Isis* in the capacity of an ordinary spiritual medi-um? I answer, Assuredly not. I have known mediums of all sorts—speaking, trance, writing, phenomena-making, medical, clairvoy-ant, and materializing, have seen them at work, attended their seances, and observed the signs of their obsession and possession. HPB's case resembled none of them. Nearly all they did she could do; but at her own will and pleasure, by day or by night, without forming "circles," choosing the witnesses, or imposing the usual conditions. Then, again, I had ocular proof that at least some of those who worked with us were living men, from having seen them in the flesh in India after having seen them in the astral body in America and Europe, from having touched and talked with them.

One of these alter egos of hers, one whom I have since personally met, wears a full beard and long moustache that are twisted, Rajput fashion, into his side whiskers. He has the habit of constantly pulling at his moustache when deeply pondering: he does it mechanically and unconsciously. Well, there were times when HPB's personality had melted away and she was "Somebody else" when I would sit and watch her hand as if pulling at and twisting a moustache that certainly was not growing visibly on HPB's upper lip, and the far-away look would be in the eyes, until presently resuming attention of passing things, the mustached Somebody would look up, catch me watching him, hastily remove the hand from the face, and go on with the work of writing. Then there was another Somebody, who disliked English so much that he never willingly talked with me in anything but French: he had a fine artistic talent and a passionate fondness for mechanical invention. Another one would now and then sit there, scrawling something with a pencil and reeling off for me dozens of poetical stanzas which embodied, now sublime, now humorous ideas. So each of the several Somebodies had his peculiarities distinctly marked, as recognizable as those of any of our ordinary acquaintances or friends. One was jovial, fond of good stories and witty to a degree; another, all dignity, reserve, and erudition. One would be calm, patient, and benevolently helpful; another testy and sometimes exasperating. One Somebody would always be willing to emphasize his philosophical or scientific explanations of the subjects I was to write upon, by doing phenomena for my edification, while to another Somebody I dared not even mention them. I got an awful rebuke one evening. I had brought home a while before two nice, soft pencils, just the thing for our desk work, and had given one to HPB and kept one myself. She had the very bad habit of borrowing penknives, pencils, and other articles of stationery and forgetting to return them: once put into her drawer or writing desk, there they would stay, no matter how much of a protest you might make over it. On this particular evening, the artistic Somebody was sketching on a sheet of common paper and chatting with me about something, when he asked

81

me to lend him another pencil. The thought flashed into my mind, "If I once lend this nice pencil it will go into her drawer and I shall have none for my own use." I did not say this, I only thought it, but the Somebody gave me a mildly sarcastic look, reached out to the pen tray between us, laid his pencil in it, handled it with his fingers of that hand for a moment, and lo! a dozen pencils of the identical make and quality! He said not a word, did not even give me a look, but the blood rushed to my temples and I felt more humble than I ever did in my life. All the same, I scarcely think I deserved the rebuke, considering what a stationery-annexer HPB was!

Now when either of these Somebodies was "on guard," as I used to term it, the HPB manuscript would present the identical peculiarities that it had on the last occasion when he had taken his turn at the literary work. If you had given me in those days any page of *Isis* manuscript, I could almost certainly have told you by which Somebody it had been written. Where, then, was HPB's self at those times of replacement? As I understood it, she herself had loaned her body as one might one's typewriter, and had gone off on other occult business that she could transact in her astral body; a certain group of Adepts occupying and maneuvering the body by turns. When they knew that I could distinguish between them, so as to even have invented a name for each by which HPB and I might designate them in our conversation in their absence, they would frequently give me a grave bow or a friendly farewell nod when about to leave the room and give place to the next relief-guard. And they would sometimes talk to me of each other, as friends do about absent third parties, by which means I came to know bits of their several personal histories, and would also speak about the absent HPB, distinguishing her from the physical body they had borrowed from her.

[In a letter to her sister Vera, Madame Blavatsky writes: "*Someone* comes and envelops me as a misty cloud and all at once pushes me out of myself, and then I am not 'I' any more—Helena Petrovna Blavatsky—but someone else. Someone strong and powerful, born in a totally different region of the world: and as to myself it is almost as if I were asleep or lying by, not quite conscious, not in my own body but close by, held only by a thread which ties me to it. However, at times I see and hear everything quite clearly: I am perfectly conscious of what my body is saying and doing—or at least its new possessor. I even understand and remember it all so well that afterwards I can repeat it and even write down his words. At such a time I see awe and fear on the faces of Olcott and others and follow with interest the way in which *he* half-pityingly regards them out of my own eyes and teaches them with my physical tongue. Yet not with my mind but his own, which enwraps my brain like a cloud" (*Path*, New York, Dec. 1894, 266). For more on this subject, consult Geoffrey A. Barborka's work *H. P. Blavatsky, Tibet, and Tulku* (Adyar, Madras: Theosophical Publishing House, 1966). —DHC]

6D. ALEXANDER WILDER
FALL 1876 –SEPTEMBER 1877, NEW YORK CITY

[Wilder 1908]

In the autumn of 1876 I had been editing several publications for Mr. J. W. Bouton, a bookseller in New York. Other engagements and associations had been laid aside.

On a pleasant afternoon I was alone in the house. The bell was rung, and I answered at the door. Colonel Henry S. Olcott was there with an errand to myself. He had been referred to me by Mr. Bouton. Madame Blavatsky had compiled a work upon occult and philosophic subjects, and Mr. Bouton had been asked in relation to undertaking its publication. Mr. Bouton meant that I should examine the work, and I agreed to undertake the task.

It was truly a ponderous document and displayed research in a very extended field. In my report to [Mr. Bouton], I stated that the manuscript was the product of great research, and that so far as related to current thinking, there was a revolution in it, but I added that I deemed it too long for remunerative publishing.

Mr. Bouton, however, presently agreed to publish the work. He placed the manuscript again in my hands, with instructions to shorten it as much as it would bear. This was a discretionary power that was far from agreeable. It can hardly be fair that a person acting solely in behalf of the publisher should have such authority over the work of an author. Nevertheless, I undertook the task. While abridging the work, I endeavored in every instance to preserve the thought of the author in plain language, removing only such terms and matter as might be regarded as superfluous and not necessary to the main purpose. In this way, enough was taken out to fill a volume of respectable dimensions.

Colonel Olcott was very desirous that I should become acquainted with Madame Blavatsky. He appeared to hold her in high regard, closely approaching to veneration, and to consider the opportunity to know her a rare favor for any one. I was hardly able to share his enthusiasm. Having a natural diffidence about making new acquaintances, and acting as a critic upon her manuscript, I hesitated for a long time. Finally, however, these considerations were passed over and I accompanied him to their establishment in Forty-seventh Street.

It was a "flat," that unhomelike fashion of abode that now extends over populous cities, superseding the household and family relationship wherever it prevails. The building where they lived had been "transmogrified" for such purposes, and they occupied a suite of apartments on an upper floor. The household in this case comprised several individuals, with separate employments. They generally met at meal-time, together with such guests from elsewhere as might happen to be making a visit.

The study in which Madame Blavatsky lived and worked was arranged after a quaint and very primitive manner. It was a large front room and, being on the side next the street, was well lighted. In the midst of this was her "den," a spot fenced off on three sides by temporary partitions, writing desk, and shelves for books. She had it as convenient as it was unique. She had but to reach out an arm to get a book, paper, or other article that she might desire that was within the enclosure. In this place Madame Blavatsky reigned supreme, gave her orders, issued her judgments, conducted her correspondence, received her visitors, and produced the manuscript of her book.

She did not resemble in manner or figure what I had been led to expect. She was tall, but not strapping; her countenance bore the marks and exhibited the characteristics of one who had seen much, thought much, traveled much, and experienced much. Her appearance was certainly impressive, but in no respect was she coarse, awkward, or ill-bred. On the other hand she exhibited culture, familiarity with the manners of the most courtly society, and genuine courtesy itself. She expressed her opinions with boldness and decision, but not obtrusively. It was easy to perceive that she had not been kept within the circumscribed limitations of a common female education; she knew a vast variety of topics and could discourse freely upon them.

I have heard tell of her profession of superhuman powers and of extraordinary occurrences that would be termed miraculous. I, too, believe, like Hamlet, that there are more things in heaven and earth than our wise men of this age are willing to believe. But Madame Blavatsky never made any such claim to me. We always discoursed of topics which were familiar to both, as individuals on a common plane. Colonel Olcott often spoke to me as one who enjoyed a grand opportunity, but she herself made no affectation of superiority. Nor did I ever see or know of any such thing occurring with anyone else.

She professed, however, to have communicated with personages whom she called "Brothers," and intimated that this, at times, was by the agency, or some means analogous to what is termed "telepathy." I have supposed that an important condition for ability to hold such intercourse was abstinence from artificial stimulation such as comes from the use of flesh as food, alcoholic drink, and other narcotic substances. I do not attach any specific immorality to these things, but I have conjectured that such abstemiousness was essential in order to give the mental powers full play, and to the noetic faculty free course without impediment or contamination from lower influence. But Madame Blavatsky displayed no such asceticism. Her table was well furnished, but without profusion, and after a manner not differing from that of other housekeepers. Besides, she indulged freely in the smoking of cigarettes, which she made as she had occasion. I never saw any evidence that these things disturbed, or in any way interfered with her mental acuteness or activity.

At my first visit, her reception was courteous and even friendly. She seemed to become acquainted at once. She spoke of the abridgments which I had made of her manuscript, extolling what I had done far beyond what it deserved. "What had been taken out was 'flapdoodle,' " she declared. My judgment, certainly, had not been so severe as that.

While she was engaged in the work, she had many books relating to the various topics, evidently for consultation. There were Jacolliot's works on India, Bunsen's *Egypt*, Ennemoser's *History of Magic*, and others. I had myself written papers upon a variety of subjects for the *Phrenological Journal* and other periodicals, and she had procured many of them. We often discussed the topics, and their various characteristics, for she was a superior conversationalist and at home on every matter about which we discoursed. She spoke the English language with the fluency of one perfectly familiar with it, and who thought in it. It was the same to me as though talking with any man of my acquaintance. She was ready to take the idea as it was expressed, and uttered her own thoughts clearly, concisely, and often forcibly. Some of the words which she employed had characteristics which indicated their source. Anything which she did not approve or hold in respect she promptly disposed of as "flapdoodle." I have never heard or encountered the term elsewhere. Not even the acts or projects of Colonel Olcott escaped such scathing, and in fact he not unfrequently came under her scorching criticism. He writhed under it, but, except for making some brief expression at the time, he did not appear to cherish resentment.

Several individuals have written letters, as though I knew something that would discredit the genuineness of the originality of *Isis Unveiled*. The manuscript which I handled I am very sure was in the handwriting of Madame Blavatsky herself. Anybody who was familiar with her, would, upon reading the first volume of *Isis Unveiled*, not have any difficulty in recognizing her as the author. Besides, a full third, or even more, of what was published, was written by Madame Blavatsky after Mr. Bouton had set about putting the work in type. She was by no means expert in preparing her material. She patched and changed, making a very large bill for "alterations." Indeed, she never actually finished the work, the publisher declared to me, till he told her that she must stop.

She always treated me with courtesy. When her work was most urgent, or she had been wearied with visitors, she commanded the woman at the door to turn off all callers. That prohibition was repeatedly spoken to me, but as she heard my voice, she would call out to admit me. This occurred when the call was not a matter of business. She was ready in conversation, and was at home on any topic. Few persons in any walk of life are as well supplied with material for discourse. Even Colonel Olcott, who was by no means inferior or commonplace, was not her equal except in his own profession.

Believing that the main body of the work would not be sufficiently attractive to purchasers, I urged her to include in it accounts of the marvelous things which she had observed in India. But this she invariably declined to do, saying that it was not permitted by the "Brothers." That was a tribunal that I could not question; my wisdom in the matter was that of the marketplace. But she was always ready to hear what I had to say, whether in relation to her work, or to philosophic questions, or to subjects of everyday life. When the printer had placed everything in type, I was employed to prepare the index.

The work was finally completed, and *Isis Unveiled* was duly issued [in September 1877].

H. P. Blavatsky about 1878

Chapter 7

MARVELS IN THE LAMASERY
AND DEPARTURE FROM
NEW YORK
1877 – December 1878

IN SEPTEMBER 1877, a powerful impact was made upon the reading and thinking public by the publication of H. P. Blavatsky's first monumental work, *Isis Unveiled*, which was issued by J. W. Bouton in New York City, the one thousand copies of the first printing being sold within ten days. The New York *Herald-Tribune* considered the work as one of the "remarkable productions of the century," many other papers and journals speaking in similar terms. *Isis Unveiled* outlines the history, scope, and development of the esoteric sciences, the nature and origin of magic, the roots of Christianity, the errors of Christian theology, and the fallacies of established orthodox science, against the backdrop of the secret teachings that run as a golden thread through bygone centuries, coming up to the surface every now and then in the various mystical movements of the last two thousand years or so.

Already a public figure, H. P. Blavatsky became increasingly well-known after the publication of *Isis*, and visitors flocked to her New York apartment, nicknamed the Lamasery, to meet the author and to witness the marvelous phenomena that she could perform or that occurred merely in her presence. The source of her abilities and her own identity became a subject of speculation, even among those who knew her well.

On July 8, 1878, H. P. Blavatsky was naturalized as a U.S. citizen, an event that received widespread publicity in various newspapers. In December of that same year, she and H. S. Olcott left for India via England.

7A. Anonymous
January 1877, New York City

["Coming Buddhist Book" 1877]

Mme. Blavatsky was found yesterday afternoon sitting by a blue window with rose-pink curtains, at a large library table, which occupied all the available space that was not taken up by a desk almost as large, in her cozy work-room. She is an affable Russian lady, no longer very young and certainly not old, who is known all over the world as a scholar in various branches of occult knowledge. Piled up on the table and desk, and strewed thick upon the floor, were hundreds upon hundreds of sheets of manuscript, and in the circumscribed space on the table, kept clear for reading and writing, were proof sheets and more manuscripts and writing materials.

"Yes. I am writing a book," she said in reply to a question from the reporter. "It is to be called 'The Veil of Isis' and is in two parts. In the first part, I attack science, and in the second part, dogmatic theology."

"Surely you do not attack science," said the startled reporter, wondering what would be left.

"No, not science as it is, but the teachings of modern scientists. Science is a true and beautiful thing, but these modern scientists have not found out what it is. They borrow theories from the ancients, and dress them up in beautiful, eloquent language, and pass them off for their own productions. The ideas that Huxley advanced while he was over here are all taken from the ancients, as I shall show in my book. But they don't any of them know what they talk about—Huxley, Tyndall, and the rest. They refuse to investigate things which are absolutely demonstrated, and they break their noses over the origin of matter, which is a correlation of spirit, and they reach, for a conclusion, the annihilation of man."

"What is your religion?" asked the reporter.

"I am a Buddhist."

"But does not Buddhism hold out annihilation as the last best good?"

"Not at all. That is simply one of the misrepresentations of ignorant theologians. The Buddhists say that whatever is beyond the power of human language to describe, beyond the reach of human intellect to conceive—whatever is impossible in any measure to understand is, so far as man is concerned, nonexistent, and what we term God is therefore nonexistent. That is, that so far as the understanding of man is concerned, God can have no existence. You see it is merely a refinement of metaphysics. And they believe in the triple nature of man; they teach that we are a material body, an astral body, and pure soul, or nous, as the Greek terms it. After the death of the material body, we lead a dual existence, and finally, when purified, the soul enters nirvana, that is, it rejoins the Creator."

"But what is this astral body you speak of?"

"It is not spirit, and yet not the matter with which we are familiar. It is imponderable matter, imperceptible to the senses."

"Believing in spirits, so you believe in what are called spiritual manifestations?"

"Certainly. The phenomena that are presented as such are perhaps often frauds. Perhaps only one in a hundred is a genuine communication of spirits, but the one cannot be judged by the others. It is entitled to scientific examination, and the reason the scientists don't examine it is because they are afraid. They explore in all directions till they come to shut doors, and they dare not open them for fear of returning to the superstitions of our ancestors, who knew far more than we do. But I believe in them because I have seen them. These mediums cannot deceive me. I know more about it than they do. I have lived for years in different parts of the East, and have seen far more wonderful things than they do.

"The day after I arrived in New York," she continued, "having left Paris suddenly (I did not think of starting until the evening before I started), I went to see Dr. [Henry] Slade [a medium]. He knew I was a foreigner by my accent, but he could not tell if I was German or French, or what. He wrote out a message in the Russian language from a friend of my childhood, who died years ago."

"But what purpose is served by spiritual manifestations?" was asked after Mme. Blavatsky had related several such incidents.

"It is proved that spirits do exist. And I have known good done in various ways by private mediums, and by mediums in the East," was the reply. "But it cannot be expected that pure spirits will communicate with us through such mediums as many of those are to whom you can go and pay 50 cents or $1 or $3 or $5. It is capable of demonstration by medical science that spirits do not communicate through healthy persons. In some way or another, mediums are all imperfect. The spirits which are forever seeking a body to inhabit, seize on those which are defective, being unable to control those which are not. So in the East, insane persons are regarded with peculiar veneration, as being possessed of spirits."

"Possessed of a devil, the Scripture has it," suggested the reporter.

"No. Daimon is the word in the Scriptures. It does not

necessarily mean a devil. It may mean a god. Socrates had a daimon, and he certainly was not possessed of a devil."

"But, as to insane persons. Can any of the medico-scientists tell the reason for insanity? Can they explain it in any way? They stop when they come to anything that requires an explanation involving the so-called supernatural—so-called because nothing can be supernatural. The whole universe is filled with spirits. It is nonsense to suppose that we are the only intelligent beings in the world. I believe there is latent spirit in all matter. I believe, almost, in the spirits of the elements. But all is governed by natural laws. Even in cases of apparent violation of these laws, the appearance comes from a misunderstanding of the laws. In cases of certain nervous diseases, it is recorded of some patients that they have been raised from their beds by some undiscoverable power, and it has been impossible to force them down. In such cases it has been noticed that they float feet first with any current of air that may be passing through the room. The wonder of this ceases when you come to consider that there is no such thing as the law of gravitation as it is generally understood."

"I don't think I catch your meaning, exactly," said the reporter faintly.

"No. The law of gravitation is only to be rationally explained in accordance with magnetic laws, as Newton tried to explain it, but as the world would not accept it. If the earth is, magnetically speaking, positive, and you can make yourself positive, you are at once repelled.

"Yes, I suppose there will be any quantity of mud thrown at me," she said, referring to the probable reception of her book by the public. "They have been throwing mud at me ever since I came here, but that has been nothing to what will come when the book appears." But she laughed heartily at the prospect, and seemed to think that the adverse criticisms which she expected from theologians and scientists would be the best compliments she could receive.

CHAPTER 7

7B. HENRY S. OLCOTT
MARCH 1877, NEW YORK CITY

[Besterman 1934, 148–54]

Putting aside [HPB's] actions, habits of thought, masculine ways, her constant asseverations of the fact . . . putting these aside, I have pumped enough out of her to satisfy me that the theory long since communicated by me to you was correct—she is a man, a very old man, and a most learned and wonderful man. Of course *she* knows just what my impressions are, for she reads my thoughts like a printed page (and others' thoughts), and it seems to me *she* is not dissatisfied, for our relations have insensibly merged into those of Master and pupil. There is not a trace left of the old *sabreur* [swordsman, slasher] Blavatsky ("Jack," as I nicknamed her to her great delight) so far as I am concerned. Now she is all sobriety, dignity, stern self-repression. Before others she is as of old, but the moment their backs are turned she is *Mejnour* [initiate hero of Bulwer-Lytton's novel *Zanoni*] and I the neophyte.

I say Isis [HPB] is a man. Let me add that *she* is (in my opinion) a Hindu man. At any rate, this thing happened tonight after my sister and her husband had gone home: Isis was leaning back in her chair, fooling with her hair, and smoking a cigarette. She got one lock in her fingers and pulled it, and fingered it in an absent way—talking the while, when lo! the lock grew visibly darker and darker until, presto! it was as black as coal. I said nothing until the thing was done, when suddenly catching her hand I asked her to let me have this neat specimen of miracle making as a keepsake. You ought to have seen her face when she saw what she had done in her brown study. But she laughed good-naturedly, called me a sharp Yankee, and cut off the lock and gave it to me. I will send you a bit of it as a talisman. Mind you, this was cut off of Isis's head in my sight and under the full blaze of the chandelier. This one lock showed against the blonde silky and crinkled hair of Blavatsky's head like a skein of black sewing-silk upon a light-brown cloth. Now what this teaches me is just this—The

Blavatsky shell is a shell tenanted by a copper-colored Hindu Solon or Pythagoras, and in this moment of abstraction his own hair—previously there only in its astral condition—became materialized and now stays so. Mind you these are my private speculations.

Why, I can't tell you the number and variety of exhibitions of magical power she has given me and others during the past four months. They exceed all I had seen before. She has done her wonders before 4, 5, and 8 persons, some of them comparative strangers. On Monday night, in the presence of Dr. Billing, Dr. Marquette, Mr. and Miss Monachesi, Mr. Curtis, and myself, these things happened in full light; she made the music of a musical box to be heard in the air. At first faint and far, far away, it grew louder and louder until it sounded as if the box were floating around the room and playing at full force. Then it died away again, again approached, and then suddenly ceased. She carelessly put out her hand, and withdrawing it showed us a long string of those perfumed Oriental beads, whose fragrance filled the room. Holding them in one hand, she asked me if I wanted some, and at once pulled *duplicates* off, one by one, until she had given me 27. I strung them and after handling them awhile laid them on my writing table (beyond her reach a good way) for a moment while I filled a pipe and upon taking them up again, there was a Turkish coin strung on the string with them! Still holding her own original necklace she pulled off (materialized) a bead mounted in gold as a scarf-pin, and upon our drawing lots, Monachesi got it and has it now. The four of the party, happening to sit so they could look out of the window into the street (a room in second story of house), saw pass the window *on the outside* the forms of two men. *One of them was a Brother I know well*, and whose portrait was materialized instantly for me some months ago. The other was a younger Brother—an advanced pupil who can travel in his [astral] double.

O'Sullivan (J. L.) has been here *en route* to Paris, and made "Mme.'s" acquaintance and even stayed all night once with us. In his presence she materialized, on two different occasions, handkerchiefs of a beautifully fine and delicate Chinese silk crepe with a satin-striped border. In the corner, marked in ink, *was the name of a certain Brother* in the ancient Zenzar character. I was present both times. I wish you might have seen O'Sullivan's consternation: he jumped for the handkerchiefs like a trout at a fly, and carried one off as a trophy. The original handkerchief was materialized two weeks ago Sunday in the presence of a French artist named Harrisse. We three were talking of the delicate fabrics of the Chinese, and Harrisse said that their crepes were much finer than those of Lyons. "Did you ever see their handkerchiefs, Madame?" he asked. "Oh! Yes—see, here is one!" she replied, quietly grabbing the very article out of the *astral wardrobe!* This specimen I retained for myself, chiefly because it was strongly impregnated with the Lodge perfume.

HPB's residence at 302 West 47th Street, New York

I saw a splendid exhibition of willpower recently. Isis and I were alone after dinner, in the parlor, when she bade me turn the gas very low and sit quiet at the other side of the room. I made the light very dim, and upon looking at her through the gloom in a few minutes, I saw beside her dark figure (she was dressed in a dark gown) a man's figure in white, or light robes, and with a shawl wound in Eastern fashion about his head. She told me to look away for a moment, and then to turn up the gas. She sat there with the very shawl transferred to her own head, and no one else visible but us two. She gave me the shawl. It was powerfully perfumed with the familiar odor. In one corner was worked the name of the same Brother above alluded to, and in the same Zensar character. It is on his portrait, in my bedroom.

7c. Henry S. Olcott
1877, New York City

[Olcott 1895, 1:377, 379–81]

Our evening's work on *Isis* was finished, I had bade good-night to HPB, retired to my own room, closed the door as usual, sat me down to read and smoke, and was soon absorbed in my book. All at once, as I read with my shoulder a little turned from the door, there came a gleam of something white in the right-hand corner of my right eye; I turned my head, dropped my book in astonishment, and saw towering above me in his great stature an Oriental clad in white garments, and wearing a head cloth or turban of amber-striped fabric, hand-embroidered in yellow floss silk. Long raven hair hung from under his turban to the shoulders; his black beard, parted vertically on the chin in the Rajput fashion, was twisted up at the ends and carried over the ears; his eyes were alive with soul fire, eyes which were at once benignant and piercing in glance. He was so grand a man, so imbued with the majesty of moral strength, so luminously spiritual, so evidently above average humanity, that I felt abashed in his presence, and bowed my head and bent my knee as one does before a god or a godlike personage. A hand was lightly laid on my head, a sweet though strong voice bade me be seated, and when I raised my eyes, the Presence was seated in the other chair beyond the table. He told me he had come at the crisis when I needed him, that my actions had brought me to this point, that it lay with me alone whether he and I should meet often in this life as co-workers for the good of mankind, that a great work was to be done for humanity, and I had the right to share in it if I wished, that a mysterious tie, not now to be explained to me, had drawn my colleague [HPB] and myself together, a tie which could not be broken, however strained it might be at times. He told me things about HPB that I may not repeat, as well as things about myself, that do not concern third parties. At last he rose, I wondering at his great height and observing the sort of splendor in his countenance—not an external shining, but the soft gleam, as it were, of an inner light— that of the spirit. Suddenly the thought came into my mind: "What if this be but hallucination; what if HPB has cast a hypnotic glamour over me? I wish I had some tangible object to prove to me that he has really been here, something that I might handle after he is gone!" The Master smiled kindly as if reading my thought, untwisted the *fehta* [turban] from his head, benignantly saluted me in farewell and was gone: his chair was empty; I was alone with my emotions! Not quite alone, though, for on the table lay the embroidered head cloth, a tangible and enduring proof that I had not been "overlooked," or psychically befooled, but had been face to face with one of the Elder Brothers of Humanity. To run and beat at HPB's door and tell her my experience was the first natural impulse, and she was as glad to hear my story as I was to tell it. I returned to my room to think, and the gray morning found me still thinking and resolving. I have been blessed with meetings with this Master and others since then.

[Note: Colonel Olcott elsewhere describes how the Master Morya left his room: "When I asked him to leave me some tangible evidence that I had not been the dupe of a vision, but that he had indeed been there, he removed from his head the *puggri* [turban] he wore, and giving it to me, vanished from my sight." H. S. Olcott, *Theosophy, Religion and Occult Science* (London, 1885), p. 123. —DHC]

7D. EMILY KISLINGBURY
AUTUMN 1877, NEW YORK CITY

[Collated from HPB: In Memory 1891,
11–3, and Kislingbury 1877, 279]

My earliest acquaintance with HPB dates from the autumn of the year 1877, when I took advantage of a three months' leave of absence from my duties in England to seek her out in New York. The Spiritualist movement, with which I was officially connected, was at that time in full swing, and the appearance of Col. Olcott's book, *People from the Other World*, was making a great stir. The part of the book which attracted me, however, was that in which Col. Olcott related the appearance on the scene of the Russian lady lately arrived from the East, and whose explanation of the phenomena was widely different from that generally received. As soon as I learned the address of Madame Blavatsky from the American Spiritualist journals, I wrote to her, and it was in consequence of our correspondence that I was induced to visit America.

Our first introduction was a singular one. I was staying at some distance from where HPB was then residing, and one afternoon, soon after my arrival, I went to call on her. After ringing three times in vain, I was about to turn away in despair, when the door was opened by HPB herself! Having already exchanged photographs, recognition was mutual, and my welcome the heartiest imaginable. We went up to the flat on the second floor. I could not remain then, for I was leaving New York the next day on a little tour to Niagara and elsewhere; but on my return three weeks later, I spent five weeks with HPB until I finally left for England.

Just at that time *Isis Unveiled* was going through the press, and many were the happy hours I spent correcting proof sheets and discussing the problems put forward in that marvelous book.

Various instances of HPB's psychical powers occurred while I was with her, but most of these are difficult to record, are in fact incommunicable. One instance is of mesmeric power exerted upon myself. I was reading, in a position from which I could see into a mirror on the opposite side of the room, and I remarked to Madame Blavatsky that the wall which was reflected in the mirror appeared to be moving up and down. She said, "That is an atmospheric effect," and went on reading her Russian newspaper. I then began to look at the mirror intently, and I saw Madame Blavatsky look at me once or twice. I was aware that she had her eye on me, but that was all. I continued to gaze, and presently the mirror became clouded and I saw distinctly, though momentarily, two different scenes. The first was that of a sea in motion, covered with ships, and might have been a port or harbor. This faded out, like a dissolving view, and was succeeded by a picture representing a group of men in Eastern costume, turbans and long garments, such as is worn by Hindus. The men seemed as if alive and conversing together. When I told Madame Blavatsky what I had seen, she said, "That is right; that is what I wished you to see; I am sorry I did not write it down, that you might have had the proof to carry away with you."

It required no special insight to perceive that communication was constantly kept up with some distant or invisible minds. Frequent signals of various kinds were heard even at the dinner table, when HPB would immediately retire to her own apartment. So familiar were these sounds, as well as the terms "Masters" and "Brothers," that when in after years so much controversy as to their reality took place, even among those calling themselves Theosophists, it never occurred to me to doubt their existence.

7E. Elizabeth L. Saxon
September 1877, New York City

[Saxon 1877]

Previous to my late visit North, a mutual friend had given me a letter to the Russian Countess, Madame H. P. Blavatsky, whose queer ideas and freely expressed opinions on spiritualism and other matters had made her a target, and the missiles fired were of all sorts, ranging from Indian arrows with poison tips to the sling and stone of petty malice, as well as good round shot, for force and logic, on the part of some of her opponents. But the Madam had held such even combat, and her ever ready pen had so stoutly defended her Russian compatriots in the daily papers of New York that, when I went to see her, the balances stood pretty even, for and against.

Some parties had essayed the task of ridicule and represented her as a sort of monster in size, as well as character and action. Of all things, I like what are called "odd or curious people." I know at once they are not cut on the "Miss Nancy or Simple Thomas pattern," and there is a chance of finding something original in the individual so marked, and you don't run the risk of finding them sewed up on all subjects but the weather.

I was invited into the famous "den," with its blue-glass windows, described by so many New York reporters, never before, I think, by a woman. Her factotum, Lucy, was so like our New Orleans Lucys that a single impulsive exclamation on my part caused Lucy to become my friend at once, and ever after she desired to give me a cup of tea when I entered that hospitable abode.

I sat down in the square room to await the lady, feeling a strange sense of a foreign atmosphere, under the unbroken rays of deep blue glass, giving a shadowy moonlight mellowness to things seen from the outside and a strange, Oriental appearance to the singular collection within.

In the four corners of the room was a long narrow mirror in a dark frame, crowned with palms. The three large windows were hung with heavily fringed blue drapery, under which a canary hung and sung in each. Over one door grinned a huge tiger's head, over another a crocodile was suspended, an asp was clinging to the wall above, and around were pictures of Russian, Japanese, and Indian friends, as well as many English and American savants and literati.

In one corner was a stuffed monkey wearing a saintly collar and snowy cravat, paper under arm and glasses astride the nose, that I heard her soon afterwards call by a professor's name, in a jocular manner. On the mantel was a gilded image of Buddha, seated on a figure of the globe, holding in his hand a flask. On a stand near, a bronze of some oriental workmanship, and a table loaded with crayons, pictures, and papers. Two cases of shelves filled with books, a huge desk loaded with papers, and three or four large lounging chairs filled up the room.

From an adjoining room M'me B——— entered, holding my letter in her hand. It was from one she respected and admired and sufficiently cordial to insure me a very friendly welcome. M'me B——— is not in appearance over forty-five, if that; she is stout, weighing about one hundred and eighty, has wavy brown hair that she combs plainly back without puffs or braids, and she is evidently a woman well accustomed to all the amenities of refined society, however much she seems disposed to throw aside many of its useless conventionalities.

She speaks English with a strong foreign accent, has a gay, melodious laugh, and certainly the prettiest hands one could wish to see, snowy white and dimpled, the taper fingers bright with diamonds, and terminated by long sharp pointed nails, as worn by the Japanese.

Like all Russians she is a great smoker; she uses many cigarettes and invariably tenders each guest one of the little rolls in the most graceful manner; and not infrequently a cup of delicious tea is also shared with her guests in an equally unceremonious way. I am free to confess I would not refuse the pipe of peace, offered in solemn conclave by an Indian brave, or the "bread and salt" of an Arab sheik. The cigarette of the Russian lady was accepted in the same spirit. What I did with it "this deponent sayeth not." We entered into an amicable discourse of the views held by our mutual friend. This led us on, and we were soon deep in discussion.

She holds stoutly to the belief that much of what is called modern spiritualism is of human origin and will so eventually be understood. That is, that the unseen living "astral spirit" performs much of it, while both medium and investigator are ignorant of the fact.

"But, Madam," I exclaimed, "there are some facts that have come under my own observation, that I cannot reconcile with this belief."

"Understand me," she said, "I do not deny the power of spirit return. I only hold that much of these manifestations are made by elementary spirits of a low order, vile beings who are neither destined to nor worthy of immortality; they are of the earth earthy, linger around until their material bodies dissolve into the elements, and they too dissolve and mingle with it."

Turning, she took up the first volume of her book [*Isis Unveiled*], fashioned in form but not yet bound, and read one or two extracts to prove her argument.

This led to a discussion of her book and its claims. I will not here express any opinion of my own, only stating that she has with daring courage undertaken to prove that modern science, religion, and spiritualism have revamped modern ideas, on ancient facts, either knowingly or in ignorance, and [she] stands forth a champion for the religion and philosophy of India.

She hurls her gage down and challenges investigation of Eastern claims. Her book reads like the wonders of the "Arabian Nights" in some of its statements, but she assured me the "half was not told," and certainly testimony of this mystic power is not wanting elsewhere. Her book comprises two large volumes of over six hundred pages each. It is issued by Bouton, and is bound to meet with large sales. I read the first volume, and would advise others to read them: whether for or against her opinions. Her long life in the East and her command of sources of information gives her great power. She is a formidable antagonist from the fact that the languages of the East are perfectly familiar to her, and their literature has been at her command.

I found her in all things genial and pleasant, her information regarding Russian matters of the best. She is in daily communion by letters and telegrams from friends, and an uncle and cousin are in the Russian service, both officers of rank. She is as earnest an advocate of her people as ever clashed a sword or wielded a pen.

I was in company one evening in her rooms with the pretty and talented wife of a prominent Southern editor—a member of the press—and a gentleman from India; Col. Olcott, whom I had met the winter before, was also present. I heard the music spoken of by reporters floating through the air; of its origin or nature I have no opinion to offer. Col. Olcott read a long letter received from an aunt of M'me B., speaking in glowing terms of her niece, Helene. M'me B. asserts that the medium is a passive instrument in the hands of the invisibles, but the "adept" commands this un-seen force by the power of will, and that she is an adept.

I shall long remember with pleasure the cordial geniality of this woman.

7F. PRINCESS HELENE VON RACOWITZA MAY 1878, NEW YORK CITY

[Racowitza 1902]

Accompanied by my husband, I pulled the bell of Madame Blavatsky's flat. The door was opened by a neat little Negress, who, showing all her teeth in a broad grin, pointed with her hand to a door closed by dark Indian curtains, through which the sound of lively conversation reached us. We went in unannounced and were greeted with a loud joyous shout of welcome by HPB—as Madame Blavatsky always liked best to be called.

She sat at her writing table in a large, comfortable armchair, which seemed as much a part of her as the flowing garments. A samovar stood beside her, from which she continually supplied her guests with the fragrant Russian national beverage, while just as perpetually her beautiful hands never ceased for a moment to roll between their graceful fingers delicate cigarettes for herself and all present, for HPB was almost more inseparable from her box of finely cut Turkish tobacco than from her Indian garments, and whenever she changed her seat, which seldom happened, the little Negress had to carry it after her. Around her sat or reclined eight or ten people, men and women of all ages and apparently belonging to every possible class of society.

As we entered, a man of very distinguished appearance was just relating to a small group his latest experiences from the "spirit-world." He was a former Ambassador of the United States, well known for his personal charm, who was then living wholly for the occult sciences. All these people sat or reclined in comfortable, careless attitudes on the low divans and cushions or on small seats, made up of boxes and chests, covered with Indian cloths and rugs.

These, with a variety of idols and oriental bric-a-brac, formed the furnishing of the room. In it there reigned a hum and buzz of conversation in various languages, and clouds of incense and tobacco smoke, streaming from oriental incense sticks and the Russian cigarettes which everyone present was smoking, so that it needed a few moments of becoming accustomed to it, before eye and ear could clearly make out what was going on.

We were instantly, as [HPB] expressed it, quite crazy for one another. She declared that I impressed her as if a bit of sunshine had got loose and were shining straight into her heart; while I found myself at once entirely under the spell of this marvelous woman. Outwardly she was quite unusually corpulent and indeed never spoke of herself otherwise than as "an old hippopotamus." But that made not the smallest unpleasant impression; she always wore loose flowing garments of a sort of Indian cut—a kind of flowing robe, which concealed the entire figure, leaving only the really ideally beautiful hands free.

Her head, standing out from the usually dark-colored woolen garments, was equally full of character, even though far sooner to be called ugly than beautiful. A genuinely Russian type: broad forehead, short, thick nose, prominent cheek bones, thin, clever, ever mobile mouth with beautiful, small teeth, brown, quite curly hair, almost like a Negroes, then still without a single silver thread in it, yellowish complexion, and—a pair of eyes, such as I have never elsewhere seen—light blue, almost water-gray, but with a look so deep, so piercing, so compelling, as if they gazed into the inmost being of things, and at times with an expression as if directed far, far above and beyond all earthly things—large, long, wonderful eyes that lit up the whole of that most singular face. To give this bodily picture is easy—but how shall I begin to describe the wonderful woman herself, how give an idea of her nature, her power, her character, of what she could do!

She was a mixture of the most heterogeneous qualities. In conversation she possessed a charm which none could withstand, and which probably lay for the most part in her keen and living appreciation of everything great and noble, and in her bubbling enthusiasm, mated with an original, often somewhat pungent humor, and a way of expressing herself which often drove into the most comical despair her Anglo-Saxon friends, who as all the world knows are rather given to prudery in the use of words.

Her contempt, nay rebellion, against all society forms and formalities made her sometimes of purpose put on a coarseness not usual with her; and she hated and battled against the convention-al lie with the heroic courage of a true Don Quixote. Yet whoever came to her poor and ragged, hungry and needing comfort, could be certain of finding a heart so warm and hand so freely and generously open as could be found with no other cultured human being however "good-mannered" he might be.

7g. Anonymous
December 10, 1878, New York City

["H. P. Blavatsky's Adieux" 1878]

Helen P. Blavatsky is leaving America, as she says, forever. A very damp reporter found his way into the pleasant French flat at Eighth avenue and Forty-seventh street this morning, and his ring was answered by a colored servant, who expressed serious doubts as to whether his mistress would see any one at so early an hour. The interviewer was, however, ushered into a breakfast room, which was in a very disordered condition, and invited to a seat on a vacant stool. The disorder was a necessary result of yesterday's auction sale, and the only semblance of occupancy left were an un-cleared breakfast table and three human occupants. Colonel Olcott sat at the table busily making memoranda in a notebook and burning his handsome moustache with a half-finished cigar that struggled ineffectually to reach beyond the outskirts of his beard.

When the reporter was finally ushered into Mme. Blavatsky's own room, he found that lady seated at the end of a letter and tobacco laden table, twisting a fragrant cigarette from a quantity of loose tobacco of a famous Turkish brand. The room was the inner temple of the Lamasery, which has become so widely known in recent years.

The reporter said: "And so you are going to leave America?"

"Yes, and the Lamasery where I have spent so many happy, happy hours. I am sorry to leave these rooms, although there is little to regret about them now," glancing about at the bare floors and walls, "but I am glad to get away from your country. You have liberty, but that is all, and of that you have too much, too much!"

The reporter asked Mme. Blavatsky: "How with your dislike for America did you come to abandon your Russian citizenship and become a resident of New York?"

"Ah, you have liberty. I had none. I could not be protected by Russian consuls so I will be protected by American consuls."

"When shall you leave?"

"I know neither the time nor the vessel, but it will be very soon. I am going first to Liverpool and London, where we have branch Theosophical societies. Then I shall go direct to Bombay. Oh! how glad I shall be to see my dear Indian home again!" and as she arose and wrapped a morning gown of strange design about her, she looked very much the Oriental priestess which she claims she is—not.

7H. ANONYMOUS
DECEMBER 1878, NEW YORK CITY

["Silence in the Lamasery" 1878]

On last Sunday night a farewell reception was given to the friends and the members of the Theosophical Society, by the famous heathen of Eighth Avenue, Madame H. P. Blavatsky, who, together with Col. H. S. Olcott and another Theosophist, sailed yesterday for Liverpool, en route for Bombay. The spacious rooms of the Lamasery were denuded of furniture, even the carpets having been torn up and sold, and the guests sat on two or three chairs hardly worth selling, and upon boxes and trunks corded and marked for transportation. The usual refreshments were provided in the usual plenty. Tea was served in rotation, only three teacups being left from the sale, but every guest had either a pipe or a cigarette.

There was much talk of the probable future of the Theosophical Society, which is expected to become a powerful factor in the development of the mental and religious freedom of the world. But, as was natural, there was far more talk of personal memories and anticipations. Madame Blavatsky carried fully her share of the conversation. Her memories of the years she has passed in America were far from cheerful. "I hate the civilization you boast of," she said emphatically. But her anticipations were rose-colored. "I shall go to Bombay, and be with my dear heathen," she said, "who are free from the yokes of Christianity at least. I shall only stop for a day or two in England to visit our branch society, and then on to India."

Presently a man came in with a phonograph which had been procured for the purpose of carrying greetings to India, without the possibility of any mistake in their delivery. A tall sculptor was dislodged from a barrel on which he sat, and the phonograph was put in position, after which the greetings were shouted into the paper funnel, and a song in pigeon Hindustani was sung into it by a jolly English artist. Charles, a huge Theosophical cat, was then induced to purr at the machine, and the various records were carefully put away.

Long after midnight the talk was kept up. On Monday and Tuesday the packing was finished, and on Tuesday night the little party gathered in the [steamer] *Canada's* saloon. Charles, in the mean time, had been sent to a good Theosophist's house, but had disappeared from the basket in transitu, and has not been seen since. "I don't know where he is," said the Hierophant [Olcott], "but I presume we will find him in Bombay when we get there."

Yesterday morning a few of the most intimate friends of the travelers went to the steamer to bid them farewell. The Hierophant wrote dozens of last dispatches on the cabin table, sending messenger after messenger away on various errands, and giving all sorts of instructions as to the future management of the society to the newly chosen officers. Madame Blavatsky held high court in her stateroom, when the inevitable cigarettes were consumed in great numbers, and when a few of her most faithful disciples were telling her of their grief at her departure.

"I am glad to go, but I am sorry to leave the few good friends I have found here," she said, and one by one they bade her what was probably their last farewell on earth.

H. P. Blavatsky about 1878

Chapter 8

LONDON, BOMBAY, AND ALLAHABAD

1879

*B*LAVATSKY AND OLCOTT, after a brief stop in England, continued their sea journey to India, arriving in Bombay in February 1879, where they established their Theosophical Headquarters. Soon after landing, they were contacted by Alfred Percy Sinnett, then Editor of the Government paper, the *Pioneer* of Allahabad. This contact soon proved of the utmost importance.

After a tour of northwestern India, the Founders returned to Bombay and started, in October 1879, their first Theosophical Journal, the *Theosophist* (still published today), with H. P. Blavatsky as editor. The Society experienced then a rapid growth, and some very remarkable people were attracted to it both in India and elsewhere.

The Theosophist, *October 1879*

8A. CHARLES C. MASSEY
JANUARY 1879, NORWOOD, NEAR LONDON

[Massey 1884]

One evening in January 1879 I had come down to Norwood by train, and found a company of some half-dozen persons assembled in the dining-room of Dr. and Mrs. Billing's house. Madame Blavatsky was not in the room when I entered, but joined us very shortly afterwards. I had hung up my overcoat in the hall outside. Madame Blavatsky turned to me and asked if I would like to name some article for myself to be produced then and there. Having for some time been in want of a card case—a want I had certainly not mentioned to any one present or, I believe, to anyone at all—I named that article.

I [was] immediately afterwards dissatisfied with that particular article I had named, as a test [and] wished to substitute another choice, but was told I was too late. I was to go into the hall, and put my hand in the pocket of my overcoat. Be it observed—and this I can state most positively—that *no one* but myself left the room after I had asked for the card case, and I went out into the hall as directed, unaccompanied by anyone. The hall was just outside the room, which had no other door than the one I went out at. I at once put my hand into the pocket of my overcoat, and there, sure enough, was an ivory card case, which I still have. It was a large, square, lady's card case, not the small oblong one used by men. The card case was not in my pocket when I entered the house. Madame Blavatsky was "not prepared" for my desire. I have long regarded the incident as inexplicable (except by occult power) on the facts present to my recollection.

8B. HENRY S. OLCOTT
JANUARY 1879, LONDON

[Olcott 1900, 2:4–6]

The most striking incident of our stay in London was the meeting of a Master by three of us as we were walking down Cannon Street. There was a fog that morning, so dense that one could hardly see across the street, and London appeared at its worst. The two who were with me saw him first, as I was next to the curb, and just then my eyes were otherwise occupied. But when they uttered an exclamation, I turned my head quickly and met the glance of the Master as he looked back at me over his shoulder. I did not recognize him for an acquaintance, but I recognized the face as that of an Exalted One; for the type once seen can never be mistaken. We three friends kept together in the City and went together back to Dr. Billing's house, yet on entering we were told by both Mrs. Billing and HPB that the Brother had been there and mentioned that he had met us three—naming us—in the City. Mrs. Billing described him as a very tall and handsome Hindu, with a peculiarly piercing eye which seemed to look her through. For the moment she was so staggered that she could not say a word, but the stranger said: "I wish to see Madame Blavatsky," and moved towards the door of the room where she sat. Mrs. Billing opened it for him and bade him enter. He did so, and walked straight towards HPB, made her an Oriental salutation, and began speaking to her in a tongue the sounds of which were totally unfamiliar to Mrs. Billing.

8C. GEORGE WYLD
JANUARY 1879, NORWOOD, NEAR LONDON

[Wyld 1903, 71–3]

It was in 1879 that, at a dinner party at the house of Mr. Billing, I first met Madame Blavatsky and Colonel Olcott. As I left the house, accompanied by a friend, he asked me what my impression was as to the character of Madame, and my reply was: "She seems to me quite the Kalmuck, and my impression is that she might have been a worn-out actress from some suburban theatre in Paris." But her undoubtedly mediumistic powers, her striking personality, her cleverness and humor, and her evidently kindly instincts interested me; and so out of curiosity, and interest, and belief in her promises, I joined her Theosophical Society, and after some two years, I became the President of the British Branch.

On one occasion when I was dining with her at the Billing's, I observed that she and Colonel Olcott ate very freely of animal food; and this startled me, for she had always taught us that those who eat animal food were never admitted to the higher circles of the occult societies, and I thought to myself, "I wonder if that woman is altogether an impostor." As I asked myself this question, she knocked on her plate with her knife, and when I looked at her she said, "Not quite so bad as that, doctor"; and we both good-humoredly laughed at the comicality of the situation. I think it was also at the same dinner party that she suddenly turned round on Colonel Olcott, who sat a few places from her, engaged in the consumption of animal food, and in an angry and loud voice exclaimed: "You baboon!" This shocked me, for Colonel Olcott was, although very credulous, yet an intelligent, self-denying, and kindly man. After dinner was over I took him aside and asked him what Madame Blavatsky meant by so coarsely addressing him at the table, and his reply was: "Dr. Wyld, her conduct is part of my training; and I do not believe there is another man in the United States who would submit as I do to the continual insults I receive at her hands."

On another occasion I was sitting at her side on the drawing room stairs when she again and again cried out and jumped about; and on my asking her what it all meant, she said: "They won't let me alone!" and when I asked: "Who won't let you alone?" she answered: "These Mahatmas are always pinching me to attract my attention!" Lastly, on one occasion when, with a most refined and interesting woman, I was in her society, and the lady asked her what her views as to the nature of Jesus Christ were, she answered: "Madame, I have not the honor of the gentleman's acquaintance."

I do not idly record these experiences, but because I think it right that her irreverence and vulgarities should be known. For, although she knew some curious Eastern occult secrets of psychical origin, yet it has always seemed to me a marvelous thing how any refined and thoughtful man or woman could continue to believe in this queer woman who smoked so incessantly, as an inspired expounder of the highest spiritual secrets of the human race.

8D. HENRY S. OLCOTT
FEBRUARY–JULY 1879, BOMBAY, INDIA

*[Collated from Olcott 1900, 2:8–25,
and Hume 1882, 78–80]*

On the 17th [of January] we left for Liverpool, after a delightful stay of a fortnight [in England] with and among our kind
friends and colleagues. The next day we passed at the Great
Western Hotel, Liverpool, and at 5 p.m. embarked on the *Speke
Hall* in a downpour of rain. The vessel was dirty and disagreeable
to see; and what with that, and the falling of rain, the smell of
damp tapestries and carpets in the saloon and cabins, and the forlorn faces of our forty fellow passengers, all equally disgusted as
ourselves, it was a wretched omen for our long voyage out to India.

Meanwhile HPB was making it lively for the servants and her
fellow passengers who, with one or two exceptions, were shocked
by her ironclad language [and] outraged by her religious hetero-
doxy. The ship being struck by a tremendous sea, HPB was pitched
against a leg of the dining-table, got her knee badly bruised, [and
was] laid up in her cabin with her lame knee.

At the rate of 250 to 300 miles a day, we sailed up the
Mediterranean, past Gibraltar, past Algiers, on to Malta. Port Said
[Egypt] was reached on 2nd February, and then came two days and
nights in the Suez Canal. [We] emerged into the Red Sea and
began the third and final stage of our sea pilgrimage to the Land
of Desire. That night the moon paved with silver the waters of the
Gulf of Suez, and we felt as if we were sailing on a dream sea.
Nothing of moment happened until the 12th, when a flue burst in
the boiler, and we had to stop for repairs. On the 15th [of
February], at noon, [we] were but 160 miles away from [the
Bombay lights], and the next morning entered Bombay Harbor.
Before sunrise I was on deck and, as we steamed rapidly towards
our anchorage, reveled in the panorama of the harbor that was
spread before me. Elephanta, ahead of us, was the first locality we
asked to be shown us, for it was the type and visible representative

of that Ancient India. Alas! as one turned towards the promontory of the Malabar Hill the dream was dispelled. The India we saw there was one of sumptuous bungalows, framed in the luxury of English flower gardens, and surrounded with all the signs of wealth gained in foreign commerce.

The ship's anchor was hardly dropped before we were boarded by three Hindu gentlemen in search of us. All seemed strangers to us, but when they pronounced their names I opened my arms and pressed them to my breast. We went ashore in their bunder boat and landed on the Apollo Bunder. The first thing I did on touching land was to stoop down and kiss the granite step; my instinctive act of puja!

The noonday Bombay sun of mid-February is a surprise to a Western visitor, and we had time to feel its full power before Mr. Hurrychund came.

The streets of Bombay charmed us with their strikingly Oriental character. The tall apartment houses in stucco, the novel dresses of the motley Asiatic population, the quaint vehicles . . . all these vivid impressions filled us with delight.

Before leaving New York, I had written Hurrychund to engage for us a small, clean house in the Hindu quarter. We were taken to a house on Girgaum Back Road, standing in a comparatively forlorn compound, and adjoining his glass-roofed photographic studio. Cocoa palms nodded their fronds over our roof, and Indian sweet-scented flowers rejoiced our sense of smell; after the dismal sea voyage it seemed like Paradise. The ladies of our friends' families called on HPB and a number of Hindu and Parsi gentlemen on our whole party; but the rush of visitors began the next morning.

We had formed one acquaintanceship on the *Speke Hall* that turned into a lasting friendship, that of Mr. Ross Scott, B.C.S., a noble fellow and an Irishman of the better sort. His long conversations with us about Eastern philosophy had resulted in his joining our Society. He called on the evening of our first day ashore and provoked HPB to doing a phenomenon that was quite new to me. They were sitting together on a sofa and I was standing with

Hurrychund at the center table, when Scott reproached HPB for her evident intention of letting him go North to his official post, without giving him the least proof of the existence of the psychical powers in men, of which she had so much spoken. She liked him very much, and so consented to comply with his request. "What shall I do for you?" she asked. He snatched the handkerchief she was holding in her hand and, pointing to her name "Heliona" embroidered across one corner, said: "Well, make that name disappear and another to take its place." "What name do you want?" she rejoined. Looking towards us, where we stood at a distance of a few paces, he pointed to our host and said: "Let it be Hurrychund's." We came over to them on hearing this, and saw what was done. She [told] Scott to hold tight in his hand the embroidered corner of her handkerchief, retaining the opposite corner herself. After a minute or so she told him to look. He did so, found the substitution of names had been made, Hurrychund's being there in the same kind of embroidery, and in the first impulse of excitement, cried out: "Where is your physical science now? This beats all the professors in the world!"

On the evening of 17th February, a reception was held at the photographic studio, at which over 300 invited guests were present. The usual welcome address, with garlands, limes, and rosewater as accompaniments, was given us.

We changed quarters, bought furniture and other necessaries, and on 7th March settled ourselves down in the little house, 108 Girgaum Back Road, for the next two years. Every evening we held an impromptu durbar, when the knottiest problems of philosophy, metaphysics, and science were discussed. Visitors kept on crowding our bungalow, and stopping until late every evening to discuss religious questions. We were completely happy in our retired cottage under the cocoa-palms. And under those umbrageous palms, we were visited in person by Mahatmas; and their inspiring presence made us strong to proceed in the path we were treading.

[On July 15, Mahatma Morya] visited me in the flesh at Bombay, coming in full daylight, and on horseback. He had me called by a servant into the front room of HPB's bungalow (she being at the time in the other bungalow talking with those who were there). He came to scold me roundly for something I had done in TS matters, and as HPB was also to blame, he telegraphed to her to come, that is to say, he turned his face and extended his finger in the direction of the place she was in. She came over at once with a rush and, seeing him, dropped on her knees and paid him reverence. My voice and his had been heard by those in the other bungalow, but only HPB and I, and the servant saw him.

[Note: In Colonel Olcott's diary for July 15, 1879, the following entry is written: "Had visit in body of the Sahib!! [He] sent Babula to my room to call me to HPB's bungalow, and there we had a most important private interview. Alas! how puerile and vain these men make one feel by contrast with them." —DHC]

8E. ANONYMOUS
FEBRUARY 16–17, 1879, BOMBAY, INDIA

["Theosophic Thaumaturgy" 1879]

Strange stories have, for several years, been rife in the American newspapers about the marvels of thaumaturgy wrought by the Countess Blavatsky, one of the Theosophical party now in Bombay. If they are credible, the inference would be that a Simon Magus in petticoats had arisen in our days. Some of them stagger belief, as for instance, her causing music to float through the air in the absence of any comprehensible cause, the instantaneous duplication of documents and articles of clothing, the causing of inscriptions in golden letters, in Oriental texts, to appear and disappear on the furniture, the rendering of herself invisible, the production of paintings and writings on paper by the mere placing of her palm upon the same. Yet all these phenomena and many equally strange have been attested by numbers of eyewitnesses, not Theosophists nor even always previous acquaintances. Of one of her magical pictures—the portrait of an Indian *yogi*,—Thomas LeClear, an eminent American painter, and William R. O'Donovan, an equally distinguished sculptor, affirmed in a London journal, that no living artist could, in their opinion, equal it in vigor, breadth, and uniqueness, while they were both unable to decide upon the nature of the coloring substance employed or the manner of its application.

Since her arrival here, the lady has been very chary of exhibiting her rare powers, but two instances have come to our hearing. These two are, however, strong enough to excite astonishment. The first was the instantaneous substitution of one name, in thread embroidery, on a fine handkerchief, for another one that was previously there. The feat was done under the very eyes of an Assistant Magistrate and the Collector of the N. W. P. who had been a fellow-passenger with the Theosophical party on the voyage hither. In fact, he held one corner of the handkerchief while the change was made, and there was a roomful of native gentlemen as onlookers, besides. The second fact was even more miraculous. Before leaving London she was requested by an English barrister [Charles C. Massey], President of the British Theosophical Society and the son of a Liberal M.P., whose name is well known throughout India, to give relief to his father's eyesight, now seriously injured. She said that upon reaching India she would try, but it being necessary to establish an electrical and magnetic current between herself and the patient, she must have some article of wearing apparel or other object that had been in close and frequent contact with his person. A pair of gloves was given her, which were put into an envelope and brought intact to India. On the 17th inst., the day after her arrival, they were taken by her from her box and in the presence of Col. Olcott, to whom she declared her intention to send one of them to the London friend. She laid the two gloves on the table in the drawing room and locked the door. This was the last that Col. Olcott saw the gloves, as he informs us.

But by the last Overland Mail came the sequel. A letter from the barrister, dated London 18th February, says that on getting to his chambers in the Temple the day before—the 17th— he found a telegram from a certain lady of good education and the highest respectability, who is what is termed a powerful "medium," but above suspicion of trickery, to be at her house at 6 PM, as her familiar "spirit" has a message for him from Madame Blavatsky. He was punctual to the appointment, and was received by the lady and her husband, who presently ushered him into a darkened room. What happened we will let the barrister himself describe. "Truth to say," he remarks,

I did not expect much, but prompt to the appointment the "spirit" came, loading the air with sweet perfume, and commencing the interview (which did not last five minutes) by flinging something light and soft in my face—a good shot in the dark. From this proceeded the perfume aforesaid. Directly I handled it I knew what was up, without being told. The glove! the glove! from *you*, from Bombay, when the papers had already informed us your ship arrived on Sunday, two days ago. What can I say—what think? The well-known signature on the inside of the kid, in the well-known blue writing, and the less known and less decipherable symbols above it.

The witnesses in this case are unimpeachable, and we really do not know what is to be said of this new trans-atmospheric mail service. The remaining glove, or what purports to be such, has been kindly given to a gentleman in Bombay to dispose of as he may elect and will be sent to London for comparison with its mate.

CHAPTER 8

8F. A. P. SINNETT
DECEMBER 1879, ALLAHABAD, INDIA

[Collated from Sinnett 1886, 221–2, 224,
226, 234, and Sinnett 1881, 42–8]

Col. Olcott['s] and Mme. Blavatsky['s] arrival in India had been heralded with a few newspaper paragraphs dimly indicating that Mme. Blavatsky was a marvelous person, associated with a modern development of "magic," and I had seen her great book, *Isis Unveiled*, which naturally provoked interest on my part in the authoress. From some remarks published in the *Pioneer*, of which I was at that time the editor, the first communications between us arose. In accordance with arrangements made by letter during the summer, she came to Allahabad to visit my wife and myself at our cold-weather home at that station in December 1879.

I well remember the morning of her arrival, when I went down to the railway station to meet her. The trains from Bombay used to come into Allahabad in those days at an early hour in the morning, and it was still but just time for *chota hozree*, or early breakfast, when I brought our guests home. She had evidently been apprehensive, to judge from her latest letters, lest we might have formed some ideal conception of her that the reality would shatter, and had recklessly painted herself as a rough, old "hip-popotamus" of a woman, unfit for civilized society; but she did this with so lively a humor that the betrayal of her bright intelligence this involved more than undid the effect of her warnings. Her rough manners, of which we had been told so much, did not prove very alarming, though I remember going into fits of laughter at the time when Col. Olcott, after the visit had lasted a week or two, gravely informed [us] that Madame was under "great self-restraint" so far. This had not been the impression my wife and I had formed about her, though we had learned already to find her conversation more than interesting.

I want to give my readers an idea of Mme. Blavatsky, as I have known her, that shall be as nearly complete as I can make it, and I shall not hesitate to put in the shadows of the picture. The first visit she paid us was not an unqualified success in all respects. Her excitability, sometimes amusing, would sometimes take an irritating shape, and she would vent her impatience, if anything annoyed her, by vehement tirades in a loud voice direct-ed against Col. Olcott, at that time in an early stage of his appren-ticeship to what she would sometimes irreverently speak of as the "occult business." No one with the least discernment could ever fail to see that her rugged manners and disregard of all conventionalities were the result of a deliberate rebellion against, not of ignorance or unfamiliarity with, the customs of refined society. Still the rebellion was often very determined, and she would sometimes color her language with expletives of all sorts, some witty and amusing, some unnecessarily violent, that we should all have preferred her not to make use of. She certainly had none of the superficial attributes one might have expected in a spiritual teacher.

Recollection of this time supplies me with a very varied assortment of memory portraits of Madame, taken during different conditions of her nerves and temper. Some recall her flushed and voluble, too loudly declaiming against some person or other who had misjudged her or her Society; some show her quiet and com-panionable, pouring out a flood of interesting talk about Mexican antiquities, or Egypt, or Peru, showing a knowledge of the most varied and far-reaching kind, and a memory for names and places and archaeological theories she would be dealing with, that was fairly fascinating to her hearers. Then, again, I remember her telling anecdotes of her own earlier life, mysterious bits of adven-ture, or stories of Russian society, with so much point, vivacity, and finish, that she would simply be the delight for the time being of everyone present.

I have said a good deal of her impetuosity and indiscretions of speech and manner and of the way in which she will rage for hours, if allowed, over trifles which a more phlegmatic, not to speak of a more philosophical, temperament would barely care to notice. But it must be understood that, almost at any time, an appeal to her philosophical intellect will turn her right off into another channel of thinking, and then, equally for hours, may any appreciative companion draw forth the stores of her information concerning Eastern religions and mythology, the subtle metaphysics of Hindu and Buddhist symbolism, or the esoteric doctrine itself.

The record of Mme. Blavatsky's residence in India is, of course, intimately blended with the history of the Theosophical Society, on which all her energies are spent, directly or indirectly, and indirectly in so far only as she was obliged during this period to do what literary work she could for Russian magazines to earn her livelihood and supplement the narrow resources on which the headquarters of the Society were kept up.

The *Theosophist*, the monthly magazine devoted to occult research, which she set on foot in the autumn of her first year in India, paid its way from the beginning and gradually came to earn a small profit, subject to the fact that its management was altogether gratuitous, and all its work in all departments performed by the little band of Theosophists at headquarters. But all the while the sneering critics of the movement in the papers would be suggesting, from time to time, that the founders of the Society were doing a very good business with "initiation fees" and living on the tribute of the faithful, Mme. Blavatsky was really at her desk from morning till night, slaving at Russian articles, which she wrote solely for the sake of the little income she was able to make in this way, and on which, in a far greater degree than on the proper resources of the Society, the headquarters was supported, and the movement kept on foot.

It has been through my acquaintance with Madame Blavatsky that I have obtained experiences in connection with occultism. The first problem I had to solve was whether Madame Blavatsky really did, as I heard, possess the power of producing abnormal phenomena.

During her first visit to my house, Madame Blavatsky was allowed to show that "raps" like those which spiritualists attribute to spirit agency, could be produced at will.

Spiritualists are aware that when groups of people sit round a table and put their hands upon it, they will, if a "medium" be present, generally hear little knocks which respond to questions and spell out messages. The large outer circle of persons who do not believe in spiritualism imagine that all the millions who do are duped as regards this impression. It must sometimes be troublesome for them to account for the wide development of the delusion, but any theory, they think, is preferable to admitting the possibility that the spirits of deceased persons can communicate in this way; or, if they take the scientific view of the matter, that a physical effect, however slight, can be produced without a physical cause. Such persons ought to welcome the explanations I am now giving, tending as these do to show that the theory of universal self-deception as regards spirit-rapping is not the only one by means of which the asserted facts of spiritualism can be reconciled with a reluctance to accept the spiritual hypothesis as the explanation.

Now, I soon found out not only that raps would always come at a table at which Madame Blavatsky sat with the view of obtaining such results, but that all conceivable hypotheses of fraud in the matter were rapidly disposed of by a comparison of the various experiments we were able to make. To begin with, there was no necessity for other people to sit at the table at all. We could work with any table under any circumstances, or without a table at all. A windowpane would do equally well, or the wall, or any door, or anything whatever which could give out a sound if hit. A half glass door put ajar was at once seen to be a very good instrument to choose, because it was easy to stand opposite Madame Blavatsky in this case, to see her bare hands or hand (without any rings) resting motionless on the pane, and to hear the little ticks come plainly, as if made with the point of a pencil or with the sound of electric sparks passing from one knob of an electrical apparatus to another. Another very satisfactory way of obtaining the raps—one frequently employed in the evening—was to set down a large glass clock shade on the hearthrug, and get Madame Blavatsky, after removing all rings from her hands and sitting well clear of the shade so that no part of her dress touched it, to lay her hands on it. Putting a lamp on the ground opposite and sitting down on the hearthrug, one could see the under surfaces of the hands resting on the glass, and still under these perfectly satisfactory conditions the raps would come, clear and distinct, on the sonorous surface of the shade.

It was out of Madame Blavatsky's power to give an exact explanation as to how these raps were produced. But the fact that the raps were obedient to the will was readily put beyond dispute, in this way amongst others working with the windowpane or the clockshade, I would ask to have a name spelled out, mentioning one at random. Then I would call over the alphabet, and at the right letters the raps would come. Or I would ask for a definite number of raps, and they would come. Or for a series of raps in some defined rhythmical progression, and they would come. Nor was this all. Madame Blavatsky would sometimes put her hands, or one only, on some one else's head, and make the raps come, audibly to an attentive listener, and perceptibly to the person touched, who would feel each little shock exactly as if he were taking sparks off the conductor of an electrical machine.

At a later stage of my inquiries I obtained raps under better circumstances again than these—namely, without contact between the object on which they were produced and Madame Blavatsky's hands at all. Madame Blavatsky used to produce the raps on a little table set in the midst of an attentive group, with no one touching it at all. After starting it, or charging it with some influence by resting her hands on it for a few moments, she would hold one about a foot above it and make mesmeric passes at it, at each of which the table would yield the familiar sound. Nor was this done only at our own house with our own tables. The same thing would be done at friends' houses, to which Madame Blavatsky accompanied us. And a further development of the head experiment was this: It was found to be possible for several persons to feel the same rap simultaneously. Four or five persons used sometimes to put their hands in a pile, one on another on a table; then Madame Blavatsky would put hers on the top of the pile and cause a current, or whatever it is which produces the sound, to pass through the whole series of hands, felt by each simultaneously, and record itself in a rap on the table beneath. Any one who has ever taken part in forming such a pile of hands must feel as to some of the hypotheses put forward by determined sceptics to the effect that the raps are produced by Madame Blavatsky's thumbnails or by the cracking of some joint—that such hypotheses are rather idiotic.

The raps gave me a complete assurance that she was in possession of some faculties of an abnormal character.

H. P. Blavatsky, Sri Lanka, 1880

Chapter 9

SRI LANKA AND BOMBAY

1880

THE FOUNDERS spent some time in Sri Lanka during May–July 1880, when Colonel Olcott laid the foundations for his later work to stimulate the revival of Buddhism. They both took Pansil, that is Pancha Sila, a formal recitation of the five precepts renouncing harmfulness, stealing, sexual immorality, lying, and alcohol, preceded by taking refuge in the Buddha, the Dharma or teaching, and the Sangha or religious community. The public ceremony of repeating these vows after a leader of the Buddhist community is the official profession of Buddhism.

9A. ANONYMOUS
MAY 1880, ON BOARD THE SS *ELLORA*,
TRAVELING FROM BOMBAY, INDIA, TO
COLOMBO, SRI LANKA

["Voyage with Mme. Blavatsky" 1891]

Early in May 1880, I took passage from Bombay for Colombo in Ceylon [Sri Lanka], on one of the comfortable little coasting steamships of the British India Navigation Company.

The fun of the trip consisted in the delight that the old woman [Madame Blavatsky] took in making life miserable for the first officer of the vessel, a huge, raw-boned, awkward Scotchman, with fiery red hair and whiskers, and an inborn hatred of anything in the way of religious belief that deviated an iota from the faith of his own Presbyterian church.

From the very first hour after sailing from Bombay harbor the first officer had wrangled with Mme. Blavatsky in argument until at last he openly declared he believed she was the only daughter of the Father of Lies, and added that he prayed to heaven that the ship bearing such an unholy person might reach port in safety. For his part he doubted it, but he prayed it might be so. This expression of the sturdy maritimer's opinion only caused the old woman to shake with laughter. Finally, one evening as we sat over coffee and raisins after dinner she told him that she was weary of his pigheaded disbelief in her powers to force natural laws to assist her in performing what he was pleased to call showmen's tricks, and that she meant to teach him then and there to hold his tongue.

"Vera well, madame, do it if ye can. I'm sure y're truly welcome to try," he replied with a sneer.

"Have you a handkerchief in your pocket?" she asked.

He unbuttoned his coat and handed her his handkerchief, a plain cotton one with a narrow blue border.

Mme. Blavatsky tossed it on the table in front of her, pushed away her plate, coffee cup, and glasses, and pulled her chair in as close to the table as she could. I was sitting directly beside her and watched her with the greatest interest, as, indeed, did all the rest, the first officer looking on from his place at the foot of the table, only a few feet away, with a very plain sneer on his rugged face.

Having cleared the space in front of her, she placed both elbows on the edge of the table, picked up the handkerchief and began to roll it into as small a compass as she could. Then having done so, she squeezed it in her two fists until she turned scarlet in the face and then almost purple. The perspiration started out on her forehead and ran down her face and neck, but still she squeezed harder and harder, with her eyes tightly shut, and as we watched her, an expression of pain came on her face, and the color rapidly faded away until she was as livid as a corpse.

I suppose all this occupied two minutes, certainly not more, and then she opened her hands and gasped as if her throat were parched from thirst. Col. Olcott motioned us to be silent, and in a few moments she opened her eyes and a faint color came back to her face. She made an effort to speak, but could only whisper, "Give it to him," at the same time pointing to the handkerchief. It was handed to the Scotchman, who looked somewhat anxious as he opened it and utterly astounded when he found his monogram most exquisitely embroidered in the center, the letters being in white silk, and enclosed in a circle of light blue of the same color as the printed border of the handkerchief. The diameter of the circle was about two inches.

For a moment the first officer looked intently at the monogram, then at the pale but triumphant old woman, who was gazing at him with blazing eyes, and then he uttered a mighty oath and walked away to his cabin on the forward deck. During the rest of the voyage he would not come near her, speak to her, nor sit at the table while she was there, and the only thing he would say about the affair was to repeat the hope that the vessel would be permitted by Providence to reach Ceylon in safety.

CHAPTER 9

9B. Henry S. Olcott
May 1880, on board the SS *Ellora*,
traveling from Bombay, India, to
Colombo, Sri Lanka, and later

[Olcott 1900, 2:154–5]

The old Captain [of the SS *Ellora*] was a fat, goodnatured person without the glimmering of a belief in things spiritual or physical. He used to joke with HPB on our notions with such a delicious ignorance of the whole subject that it only made us laugh. One day she was playing her favorite solitary game of Patience, when the Captain broke in upon her meditations with a challenge that she should tell his fortune with the cards. She at first refused, but at last consented, and, making him cut, laid out the cards on the table. She said, "This is very strange: it can't be so!" "What?" asked the Captain. "What the cards say. Cut again." He did so, and with the same result, apparently, for HPB said the cards prophesized such a nonsensical thing that she didn't like to tell him. He insisted; whereupon she said that the cards foretold that he would not be much longer at sea; he would receive an offer to live ashore, and would throw up his profession. The big Captain roared at the idea, and told her that it was just as he anticipated. As for his quitting the sea, nothing would please him more, but there was no such good luck in store for him. The thing passed off without further remark beyond the Captain's repeating the prophecy to the Chief Officer, through whom it became the laugh of the ship. But there was a sequel.

A month or two after our return to Bombay, HPB received a letter from Captain Wickes, in which he said he owed her an apology for his behavior about the card prophecy, and must honestly confess that it had been literally fulfilled. After dropping us at Ceylon, he continued his voyage to Calcutta. On arrival, he had the offer of the appointment of Harbor Master (Port Officer) at Karwar (I think it was, or if not, then Mangalore), had accepted it, and had actually returned as passenger in his own ship! This is

132

a specimen of a great many card prophecies HPB made. I do not suppose the cards had anything to do with it save that they may have acted as a link between her clairvoyant brain and the Captain's personal aura, thus enabling her clairvoyant faculty of prescience to come into play. Yet psychically endowed as she was, I scarcely remember her having foreseen any one of the many painful events that happened to her through treacherous friends and malicious enemies. If she did, she never told me or anybody else so far as I ever heard. A thief stole something she valued once, at Bombay, but she could not find out the culprit, nor help the police whom she called in.

9c. Henry S. Olcott
May–July 1880, Sri Lanka

[Olcott 1900, 2:151–205]

A visit to Ceylon, long urgently requested by the leading priests and laity of the Buddhist community, had been determined upon, and the preparations occupied us.

Everything being ready, we embarked on 7th May in a British India coasting steamer for Ceylon. The party consisted of the two Founders, Mr. [Edward] Wimbridge, Damodar K. Mavalankar, [and others].

We dropped anchor in Colombo harbor on the morning of 16th May, and after a while a large boat came alongside bringing Mohottiwatte Gunananda, the Buddhist orator-priest, John Robert de Silva, and some junior priests. We found the famed Mohottiwatte a middle-aged, shaven monk, of full medium stature, with a very intellectual head, a bright eye, very large mouth, and an air of perfect self-confidence and alertness, the most brilliant polemic [Buddhist] orator of the Island, the terror of the [Christian] Missionaries. HPB had sent him from New York a presentation copy of *Isis Unveiled,* and he had translated portions where she describes some of the phenomena she had personally witnessed in the course of her travels. His greeting to us was especially cordial. He requested us to proceed with the steamer to Galle, where arrangements had been made for our reception; he himself would go that evening by train.

Before dawn on the 17th we were off Galle. The monsoon burst, and there was tremendous wind and rain, but the view was so lovely that we stopped on deck to enjoy it. A beautiful bay; a verdant promontory to the north, against which the surf dashed and in foamy jets ran high up against the rocky shore; a long, curved sandy beach bordered with tile-roofed bungalows almost hidden in an ocean of green palms; the old fort, custom house, lighthouse, jetty, and coaling sheds to the south, and to the east the tossing sea with a line of rocks and reefs walling it out from the harbor. Far away inland rose Adam's Peak and his sister mountains.

After breakfast, in a lull of the storm, we embarked in a large boat decorated with plantain trees and lines of bright-colored flowers, on which were the leading Buddhists of the place. On the jetty and along the beach a huge crowd awaited us. A white cloth was spread for us from the jetty steps to the road where carriages were ready, and a thousand flags were frantically waved in welcome. The multitude hemmed in our carriages, and the procession set out for our appointed residence, the house of Mrs. Wijeratne. The roads were blocked with people the whole distance, and our progress was very slow. At the house three Chief Priests received and blessed us at the threshold. Then we had a levee and innumerable introductions, the common people crowding every approach, filling every door, and gazing through every window. This went on all day. Our hostess and her son, the Deputy Coroner of Galle, lavished every hospitality upon us.

The monks, who had read [Mohottiwatte's] excerpts from HPB's book, pressed her to exhibit her powers, and young Wijeratne, on hearing about the handkerchief phenomenon on board ship, asked her to repeat it for him. So she did, and again for a Mr. Dias; each time obliterating her own embroidered name and causing theirs to replace it. The excitement, of course, rose to fever heat and culminated when she made some fairy bells ring out sharp in the air, near the ceiling and out on the verandah. I had to satisfy the crowd with two impromptu addresses during the day.

Our rooms were packed with visitors all day. There were no end of metaphysical discussions with the aged High Priest Bulatgama Sumanatissa. Old Bulatgama was a particularly persistent disputant, very voluble and very kind. Among other topics of discussion was that of the psychical powers, and HPB, who thoroughly liked him, rang bells in the air (one a booming explosion like the striking of a large steel bar), made spirit raps, caused the great dining table to tremble and move, etc., to the amazement of her select audience.

This was the prologue to such a drama of excitement as we had not dreamt we should ever pass through. In a land of flowers and ideal tropical vegetation, under smiling skies, along roads shaded by clustering palm trees, the people could not do enough for us; nothing seemed to them good enough for us; we were the first white champions of their [Buddhist] religion, speaking of its excellence and its blessed comfort from the platform, in the face of the [Christian] missionaries, its enemies and slanderers.

On 25th May, HPB and I "took *pansil*" from the venerable Bulatgama, at a temple of the Ramanya Nikaya and were formally acknowledged as Buddhists. We had previously declared ourselves Buddhists long before, in America, both privately and publicly, so that this was but a formal confirmation of our previous professions. HPB knelt before the huge statue of the Buddha, and I kept her company. We had a good deal of trouble in catching the Pali words that we were to repeat after the old monk. A great crowd was present and made the responses just after us, a dead silence being preserved while we were struggling through the unfamiliar sentences. When we had finished the last of the *Silas*, and offered flowers in the customary way, there came a mighty shout to make one's nerves tingle, and the people could not settle themselves down to silence for some minutes, to hear the brief discourse which, at the Chief Priest's request, I delivered.

The next morning we began our journey northward in carriages supplied by the fishermen of Galle. Almost the entire Buddhist population of Galle massed together to see us leave town, and rent the air with friendly shouts.

At Panadure we were lodged [in a] building comprising small bedrooms opening on a verandah which extended on all sides, and one small hall through the middle. There were no bathrooms. The windows were furnished only with wooden shutters, and when they were shut in the daytime, the rooms were dark. HPB had one of the rooms in the south end. She wanted to bathe, and, as there was no other place, I arranged for a tub in her own room. As she would be in pitch darkness if the shutters were closed, I tied a large soft mat across the end of the shutters, left standing open, and she began her toilet. The rest of us were sitting around the corner, on the other verandah, chatting, when I heard my name shouted, and ran around to see what was the matter. At that moment three Sinhalese women were in the act of creeping out beneath the edge of the mat, and the old lady was abusing them in grand style. On hearing my voice, she said that these impertinent creatures, to gratify their curiosity, had actually crept under the mat and, when she happened to turn her head, she saw them standing close against the window sill, calmly watching her ablutions. Her indignation was so tragic that, while hustling the intruders away, I could not help laughing heartily. Poor things! they meant no harm.

We left for Kandy by train on the 9th [of June], and after the run of one and a half hours through one of the most picturesque tracts of country in the world, arrived at about 7 p.m. Along with the usual crowd, a deputation of Kandyan Chiefs received us at the station and accompanied us to our quarters in a great procession, bright with torches and ear-splitting with tom-toms and native trumpets. Two addresses were made to us, by the Chiefs' Committee and by a society of Buddhists connected with the Temple of the Sacred Tooth of Buddha, the Dalada Maligawa. We went to the temple at 2 p.m. for my lecture. [On the] morning [of June 14th], the unusual honor was conferred upon us of admitting us to a special exhibition of the Buddha Tooth Relic. This is kept in a separate tower, protected by a thick door of entrance studded with iron and fastened with four great locks. The relic is of the size of an alligator tooth, is supported by a gold wire stem rising from a lotus flower of the same metal, and is much discolored by age. If genuine, it would, of course, be twenty-five centuries old. On our return to our lodgings, the educated Sinhalese about us were eager to know HPB's opinion as to the genuineness of the relic, whether it is or is not a real tooth of the Buddha. This was a nice, not to say ticklish, question. HPB's jovial answer to her interrogators [was]: "Of course, it is his tooth: one he had when he was born as a tiger!"

At 2 p.m. [we] took train for Colombo. [Then] we proceeded on to Bentota. The trip was delightful, both by rail along the sea beach, where the track skirts almost the wash of the surf, and by road through the continuous groves of palms. Our reception at Bentota was princely indeed. There was a procession a mile long, at least ten miles of decorations along the roads and lanes. I lectured from a large decorated pavilion or platform. We passed the night at the rest house, or travelers' bungalow, a Government affair. We were all agreed that we had never seen so delightful a house in the tropics. The lofty ceilings, the floors of red tiles, the walls of laterite, thick and cool, a wide verandah at the back just over the rocky shore of the sea, the rooms at least thirty feet square, the sea breeze sweeping through them night and day, a bathing place on the beach, abundance of flowers...HPB declared she should like to pass a whole year there.

[Finally returning to Galle,] the 12th [of July] was our last day in the Island [of Sri Lanka]; on the 13th our steamer arrived, and at two we embarked, leaving many weeping friends behind, and taking away with us many recollections of gracious kindnesses, cheerful help, lovely journeys, enthusiastic multitudes, and strange experiences.

CHAPTER 9

9D. ANAGARIKA DHARMAPALA
JUNE 1880,
COLOMBO, SRI LANKA

[Dharmapala 1927, 723]

When I was ten years old, I attended a great debate in a temple pavilion sixteen miles from [Colombo] Ceylon, where the Christians on one side and [the Buddhist Mohottiwatte] Gunananda on the other argued out the truths of their respective religions. Thousands came from the most distant parts of the island to hear this famous debate. Mohottiwatte Gunananda supplied the oratory; and the Venerable Sumangala furnished him with the scholarly material and references. The debate lasted three days.

Dr. J. M. Peebles, an American Spiritualist, who was visiting Colombo at the time, obtained an English report of the controversy between the Buddhists and Christians and, upon his return to the U.S., showed it to Colonel Henry S. Olcott and Madame H. P. Blavatsky, who had organized the Theosophical Society in New York in 1875. Deeply impressed, they wrote to Gunananda and Sumangala that, in the interest of universal brotherhood, they had just founded a society inspired by oriental philosophies and that they would come to Ceylon to help the Buddhists. The letters from Colonel Olcott and Madame Blavatsky were trans-lated into Sinhalese and widely distributed. My heart warmed toward these two strangers, so far away and yet so sympathetic, and I made up my mind that, when they came to Ceylon, I would join them.

They did come to Colombo a few years later, when I was sixteen. The Buddhists entertained them royally. I remember going up to greet them. The moment I touched their hands, I felt overjoyed. The desire for universal brotherhood, for all the things they wanted for humanity, struck a responsive chord in me. I began to read their magazine. As I walked in the gardens overgrown with fragrant plants or along the shore shaded by teak and coco palms, I pondered on the conversations I had had with the two Theosophists. I made up my mind not to entangle myself in the net of worldly desires. I would endeavor from then on to devote my life to the welfare of others. Exactly how I was to carry out my resolve, I was not certain, but I felt that somehow the way would be found in the writings of Madame Blavatsky.

9E. DAMODAR K. MAVALANKAR
JUNE 23–JULY 1880,
SRI LANKA (CEYLON) AND
THEN ON SHIP BACK TO BOMBAY

[Mavalankar 1965, 55–8]

In Ceylon [in a] particular village, HPB, Col. Olcott, and myself were the only three persons that stopped one night, the rest of our party having gone to a further place. We were all busy there initiating people and forming a branch of our [Theosophical] Society till about 12 in the night. HPB and Col. Olcott went to bed at about one. As we had to stay in the village only one night, we had got down in the Rest House where comfortable accommodation can be had only for two travelers. I had therefore to lie down in an armchair in the dining room. I had scarcely locked the door of the room from the inside and laid myself in the chair when I heard a faint knock at the door. It was repeated twice before I had time enough to reach the door. I opened it and what a great joy I felt when I saw [Mahatma Morya] again! In a very low whisper he ordered me to dress myself and to follow him. At the back door of the Rest House is the sea. I followed him as he commanded me to do. We walked about three quarters of an hour by the seashore. Then we turned in the direction of the sea. All around there was water *except the place we were walking upon which was quite dry!!* He was walking in front and I was following him. We thus walked for about seven minutes when we came to a spot that looked like a small island. On the top of the building was a triangular light. From a distance, a person, standing on the seashore would think it to be an isolated spot which is covered all over by green bushes. There is only one entrance to go inside. After we reached the island, we came in front of the actual building. There in a little garden in front, we found one of the Brothers sitting. I had seen him before, and it is to him that this place belongs. [Mahatma Morya] seated himself near him and I stood before them. We were there for about half an hour. I was shown a part of the place. How very pleasant it is! And inside this place he has a small room where the body remains when the *spirit* moves about. What a charming, delightful spot that is! What a nice smell of roses and various sorts of flowers! The half hour was finished and the time for our leaving the place was near. The master of the place, whose name I do not know, placed his blessing hand over my head, and [Mahatma Morya] and I marched off again. We came back near the door of the room wherein I was to sleep and he suddenly disappeared there on the spot.

I omitted to mention to you the two other places where I was taken. One of them is near Colombo, a private house of [Mahatma Morya], and the other one near Kandy, a library.

One evening on the steamer on our way back to Bombay [in July 1880], we finished our dinner [and] I went in [my cabin] and put on [my] coat. Without thinking I put my hands into my pockets as I usually do and lo! in the right-hand one I felt some paper. I took it out, and to my surprise I found a letter addressed to Mme. Blavatsky. I took it nearer to the light. The cover was open and on it were written in red the words: "For Damodar to read." I then read the letter. Thinking all the time of this matter, I lay down in my bed. Absorbed in deep thought, I was startled on the sound of footsteps *in the* cabin which I had locked from inside. I looked behind and there was [Mahatma Morya] again and two others! What a pleasant evening that was! Speaking of various things in regard to knowledge and philosophy for about half an hour!

9F. HENRY S. OLCOTT
JULY–AUGUST 1880, BOMBAY

[Olcott 1900, 2:206–8, 213, 215, 225]

By way of contrast to the pleasant experiences of the Ceylon tour, we had a terribly rough sea passage from Galle to Colombo, and all of us were miserably seasick. It rained cats and dogs on the last day of our return voyage—as it had nearly every day; the decks were wet. HPB made absurd efforts to write at a table placed for her by the accommodating Captain on a couple of gratings, in a comparatively dry spot, but used more strong words than ink, her papers were so blown about by the gusts that swept the ship. At last we entered Bombay harbor and in due course had solid ground under our feet.

On the evening of 4th August, Mahatma [Morya] visited HPB, and I was called in to see him before he left. He dictated a long and important letter to an influential friend of ours at Paris, and gave me important hints about the management of current [Theosophical] Society affairs. I was sent away before his visit terminated, and left him sitting in HPB's room.

H. S. Olcott at his desk, May 1903

[Then] we received from Mr. Sinnett an invitation to visit them at Simla. We—HPB and I, with our servant Babula—left Bombay for the North by the evening mail train of 27th August. We came in sight of Simla just before sunset [on September 8th]. A servant of Mr. Sinnett's met us as we entered the town, with *jampans*—chairs carried by porters by long poles—and we were soon under the hospitable roof of our good friends the Sinnetts, where a hearty welcome awaited us.

9G. DAMODAR K. MAVALANKAR
SEPTEMBER 1880, BOMBAY, INDIA

[Mavalankar 1965, 58–62]

[On] Aug. 27, 1880, HPB and Col. O. left Bombay for Simla and other places in the North [of India]. I worked all alone in HPB's compartments. [One day in September] at about 2 in the morning after finishing my work, I locked the door of the room and lay in my bed. Within about 2 or 3 minutes I heard HPB's voice in her room calling me. I got up with a start and went in. She said "some persons want to see you" and after a moment added, "Now go out, do not look at me." Before however I had time to turn my face, I saw her gradually disappear on the spot and from that very ground rose up the form of [Mahatma Morya]. By the time I had turned back, I saw two others dressed in what I afterwards learned to be Tibetan clothes. One of them remained with [Mahatma Morya] in HPB's room. The other one I found seated on my bed by the time I came out. Then he told me to stand still for some time and began to look at me fixedly. I felt a very pleasant sensation as if I was getting out of my body. I cannot say now what time passed between that and what I am now going to relate. But I saw I was in a peculiar place. It was the upper end of Cashmere at the foot of the Himalayas. I saw I was taken to a place where there were only two houses just opposite to each other and no other sign of habitation. From one of these came out the person [Koot Hoomi, who] ordered me to follow him. After going a short distance of about half a mile, we came to a natural subterranean passage. After walking a considerable distance through this subterranean passage, we came into an open plain. There is a large massive building thousands of years old. The entrance gate has a large triangular arch. Inside are various apartments. I went up with my *Guru* to the Great Hall. The grandeur and serenity of the place is enough to strike anyone with awe. While standing there, I do not know what happened, but suddenly I found myself in my bed. It was about 8 in the morning. What was that I saw? Was it a dream or a reality? Perplexed with these ideas, I was sitting silent when down fell a note on my nose. I opened it and found inside that it was not a dream but that I was taken in some mysterious way in my astral body to the real place of Initiation.

A. P. Sinnett

Chapter 10

SIMLA

1880

*H*PB AND COLONEL OLCOTT visited A. P. Sinnett and his wife Patience at Simla in northern India in September and October 1880. The serious interest of Sinnett in the teachings and the work of the Theosophical Society prompted H. P. Blavatsky to establish a contact by correspondence between Sinnett and the two Adepts who were sponsoring the Society, Mahatmas KH and M. From this correspondence Sinnett wrote *The Occult World* (1881) and *Esoteric Buddhism* (1883), both of which had an enormous influence in generating public interest in Theosophy. The replies and explanations given by the Mahatmas to the questions by Sinnett are embodied in their letters from 1880 to 1885, published in 1923 as *The Mahatma Letters to A. P. Sinnett*. The original letters from these Teachers are the prized possession of the British Library, where they can be viewed by special permission in the Department of Rare Manuscripts.

10A. A. P. SINNETT
OCTOBER 3, 1880, SIMLA, INDIA

[Sinnett 1881, 66–84]

We set out at the appointed time next morning. We were originally to have been a party of six, but a seventh person joined us just before we started. After going down the hill for some hours a place was chosen in the wood near the upper waterfall for our breakfast: the baskets that had been brought with us were unpacked, and the servants at a little distance lighted a fire and set to work to make tea and coffee. Concerning this some joking arose over the fact that we had one cup and saucer too few, on account of the seventh person who joined us at starting, and some one laughingly asked Madame Blavatsky to create another cup and saucer. When Madame Blavatsky said it would be very difficult, but that if we liked she would try, attention was of course at once arrested. Madame Blavatsky, as usual, held mental conversation with one of the Brothers, and then wandered a little about in the immediate neighborhood of where we were sitting—that is to say, within a radius of half a dozen to a dozen yards from our picnic cloth—I closely following, waiting to see what would happen. Then she marked a spot on the ground, and called to one of the gentlemen of the party to bring a knife to dig with. The place chosen was the edge of a little slope covered with thick weeds and grass and shrubby undergrowth. The gentleman with the knife [Major Philip Henderson] tore up these in the first place with some difficulty, as the roots were tough and closely interlaced. Cutting then into the matted roots and earth with the knife, and pulling away the debris with his hands, he came at last, on the edge of something white, which turned out, as it was completely excavated, to be the required cup. A corresponding saucer was also found after a little more digging. Both objects were in among the roots, which spread everywhere through the ground, so that it seemed as if the roots were growing round them. The cup and saucer both corresponded exactly, as regards their pattern, with those that had been brought to the picnic, and constituted a seventh cup and saucer when brought back to where we were to have breakfast. Afterwards, when we got home, my wife questioned our principal khitmutgar as to how many cups and saucers of that particular kind we possessed. In the progress of years, as the set was an old set, some had been broken, but the man at once said that nine teacups were left. When collected and counted that number was found to be right, without reckoning the excavated cup. That made ten, and as regards the pattern, it was one of a somewhat peculiar kind, bought a good many years previously in London, and which assuredly could never have been matched in Simla.

If the phenomenon was not what it appeared to be—a most wonderful display of a power of which the modern scientific world has no comprehension whatever—it was, of course, an elaborate fraud. That supposition will only bear to be talked of vaguely. The cup and saucer were assuredly dug up in the way I describe. If they were not deposited there by occult agency, they must have been buried there beforehand. Now, I have described the character of the ground from which they were dug up; assuredly that had been undisturbed for years by the character of the vegetation upon it. But it may be urged that from some other part of the sloping ground a sort of tunnel may have been excavated in the first instance through which the cup and saucer could have been thrust into the place where they were found. If the tunnel had been big enough for the purpose, it would have left traces, which were not perceptible on the ground—which were not even discoverable when the ground was searched shortly afterwards with a view to that hypothesis. But the truth is that the theory of previous burial is untenable in view of the fact that the demand for the cup and saucer—of all the myriad things that might have been asked for—could never have been foreseen. It arose out of circumstances themselves the sport of the moment. If no extra person had joined us at the last moment, the number of cups and saucers packed up by the servants would have been sufficient for our needs, and no attention would have been drawn to them. It was by the servants, without the knowledge of any guest, that the cups taken were chosen from others that might just as easily have been taken. Had the burial fraud been really perpetrated, it would have been necessary to constrain us to choose the exact spot we did actually choose for the picnic with a view to the previous preparations, but the *exact* spot on which the ladies' jampans were deposited was chosen by myself in concert with [Mr. Henderson], and it was within a few yards of this spot that the cup was found. Thus who could be the agents employed to deposit the cup and saucer in the ground, and when did they perform the operation? Madame Blavatsky was under our roof the whole time from the previous evening, when the picnic was determined on, to the moment of starting. The one personal servant she had with her, a Bombay boy and a perfect stranger to Simla, was constantly about the house the previous evening, and from the first awakening of the household in the morning. Colonel Olcott, also a guest of ours at the time, was certainly with us all evening and was also present at the start. To imagine that he spent the night in going four or five miles through forest paths difficult to find, to bury a cup and saucer of a kind that we were not likely to take, in a place we were not likely to go to, in order that in the exceedingly remote contingency of its being required for the perpetration of a hoax it might be there, would certainly be a somewhat extravagant conjecture. Another consideration—the destination for which we were making can be approached by two roads from opposite ends of the upper horseshoe of hills on which Simla stands. It was open to us to select either path, and certainly neither Madame Blavatsky nor Colonel Olcott had any share in the selection of that actually taken. Had we taken the other, we should never have come to the spot where we actually picnicked.

[Mr. Henderson] had been a good deal with us during the week or two that had already elapsed since Madame Blavatsky's arrival. Like many of our friends, he had been greatly impressed with much he had seen in her presence. He had especially come to the conclusion that the Theosophical Society was exerting a good influence with the natives. He had declared his intention of joining this Society as I had done myself. Now, when the cup and saucer were found most of us who were present, [Mr. Henderson] among the number, were greatly impressed, and in the conversation that ensued the idea arose that [Mr. Henderson] might formally become a member of the Society then and there.

The proposal that [Mr. Henderson] should then and there formally join the Society was one with which he was quite ready to fall in. But some documents were required—a formal diploma, the gift of which to a new member should follow his initiation into certain little Masonic forms of recognition adopted in the Society. How could we get a diploma? Of course for the group then present a difficulty of this sort was merely another opportunity for the exercise of Madame's powers. Could she get a diploma brought to us by "magic"? After an occult conversation with the Brother who had then interested himself in our proceedings, Madame told us that the diploma would be forthcoming. She described the appearance it would present—a roll of paper wound round with an immense quantity of string, and then bound up in the leaves of a creeping plant. We should find it about in the wood where we were, and we could all look for it, but it would be [Mr. Henderson], for whom it was intended, who would find it. Thus it fell out. We all searched about in the undergrowth or in the trees, wherever fancy prompted us to look, and it was [Henderson] who found the roll, done up as described.

We had had our breakfast by this time. [Mr. Henderson] was formally "initiated" a member of the society by Colonel Olcott, and after a time we shifted our quarters to a lower place in the wood where there was the little Tibetan temple, or rest house. We amused ourselves by examining the little building inside and out, "bathing in the good magnetism," as Madame Blavatsky expressed it, and then, lying on the grass outside, it occurred to someone that we wanted more coffee. The servants were told to prepare some, but they had used up all our water. The water to be found in the streams near Simla is not of a kind to be used for purposes of this sort, and for a picnic, clean filtered water is always taken out in bottles. It appears that all the bottles in our baskets had

149

been exhausted. This report was promptly verified by the servants by the exhibition of the empty bottles. The only thing to be done was to send to a brewery, the nearest building, about a mile off, and ask for water. I wrote a pencil note and a coolie went off with the empty bottles. Time passed, and the coolie returned, to our great disgust, without the water. There had been no European left at the brewery that day (it was a Sunday) to receive the note, and the coolie had stupidly plodded back with the empty bottles under his arm, instead of asking about and finding someone able to supply the required water. At this time our party was a little dispersed. [Mr. Henderson] and one of the other gentlemen had wandered off. No one of the remainder of the party was expecting fresh phenomena, when Madame suddenly got up, went over to the baskets, a dozen or twenty yards off, picked out a bottle—one of those, I believe, which had been brought back by the coolie empty—and came back to us holding it under the fold of her dress. Laughingly producing it, it was found to be full of water. Just like a conjuring trick, will someone say? Just like, except for the conditions. For such a conjuring trick, the conjurer defines the thing to be done. In our case the want of water was as unforeseeable in the first instance as the want of the cup and saucer. The accident that left the brewery deserted by its Europeans, and the further accident that the coolie sent up for water should have been so stupid to come back without, because there happened to be no European to take my note, were accidents but for which the opportunity for obtaining the water by occult agency could not have arisen. And those accidents supervened on the fundamental accident, improbable in itself, that our servants should have sent us out insufficiently supplied. That any bottle of water could have been left unnoticed at the bottom of the baskets is a suggestion that I can hardly imagine any one present putting forward, for the servants had been found at fault with for not bringing enough; they had just before had the baskets completely emptied out, and we had not submitted to the situation till we had been fully satisfied that there really was no more water left. Furthermore, I tasted the water in the bottle Madame Blavatsky produced, and it was not water of the same kind as that which came from our own filters. It was an earthy-tasting water, unlike that of the modern Simla supply, but equally unlike, I may add, though in a different way, the offensive and discolored water of the only stream flowing through those woods.

How was it brought? The fact is there whether we can explain it or not. The rough, popular saying that you cannot argue the hind leg off a cow, embodies a sound reflection, which our prudent skeptics in matters of the kind with which I am now dealing are too apt to overlook. You cannot argue away a fact by contending that by the light in your mind it ought to be something different from what it is. Still less can you argue away a mass of facts like those I am now recording by a series of extravagant and contradictory hypotheses about each in turn. What the determined disbeliever so often overlooks is that the skepticism which may show an acuteness of mind up to a certain point, reveals a deficient intelligence when adhered to in face of certain kinds of evidence.

[Mr. Henderson], I should add here, afterwards changed his mind about the satisfactory character of the cup phenomenon, and said he thought it vitiated as a scientific proof by the interposition of the theory that the cup and saucer might have been thrust up into their places by means of a tunnel cut from a lower part of the bank. I have discussed that hypothesis already, and mention the fact of [Mr. Henderson's] change of opinion, which does not affect any of the circumstances I have narrated, merely to avoid the chance that readers might think I was treating the change of opinion in question as something which it was worth while to disguise.

It was on the evening of the day of the cup phenomenon that there occurred an incident destined to become the subject of very wide discussion in all the Anglo-Indian papers. This was the celebrated "brooch incident." The facts were related at the time in a little statement drawn up for publication and signed by the nine persons who witnessed it. This statement will be laid before the reader directly, but as the comments to which it gave rise showed that it was too meager to convey a full and accurate idea of what occurred, I will describe the course of events a little more fully.

We, that is, my wife and myself with out guests, had gone up the hill to dine, in accordance with previous engagements, with Mr. and Mrs. Hume. We dined, a party of eleven, at a round table, and Madame Blavatsky, sitting next [to] our host, tired and out of spirits as it happened, was unusually silent. During the beginning of dinner she scarcely said a word, Mr. Hume conversing chiefly with the lady on his other hand. At Indian dinner-tables [there are] little metal plate warmers with hot water before each guest, on which each plate served remains while in use. Such plate warmers were used on the evening I am describing, and over hers—in an interval during which plates had been removed—Madame Blavatsky was absently warming her hands. Now, the production of Madame Blavatsky's raps and bell sounds we had noticed sometimes seemed easier and the effects better when her hands had been warmed in this way; so some one, seeing her engaged in warming them, asked her some question, hinting in an indirect way at phenomena. So, merely in mockery, when asked why she was warming her hands, she enjoined us all to warm our hands too and see what would happen. Some of the people present actually did so, a few joking words passing among them. Then Mrs. Hume raised a little laugh by holding up her hands and saying, "But I have warmed my hands, what next?" It appears from what I learned afterwards that just at this moment, or immediately before, [HPB] suddenly perceived by those occult faculties of which mankind at large have no knowledge, that one of the Brothers was present "in astral body" invisible to the rest of us in the room. It was following his indications, therefore, that she acted in what followed; of course no one knew at the time that she had received any impulse in the matter external to herself. What took place as regards the surface of things was simply this: When Mrs. Hume said what I have set down above, and when the little laugh ensued, Madame Blavatsky put out her hand across the one person sitting between herself and Mrs. Hume and took one of that lady's hands, saying, "Well then, do you wish for anything in particular?" I cannot repeat the precise sentences spoken, nor can I say now exactly what Mrs. Hume first replied before she quite understood the situation; but this was made clear in a very few minutes. Some of the other people present catching this first, explained, "Think of something you would like to have brought to you; anything you like not wanted for any mere worldly motives; is there anything you can think of that will be very difficult to get?" Remarks of this sort were the only kind that were made in the short interval that elapsed between the remark by Mrs. Hume about having warmed her hands and the indication by her of the thing she had thought of. She said then that she had thought of something that would do. What was it? An old brooch that her mother had given her long ago and that she had lost.

Now, when this brooch, which was ultimately recovered by occult agency, as the rest of my story will show, came to be talked about, people said: "Of course Madame Blavatsky led up the conversation to the particular thing she had arranged beforehand to produce." I have described *all* the conversation which took place on this subject, before the brooch was named. There was no conversation about the brooch or any other thing of the kind whatever. Five minutes before the brooch was named, there had been no idea in the mind of any person present that any phenomenon in the nature of finding any lost article, or of any other kind, indeed, was going to be performed. Nor while Mrs. Hume was going over in her mind the things she might ask for, did she speak any word indicating the direction her thoughts were taking.

From the point of the story now reached, the narrative published at the time tells it almost as fully as it need be told, so I reprint it here.

On Sunday, the 3rd of October, at Mr. Hume's house at Simla, there were present at dinner Mr. and Mrs. Hume, Mr. and Mrs. Sinnett, Mrs. Gordon, Mr. F. Hogg, Captain P. J. Maitland, Mr. Beatson, Mr. Davidson, Colonel Olcott, and Madame Blavatsky. Most of the persons present having recently seen many remarkable occurrences in Madame Blavatsky's presence, conversation turned on occult phenomena, and in the course of this Madame Blavatsky asked Mrs. Hume if there was anything she particularly wished for. Mrs. Hume at first hesitated, but in a short time said there was something she would particularly like to have brought her, namely, a small article of jewelry that she formerly possessed, but had given away to a person who had allowed it to pass out of her possession. Madame Blavatsky then said if she would fix the image of the article in question very definitely on her mind, she, Madame Blavatsky, would endeavor to procure it. Mrs. Hume then said that she vividly remembered the article, and described it as an old-fashioned breast brooch set round with pearls, with glass at the front, and the back made to contain hair. She then, on being asked, drew a rough sketch of the brooch. Madame Blavatsky then wrapped up a coin attached to her watch chain in two cigarette papers, and put it in her dress, and said that she hoped the brooch might be obtained in the course of the evening. At the close of dinner, she said to Mr. Hume that the paper in which the coin had been wrapped was gone. A little later, in the drawing room, she said that the brooch would not be brought into the house, but that it must be looked for in the garden, and then as the party went out accompanying her, she said she had clairvoyantly seen the brooch fall into a star-shaped bed of flowers. Mr. Hume led the way to such a bed in a distant part of the garden. A prolonged and careful search was made with lanterns, and eventually a small paper packet, consisting of two cigarette papers, was found amongst the leaves by Mrs. Sinnett. This being opened on the spot was found to contain a brooch exactly corresponding to the previous description, and which Mrs. Hume identified as that which she had originally lost. None of the party, except Mr. and Mrs. Hume, had ever seen or heard of the brooch. Mr. Hume had not thought of it for years. Mrs. Hume had never spoken of it to anyone since she parted with it, nor had she, for long, even thought of it. She herself stated, after it was found, that it was only when Madame asked her whether there was anything she would like to have, that the remembrance of this brooch, the gift of her mother, flashed across her mind.

Mrs. Hume is not a spiritualist, and up to the time of the occurrence described was no believer either in occult phenomena or in Madame Blavatsky's powers. The brooch is unquestionably the one which Mrs. Hume lost. Even supposing, which is practically impossible, that the article, lost months before Mrs. Hume ever heard of Madame Blavatsky, and bearing no letter or other indication of original ownership, could have passed in a natural way into Madame Blavatsky's possession, even then she could not possibly have foreseen that it would be asked for, and Mrs. Hume herself had not given it a thought for months.

This narrative, read over to the party, is signed by:

A. O. Hume	Alice Gordon	P. J. Maitland
M. A. Hume	Wm. Davidson	A. P. Sinnett
Fred R. Hogg	Stuart Beatson	Patience Sinnett

When this narrative was published, the nine persons above mentioned were assailed with torrents of ridicule. Floods of more or less imbecile criticism have been directed to show that the whole performance must have been a trick; and for many persons it is now, no doubt, an established explanation that Mrs. Hume was adroitly led up to ask for the particular article produced, by a quantity of preliminary talk about a feat which Madame Blavatsky specially went to the house to perform. A further established opinion is that the brooch which Mrs. Hume gave to her daughter, and which her daughter lost, must have been got from that young lady about a year previously, when she passed through Bombay, where Madame Blavatsky was living, on her way to England. The young lady's testimony to the effect that she lost the brooch before she went to Bombay, or ever saw Madame Blavatsky, is a little feature of this hypothesis which its contented framers do not care to inquire into.

10B. P. J. MAITLAND
OCTOBER 13, 1880, SIMLA, INDIA

[Sinnett 1881, 88–90]

On the evening of [October 13th] I was sitting alone with Madame Blavatsky and Colonel Olcott in the drawing room of Mr. Sinnett's house in Simla. After some conversation on various matters, Madame Blavatsky said she would like to try an experiment in a manner which had been suggested to her by Mr. Sinnett. She, therefore, took two cigarette papers from her pocket and marked on each of them a number of parallel lines in pencil. She then tore a piece off the end of each paper across the lines, and gave them to me. At that time Madame Blavatsky was sitting close to me, and I intently watched her proceedings, my eyes being not more than two feet from her hands. She declined to let me mark or tear the papers, alleging that if handled by others they would become imbued with their personal magnetism, which would counteract her own. However, the torn pieces were handed directly to me, and I could not observe any opportunity for the substitution of other papers by sleight of hand. The genuineness or otherwise of the phenomena afterwards presented appears to rest on this point. The torn-off pieces of the paper remained in my closed left hand until the conclusion of the experiment. Of the larger pieces, Madame Blavatsky made two cigarettes, giving the first to me to hold while the other was being made up. I scrutinized this cigarette very attentively, in order to be able to recognize it afterwards. The cigarettes being finished, Madame Blavatsky stood up, and took them between her hands, which she rubbed together. After about twenty or thirty seconds, the grating noise of the paper, at first distinctly audible, ceased. She then said: "The current is passing round this end of the room, and I can only send them somewhere near here." The theory is that a current of what can only be called magnetism can be made to convey objects, previously dissipated by the same force, to any distance, and in spite of the intervention of any amount of matter. A moment afterwards she said one had fallen on the piano, the other near that bracket. As I sat on a sofa with my back to the wall, the piano was opposite, and the bracket, supporting a few pieces of china, was to the right, between it and the door. Both were in full view across the rather narrow room. The top of the piano was covered with piles of music books and it was among these Madame Blavatsky thought a cigarette would be found. The books were removed, one by one, by myself, but without seeing anything. I then opened the piano, and found a cigarette on a narrow shelf inside it. This cigarette I took out and recognized as the one I had held in my hand. The other was found in a covered cup on the bracket. Both cigarettes were still damp where they had been moistened at the edges in the process of manufacture. I took the cigarettes to a table, without permitting them to be touched or even seen by Madame Blavatsky and Colonel Olcott. On being unrolled and smoothed out, the torn, jagged edges were found to fit exactly to the pieces that I had all this time retained in my hand. The pencil marks also corresponded. It would therefore appear that the papers were actually the same as those I had seen torn. Both the papers are still in my possession. It may be added that Colonel Olcott sat near me with his back to Madame Blavatsky during the experiment, and did not move till it was concluded.

10c. A. P. Sinnett
October 15, 1880, Simla, India

[Sinnett 1881, 92–5]

One day I asked Madame Blavatsky whether, if I wrote a letter to one of the Brothers, she could get it delivered for me. I hardly thought this was probable, as I knew how very unapproachable the Brothers generally are; but as she said that at any rate she would try, I wrote a letter, addressing it "to the Unknown Brother," and gave it her to see if any result would ensue. It was a happy inspiration that induced me to do this, for out of that small beginning has arisen the most interesting correspondence in which I have ever been privileged to engage.

The idea I had specially in mind when I wrote the letter above referred to was that of all test phenomena one could wish for, the best would be the production in our presence in India of a copy of the London *Times* of that day's date. With such a piece of evidence in my hand, I argued, I would undertake to convert everybody in Simla who was capable of linking two ideas together, to a belief in the possibility of obtaining by occult agency physical results which were beyond the control of ordinary science.

A day or two elapsed before I heard anything of the fate of my letter, but Madame Blavatsky then informed me that I was to have an answer. She had not been able at first to find a Brother willing to receive the communication. Those whom she first applied to declined to be troubled with the matter. At last her psychological telegraph brought her a favorable answer from one of the Brothers with whom she had not for some time been in communication. He would take the letter and reply to it.

A day or two after, I found one evening on my writing table the first letter sent me by my new correspondent. He was a native of the Punjab who was attracted to occult studies from his earliest boyhood. He was sent to Europe whilst still a youth at the intervention of a relative—himself an occultist—to be educated in Western knowledge, and since then has been fully initiated in the greater knowledge of the East.

My correspondent is known to me as Koot Hoomi Lal Sing. This is his "Tibetan Mystic name"—occultists taking new names on initiation.

The letter I received began about the phenomenon I had proposed. "Precisely," Koot Hoomi wrote, "because the test of the London newspaper would close the mouths of the skeptics," it was inadmissible. "See it in what light you will, the world is yet in its first stage of disenthrallment, hence unprepared. Very true we work by natural, not supernatural, means and laws. But, as on the one hand science would find itself unable, in its present state, to account for the wonders given in its name, and on the other the ignorant masses would still be left to view the phenomenon in the light of a miracle, everyone who would thus be made a witness to the occurrence would be thrown off his balance, and the results would be deplorable. Believe me, it would be so especially for yourself, who originated the idea, and for the devoted woman [HPB] who so foolishly rushes into the wide, open door leading to notoriety. This door, though opened by so friendly a hand as yours, would prove very soon a trap—and a fatal one, indeed, for her. And such is not surely your object."

[Note: The correspondence between A. P. Sinnett and the Master Koot Hoomi extended from October 1880 to March-April 1885. In 1923, Master KH's letters (as well as the letters of Master Morya) were published in London under the title *The Mahatma Letters to A. P. Sinnett.* —DHC]

10D. A. P. SINNETT
OCTOBER 20, 1880, SIMLA, INDIA

[Sinnett 1881, 108–113]

Accompanied by our guests [Madame Blavatsky, Colonel Olcott, and Alice Gordon], we went to have lunch one day on the top of a neighboring hill. The night before, I had had reason to think that my correspondent, Koot Hoomi, had been in what I may call subjective communication with me.* After discussing the subject in the morning, I found on the hall table a note from Koot Hoomi, in which he promised to give me something on the hill which should be a token of his (astral) presence near me the previous night.

We went to our destination, camped down on the top of the hill, and were engaged on our lunch, when Madame Blavatsky said Koot Hoomi was asking where we would like to find the object he was going to send me. Up to this moment there had been no conversation in regard to the phenomenon I was expecting. The usual suggestion will, perhaps, be made that Madame Blavatsky "led up" to the choice I actually made. The fact of the matter was simply that in the midst of altogether other talk Madame Blavatsky pricked up her ears on hearing her occult voice—at once told me what was the question asked, and did not contribute to the selection made by one single remark on the subject. In fact, there was no general discussion, and it was by an absolutely spontaneous choice of my own that I said, after a little reflection, "inside that cushion," pointing to one against which one of the ladies present was leaning. I had no sooner uttered the words than my wife cried out, "Oh no, let it be inside mine," or words to that effect. I said, "Very well, inside my wife's cushion"; Madame Blavatsky asked the Mahatma by her own methods if that would do, and received an affirmative reply. My liberty of choice as regards the place where the object should be found was thus absolute and unfettered by conditions. The most natural choice for me to have made under the circumstances, and having regard to our previous experiences, would have been up some particular tree, or buried in a particular spot of the ground; but the inside of a sewn-up cushion, fortuitously chosen on the spur of a moment, struck me, as my eye happened to fall upon the cushion I mentioned first, as a particularly good place; and when I had started the idea of *a* cushion, my wife's amendment to the original proposal was really an improvement, for the particular cushion then selected had never been for a moment out of her own possession all the morning. It was her usual jampan cushion; she had been leaning against it all the way from home, and leaning against it still, as her jampan had been carried right up to the top of the hill, and she had continued to occupy it. The cushion itself was very firmly made of worsted work and velvet, and had been in our possession for years. It always remained, when we were at home, in the drawing room, in a conspicuous corner of a certain sofa, whence, when my wife went out, it would be taken to her jampan and again brought in on her return.

When the cushion was agreed to, my wife was told to put it under her rug, and she did this with her own hands, inside her jampan. It may have been there about a minute, when Madame Blavatsky said we could set to work to cut it open. I did this with a penknife, and it was a work of some time, as the cushion was very securely sewn all round, and very strongly, so that it had to be cut open almost stitch by stitch, and no tearing was possible. When one side of the cover was completely ripped up, we found that the feathers of the cushion were enclosed in a separate inner case, also sewn round all the edges. There was nothing to be found between the inner cushion and the outer case; so we proceeded to rip up the inner cushion; and this done, my wife searched among the feathers.

The first thing she found was a little three-cornered note, addressed to me in the now familiar handwriting of my occult correspondent. It ran as follows:

My "Dear Brother,"

This brooch No. 2—is placed in this very strange place simply to show to you how very easily a real phenomenon is produced and how still easier it is to suspect its genuineness.

The difficulty you spoke of last night with respect to the interchange of our letters I will try to remove. An address will be sent to you which you can always use; unless, indeed, you really would prefer corresponding through—pillows.

Koot Hoomi Lal Sing.

While I was reading this note, my wife discovered, by further search among the feathers, the brooch referred to, one of her own, a very old and very familiar brooch which she generally left on her dressing table when it was not in use. The whole force and significance to us of the brooch thus returned, hinged onto my subjective impressions of the previous night. The reason for selecting the brooch as a thing to give us dated no earlier than then. On the hypothesis, therefore, that the cushion must have been got at by Madame Blavatsky, it must have been got at since I spoke of my impressions that morning, shortly after breakfast; but from the time of getting up that morning, Madame Blavatsky had hardly been out of our sight, and had been sitting with my wife in the drawing room. She had been doing this, by the by, against the grain, for she had writing which she wanted to do in her own room, but she had been told by her voices to go and sit in the drawing room with my wife that morning, and had done so, grumbling at the interruption of her work, and wholly unable to discern any motive for the order. The motive was afterwards clear enough, and had reference to the intended phenomenon. It was desirable that we should have no *arriere pensee* [after thought, mental reservation, suspicion] in our minds as to what Madame Blavatsky might possibly have been doing during the morning, in the event of the incident taking such a turn as to make that a factor in determining its genuineness. Of course, if the selection of the pillow could have been foreseen, it would have been unnecessary to victimize our "old Lady," as we generally called her. The presence of the famous pillow itself, with my wife all the morning in the drawing room, would have been enough. But perfect liberty of choice was to be left to me in selecting a cache for the brooch; and the pillow can have been in nobody's mind, any more than in my own, beforehand.

*[Note: A. P. Sinnett writes: "I saw K. H. in astral form on the night of 19th of October, 1880—waking up for a moment but immediately afterwards being rendered unconscious again (in the body) and conscious out of the body in the adjacent dressing room, where I saw another of the Brothers afterwards identified with one called Serapis by Olcott." *The Mahatma Letters*, p. 10. —DHC]

10E. ALICE GORDON
SEPTEMBER–OCTOBER 1880 AND
SEPTEMBER–OCTOBER 1881,
SIMLA, INDIA

[Gordon 1890]

I returned to India from England at the end of 1878, having, during that year, investigated the phenomena of Spiritualism and convinced myself of their truth, and in 1879 I published in a leading newspaper there an account of some seances held in my house in London. Mr. Sinnett was the editor of that paper, and the connection thus began led eventually to my acquaintance with Madame Blavatsky, to see whom I took a long journey of nearly thirty hours to Allahabad, and at the same time I met for the first time Mr. and Mrs. Sinnett and Mr. and Mrs. Hume. This was in the winter of 1879–80. During this visit, I heard raps produced at will on tables, glass doors, and elsewhere, and a large glass clock shade was often used, we being able to see the hands from underneath this, and so be certain that they did not move. From Allahabad, Madame Blavatsky, Colonel Olcott, the Sinnetts, and myself went to Benares for a few days, a Rajah there having lent us a house. Probably most of you have read Mr. Sinnett's book, *The Occult World*, in which this visit is recorded.

In the summer of 1880, I went to Simla on a visit to Mr. and Mrs. Hume. Madame Blavatsky was there part of the season, the guest of Mr. and Mrs. Sinnett. In *The Occult World* much of the phenomenon is recorded [by Mr. Sinnett], and, probably, you have all heard of the cigarettes which were disintegrated and reintegrated. I saw this done several times, but will only mention in detail the one cigarette which was especially made and manipulated for me. I went one morning unexpectedly to see Madame, and found her alone in her room. Our conversation turned on phenomena, and I asked her whether she could send anything to my husband now, or to me after I returned home. She said she could not, as she must know the place in order to direct her thought there. But she added that as I never bothered her for phenomena, she would like to do something for me, and suddenly remembering that she had been somewhere that morning (to the dentist) suggested sending a cigarette there if I would go directly and fetch it, to which I consented. She then took out a cigarette paper, and in broad daylight, I standing quite close watching her, she tore off a corner and gave it to me, telling me to take care of it, which I did, putting it into my purse at once. She made a cigarette with the other piece of the paper, and was on the point of crushing it between her hands, when she bethought her to try a new experiment, saying, if it failed it was of no consequence, as it was for me, and so she put it into the fire. In a few seconds she said it was all right, and told me where I should find it. I started at once for the house, and astonished my friends by asking them to look under a cloth on a table in a certain room for a cigarette, and there sure enough we found one. On opening it and comparing the paper with the piece I had with me, they fitted exactly. Of course, it sounds like a conjuring trick, but I feel quite sure that I saw the piece of paper I held torn off the very paper from which the cigarette was made.

You have doubtless read of the so-called astral bells. These I have often heard in Madame Blavatsky's presence, both indoors and out of doors. The nearest approach to the sound is that produced by striking softly a thin wineglass, which produces a clear, musical sound. Sometimes there were several sounds in succession, forming a cadence. I remember on one occasion a gentleman going into the next room to that in which Madame Blavatsky was sitting, and there he also heard the bell-like sound. We had at that time phenomena almost daily and were almost always on the lookout for something to happen. One day it suddenly occurred to me that I should like to write to Koot Hoomi. We seemed to know him so well, there being so many communications from him; so I wrote a letter, and took it straight to Madame's room and asked her if she thought he would take it from me; I did not expect him to do so, I admit. She said she did not know. I then showed her an envelope which contained the one I had written, and she told me to place it under the tablecloth at the place where she always sat when writing, and see if it was taken. I did so. There was no one in the room but ourselves, and she then suggested that I should not lose sight of her, which I did not. We went to luncheon, and on our return she told me to look under the cloth. My letter was no longer there. I received an answer from Koot Hoomi, but it was given me by Madame Blavatsky. I believe that letter was taken by occult means, though the evidence would not be very conclusive to an outsider; one must always appear too credulous when not entering into details and giving reasons.

I will now relate a phenomenon of which I was the sole witness with Madame Blavatsky. I had gone unexpectedly to her room when we were both staying at Mr. Hume's in Simla, in 1881. She was sitting writing at her table, which was placed close to a small window. The room being very warm, I suggested a little fresh air and proposed opening the window, which swung from the top on hinges. With some difficulty I pushed it out from below, but in swinging back it came down onto the piece of wood intended to hold it open, which went through the glass. Madame became excited, and I, thinking it was because the glass was broken, said, "Never mind, we can get it mended." She exclaimed, "No, no, keep still; I saw a hand; something is going to happen." I was standing close to the window ledge, between Madame and the window. Presently she said, "Draw the curtain"—a small one just coming as far as the ledge, but I had scarcely pulled it across when she said, "Draw it back," and there in front of me was a letter directed to Mr. Hume, and "Favored by Mrs. Gordon," in the handwriting so well known to me as that of Koot Hoomi. This I concluded was done that Mr. Hume might have evidence that the letters really arrived phenomenally, and I am perfectly certain that the letter was not in the place where I found it one half minute before, and quite as certain that no human hand in the flesh put it there.

William Eglinton

Chapter 11

BOMBAY AND THE
VEGA PHENOMENON
1881–1882

ADAME BLAVATSKY and Colonel Olcott were at Bombay, residing in a house called "The Crow's Nest," while they pursued considerable activity in propagating the Theosophical Society. That propagation included having certain persons, both Easterners and Westerners, get into touch with the Mahatmas, by either correspondence or personal visitations. The contact of those persons with the Mahatmas was sometimes arranged by HPB, but was often independent of her, as in the case of the distinguished Spiritualist and medium, William Eglinton. He had a paranormal encounter with the Mahatma KH on board the SS Vega and subsequently sent a written communication by paranormal means from the ship to Calcutta via Bombay (selections 11e and 11f).

CHAPTER 11

11A. MARTANDRAO BABAJI NAGNATH
APRIL 1881, BOMBAY, INDIA

[Hume 1882, 103–5]

I have had constant occasions to visit [Theosophical] headquarters at Breach Candy, Bombay. My connection with the
Founders of the Society has been close, and my opportunity good
for studying Theosophy. I am therefore inclined, for my satisfaction and for the information of students of Nature, to record here
my experiences of certain phenomena, which came under my
observation on several occasions in the presence of brother
Theosophists and strangers. I have also had the rare privilege to
see the so-called and generally unseen Brothers [Mahatmas] of the
1st section of the Theosophical Society.

In the month of April 1881, on one dark night, while talking
in company with other Theosophists with Madame Blavatsky
about 10 PM in the open verandah of the upper bungalow, a man,
six feet in height, clad in a white robe, with a white [turban] on
the head, made his appearance on a sudden, walking towards us
through the garden adjacent to the bungalow from a point—a
precipice—where there is no path for any one to tread. Madame
then rose up and told us to go inside the bungalow. So we went in,
but we heard Madame and he talking for a minute with each other
in an Eastern language unknown to us. Immediately after, we
again went out into the verandah, as we were called, but the
Brother had disappeared.

On the next occasion, when we were chatting in the above
verandah as usual, another Brother, clothed in a white dress, was
suddenly seen as if standing on a branch of a tree. We saw him
then descending as though through the air, and standing on a
corner edge of a thin wall. Madame then rose up from her seat
and stood looking at him for about two minutes, and—as if it
seemed—talking inaudibly with him. Immediately after, in our
presence, the figure of the man disappeared, but was afterwards

seen again walking in the air through space, then right through the tree, and again disappearing.

Group at the Theosophical Society convention, Bombay, 1882

11B. SORAB J. PADSHAH
JULY 15–16, 1881, BOMBAY, INDIA

[Theosophical Society 1885, 70]

I have received two letters in all from the revered Mahatma [Koot Hoomi]. The first [letter] I received on the evening of the 15th July, 1881. I copy the endorsement which I immediately made on the back of the envelope which contained the letter: "Received about ten minutes to ten—a little while after Madame

[Blavatsky] had retired and Babula had left the lamp on the table. I had just written the first two lines of a poem I was composing on the Brothers, and was thinking how to finish the third, when I heard a sound as if a large butterfly had fallen on the table. It was this letter. It fell from some height. The doors of the room and shutters were closed. My gratitude and thanks. 15-7-81, S.J.P." After I had examined the room to see that there was no trickery in the affair, and satisfying myself that none was possible, I fell on my knees and uttered some words to myself mentally. The following morning I saw Madame Blavatsky in her study. After some conversation she told me she was satisfied that I was devoted to the [Theosophical] cause, for the Master had watched me and she proceeded to relate all that had happened in my room *after* I had received the letter, startling me at the same time *by reciting word for word my unspoken thought.*

11c. A. P. SINNETT
JULY–AUGUST 1881, BOMBAY
AND THEN LATER ON THE ROAD TO SIMLA

[Sinnett 1886, 236–9, 241–3]

During [July] 1881 I returned to India from a visit to England, and on landing at Bombay spent a few days with Mme. Blavatsky at the headquarters of the Theosophical Society, then established at Breach Candy, in a bungalow called the Crow's Nest, perched up on a little eminence above the road. It had been unoccupied for some time I heard, discredited by a reputation for snakes and ghosts, neither of which encumbrances greatly alarmed the new tenants.

The building was divided into two portions—the lower given over to the Society's service and to Colonel Olcott's Spartan accommodation; the upper part, reached by a covered stairway, corresponding to the slope of the hill, to Mme. Blavatsky and the office work of the *Theosophist*. There was also a spare room in this upper portion, all the rooms of which were on one level, and opening on to a broad covered-in verandah, which constituted Mme. Blavatsky's sitting, eating, and reception room all in one. Opening out of it at the further end she had a small writing-room. The covered verandah was all day long and up to late hours in the evening visited by an ebb and flow of native guests, admiring Theosophists who came to pay their respects to Madame.

She would generally be up at an early hour writing at her Russian articles or translations, or at her endless letters she sent off in all directions in the interest of the Society, or at articles for the *Theosophist*; then during the day she would spend a large part of her time talking with native visitors in her verandah room, or getting back to her work with wild protests against the constant interruption she was subject to, and in the same breath calling for her faithful Babula, her servant, in a voice that rang all over the house, and sending for some one or another of the visitors she knew to be waiting about below and wanting to see her.

Then in the midst of some fiery argument with a pundit about a point of modern Hindoo belief that she might protest against as inconsistent with the real meaning of the Vedas, or a passionate remonstrance with one of her aides of the *Theosophist* about something done amiss that would for the time overspread the whole sky of her imagination with a thundercloud, she would perhaps suddenly "hear the voice they did not hear"—the astral call of her distant Master or of one of the other "Brothers" and forgetting everything else in an instant she would hurry off to the seclusion of any room where she could be alone for a few moments, and hear whatever message or orders she had to receive.

She never wanted to go to bed when night came. She would sit on smoking cigarettes and talking—talking with a tireless energy that was wonderful to watch—on Eastern philosophy of any sort, on the mistakes of theological writers, on questions raised (but not settled) in *Isis*, or, with just as much intensity and excitement, on some wretched matter connected with the administration of the Society, or some foolish sarcasm leveled against herself and the attributes imputed to her in one of the local newspapers.

She joined me at Allahabad a few [weeks] after my return to India in 1881, and went up to Simla with me to be the guest for the remainder of that season of Mr. A. O. Hume. She was far from well at the time, and the latter part of the journey—a trying one for the most robust passenger—was an ordeal that brought out the peculiar characteristics of her excitable temper in an amusing way; for the "tongas," in which the eight hours' drive up the mountain roads from Kalka at the foot of the hills to the elevated sanatorium [Simla] is accomplished, are not luxurious conveyances. They are low two-wheeled carts hung on a crank axle, so that the foot boards are only about a foot above the road, with seats for four persons, including the driver, two and two back to back—just accommodation enough in each for one passenger with his portmanteau (equivalent, if he has one with him, to a passenger), and a servant. We had two tongas between us, putting our servants with some of the luggage in one, while Mme. Blavatsky and I occupied the back seat of the other with a portmanteau on the seat beside the driver.

A tonga gets over the ground rapidly, and the ponies, frequently changed, trot or canter up all but the steepest gradients. The traveler is jolted frightfully, but he is not likely to be capsized, though even that happens sometimes, for the mountain roads are very rough, and the ponies apt to be troublesome. The animals are attached to the vehicle by a strong crossbar resting in sockets on saddles they carry for the purpose, and though on this system ponies and cart are as firmly united as a bunch of keys by its steel ring, still they are no less loosely linked together, and a nervous passenger is liable to be disturbed by the extraordinary positions into which they get during any little disagreement between the team and the driver.

One such disagreement arose soon after our start on the journey, and Madame's impassioned anathemas directed against the whole service of the tonga dak and the civilization of which it formed a part, ought not, I remember thinking at the time, to have had their comicality wasted upon an audience of one. Then as the day and the weary drive wore on, Madame's indignation at the annoyance of the situation only waxed more vehemently. Especially incensed whenever the driver sounded his ear-piercing horn close behind us, she would break off whatever she was talking about to launch invectives at this unfortunate "trumpet."

11D. JOHN SMITH
JANUARY 31, 1882, BOMBAY, INDIA

[Hume 1882, 97–8]

On the evening of 31st January, when the daily batch of letters was being opened, one was found to contain some red writing different from the body of the letter. Col. Olcott then took two unopened letters and asked Madame Blavatsky if she could perceive similar writing in them. Putting them to her forehead, she said one contained the word "carelessly" and the other something about Col. Olcott and a branch at Cawnpore. I then examined these letters and found the envelopes sound. I opened them and saw the words mentioned. One letter was from Meerut, one from Cawnpore, and one from Hyderabad.

Next day Col. Olcott remarked that if I were to get any letters while here, there might be some of the same writing in them. I replied that there would be *"no chance* of that, as no one would write to me." Madame Blavatsky then, looking fixedly for a little, said: "I see a Brother here. He asks if you would like some such token as that we have been speaking of." I replied that I would be much gratified. She rose from the table and told us to follow her. Taking my hand, she led me along the verandah, stopping and looking about at some points till we reached the door of my bedroom. She then desired me to enter alone and look round the room to see if there was anything unusual, and to close the other doors. I did so, and was satisfied the room was in its usual condition.

She then desired us to sit down, and in doing so took my hands in both of hers. In a few seconds a letter fell at my feet. It seemed to me to appear first a little above the level of my head. On opening the envelope I found a sheet of notepaper, headed with a Government stamp of the Northwestern Provinces and Oudh, and the following words written with red pencil, *in exactly the same handwriting as that in the letters of the previous evening* "NO CHANCE of writing to you inside your letters, but I can write *direct*. Work for us in Australia, and we will not prove ungrateful, but will prove to you our actual existence, and thank you." A fair review of the circumstances excludes, in my opinion, any theory of fraud.

11E. WILLIAM EGLINTON
MARCH 22–24, 1882,
SS VEGA, INDIAN OCEAN,
WEST OF SRI LANKA (CEYLON)

[Collated from Eglinton 1882, 301,
and Eglinton 1886]

It was not until the last week of my stay in India that I began to receive evidence of the existence of the beings designated the "Himalayan Brothers." One night I was sitting with Colonel and Mrs. Gordon at their house in Howrah [a suburb of Calcutta] when my [spirit] guide, "Ernest," came and informed us that he had been in communication with certain of the Brotherhood. This aroused my curiosity, because I knew I could depend upon a statement so made, but nothing more happened to convince me until I was homeward bound on board the SS *Vega*.

174

On the 22nd March, 1882, I was at sea, having left [Colombo,] Ceylon about 6 p.m. the same day. I occupied a deck cabin forward under the bridge. About ten o'clock I was in this cabin undressing preparatory to sleeping on deck, my back being to the open door. On turning round to make my exit, I found the entrance barred by what I took, at first sight, to be a khitmaghur or native butler.

Thinking he had come on some message, I waited for him to speak, but as he did not do so, and deeming his manner insolent from his not having demanded entrance, and not paying the deference usual to Europeans, I angrily told him, in Hindustani, to go away; whereupon he stepped into the cabin, grasped me by the right hand, and gave me the grip of a Master Mason before I had sufficiently recovered from my astonishment. I requested him to tell me why he had intruded upon me and to state his business.

Speaking in perfect English, he deliberately informed me he was "Koot Hoomi Lal Singh," and I was at the moment so profoundly impressed with his general appearance, his knowledge of Freemasonry, and the statement that he really was the person, mystic, or Adept of whom I had heard so much during my residence in India, that without hesitation I accepted him as such. We then entered into conversation of some length, of no particular importance to anyone but myself, but it proved to me that he was intimately acquainted with both the Spiritualistic and Theosophical movements, as well as with friends of mine in India.

He was in every respect an intelligent man, perfectly formed, and in nowise differing, in outward semblance at any rate, from the thousands of natives one sees in the East. Nor was it hallucination, for I was in full possession of all my faculties; and that it was not a subjective vision is proved by the grasp of the hand, and the very evident materiality of the figure. Some little thing attracted my attention from him for a moment, for I was criticizing him keenly, and when I turned my head again—he was gone! Two steps took me to the open door, where I had the advantage of scanning both the fore and aft decks, but I could observe no one in the act of retreating, although no living being could have in the time escaped from the range of my vision.

The next day I searched the ship, even going down into the shaft tunnel to find a person in appearance like the man I had seen on the previous night, but without obtaining the slightest clue to his identity, although my mind was then dwelling upon the possibility of a man having been commissioned to come on board at Ceylon on purpose to deceive me. But the more I reflected the more difficult I found it to accept such a theory, and two days after I penned the hasty and enthusiastic letter which appears in *The Occult World*.

"Koot Hoomi" had promised to take a letter to Mrs. Gordon, at Howrah, if I would write one when on board. I thought my having seen the "figure" a good opportunity to convey the news in the manner suggested, and I accordingly wrote, asserting my complete belief that the person I had seen was none other than the Great Master. After I had written the letter, I went onto the deck, and knowing a certain lady to be on board who was much interested in psychical matters, I read her the letter, and invited her to mark the envelope as a little test between ourselves and those at the "other end of the line." This she did.

On my return to the smoking room I told some of my fellow passengers what I had done, whereupon a gentleman who claimed to be a Theosophist and acquainted with Madame Blavatsky, asked why, if I could send a letter, could he not do the same? I saw no objection to his doing so, and he at once wrote a short note. I opened the envelope and enclosed both letters in another, and again sought the lady to re-mark it. She was not on the deck at the time, so I returned to the smoking room, and on mentioning the matter to those assembled, one said, "Put a cross upon it"; another remarked, "Add a second"; and a third person wished that three crosses should be put. As each one spoke I added the cross, until there were three in all, and I then took the envelope, placed it in my locked writing case, and put it (the case) upon a shelf in my cabin. I opened it at intervals to see whether the envelope was still there, and I last saw it, to the best of my recollection, about four p.m., for when I looked again just before dinner it was gone.

The same night, in the presence of Colonel Olcott and Colonel and Mrs. Gordon, an envelope marked with three crosses and stated to contain my letter, was dropped from the ceiling of the bedroom I had occupied when at Howrah. I have not been able to verify whether the letter was in my writing, but I imagine it to be mine as the letter was similar in terms to the one written by me—in addition to which Mrs. Gordon was intimately acquainted with my writing.

11F. MRS. ALICE GORDON
MARCH 23–24, 1882,
HOWRAH, A SUBURB OF
CALCUTTA, INDIA

[Gordon 1882]

Colonel Olcott told me that he had had an intimation in the night from his Chohan (teacher) that KH had been to the *Vega* and seen Eglinton. This was at about eight o'clock on Thursday morning, the 23rd [of March]. A few hours later a telegram, dated at Bombay 9 minutes past 9 PM on Wednesday evening, came to me from Madame Blavatsky, to this effect: "KH just gone to *Vega.*" It corroborated, as will be seen, the message of the previous night to Colonel Olcott. We then felt hopeful of getting the letter by occult means from Mr. Eglinton. A telegram [from Mme. Blavatsky] later on Thursday asked us to fix a time for a sitting, so we named 9 o'clock Madras time, on Friday 24th.

At this hour we three—Colonel Olcott, Colonel Gordon, and myself—sat in the room which had been occupied by Mr. Eglinton. We had a good light, and sat with our chairs placed to form a triangle, of which the apex was to the north. In a few minutes Colonel Olcott saw outside the open window the two

"Brothers" and told us so; he saw them pass to another window, the glass doors of which were closed. He saw one of them point his hand towards the air over my head, and I felt something at the same moment fall straight down from above on to my shoulder, and saw it fall at my feet in the direction *towards* the two gentlemen. I knew it would be the letter, but for the moment I was so anxious to see the "Brothers" that I did not pick up what had fallen. Colonel Gordon and Colonel Olcott both saw and heard the letter fall. Colonel Olcott had turned his head from the window for a moment to see what the "Brother" was pointing at, and so noticed the letter falling from a point about two feet from the ceiling. When he looked again the two "Brothers" had vanished.

There is no verandah outside, and the window is several feet from the ground.

I now turned and picked up what had fallen on me, and found a letter in Mr. Eglinton's handwriting, dated on the *Vega* the 24th. We opened the letter carefully, by slitting up one side, as we saw that someone had made on the flap in pencil three Latin crosses, and so we kept them intact for identification. The letter is as follows:

My Dear Mrs. Gordon, —At last your hour of triumph has come! After the many battles we have had at the breakfast-table regarding KH's existence, and my stubborn skepticism as to the wonderful powers possessed by the "Brothers," I have been forced to a *complete belief* in their being living distinct persons. I am not allowed to tell you all I know, but KH *appeared* to me in person two days ago, and what he told me dumbfounded me.

[Colonel Olcott in his diary for March 24, 1882, pens the following: "At 9 the Gordons and I sat together. Morya and KH appeared at the windows and notes from Eglinton (from on board the Vega), Morya, KH and HPB, tied together, dropped through the air on Mrs. Gordon's shoulder. A stupendous phenomenon all round. E. says in his note that he is sending it off by the Brothers to HPB after showing it to a fellow passenger, Mrs. Boughton, and having her mark the envelope." —DHC]

11G. NORENDRO NATH SEN
APRIL 6–10, 1882, CALCUTTA, INDIA

[Sen 1882]

Spiritualism, which, for sometime past, had been secretly and slowly, but steadily, gathering disciples among the educated and intelligent classes of Hindu society, suddenly received a strong impulse to the investigation of its mysteries from the time that Mr. Eglinton arrived in Calcutta and began to manifest his rare powers as a medium. At his departure from India, he left this branch of occult science in a somewhat advanced state of development; and it is to be hoped that the prosecution of the investigations, set on foot under his auspices, will in time lead to such further progress as may prove that spiritualism is not the idle or deluding thing most people, who have not scientifically studied it, are disposed to take it to be. The stir which Mr. Eglinton had created had hardly subsided when men's minds were roused into eager curiosity by the advent, first of Colonel Olcott and shortly afterwards of Madame Blavatsky at Calcutta. Both these distinguished personages have been residing in India for three years; but though they have visited most parts of the country during this period, they have now come to the metropolis of the Indian Empire for the first time. It is hardly necessary to say that a most intense feeling of anxiety to see them here had been pervading the educated classes of Hindu society. Now that they are here, we hope that the fullest opportunity will be taken of their present visit, however brief, to ascertain the nature and objects of the science of Theosophy to the utmost extent possible. We are perfectly aware that many intelligent and well-informed people entertain very vague and hazy notions regarding this science. It would be well if no time were lost in dispelling crude and misleading conceptions on a subject of so much importance.

Since their arrival here, we have had frequent opportunities of seeing Colonel Olcott and Madame Blavatsky, and conversing with them both. Colonel Olcott seems to be a man of vast erudition and considerable thought. He is a clever man, who was a Counselor at Law in his country, and held several important offices there, having, besides, been connected with several local newspapers. It is an undoubted fact that he has made considerable sacrifices in the interests of Theosophy. It is always a pleasure to hear Colonel Olcott dilate on Theosophy and cognate subjects, in which he is evidently well versed. As for Madame Blavatsky, she is unquestionably a remarkable lady. Without exaggeration, she may be described as a book in herself. She is well grounded in abstruse and recondite studies. In Theosophy though, Colonel Olcott, however clever and able, seems as if he were only a tyro in comparison. She is also well up in several languages, and though she is not as proficient in English as in her own mother tongue or in French, she can express herself far better than many people well acquainted with the English language. It is well known that she is the Editor of the *Theosophist*—a journal which is conducted with remarkable ability and success. We have often been struck by Madame Blavatsky's rare powers of carrying on a controversy, whether in writing or viva voce. She seems to have acquired her command over her thoughts and her language from the extensive experience she has enjoyed as a journalist.

Colonel Olcott's lecture on the 6th instant was, to all Hindus at least, the most interesting that was ever heard. We know that many people listened to it with much satisfaction and derived considerable instruction from it. There can be no two opinions as to the ability manifest in every line of the lecture and in the style in which it was set out. It was a unique and striking thing altogether to hear a foreigner—a white man hailing from the United States—speak so appreciatively, as Colonel Olcott did, of our ancient religion, of our *rishis* of old, and of our grand institutions. The Hindus ought to feel the greatest interest in this movement. Theosophy, though a new, is a most attractive study; and even such as are skeptical about it should inquire into it before condemning or ridiculing it. Madame Blavatsky is anxious that people should interest themselves more in the nature than in the phenomena of Theosophy, and very rightly so. The phenomena would look more like conjuring tricks and would be attended with few practical results, unless the philosophy underlying them were thoroughly understood and appreciated. A branch of the Theosophical Society has been established in Calcutta.

Many phenomena in connection with Theosophy have not yet been seen in Calcutta. But we shall describe a few of those which we ourselves have witnessed. As for the rappings which spiritualists produce, we have seen Madame Blavatsky cause them to be produced in any number, merely by the force of her will and her magnetic power, sometimes even without touching an object, but merely by waving her hands across it. We have seen her produce raps on the human head, on a glass shutter, and on other articles. They are much louder than the spiritualistic raps, and are given precisely up to the number, indicated by Madame Blavatsky, at the request of any bystander.

Then, again, on the 6th instant, in the presence of several gentlemen, the following phenomenon was disclosed. A native gentleman of Lucknow, who is practicing as a pleader in the local court, sometime ago lost his wife and children, and being utterly brokenhearted, had determined to abandon the world and give himself up to the service of Theosophy. Accordingly, he wrote a letter from Lucknow, bearing date the 1st instant, to the address of Colonel Olcott, saying that he had followed him to Allahabad and other places, that he was anxious to see him, and inquiring where he could be found. As he thought that the Colonel had returned to the headquarters of the Society, he directed his letter to Bombay. On the day in question, some letters by post were brought in to Colonel Olcott, in the presence of several gentlemen, by a servant of the house where he is staying. Among them was this identical letter. Another letter by post came on the same day immediately following the other one, and while he was reading it. It was a printed circular from a paral [apparel, goods?] tradesman of Bombay. It was delivered to the Colonel who opened it before the same gentlemen. Across this letter appeared some writing in blue pencil, and signed KH (Koot Hoomi), one of the Himalayan Brothers. It was also signed by Colonel Olcott's own Guru. It ordered him to telegraph for the Lucknow pleader (mentioning him by name) to come to Calcutta, and to postpone till the 19th instant his visit to Madras, for which place Colonel Olcott had already taken a passage by the SS *Khandalah*, intending to proceed on board that very night. Both the letters, as we have said, were brought in by post. They bore the usual postmarks, and it was certainly impossible that the letter across which the message in blue pencil from KH appeared could have been tampered with, in the ordinary course, in its passage from Bombay. The writing in blue pencil was in the hand of Koot Hoomi. Mr. Sinnett, the editor of the *Pioneer*, we are told, recently met with a similar experience in the case of a telegram which was sent to him from Calcutta under the usual official cover, thoroughly secured in the usual official manner. When the cover was opened, besides the telegram, it was found to contain a separate note from the hand of Colonel Olcott's Guru.

We have already said that Madame Blavatsky is very justly averse to give manifestations of her occult powers. She rightly holds that if Theosophy cannot assert and maintain its authority by the soundness and beneficence of its principles, it would be idle to try to bolster it up by the exhibition of phenomena which, unless cause and effect are thoroughly understood, might be construed into vulgar conjuring tricks. She wishes that the science with whose promotion she has so thoroughly identified herself should stand or fall on its own merits. It is her hope that men of education and intelligence will make Theosophy the object of careful and scientific study. If the science does not fulfill the promises it holds out, it will be easy for a student to give up the study when he finds his expectations disappointed.

On the morning of the 10th instant, we called on Madame Blavatsky with a full determination not to express our wish to witness any phenomena. Besides Madame Blavatsky and ourselves, there were present in the room Babus Peary Chand Mittra and

Mohini Mohun Chatterji, M.A. While we were engaged in general conversation, Madame Blavatsky suddenly fixed her eyes on a certain spot. She asked Babu Mohini Mohun to go outside the room and see if anyone was concealed in the adjoining hall. The Babu accordingly did as he was directed, but he found nobody. Scarcely he had resumed his seat when a small billet of paper was visibly shot by some unseen agency from a point above the top of a lofty wooden partition obliquely, and it fell near the spot where Colonel Olcott was seated, after a flight of 20 feet. At the desire of Madame Blavatsky, Babu Mohini Mohun picked up the paper, and its contents were found to run as follows:

Degrade not Truth by forcing it upon unwilling minds. Seek not to secure help from those whose hearts are not patriotic enough to unselfishly work for the good of their countrymen. "What good can we do?"— is asked. "What benefit can we confer upon humanity, or even our own country?" Lukewarm patriots, verily, are they. In the presence of his country perishing in its nationality for want of vitality, and the infusion of fresh forces, a *real patriot* catches at a straw. But are there any *true patriots* in Bengal? Had there been many, we would have sent you here before now; we would have hardly allowed you to remain three years in India, without visiting Calcutta, the city of great intellects and—no hearts. You may read this to them.

K. H.

Neither Madame Blavatsky nor Colonel Olcott expected such a letter; and neither certainly was concerned in the mysterious manner in which it was conveyed into the room. The thing may seem almost incredible; but it is nevertheless an undoubted fact.

[The letter from Master KH quoted in Sen's article was finally published as Letter 12 in *Letters from the Masters of Wisdom 1870-1900*, First Series, transcribed and compiled by C. Jinarajadasa (Adyar, Madras, India: Theosophical Publishing House). Sen was the editor of *The Indian Mirror*. —DHC]

Damodar K. Mavalankar

Chapter 12

INDIA:
REACTIONS OF
BELIEF AND SKEPTICISM
1882

*B*LAVATSKY'S ABILITY to produce phenomena was remarkable, but she sometimes used it in a joking way, as in her spontaneous materialization of a letter in the handwriting of an antagonist to the Society, purporting to be his application for membership (selection 12a). Her phenomena and the reality of her teachers were both controversial matters, eliciting both believing acceptance (sometimes with independent confirmation) and skeptical rejection, as the following selections illustrate.

CHAPTER 12

12A. HENRY S. OLCOTT
JUNE 19, 1882, BARODA, INDIA

[Olcott 1900, 2:363–7]

In June 1882, HPB and I accepted an invitation to visit Baroda, the flourishing capital of H. H. the Gaikwar. Judge Gadgil and other high officials met us at the station, and took us to a bungalow adjoining the new and splendid palace. We had many visitors [and] our reception room [was] crowded with inquirers day and evening.

I had been out to see the Gaikwar, and on my return found [Mr.] Kirtane and [Judge] Gadgil standing at the threshold of HPB's open door, while she was in the middle of the room with her back towards us. Our two friends told me not to step inside, as Madame B. was doing a phenomenon and had just turned them out on the verandah where I found them. The next minute she came towards us, and, taking a sheet of paper from the table, told the gentleman to mark it for identification. Receiving it back, she said: "Now turn me in the direction of his residence." They did so. She then laid the paper between her palms (held horizontally), remained quiet a moment, then held it towards us and went and sat down. Cries of amazement broke from the two on seeing on the just before clean sheet of paper, a letter addressed to me in the handwriting and bearing the signature of the then British Resident at that Court. It was a most peculiar, small calligraphy, and the signature more like a tiny tangle of twine than a man's name.

They then told me the story. It seems that they were asking HPB to explain the scientific rationale of the process of precipitating upon paper, cloth, or any other surface, a picture or writing, then invisible to the onlooker, and without the help of ink, paints, pencils, or other mechanical agents. She told them that inasmuch as the images of all objects and incidents are stored in the Astral Light, it did not require that she should have seen the person or known the writing, the image of which she wished to precipitate; she had only to be put on the trace and could find and see them for herself and then objectivate them. They urgently begged her to do the thing for them. "Well, then," she finally said, "tell me the name of some man or woman most unfriendly to the Theosophical Society, one whom neither Olcott nor I could have ever known." At once, they mentioned Mr ... the British Resident, who held us and our Society in especial hatred, who never missed the chance of saying unkind things of us, and who had prevented the Gaikwar from inviting HPB and myself to his enthronement, as he had otherwise intended, on the suggestion of Judge Gadgil. They thought this a poser. That it was not, the sequel proved.

I thought they would explode with laughter when they read the contents of the note. It was addressed to "My dear Colonel Olcott," begged my pardon for the malicious things he had said against us and said he wished to become a member of the Theosophical Society; it was signed "Yours sincerely" and with his name. She had never seen a line of the gentleman's writing nor his signature, never met him in the flesh, and the note was precipitated on that sheet of paper, held between her hands, as she stood in the middle of the room, in broad daylight, with us three witnesses looking on.

12B. R. CASAVA PILLAI
MAY–OCTOBER 1882, NELLORE, BOMBAY, AND DARJEELING, INDIA

[Pillai 1885]

In 1881, I had the good fortune to come in contact with a chela, who was then in the lower stages of his spiritual development at Nellore. He is a Vaishnava by caste, and had lived for some time before 1881 with a Mahatma in the North, having left his parents and family from whom he has now separated himself for good. He is a chela of a high order. His friendship with me brought me in contact with Brother Damodar K. Mavalankar, FTS, early in 1881. Just at this time, the familiar and sacred face of my Guru Deva [Koot Hoomi] used to appear before me oftener in my dreams, and with a more gracious and approving countenance.

Early in 1882, under the auspices of the chela I have above referred to—who then happened to be at the headquarters of the Theosophical Society at Bombay—arrangements were made for the organization of the Nellore Branch. On an application from the members here, Madame Blavatsky and Colonel Olcott arrived at Nellore [in May 1882], and this branch has been opened. While the Founders were here, I received, for the first time, a letter from Mahatma M, addressed to me and some Theosophists, containing certain instructions as to the management of this Branch &c. Myself, Mr. Narayana Swamy Naidu, FTS, G. Subbia Chetty Garu, FTS (Madras Branch), and Singaravelu Mudalyar, B.A., FTS, of the Guntar Branch, were present in the Apstani Hall; Madame Blavatsky was writing at the table, we were seated, and on her telling us that she felt the presence of her Guru in the room, we all looked up, and then within a minute or two, a letter fell before us from the ceiling in broad daylight at about 3 PM. There were no contrivances or trapdoors to perform the phenomena at the time.

That very day, an hour afterwards, in the presence of about a dozen or more persons (both Theosophists and non-Theosophists), the subject of conversation was to know a certain date, and then one of us (I believe it was G. Subbia Chetty) suggested that Madame might be requested to give us an almanac, and another suggested that it should be one not available at Nellore. Then all of us joined in the request. Madame Blavatsky remarked that she would try, as a high chela, Jwalkool, was present in his astral body somewhere near. We were all seated in the same hall, and a verandah adjoining opened to the roof with nothing but the sky overhead. She then called out for the chela to make us a gift of an almanac, and within 3 or 4 minutes one "Almanac for 1882 and Diary Phoenix" were flung at us with some force as if it fell from the sky overhead, and this was handed to me by Madame Blavatsky, and it is with me still.

Madame Blavatsky told me, while she was at Nellore, that the Brothers had spoken to her about me, and that they were watching me long before this, and I replied that I knew it to be the case. This conversation took place while T. V. Charlu, FTS, and C. Kotiah Chetty Garu, FTS, Deputy Inspector of Schools, and some others were present. It was after this that I really thought more seriously of the appearance of the Mahatmas before me in dreams and otherwise. I then began to concentrate my attention upon the beautiful features of the latter Mahatma, my most revered Guru Deva, whom I then knew to be Mahatma Koot Hoomi. It was not in vain I did so. Within four or five days I had a response to my prayer. The blessed Mahatma from that time forward used to give me instructions in my dreams—not exactly dreams—but a state of half-wakefulness—for want of a better word I call them dreams—and in one—I believe it was about the end of May—I fervently prayed to Him that I might be allowed the happiness of seeing Him in his physical body, to which, after a moment's consideration, the Guru Deva replied that I should have to cross the Himalayas *alone*.

I left Madras on the evening of the 11th September 1882 by the mail train, and reached the [Theosophical] Society's head-quarters at Bombay on the 13th September.

That day in the afternoon, in the presence of Madame Blavatsky, Madame Coulomb, Mr. Tukaram Tatya, Damodar K. Mavalankar, and another Theosophist whose name I do not know, I received a letter which fell just on my head from the ceiling. It was from my *Guru*—in reply to which I kept my letter in the presence of the above persons (except Tukaram Tatya who had left the place then) just near the statue of Lord Buddha over the shelf in the hall. And in our presence, the letter disappeared. That very night while I was going to bed in Col. Olcott's room, with all doors closed, and in good lamplight, I was startled to see coming out, as it were, of the solid wall, the astral form of my most revered Guru Deva, and I prostrated before him, and he blessed me and desired me to go and see him beyond the Himalayas, *in good Telugu language*. The conversation that passed between us is too sacred to be mentioned here. He disappeared in the same way as he appeared.

On the following day, the 15th September, myself and Madame Blavatsky started for the North. Mr. and Mrs. Coulomb, Damodar K. Mavalankar, Mr. Tukaram Tatya, and another Theosophist (all in three carriages) accompanied us to the platform.

On our way, on the 16th idem, beyond the Bhosawal Junction between the Stations of Chandani and Khandwa, I found the bridges over a small tributary of the Tapti had been washed away by the overflow of the latter river; and the road for about two miles or so suffered therefrom. Then we had to get down and cross the river by a boat. Some boxes of Madame Blavatsky containing her clothing and other necessary articles were left behind by mistake in the boat, and we all got into the train on the other side of the river, without noticing the boxes so left behind. After passing the Khandwa Station, I believe, Madame found out that some boxes were missing, and she got down with her servant, Babula, and things. The train left for the North, leaving Madame &c. behind, I myself traveling in a 3rd-class carriage. So I had to meet her again at Allahabad on the 18th September. On the 17th idem, when I was some few stations south of Allahabad, with only two or three passengers in the compartment, I had the good fortune of seeing a letter falling over me from the top of the carriage. Madame Blavatsky at that time must have been somewhere between Sahagpore and Jabbalpore, about 250 miles distant from me. This letter was in the familiar hand of my Mahatma, having reference to a letter I had sent at Bombay, which disappeared from the statue of Lord Buddha.

On my meeting Madame Blavatsky at Allahabad, we both, along with Babula, started for the North, and reached Chandernagore on the morning of the 19th idem by the mail train.

I there left Madame Blavatsky and her servant near the railway station, and crossed the Hughly by a boat to the other side, and walked about 5 miles to the Nalhati Station, and then took the mail train for Siliguri, which I reached on the 20th idem early in the morning, and took the rail for Darjiling, which place I reached about evening and met Babaji Dharbagirinath that very night, just when I was in the greatest fix to find my way to the North.

We were both together until the 28th idem. We traveled together, both on horseback and on foot in Bhutan, Sikkim, &c. We visited several "Gumpas" (temples). I had to cross and recross the Ranjit River more than twice, by the swinging bridge as well as the ferryboat.

In the course of these travels, just about Pari or Parchong on the northern frontier of Sikkim, I had the good fortune and happiness to see the blessed feet of the *most venerated Masters Koot Hoomi and M[orya]* in their physical bodies. The very identical personages whose astral bodies I had seen in my dreams &c. since 1869, and in 1876 in Madras, and on the 14th September 1882 in the headquarters at Bombay. Besides, I have also seen a few advanced chelas, and among them, the blessed Jwalkool who is *now* a Mahatma.

On the 26th September evening, we both having heard that Madame Blavatsky and Ramaswamy Iyer had come to Darjiling and were putting up in Babu Parvati Churn Roy's (Deputy Collector and Deputy Magistrate, and Superintendent of the Dehra-Dhun Survey) bungalow—"Willow-Cot," we met them there.

I took leave from Madame Blavatsky and my other friends at Darjiling on the 28th idem and took the train for Siliguri at 10 AM, and reached it at 7 PM. On the 29th, I got into the train for Calcutta, and reached the place on the morning of the 30th idem.

I reached Madras on the morning of the 9th October 1882.

On the 10th October 1882, I visited Mr. G. Muttu Swamy Chetty, Small Cause Court Judge, Madras, and informed him and his sons Mr. Lalpett, and Mr. Rajulu Naidu, FTS, that I had seen the Mahatmas.

On the 11th idem, I saw my esteemed friend, T. Velayudam Mudelliar, Tamil Pundit, Presidency College, Madras, to whom also I told the fact of my having seen the Mahatmas.

On my reaching Nellore and joining my office on the 16th idem, a meeting of the members of the Nellore Branch Society was convened, when I informed my brothers how I had seen the astral body of my Guru at the Bombay headquarters, and also how I had been blessed in being allowed to see and be in company of the Most Revered Mahatmas.

In conclusion, let me say that I am, owing to the grace of my Guru Deva, in direct correspondence with Him and have received several letters from Him since 1882, and that even so late as January 1885, I received a letter directly from Him, permitting me to publish an account of my travels.

12C. PARBATI CHURN ROY
SEPTEMBER–OCTOBER 1882,
DARJEELING, INDIA

[Roy 1896, 36–46]

I felt great interest in Spiritualism from the time that it first came to India from America. The arrival, in 1879, of Madame H. P. Blavatsky in Bombay and the accounts of her wonderful doings awakened in my mind fresh interest towards it. What I would not accept as true from Hindus, whom I looked upon as too credulous and superstitious, I was prepared to accept as such when it came from Europeans. I once intended to go to Bombay to satisfy my curiosity, but through some cause or other, chiefly because my skepticism was increasing more and more, I did not carry out my intention. I could not, however, rest quiet; something within always prompted me to continue my spiritual inquiries, and so I wished I could have an interview with Madame Blavatsky.

She was at first suspected by the Government to be a Russian spy, but, far from being a spy, she was an admirer of the British rule. In her opinion, it was the best Government that India could have in her present condition.

In the autumn of 1882, Madame Blavatsky, accompanied by several of her disciples, came to Darjeeling, a hill station in Bengal, in the course of her Theosophical tour. Some Hindu friends, who were looking for a place for her accommodation, asked me if I could not put her up in my house for a few days. I had longed for an opportunity to see her, and nothing could be more desirable than that I should do so in my own house, and so I readily complied with the request.

Though I had adopted the English way of living, I was quite ignorant of English manners and customs, and, therefore, I felt somewhat anxious as to the manner in which Madame Blavatsky was to be entertained during her stay at my cottage. My anxieties were, however, put to rest as soon as I met her. There could not be a more simple, unostentatious, openhearted, and unceremonious person than HPB. Her heart was full of love and kindness for others.

Her dress was plain and simple; her food and drink also being of the simplest possible. In the morning she made a hearty breakfast of coffee, milk, and bread. After breakfast, she shut herself up in her room and spent till luncheon, at 1:00 PM, in reading and writing. Neither at luncheon nor at dinner did she eat a full meal, and ate but very little meat. At teatime she again had her coffee, milk, and bread; in fact, her chief meals were taken at breakfast and tea.

As is well known, she was a great smoker of cigarettes, at the making of which she was an expert. She always wore a kind of loose gown, over which she sometimes put a yellow robe like what is used by the Buddhist nuns. She often had a rosary in her hand, which she counted as she inaudibly repeated to herself certain words.

On the night of her arrival, in fact, the very moment that she stepped inside my threshold, I began to talk disparagingly of everything spiritual, while I lauded to the skies the teachings of the materialists and agnostics. She smiled and, touching a pane of glass with her hand, produced a soft tinkling sound, which she asked me to explain. Of course, I was not able to explain, nor could I find any explanation of it in any of my scientific books. She gave an explanation which was quite unintelligible to me. So far as I remember now, she said something about *akas* (ether). She also sent down, from the tips of her fingers, something like electric currents to the head of my cousin Babu Kali Mohun Das, Vakeel of the Calcutta High Court, without touching it. Babu Kali Mohun Das said that he felt a sort of burning sensation in his head by the very fact of Madame Blavatsky's fingers being pointed towards it. I watched her hand carefully and saw that the tips of her fingers were two or three inches above the head.

On the day following Madame Blavatsky's arrival at "Willow Dale," the cottage occupied by me, as we were sitting at luncheon we heard in the air a soft tinkling sound as that of a bell. No sooner she heard the sound than she rose up hurriedly from her chair, saying, "I am called, I am called," and in a most agitated manner proceeded towards her room. As she was going out of the dining room, another sound like the first was heard immediately over her head. She then shut herself in her room for some time.

In the course of conversation on the very night of her arrival, Madame Blavatsky inquired if I knew anything about Theosophy. I replied in the negative, and she presented me Mr. A. O. Hume's *Hints on Esoteric Theosophy* and Mr. A. P. Sinnett's *Occult World*. In the first page of the latter, she wrote these words—"To my skeptic and quarrelsome brother." Though she was hardly more than forty-eight hours in my house, I had already begun to quarrel with her. In my admiration for the civilization of the English, I cried down that of the Hindu. I also had no sympathy for the exclusiveness of the Tibetans, who would not let any foreigners visit their country, and so I wished that the English might go and conquer them and throw their country open to us. She felt greatly pained at my then attitude of mind and said that I was an unworthy descendant of the great Aryans.

The things related to have happened [in *The Occult World*] could not be explained by any known laws of nature—laws known to the great scientists of the West; and, therefore, I argued, they could not be accepted as true. Though there was a sort of impulse from within to believe that the book gave an account of things that actually happened, I hesitated to act on my intuition, and so told Madame Blavatsky that I could not be a member of the Theosophical Society, as I could not believe in Mahatmas. On this she said that a belief in Mahatmas was not essential for becoming a Theosophist. She then gave me the Rules, from which I found that the following were the objects of the Society:

1. To form the nucleus of a Universal Brotherhood of Humanity, without distinction of race, creed, sex, caste or color.
2. To promote the study of Aryan and other Eastern literatures, religions, philosophies, and sciences, and demonstrate the importance of that study.
3. To investigate unexplained laws of nature, and the psychic powers latent in man.

I had no objection to the first object, but I strongly protested against attaching any importance to objects 2 and 3. Madame Blavatsky said that, if I believed in the importance of forming a Society to promote brotherly feelings, that would be sufficient, that I might put off the two others until I was convinced of their importance. As I felt that by standing aloof, I should be wounding the feelings of a lady who was, according to her light, working for the good of humanity, and was in my house as a guest, I signed a "Form of Application," and HPB granted me a diploma of membership in the Theosophical Society.

Before the arrival of Madame Blavatsky at my cottage, I invited two friends to come up from Calcutta and spend with me a few days during the Court vacation. One of these was my cousin, Babu Bhuban Mohan Das, who was editor of the *Brahmo Public Opinion*, and the other was my friend Babu Tariny Kumar Ghose, a graduate of the Calcutta University. The former was a leading member of the Sadharan Brahmo-Somaj, or the Constitutional

Theistic Church; and the latter, a very learned agnostic. When these guests arrived, we were pressed for room, and Madame Blavatsky was put to much inconvenience, but she did not mind it. These friends, however, did not like her presence, as they looked upon her as an impostor. And, though I myself had noticed nothing against her conduct, I began to doubt my own senses, especially as I believed my friends to be men of very sound judgment. I gradually began to think that it would be well if HPB were to leave Willow Dale.

One night, when my feelings against the Mahatmas had been worked up by the sneers and taunts of my theistic and agnostic friends mentioned above, I had a most heated discussion with Nobeen Babu [a friend of HPB's]. The quarrel, for so it was, arose in this wise: I began by finding fault with the Mahatmas for not coming forward before the public and explaining their doctrines by means of experiments like the scientists in the West. If what they were said to be capable of doing was true, surely truth would not suffer by being publicly made known to the world. To this Nobeen Babu replied by saying that the truths taught by the Mahatmas were far too transcendental to be understood and appreciated by anyone who had not gone through a course of preparatory training; that just as a boy who had no knowledge of chemistry and physics would be incapable of understanding the highest teachings of those sciences; as one whose knowledge of mathematics was confined only to arithmetic would be incapable of appreciating the high mathematical teachings of Sir W. Thomson's vortex theory; so a person uninitiated in the mysteries of the spiritual world would be incapable of understanding the teachings of the Mahatmas. And that, even if the Mahatmas were to appear before the public and exhibit their powers, they would be considered as no better than jugglers, who often perform tricks which baffle the understanding of even men of science.

I lost my temper and began to speak loudly and angrily, while Nobeen Babu continued calm and dignified. Just as I was speaking disparagingly of the Mahatmas, the soft tinkling sound of a bell, like that which was heard on the day following Madame

Blavatsky's arrival, was heard over our head. On hearing this, Madame Blavatsky, who was quietly listening to our discussion in a lounging chair in the adjoining room, desired us to shut the door opening into it. This was immediately done. We were quite startled by this bell phenomenon, and an end was put to the discussion. A little while after, the door was again opened by HPB's desire. She did not tell us what took place in the room when the door was closed, but it is believed that she had a visit from her Guru (Teacher) in his astral body. Next morning HPB left my house. To my entreaties for her to stay, she said that she had been ordered to leave and that her stay at Willow Dale was causing inconvenience to the friends whom I had invited to come up before I expected her arrival.

When Madame Blavatsky was gone, I felt somewhat uncomfortable in mind. In spite of my skepticism and the sneers and taunts of my friends, I could not get over the impression that her conduct was far different from that of an impostor; that she was earnest and sincere in the cause for which she was working; and that there was no earthly motive associated with her work. I was anxious to know more about her but was afraid that my agnostic friend would regard me as a dupe and a fool. I was also ashamed to appear before HPB after the disgraceful squabble I had with Nobeen Babu, which was the immediate cause of her leaving my house.

Some days after HPB had removed to her new house, which was the one occupied by Nobeen Babu and his family, my friend Tariny Babu and I went one afternoon to pay her a call. This house was much smaller than mine and was situated in a crowded part of the town, and I could easily perceive that she had there to put up with much inconvenience. She was in her room busy with writing when we went, but, on learning of our arrival, she came out into the sitting room and talked about various matters. She seemed to be very happy in her new quarters. It being teatime, Nobeen Babu entertained us with tea. Besides ourselves, there were several other visitors present. There not being sufficient accommodation for all of us at the table, Madame Blavatsky, Tariny Babu, and myself took our tea there, while Nobeen Babu and other friends had theirs on the verandah in front of us. They sat on the floor at a distance of ten or twelve feet from us.

When the tea was over and my friend and I were about to take leave, HPB asked us to stay a little while longer as she felt that some news was coming from Tibet. We waited in an expectant attitude, when the friends in the verandah suddenly cried out—"A letter, a letter!" We immediately turned our eyes to the verandah, and saw a letter standing in the teacup of Nobeen Babu, who, at the desire of Madame Blavatsky, brought it to us. The letter was addressed to "Babu Nobeen" in the same handwriting as that of the one I saw in Madame Blavatsky's room at my house! We were at a loss how to account for the appearance of this letter, which had, so to speak, dropped from the air before our very eyes. It is true that none of us saw it while in the act of falling, but the time taken in dropping from the ceiling into the teacup could not have been even half a second, as the distance was only six or seven feet. The letter could not have been thrown into the teacup by Madame Blavatsky, as we were looking at her. But even supposing that she managed to throw it without our being able to observe the act, it was impossible that the letter could fall perpendicularly into the teacup, seeing that she was sitting only about two feet higher than Nobeen Babu, at a distance of ten or twelve feet. This was a puzzle to me, skeptic as I was.

My friend Babu Tariny Kumar Ghose afterwards pointed out to me that the address on the envelope was sufficient against the supposition that the letter came from an Indian. If an Indian Mahatma had written it, he would have addressed "Nobeen Babu," and not "Babu Nobeen;" the former being the familiar way in which one Bengali gentleman addresses another. Though he could not explain how the letter came to be in the teacup, he had no doubt that it was the doing of Madame Blavatsky, and I believed at the time that he was right. But I have since come across two letters written to me by HPB, from which it appears that she was not ignorant of the familiar mode of addressing a Bengali gentleman. In a letter dated "Allahabad, November 15, 1882," and in another dated "Madras, November, 17, 1883,"

Madame Blavatsky, when speaking of a brother Theosophist, calls him "Kanti Babu," and not "Babu Kanti." The writer of the address must, therefore, have been not Madame Blavatsky, but someone else. It is not unusual for Hindus in the Upper Provinces of India to call a Bengali gentleman "Babu so and so," and not "so and so Babu." As the Mahatmas are said to come from those Provinces, it is quite reasonable to suppose that they would very naturally address the letter as it was addressed.

On returning home from the above visit to Madame Blavatsky, I found a telegram waiting for me with the news that my wife was seriously ill at Dacca. I had, therefore, to leave Darjeeling by the next down train; but before leaving I wrote a letter to HPB informing her of my sudden departure, to which she replied as follows:

My Dear Brother,—I am sorry to lose you. I hope you will allow us to hear from you occasionally. You are a member of our Society, hence no real evil can befall you, and I do fervently hope and pray that some day will find you a good Aryan, and in your *dhoti* (Indian dress) again.

Take care of yourself. Thanking you for the brotherly services rendered, and all your attentions.

Believe me,
Yours sincerely and fraternally,
H. P. Blavatsky.

12D. S. RAMASWAMIER
SEPTEMBER–OCTOBER 1882,
DARJEELING, INDIA, AND SIKKIM

[Ramaswamier 1882]

My health having been disturbed by official work and worry, I applied for leave on medical certificate and it was duly granted. One day in September last, while I was reading in my room [in the

Sketch of the Master Morya

town of Tinnevelly, southern India], I was ordered by the audible voice of my blessed Guru, [Morya], to leave all and proceed immediately to Bombay, whence I had to go in search of Madame Blavatsky wherever I could find her and follow her wherever she went. Without losing a moment, I closed up all my affairs and left the station. Arrived at Bombay, I found Madame Blavatsky gone. Really not knowing whither I had best go, I took a through ticket to Calcutta; but, on reaching Allahabad, I heard the same well-known voice directing me to go to Berhampore.

On the 23rd [of September], I was brought by Nobin Babu from Calcutta to Chandernagore, where I found Madame Blavatsky, ready to start with the train. When the train arrived, she got into the carriage. I myself had barely the time to jump into the last carriage.

The first days of her arrival [at Darjeeling] Madame Blavatsky was living at the house of a Bengalee gentleman, a Theosophist; was refusing to see any one. To all our importunities we could get only this answer from her: that we had no business, *to stick to and follow her*, that she did not want us, and that she had no right to disturb the Mahatmas with all sorts of questions.

In despair, *I determined, come what might*, to cross the frontier, which is about a dozen miles from here, and find the Mahatmas, or—DIE. Without breathing a word of my intentions to anyone, one morning, namely, October 5, I set out in search of the Mahatma. The same afternoon I reached the banks of the Rungit River, which forms the boundary between the British and Sikkim territories.

That whole afternoon I traveled on foot, penetrating further and further into the heart of the Sikkim Territory, along a narrow foot-path. I traveled before dusk not less than twenty or twenty-five miles. Throughout, I saw nothing but impenetrable jungles and forests on all sides of me, relieved at very long intervals by solitary huts belonging to the mountain population.

At dusk I began to search around me for a place to rest in at night. After a sound sleep, undisturbed by any dream, I woke and found it was just dawning.

I lost no time. When it became quite light, I wended my way on through hills and dales.

It was, I think, between eight and nine AM, and I was following the road to the town of Sikkim, whence, I was assured by the people I met on the road, I could cross over to Tibet easily in my pilgrim's garb when I suddenly saw a solitary horseman galloping towards me from the opposite direction. From his tall stature and the expert way he managed the animal, I thought he was some military officer of the Sikkim Raja. Now, I thought, am I caught. But as he approached me, he reined the steed. I looked at and recognized him instantly. I was in the presence of my own revered *Guru*. The very same instant saw me prostrated on the ground at his feet. I arose at his command and, leisurely looking into his face, I forgot myself entirely. I knew not what to say: joy and reverence tied my tongue. I was at last face to face with "the Mahatma of the Himavat" and he was no myth. It was no night dream; it is between nine and ten o'clock of the forenoon. There is the sun shining and silently witnessing the scene from above.

He speaks to me in accents of kindness and gentleness. Nor was it until a few moments later that I was drawn to utter a few words, encouraged by his gentle tone and speech. Never have I seen a countenance so handsome, a stature so tall and so majestic. He wears a short black beard, and long black hair hanging down to his breast. He wore a yellow mantle lined with fur, and, on his head a yellow Tibetan felt cap.

When the first moments of rapture and surprise were over and I calmly comprehended the situation, I had a long talk with him. He told me to go no further, for I would come to grief. He said I should wait patiently if I wanted to become an ac-cepted Chela.

The Mahatma, I found, speaks very little English—or at least it so seemed to me—and *spoke to me in my mother-tongue—Tamil.* I asked the blessed Mahatma whether I could tell what I saw and heard to others. He replied in the affirmative. He was pleased to say when I offered my farewell *namaskarams* (prostration) that he approached the British Territory to see [HPB].

Before he left me, two more men came on horseback, his attendants I suppose, probably Chelas, for they were dressed like himself, with long hair streaming down their backs. They followed the Mahatma, as he left, at a gentle trot.

For over an hour I stood gazing at the place that he had just quitted, and then, I slowly retraced my steps. I had eaten nothing since the day before, and I was too weak to walk further. My whole body was aching in every limb. At a little distance I saw petty traders with country ponies, taking burden. I hired one of these animals. In the afternoon I came to the Rungit River and crossed it. A bath in its cool waters renovated me. I purchased some fruit in the only bazaar there and ate them heartily. I took another horse immediately and reached Darjeeling late in the evening.

I could neither eat, nor sit, nor stand. Every part of my body was aching. My absence had seemingly alarmed Madame Blavatsky. She scolded me for my rash and mad attempt to try to go to Tibet, after this fashion. I recounted all that had happened to me.

Theosophical Society Headquarters, Adyar, 1884

Chapter 13

ADYAR AND OOTACAMUND
1882–1883

HE FOUNDERS bought a large estate in southern India on the Adyar River, near Madras, in May 1882 and moved the Theosophical headquarters there at the end of the year. This center soon became the radiating point for worldwide activity. During 1883, Madame Blavatsky and Colonel Olcott traveled from Adyar to various outlying districts, founded Branches, received visitors, conducted an enormous correspondence with inquirers, and filled their journal with valuable and scholarly material. The main purpose of that material was to revitalize the dormant interest on the part of Indians in the spiritual worth of their own ancient scriptures and culture.

Emma Coulomb later claimed that she collaborated with HPB at Adyar, as she had earlier in Bombay, in producing false phenomena; however, her descriptions of what she did are not consistent with the observations of others who witnessed the phenomena, both Indians and Westerners, as some of the following selections demonstrate.

CHAPTER 13

13a. A. P. Sinnett
December 1882 – March 1883,
Adyar, Madras, India

[Sinnett 1886, 255, 257–8]

On the 16th of December 1882, a farewell entertainment was given by native friends to the founders of the Theosophical Society, just before their departure from Bombay to take up their residence at Adyar, Madras, where a house had been purchased for the Society by subscription.

The house at Madras was a great improvement on the cramped and comfortless bungalow at Bombay. Madras is a station of enormous extent, straggling along seven or eight miles of the seashore. Adyar is a suburb at the southern extremity, through which a small stream finds its way to the sea, and just before it reaches the beach spreads out into a broad shallow expanse of water, beside which the Theosophical house stands in extensive grounds. Here we found Mme. Blavatsky and her heterogeneous household comfortably installed when my wife and I visited her on our way home [to England] from India in March 1883.

The upper rooms of the house were her own private domain. [One of these rooms] just built was destined by Madame to be her "occult room," her own specially private sanctum. She had especially devoted herself to decorating a certain hanging cupboard to be kept exclusively sacred to the communications passing between [the] Masters and herself, and bestowed upon it the designation the Shrine. Here she had established some simple occult treasures, two small portraits she possessed of the Mahatmas, and some other trifles. The purpose of this special receptacle was of course perfectly intelligible to everyone familiar with the theory of occult phenomena. A place kept pure of all "magnetism" but that connected with the work of integrating and disintegrating letters, would facilitate the process, and the "shrine" was used for the transaction of business between the Masters and the chelas.

206

13B. WILLIAM Q. JUDGE
DECEMBER 1882, ADYAR, MADRAS, INDIA

[Collated from Judge 1890 and Judge 1892,
pen and ink drawings by Wm. Q. Judge]

The Headquarters of the [Theosophical] Society in India are in a suburb of Madras called Adyar, so named from the Adyar river [which] runs past the building, washes, indeed, the base of the wide piazza at the back. The building is made of brick and plaster, painted white, except some rooms erected upon the roof. The grounds comprise about twenty-one acres, bounded in front of the house by a large grove of trees, on the back by the river, and on one side by the main road leading out of Madras. There are numerous mango trees in the compound between the house and the main road, and these afford a grateful shade, their spreading branches covering great distances around their trunks.

[The picture above gives] the point of view as you come up the drive from the entrance gate. It shows the front of the building as it faces the compound. The porte cochere is seen in perspective. It gave a grand air to the front. The whole building was of a white color, appearing at a distance like a marble structure, but in reality is constructed of brick plastered white, as is very usual in India.

Just appearing over the ornamental balustrade which encloses the roof is the front of HPB's own room, which led into the shrine room shown in the second picture. Her room was an addition to the building, and in a way served to join the two towers which rise at the back corners at either end. The stairs of the tower illustrated [in the picture below] were the means of communication with her apartment, although the other tower had also a stairway.

That part of the compound extending from the entrance gate on the highway was full of mango trees, and through them the driveway brought you up to the house and under the porte cochere. Alighting there, a short flight of steps took you up to the entrance hall, where the floor was of black and white marble. Here there were two tables, sofas, and some chairs, and on the floor many a night slept Damodar K. Mavalankar, together with several others.

Part of the end of the building on the side near the main road is given [in the above picture]. It is a continuation of the corner seen in the first cut. The tower finished the river end of the building, and the river itself can be just seen at the back. On the top is the occult room with the extension or verandah. The roof of the "occult room" was slanting and tiled in red, the plaster being tinted yellow. In this was the shrine. It was entered from the other side, and, being a few feet lower than the rooms used by HPB, a short flight of steps ran down into it. In the tower is a winding brick stairway.

Damodar's room was in this tower at the top as you came up the narrow stairs. A corridor, as you might call it, ran across the back of HPB's rooms from tower to tower, open to the river and giving a view of the little island opposite and the long bridge which carries the highway across the river.

[The illustration on page 204] is reproduced from a photograph of the back of the building taken from the little island. It shows the other tower, companion to that in which was Damodar's room. The lower floor under the roof was the back part of the middle of the building, and was occupied by the *Theosophist* magazine. Trees and shrubs almost hid the view. A plastered embankment ran for a short distance along this side so as to protect the foundations.

These pictures give a very correct idea of the house when HPB lived in it.

13c. G. SOOBIAH CHETTY
DECEMBER 24, 1882, ADYAR, MADRAS, INDIA

[Chetty 1928]

HPB and Col. Olcott arrived in Madras on December 19, 1882. A few days after their arrival, on a Sunday morning, Madame Blavatsky was unpacking, assisted by "the boys"— Damodar K. Mavalankar, Narasimhulu and Soobiah Chetty, and Krishnaswami, known as "Bhavaji." Among the articles were found two portraits; and Narasimhulu and Soobiah were examining them intently, as they recognized in one of them a sadhu they had seen some years before. Noticing them handling the pictures, HPB pounced upon them and forbade it, saying they were pictures of the Masters. The two brothers said they had seen the person portrayed in one of them. HPB declared this could not be true; but a fortnight later she was told that they had indeed seen the Master M in 1874; that He had visited the city of Madras in His physical body; and that they were two of the four persons who had seen Him then. She asked them to describe the visit.

They said that early one morning a sadhu entered their home unannounced. A strikingly tall man, clothed in a long white dress and white pagri, with black hair falling on his shoulders, and black beard, stood within the door. Of the three persons present, one left the room, and the other two—Narasimhulu and Soobiah—drew near to him. He made certain signs which the brothers did not understand, but remembered vividly. He asked for one pice; and when they went to the moneybox they found it contained exactly one pice, which they gave to Him. He turned and left the house, followed by the two brothers, and suddenly disappeared, to their great astonishment. They could find no trace of Him in the street. It was this sudden and mysterious disappearance that impressed the visit so deeply upon them that they always remembered it in detail.

HPB added the information that He was on His way to Rameshvaram, one of the great places of pilgrimage in India.

13D. EMMA COULOMB
MARCH 1880 – MARCH 1883

[Coulomb 1884, 7–9, 30–1, 34–6, 46–8, 52–3]

Arriving at Bombay by a P. and O. steamer on the 28th of [March 1880] we landed and, after having taken a room and dinner in the hotel, we drove in a tram-cart up to the terminus of Girgaum, where we asked a gentleman who was in the same cart with us to show us the way to Girgaum Back Road, to the head-quarters of the Theosophical Society. He did so, and we went. As soon as Madame Blavatsky saw me she gave a loud cry to joy, and instantly asked us to take up our abode at the headquarters. I need not here say how this offer consoled my afflicted heart. That evening we slept at the hotel, and the next day at noon we moved into the headquarters of the Theosophical Society.

The first few days we were very happy indeed; the company was very agreeable and we thought ourselves in heaven. On the 5th of April Colonel Olcott came into my room and asked me if I would undertake to direct the domestic affairs, as the lady who looked after them did not wish to do so anymore. I accepted with great pleasure this charge, as it gave me the chance of making myself useful. We had already been initiated and had joined the Society. The pleasure we had of being in company with [Madame Blavatsky,] whom we had known in better days [in Egypt, and] the gentlemanly and kind behavior of Colonel Olcott towards us made us really desirous to do all that lay in our power to show our gratitude and contentment. There was not a thing that we were asked to do that we did not do with the greatest pleasure.

Madame Blavatsky, seeing our earnest desire to please her in everything, one evening, taking hold of my arm and walking up and down in the library compound, all of a sudden said: "Look here, run and tell the Colonel that you have seen a figure in the garden." "Where is the figure?" I asked. "Never mind," she said, "run and tell him so; we shall have some fun." Thinking this to be a joke, I ran to him and told him. As the Colonel came up, Madame began to laugh, saying, "See, she has been afraid of an apparition," and so they both went on laughing and, going up to the other bungalow, related the story to the rest of the people who were there. I must conscientiously say that I did not know what they meant by this joke.

My readers will think that I did not show much gratitude to

Colonel for his kindness to me by helping Madame to perform such tricks and thus impose on his bona fides. In order to justify my apparent bad behavior, I must say that Madame had told me that she did all these things to divert the Colonel's mind from certain painful occurrences that he had experienced in America.

We worked incessantly, and very often we used to go to bed so tired that we could not sleep. Yet it did not fully satisfy Madame's Theosophical object; she wanted work of another kind, but did not dare to express her wish in so many words. So she used to get cross, despise everything, and hate everybody; and as we could not understand what she really wanted, she vented her rage on us by forbidding that a sufficient quantity of bread should be brought into the house, saying that if we wanted more we were to buy it with our own money—and this, after we had worked like slaves for her!

Sometimes when awake in bed, I used to torture my brain to find out what I could do to please her—for, bad as the place was, yet it was better than none; and although she was unjust, yet at times she used to have a good fit for two or three days, at which times she was more tractable, which made up for the past, and we pushed on. In one of these moods she called me up and told me: "See if you can make a head of human size and place it on that divan," pointing to a sofa in her room, "and merely put a sheet round it; it would have a magic effect by moonlight." What can this mean? I wondered. But knowing how disagreeable she could make herself if she was stroked on the wrong side, I complied with her wish.

She cut a paper pattern of the face I was to make, which I still have; on this I cut the precious lineaments of the beloved Master, but, to my shame, I must say that, after all my trouble of cutting, sewing, and stuffing, Madame said that it looked like an old Jew—I suppose she meant Shylock. Madame, with a graceful touch here and there of her painting brush, gave it a little better appearance. But this was only a head, without bust, and could not very well be used, so I made a jacket, which I doubled, and between the two cloths I placed stuffing, to form the shoulders and chest; the arms were only to the elbow, because, when the thing was tried on, we found the long arm would be in the way of him who had to carry it. This beauty finished, made Madame quite another person. Now the philosopher's stone was found! Let us see what I can do with it, thought I to myself, and, if it is only this she wants, and this is to assure us a home, she shall certainly have as many as she likes.

Let us see for what purpose the doll was made. This was to give a convincing and material proof of the existence of the brothers [the Mahatmas], as their (*said*) invisible presence did not fully satisfy the truth-seekers.

Among the many apparitions to which this doll has been instrumental, I will choose one seen by Mr. Ramaswamier, in December 1881. The Mahatma he saw in his astral body on the balcony at the headquarters of the Theosophical Society in Bombay, on the memorable night of December 1881, was no one else than Monsieur Coulomb, with the doll's head on his own.

The doll plays the greatest part in these apparitions, and, as I have already explained, it is carried on somebody's head; but at times it is placed on the top of a long bamboo, and raised to show that it is an astral body; but when the doll has not been at hand, even a white cloth wrapped round the person who was to perform the Mahatma was at times used, and answered the purpose.

At this period, having satisfied myself that neither phenomena nor apparitions were genuine, I began to think more seriously on the matter, and finally I asked her why she did these things, to which she answered as follows: "But do you know that you are a great '*Seccatura*' [nuisance]? What a bigot you are! Do not be afraid, I do no harm; but on the contrary, a great deal of good. See," she added, "Mr. Somebody, who for eight years was careless of his wife and child, by this means has been brought back to the fold, and now, as you see him, he cares for both; and, moreover, the same gentleman, who, before joining the Society, was so proud and so hard with the natives, now shakes hands with them, and even remains in their company." And she related to me many instances of good results from such foolish practices.

I must say that I like to see good done, but I confess that I could not understand how people of sense could believe in such stuff, and how they could accept such doctrines, which are so much at variance with the known laws of nature; this is blind belief, and not investigation of truth. However, if a phantom is sufficient to make a man change his conduct from bad to good, then, I say, hurrah, to Koot Hoomi, Moria, and all the host of the Himalayan brothers.

So far as the natives were concerned, I did not mind, because Madame had told me that they believed in these things and that the Mahatmas and their wonderful power was part of their belief. But I must say that when the turn came for the Europeans, I did not like it, and had I not feared to do more harm than good, I certainly would have warned them of the deceit, but, as I was shown to everyone in the light of an intolerant bigoted Christian, no one would have listened to me if I had done so, as it finally came to be. However, such was our position and [we had] to keep silent.

I shall [now] speak of the apparition which Mr. Sinnett saw on the terrace of Colonel Olcott's bungalow [at Adyar, Madras, in March 1883]; and for precision's sake it behooves me to give here a short description of what took place on the arrival of Mr. Sinnett at headquarters.

Madame told me: "What are we to do now? Mr. Sinnett wants to go and sleep in Colonel's bungalow." To this I answered that I was very sorry, because I knew that Colonel did not like anyone to occupy his rooms; but Madame said, "He wants to go there because he expects a visit from the Mahatma." I shrugged my shoulders. A little later in the day she asked me to go upstairs. I went. "Come here," she said. "See, Mr. Sinnett would go into the Colonel's bungalow to sleep, because, as I told you, he expects a visit from the Mahatma. Do you think it would be possible for Mr. Coulomb to go quietly in the night, and through the window close to his bed pass a letter and go away, or even show himself at a distance? Mr. Sinnett would never dare to move if I tell him not." I answered that I would ask my husband, but that I was sure he would not do it, because Mr. Sinnett was not a simpleton: he might go after the apparition and find out what it was, and then what would become of her? I told my husband, and he refused pointblank, saying that he would not do it. Whether anyone else did it instead, or not, this I could not say; but what I can affirm is, that Mr. Sinnett did not stay very long in the bungalow, and I heard him say that it was no use staying any longer.

A few days after this, Madame asked to have Koot Hoomi shown on Colonel's bungalow. Babula, Madame's servant, took the Christofolo [the nickname for the "doll"], all wrapped up in a shawl, and with Mr. Coulomb went all along the compound on the side of the swimming bath to the end of the pasture, returning in a straight line back to Colonel's bungalow up to the terrace, where it was lifted up and lowered down to give it a vapory appearance. I went up to Madame to say that all was ready, and found her at the window, in company with Mr. and Mrs. Sinnett, looking through an opera glass; I was very much annoyed that she should be so imprudent, but this is her nature.

Another day, she asked that the Mahatma should be taken to the island in the middle of the [Adyar] river opposite the main bungalow. It was impossible to oblige her at this time, because the tide was high and the moonlight as bright as day, so that the servant, who had to carry the bundle, could not cross the river; consequently the apparition did not take place, to Madame's great annoyance, because she had already invited Mr. and Mrs. Sinnett to go up and see.

13E. DAMODAR K. MAVALANKAR
APRIL 1883, ADYAR, MADRAS, INDIA

[Mavalankar 1907]

Last night was a memorable one. Narasimhulu Chetty and myself were seated on a chair quite close to Mme. Blavatsky's bed, fanning her and talking together, so as gradually to induce sleep in her. Suddenly Mme. B. gave a start and exclaimed, "I feel him [Mahatma Morya]." She enjoined on us strictly not to leave our places, nor to get excited, but remain where we were and be perfectly calm and quiet. Suddenly she asked for our hands and the right hand of each of us was held by her.

Hardly two minutes had elapsed and we saw him coming from the screen door of Mme. B.'s bed-room and approaching her. His manner of walking was so gentle that not a footstep, not the slightest sound, was audible; nor did he *appear* to move, by his gestures. It was only the change of position that made us see he had come nearer and nearer. He stood exactly opposite Mme. B.—*not quite an arm's length from us*. We were on this side of the bed; he on the other.

You know I have seen him often enough to enable me to recognize him at once. His usual long white coat, the peculiar Pagri [turban], long black hair flowing over the broad shoulders, and long beard were as usual striking and picturesque. He was standing near a door, the shutters of which were open. Through these the lamplight, and through the windows which were all open, the moonlight, were full upon him. And we being in the dark, i.e., having no light on our eyes—we being turned against the windows through which the moonlight came—we could see distinctly and clearly.

He held out and put his hands twice over Mme. B.'s head. She then stretched out her hand *which passed through* his—a fact proving that what we saw was a *mayavi rupa* [apparitional body], although so vivid and clear as to give one the impression of a material physical body. She immediately took the letter from his hands. It crumpled, as it were, and made a sound. He then waved his hands toward us, walked a few steps, *inaudibly and imperceptibly as before*, and disappeared! Mme. B. then handed the letter to me, as it was intended for me. Never shall I forget last night's experience; so clear, so vivid and tangible it was!

13F. HENRY S. OLCOTT
AUGUST–SEPTEMBER 1883, OOTACAMUND, INDIA

[Olcott 1900, 2:463–6; and Olcott 1929, 3:11, 18]

I went to Ootacamund to rejoin my dear colleague HPB, at the hospitable home of Major-General and Mrs. Morgan. The railway ends at the foot of the Nilgiri Hills, and the traveler proceeds up the well-metaled [well-paved] mountain road in a horse tonga, or two-wheeled mail cart drawn by a pair of galloping ponies. The ride up is simply charming, and passing through forests, by banks of flowers, and past swarms of lovely painted butterflies, the air grows cooler and cooler, until midway one is obliged to stop at the rest house and change one's light tropical costume for heavy woolens and even put on a topcoat. At almost every turn in the winding road splendid panoramas of scenery present themselves to view, while one finds Ootacamund a lovely village of picturesque houses, spreading over the foot slopes of the grassy and forest-covered adjacent hills, the roads lined with roses, the enclosures joyous with lilies, verbenas, heliotropes.

At the tollgate on the Coonoor Road, HPB met me in company with our dear Mrs. Morgan, Mrs. Batchelor, and others of the family, the General being absent from home temporarily. My old "chum" seemed really overjoyed to see me and rattled on in her affectionate way like one who greets a long-absent relative. She was looking well; the champagne-like mountain air set her blood to leaping through her body, and she was in the highest spirits about the civilities that were being shown her by some of the high officials and their families. She worked off some of her excitement that same night by keeping me up until 2 a.m. to read proofs and correct her MS! What an amusing creature she was when in the mood; how she would make a roomful of people hang on her lips as she would tell stories of her travels and adventures in search of the wonderworkers in Magic and Sorcery; and their eyes open in amazement when she would, now and again, ring some astral bell, or make some raps, or do some other minor phenomenon!

Our joint desk work went on and the hard labor was diversified with her bright talk and frequent grumblings at the cold. Certainly with cause, for the mercury marked forty degrees more of cold than we feel on the plains, the houses are heated with wood fires in open fireplaces, the winds blow in gusts down the open throated chimneys, filling the rooms with smoke and dusting one's paper and books with fine ashes. HPB wrote in a fur coat, with a woolen shawl on her head and her feet wrapped in a travelling rug—a funny sight. Part of her work was the taking from dictation, from her invisible teacher, of the "Replies to an English F.T.S." That she was taking down from dictation was fully apparent to one who was familiar with her ways.

[On September 16th] we two left beautiful Ooty in tongas for Coimbatore [and then on to Pondicherry]. We left Pondicherry for Madras, September 23rd, and got home that afternoon, rejoiced to see the dear place again.

13G. T. C. Rajamiengar
September 1883, Adyar, Madras, India

[Rajamiengar 1884]

In regard to the charge made, in *Christian College Magazine* for September 1884 against Madame Blavatsky, that occult phenomena produced at Adyar (Madras), India, are fraudulent ones, done by means of a backdoor attached to the shrine at that place, permit me to make the following observations.

I make bold to make them as I am personally acquainted with the lady, whose character was traduced in that journal, and I am very familiar with the place which has been a subject of much slanderous misrepresentations.

The facts relating to this matter, so far as I know them, are these: I have known the shrine at Adyar since February 1883. But it was in September 1883 that I had actually an opportunity of closely examining the structure of the shrine, so as to see whether the trickery, now pretended to be exposed, has ever any existence. I may say that I entered the room containing the shrine with the mind of an out-and-out skeptic; indeed, all this time I may say I was an unbeliever, though I had constantly met the Founders of the Theosophical Society and read much of their writing. What struck me about the doings of the Theosophists was, "What necessity is there for these modern Theosophists to perform their phenomena in a particular locality, and that in a shrine, while our ancient sages did all we have known in open places." I was soon quieted by an invitation on the part of Madame Blavatsky to inspect the shrine and satisfy myself about it.

I shall now give a brief description of the shrine and its situation in order that the outside public may see whether it is possible that the enlightened members of the Society could have been subjected to the trickery that the Coulombs now boast of exposing.

Madame Blavatsky had her sleeping apartment in the hall upstairs in the Adyar premises. There is a doorway leading from this hall to a room where the shrine is suspended, the shrine itself (a cupboard as they call it) being on the wall about four feet above the ground. I opened the doors of this shrine and found in it some photos and a silver cup and a few other things. I clearly examined every portion of this shrine from within, tapping with my hands every part of it, and nowhere could I find room for suspicion. Not satisfied with this, I examined the outside of the shrine, the front and the sides, and the top; and they stood the test. For fear of disarranging the things, I did not move the shrine about, but what was more satisfactory, I examined the back portion of the wall on which rested the shrine (which was inside the hall containing Madame Blavatsky's sleeping apartment) and found that there could not be the slightest room for suspicion in any direction, as far as the matter of the structure of the shrine is concerned.

After this Madame Blavatsky had the kindness to ask if any of us (we were then about five there) had any letter to send to Mahatmas. One of us immediately produced a letter; I took up the cup from the shrine, having carefully examined it, and the gentleman dropped the letter into it. I placed the cup with the letter in the shrine and closed it, as desired by the above lady. Two or three minutes after, Madame Blavatsky, who was standing about two yards off from the shrine, said she felt an answer came, and on opening the shrine we found a letter addressed to the sender, containing four pages with not less than 20 lines on each, which would occupy any mortal writer, simply to copy it in not less than half an hour. It must be remembered that there must have been time for one to read the letter and then to prepare an answer, which may take up another 15 minutes. But all this took place in the course of two or three minutes.

I shall now give an account of the so-called trapdoor. I found this trapdoor in an incomplete state for the first time in June 1884, a few months after the departure of the Founders. It is so small a door that a thin spare boy of 10 or 12 could hardly enter through it. It is intended to be understood the phenomenal letters were ushered into the shrine through this passage, but anyone, seeing the passage for himself, would be convinced of the impossibility of the thing being done.

I must, therefore, take this occasion to represent what I know of these matters to allow Truth to triumph; and I feel it specially necessary now that every one of us should speak out his experience of the Theosophists and their doings, that they may furnish, however lightly it may be, answers to the attacks of the Coulombs upon the conduct of persons too far away to justify themselves.

13H. WILLIAM T. BROWN
SEPTEMBER–DECEMBER 1883, INDIA

[Brown 1884, 5–7, 10–11, 12, 13, 15–17]

I sailed [from England] for India upon the 25th of August. [On September 29th] I reached the Headquarters of the Theosophical Society at Adyar, Madras, and was welcomed by Madame Blavatsky, the learned author, editor, and Corresponding Secretary. I was established in a bungalow, situated beautifully by the riverside, and felt at home in a very short time.

In regard to Madame Blavatsky, never before have I met anyone who evidences such vast and varied learning, nor one who is more large hearted.

One evening, shortly after my arrival at Adyar, some letters were being sent by Chelas to their Masters, and I was permitted to enter the "Occult Room" and see the process going on. The letters were put into an almirah, in a richly ornamented recess called by some "the Shrine." There were some seven of us then present, four of whom were Chelas. These gentlemen, after placing their letters as aforesaid, offered up incense and prostrated themselves according to the Hindu manner of evincing devotion and respect. In about two minutes Madame, who was standing by my side in an attentive attitude, received a psychic telegram, and indicated that the answers had come to hand. The almirah was accordingly opened, and, in place of the letters "posted," others were there, enclosed in Tibetan envelopes and written on Tibetan paper. D[amodar] K. M[avalankar] (a Chela of the Master Koot Hoomi) discovered something more than was expected, and exclaimed, "Here is a letter from my Master to Mr. Brown." I then received from his hands a memorandum, written with blue pencil.

I need scarcely say how honored and grateful I felt at being noticed by the Mahatma, whose teachings had so strongly impressed me. I rose, and going forward, reverently said, "Mahatma Koot Hoomi! I sincerely thank you." Immediately all those present in the room said, "There's a bell—did you hear it?" I said that I had *not*. Madame B. then expressed regret that I had not observed the Master's acknowledgement of having heard my words, and said "Oh Master! let us hear the bell, once more, if it be possible." We stood silently for about a minute and then there was distinctly heard by all of us (myself included) the sound of a bell.

After a railway journey [from Madras] of six and twenty hours, I joined Colonel Olcott at the town of Sholapur. I shall confine myself to speaking of a few of the places on our journey [to Northern India] which call for special mention.

We arrived at Jubbulpore [and] on the evening of the lecture, Colonel Olcott, Damodar, several fellows of the Society, and I drove together to the place of the public meeting. There the Colonel delivered an impressive address to a large audience. During the lecture some three or four majestic figures had attracted my particular attention. They did not seem to hang upon the lips of the speaker, as did the rest of the audience, but remained calmly dignified, occasionally only exchanging pleasant glances. I was not surprised to learn afterwards that some Mahatmas had been present at the meeting in astral form.

And now let us proceed to Allahabad. At this ancient city a most stirring lecture was delivered. Here I saw and *recognized* the Mahatma [Koot Hoomi].

Although I was enabled to look at him but for a minute, I knew that it was he and recognized him by his portrait, which I had scrutinized some weeks before. On our return to the bungalow at which we were being entertained, my impression was corroborated by Damodar, who volunteered the remark that his master had been there. Damodar, I may remark, had not been at the lecture.

The place to which our narrative really next pertains is the city of Lahore. Here, as elsewhere, Colonel Olcott delivered stirring addresses to large audiences; but Lahore has a special interest, because there we saw, in his own physical body, Mahatma Koot Hoomi himself.

On the afternoon of the 19th November, I saw the Master in broad daylight, and recognized him, and on the morning of the

20th he came to my tent, and said, "Now you see me before you in the flesh; look and assure yourself that it is I," and left a letter of instructions and silk handkerchief.

This letter is as usual written seemingly with blue pencil, is in the same handwriting as that in which is written communications received at Madras, and has been identified by about a dozen persons as bearing the calligraphy of Mahatma Koot Hoomi. The letter was to the effect that I had first seen him in visions, then in his astral form, then in body at a distance, and that finally I now saw him in his own physical body, so close to me as to enable me to give to my countrymen the assurance that I was from personal knowledge as sure of the existence of the Mahatmas as I was of my own.

On the evening of the 21st, after the lecture was over, Colonel Olcott, Damodar, and I were sitting outside the *shamiana* (pavilion or pandal [a temporary, open-sided shelter roofed with bamboo matting]), when we were visited by Djual Khool, the Master's head Chela, who informed us that the Master was about to come. The Master then came near to us, gave instructions to Damodar, and walked away.

On leaving Lahore the next place visited was Jammu, the winter residence of His Highness the Maharajah of Cashmere.

We enjoyed a most inspiring holiday in full view of the Himalayan Mountains.

At Jammu I had another opportunity of seeing Mahatma Koot Hoomi in *propria persona*. One evening I went to the end of the "compound" (private enclosure), and there I found the Master awaiting my approach. I saluted in European fashion, and came, hat in hand, to within a few yards of the place on which he was standing. After a minute or so he marched away, the noise of his footsteps on the gravel being markedly audible.

Group at the Theosophical Society convention, Adyar, 1884. Standing at the back are Bawaji and H. S. Olcott. In the second row, seated on the veranda, are (left to right) Maj.-Gen. H. R. Morgan, W. T. Brown, T. Subba Row, Damodar K. Mavalankar, H. P. Blavatsky, Dr. Franz Hartmann, and Rudolf Gebhard. In the first row, seated on the mat, are (left to right) Bhavani Shankar, Norendro Nath Sen, T. V. Charlu, S. Ramaswamier, Tukaram Tatya, P. Srinivasa Row, and V. C. Iyer.

Chapter 14

LAHORE AND ADYAR
1883–1884

MANY INDIANS AND WESTERNERS had contact, either by writing or in person, with the Mahatmas at this time and left personal accounts of those contacts. Others, especially some Western visitors (14c), had no such experiences and responded incredulously to the reports of others.

Colonel Olcott practiced mesmeric healing on a wide scale until February 1884, when he left for London to petition the British Government on behalf of the Buddhists of Sri Lanka. H. P. Blavatsky, then in poor health, decided to travel with him to Europe.

CHAPTER 14

14A. HENRY S. OLCOTT
NOVEMBER 19–20, 1883,
LAHORE, INDIA

[Olcott 1929, 3:37–9, 43–5]

[In Colonel Olcott's diary for Tuesday, November 20, 1883, the entry reads: "1:55 a.m. Koot Hoomi came in body to my tent. Woke me suddenly out of sleep, pressed a note (wrapped in silk) into my left hand, and laid his hand upon my head. He then passed into Brown's compartment and integrated another note in his hand (Brown's). He spoke to me." —DHC]

My camp was thronged with visitors during the three days of our stay, and I gave two lectures under the largest *shamiana* to multitudes, with great pots of fire standing along the sides to modify the biting November cold.

I was sleeping in my tent, the night of the 19th, when I rushed back towards external consciousness on feeling a hand laid on me. The camp being on the open plain, and beyond the protection of the Lahore Police, my first instinct was to protect myself from some possible religious fanatical assassin, so I clutched the stranger by the upper arms, and asked him in Hindustani who he was and what he wanted. It was all done in an instant, and I held the man tight, as would one who might be attacked the next moment and have to defend his life. But the next instant a kind, sweet voice said: "Do you not know me? Do you not remember me?" It was the voice of the Master KH. A swift revulsion of feeling came over me, I relaxed my hold on his arms, joined my palms in reverential salutation, and wanted to jump out of bed to show him respect. But his hand and voice stayed me, and after a few sentences had been exchanged, he took my left hand in his, gathered the fingers of his right into the palm, and stood quiet beside my cot, from which I could see his divinely benignant face by the light of the lamp that burned on a packing case at his back.

Presently I felt some soft substance forming in my hand, and the next minute the Master laid his kind hand on my forehead, uttered a blessing, and left my half of the large tent to visit Mr. W. T. Brown, who slept in the other half behind a canvas screen that divided the tent into two rooms. When I had time to pay attention to myself, I found myself holding in my left hand a folded paper enwrapped in a silken cloth. To go to the lamp, open and read it, was naturally my first impulse. I found it to be a letter of private counsel. On hearing an exclamation from [Brown's] side of the screen, I went in there and he showed me a silk-wrapped letter of like appearance to mine though of different contents, which he said had been given him much as mine had been to me, and which we read together.

The next evening, after the visits to Mr. Brown and myself, we two and Damodar sat in my tent, at 10 o'clock, waiting for an expected visit from Master KH. The camp was quiet, the rest of our party dispersed through the city of Lahore. We sat on chairs at the back of the tent so as not to be observed from the camp: the moon was in its last quarter and had not risen. After some waiting we heard and saw a tall Hindu approaching from the side of the open plain. He came to within a few yards of us and beckoned Damodar to come to him, which he did. He told him that the Master would appear within a few minutes, and that he had some business with Damodar. It was a pupil of Master KH. Presently we saw the latter coming from the same direction, pass his pupil— who had withdrawn to a little distance—and stop in front of our group, now standing and saluting in the Indian fashion, some yards away. Brown and I kept our places, and Damodar went and conversed for a few minutes with the Teacher, after which he returned to us and the king-like visitor walked away. I heard his footsteps on the ground. Before retiring, when I was writing my diary, the pupil lifted the *portiere*, beckoned to me, and pointed to the figure of his Master, waiting for me out on the plain in the starlight. I went to him, we walked off to a safe place at some distance where intruders need not be expected, and then for about a half hour he told me what I had to know. There were no miracles done at the interview, just two men talking together, a meeting, and a parting when the talk was over.

14B. DAMODAR K. MAVALANKAR
NOVEMBER–DECEMBER 1883, LAHORE,
INDIA, AND LATER AT JAMMU, KASHMIR

[Mavalankar 1883–4]

While on my tour [of northern India] with Col. Olcott, we reached Lahore, where we expected to meet in body my Master [Koot Hoomi]. *There I was visited by him in body, for three nights consecutively* and, in one case, even went outside the house meeting [the Master] in the compound, re-entering the house with him, offering him a seat, and then holding a long converse. Moreover, him whom I saw in person at Lahore was the same I had seen in astral form at the Headquarters of the Theosophical Society, and the same again whom I, in my visions and trances, had seen at his house, thousands of miles off, to reach which in my astral Ego, I was permitted, owing, of course, to his direct help and protection. In those instances with my psychic powers hardly developed yet, I had always seen him as a rather hazy form, although his features were perfectly distinct and their remembrance was profoundly graven on my soul's eye and memory; while now at Lahore, Jammu, and elsewhere, the impression was utterly different. In former cases, when making *pranam* (salutation) my hands passed through his form, while on the latter occasions they met solid garments and flesh.

I shall not here dwell upon the fact of his having been corporeally seen by both Col. Olcott and Mr. Brown separately, for two nights at Lahore. [Later at] Jammu I had the good fortune of being sent for, and permitted to visit a sacred *ashram* where I remained for a few days in the blessed company of several of the much doubted Mahatmas of Himavat and their disciples. There I met not only my beloved Gurudeva [Koot Hoomi] and Col. Olcott's Master [Morya], but several others of the Fraternity, including one of the highest. Thus, I saw my beloved Guru not only as a *living* man, but actually as a young one in comparison with some other Sadhus of the blessed company, only far kinder, and not above a merry remark and conversation at times.

Thus on the second day of my arrival, after the meal hour I was permitted to hold an intercourse for over an hour with my Master. Asked by Him smilingly, what it was that made me look at him so perplexedly, I asked in my turn: "How is it, Master, that some of the members of our Society have taken into their heads a notion that you were 'an elderly man,' and that they have even seen you clairvoyantly looking an old man passed sixty?" To which he pleasantly smiled and said that this latest misconception was due to the reports of a certain pupil of a Vedantic Swami. As to his being perceived clairvoyantly as an "elderly man," that could never be, he added, as *real* clairvoyance could lead no one into such mistaken notions; and then he kindly reprimanded me for giving any importance to the age of a Guru, adding that appearances were often false, etc., and explaining other points.

14c. Moncure D. Conway
EARLY JANUARY 1884, ADYAR, MADRAS, INDIA

[Conway 1884]

And what or where is Adyar? It is the center of the new cult called Theosophy, whose believers see in it the fulfillment of past visions and prophecies, while unbelievers find a repetition of the pious frauds which have attended the history of religious enthusiasm in all time. One hears stories of able men—European as well as Hindu—who have abandoned fair prospects, left family and friends, to devote themselves to this new movement. One hears rumors of a new pythoness and a thaumaturgist, by whom are fulfilled old fables, so that the tree so long deemed mythological, which yields whatever is asked of it—rubies or rupees included—is actually at Adyar. When I smiled at these rumors, my convinced friends in Australia said, "Only go and investigate the matter for yourself." And so, bearing a letter from one of them, I made my way from the revered footprint of the doubting disciple at St. Thomas's Mount to this shrine of the undoubting. As I approached Adyar bridge, I stopped to inquire for the residence of the "Countess Blavatsky," that being the name on my letter of introduction. Every native on the roadside knew the place, and a girl trotted beside the carriage to make sure of my entering the right gate. On it was written "Headquarters of the Theosophical Society."

Just inside the gate was the dilapidated carcass of a big blue pasteboard elephant, one of two, as I afterward learned, which some Madras gentlemen had set up at the gate on the occasion of a recent Theosophist anniversary. The carriage road winds through a large and leafy park up to a handsome mansion. The spacious veranda displayed every elegance, but it was unoccupied. For a time my coolies vainly tried to find someone about the place, and I was conscious of a half hope that no one might be at home. I had promised several friends in Ceylon interested in Spiritualism and its dark-complexioned sister, Theosophy, that I would make this call and heed whatever fact or truth might be offered but had no faith that anything lay for me in "occultism," after thirty years' observation of similar "phenomena." I was afraid of being out of place among enthusiasts of a movement I believed superstitious, but at the same time had already recognized Theosophy as an important contemporary phenomenon in India. Buddhist Ceylon was ablaze with it, the Theosophical Society at Colombo being united with the Freethinking Association of the same place.

My hesitation between fear of obtruding on those whose belief I was little likely to share and the feeling that I ought to know whatever they could show or tell me was ended by the appearance of a gracious young Babu, who came to bring me the Countess Blavatsky's welcome and to say she would presently receive me. Next, a youth of more remarkable appearance, delicate and almost maidenly, advanced, but when, in response to his greeting, I offered my hand, he said, gently, "I cannot shake hands with you." I afterwards learned that this youth is what his mystical faith terms "a lay Chela," that he already possesses the power of appearing at a distance in his astral body, and that he fears to shake hands lest his magnetism, or whatever his occult virtue is termed, may depart. Colonel Olcott was absent, founding in some distant place a new branch of the society of which he is President. The Countess was cordial and urged my remaining until the morning. I agreed to remain during the rest of the evening and consequently was with her and her co-workers for near six hours.

Besides the two mentioned, other Indian gentlemen were present, among them Mr. Norendro Nath Sen, Sr., known to me by reputation as editor of the *Indian Mirror*. America was represented in the company of Dr. Hartmann of Colorado. Another person present was W. T. Brown of Glasgow, a young man of education and pleasant manners, who told me some of his marvelous experiences. Indeed, they all told me their own marvelous experiences, but when I hinted that I would like to carry away some little marvel of my own experience the reply unpleasantly recalled vain attempts made these many years to witness a genuine spiritualistic phenomenon. I was once more put off with narratives of what had occurred before I came and predictions of what might occur if I should come again—in the great "by-and-by." A cabinet shrine was pointed out, in which letters were deposited and swift answers received from the wonderful Mahatmas far away in the Himalayas; but when I proposed to write a note, I was told that only a few days before the Mahatmas had forbidden any further cabinet correspondence. Just my luck! The Countess Blavatsky, as I have since learned, had been forewarned of my visit by one of her friends in Sydney, and it seems a little unreasonable that the Mahatmas, with whom she is in daily communication, should have terminated their cabinet miracles just when one was coming who needed them more than the convinced already, to whom, apparently, the signs were limited.

The Theosophists said that probably even if an occult phenomenon occurred, I would have suspected it of being a trick, but in this they were mistaken. If a Mahatma, or the Countess, or anybody else, can answer a note I can write, and show that they understand the matter to which it should refer, I will believe in Theosophy. Though I was not shown any evidence of occult phenomena beyond the familiar testimony which would equally confirm the miracles of Romanism (and they are none the less miracles because the Theosophists say they are not miraculous), I was not to go away without experiences of a startling kind. I was invited to see the cabinet shrine. It was tastefully, not to say aesthetically, decorated, and when the doors were opened, richly wrought metalwork was displayed. In the midst sat a small figure of Buddha, and on each side was the portrait of a Mahatma, in frames about seven inches high, done, as I was given to understand, by some "occult" process. These faces were not without a certain beauty, but, had I not been told they were actual men, I should say they are ideals on their way to conventionalization, like the face of Buddha. One of the two is the famous Koot Hoomi, or Khothume (as I saw it written on a document in the house). He holds a praying machine in his hand!

The burning question in certain circles is, Does Koot Hoomi really exist? Theosophists declare that Koot Hoomi is the descendant of Rajput kings, chief successor of the most venerable Rishis, or Rahats, heir of their power over nature, able to render himself invisible and to visit a man in New York or elsewhere by his "astral" body, while his physical form is in Tibet. On the other hand, the Chief Priest of Ceylon, though friendly to the Theosophists, affirmed in my hearing that the last Rahat died a thousand years after Buddha, that no such being can now exist. Skeptics declare that Koot Hoomi is a name made up of the last part of Colonel Olcott's name, combined with that of Allen Hume (now undergoing Theosophic austerities at Simla), these two (Cott-Hume) being Mme. Blavatsky's particular friends. (I have been informed by an eminent Oriental scholar that the name lies completely outside the analogies of any language ever spoken in India). The skeptics also challenge Theosophites to name the spot where Koot Hoomi resides. Theosophists reply that their Mahatma or Master must conceal himself and reserve the secret of his powers, lest that secret become the possession of unworthy persons, who might use them for evil or selfish purposes. Against this I have heard it argued that, *ex hypothesi*, the powers can only be used by one who has reached the sanctification implied in the title Rahat, and, by all Buddhist orthodoxy, a Rahat cannot use any power for evil ends.

The evidence for Koot Hoomi's existence would be complete if the testimony of those I met at Adyar be accepted. Nearly all declared they had seen him, and there is no need to doubt their good faith in so declaring; but, when cross-examined, their experiences appeared too largely subjective to be of value to others but themselves. Some of them had seen Koot Hoomi only in his "astral" body, and one familiar with the phenomena of visions and dreams can attach only pathological or psychological significance to such testimony. Three affirmed that they had seen Koot Hoomi in his material body, but the only such witness whom I was able to question closely or satisfactorily (Mr. Brown of Glasgow) gave a narrative of his meetings with the mysterious Mahatma which raised grave doubts. There were two or three such meetings, at one of which Mr. Brown was so overwhelmed with religious awe and emotion that he "could not look upon him"; at another the Master was at some little distance, his head and lower face being covered, after the manner of Rajput Rajas; the third occasion was at night, Mr. Brown being in bed, and he knew that the Master had visited him only by finding in his hand a letter and a handkerchief with "K.H." on it. (It may be that the second of these meetings was that of another person present). Mr. Brown evidently told me exactly what he believed true, and I think must have felt that no such testimony could prove Koot Hoomi's existence in a court of law, for he made much more of certain letters he had received signed "K.H." The force of the letters could not, of course, be felt by one to whom the nature of their revelations was unknown.

Two of the young men (natives) prostrated themselves on the floor before the cabinet with their heads towards the portrait of Koot Hoomi. It struck me then that whatever its origin, Theosophy is becoming a purely Oriental thing. It can hardly be expected that Western people should take seriously the notion of a thaumaturgic sage, greater than any other man of our time, who yet carries a praying machine, permits physical abasement before himself, and unlike Buddha, or any other recognized "master" of ancient or modern times, lurks and hides and keeps himself apart from the people. It is probable that the goddess Maya, whom we call "Glamour," is weaving her spells around these gentle Hindu pilgrims from a crumbling to an ideal temple. For a time, at any rate, they have found refuge in a spiritual air castle, whose solidity they do not doubt. One of them ascribed the skepticism of English people concerning "occultism" to their consumption of beef. However that may be, I had to remind the Countess Blavatsky that the footprint of the disciple that doubted the existence of his Mahatma is on the neighboring hill, where I had just seen it. If I could accept Koot Hoomi and his miracles there would be no difficulty in taking Rome in on my way home and submitting myself to the Pope. She promised to visit me in London in her "astral" form, and then, no doubt, the misgivings of this letter will appear to me as ridiculous as to those who believe so devoutly in the wonder-working Mahatmas.

I was considerably surprised on the morrow of my visit to Adyar to hear from a Theosophist that the young man had heard a mysterious bell ringing when I went into the room where the cabinet is. This ringing of a bell, where no bell is, I had heard of as one of the more frequent signs and wonders accompanying the Countess, but I certainly heard nothing of the kind. If it occurred, it seems unaccountable that some one of the persons present did not mention it at a time when it could be investigated. I was a day out at sea before I heard of it. But probably the

Countess knew that a bell ringing in a strange house would be a rather absurd apology for an evidence of occultism. I saw and heard nothing favorable to Theosophy or occultism at Adyar, but I carried away from my interview with these young men an impression that Theosophy is taking a deeper hold on the mind of young India than is generally supposed. There seems to be little doubt that Colonel Olcott has a great deal of personal force among these Orientals.

Certain sympathizers with Theosophy in both Ceylon and India have expressed to me grave doubts of "occultism" and their regret that the movement should be committed to anything beyond an ethical and religious propaganda. Undoubtedly this American has shown the vast possibilities of a new non-Christian agitation that should strike the Indian heart and imagination. These Hindu scholars have always been aware that they have a great history and religious literature. After all the generations in which missionaries sent here have ignored that literature, despised their philosophy, counted their religion mere idolatry and them as idolaters on their way to hell—there has risen a new race of scholars like Max Müller, who have shown the high value and profound religious idealism of their systems.

While this revival of Orientalism has gone on in the universities of Europe, the missionaries have not been influenced by it, but have gone on with the same old denunciations of Hindu and Buddhist ideas and beliefs. But now there have appeared a few people of position (a "Countess" and a "Colonel") from the centers of Christendom, who formally give in their adhesion to an Oriental religion. They solemnly repudiate every form of Christianity and fix their abode in India, to lead in the work of resisting the missionaries and reviving the faith of Buddha and Krishna. In two or three years they have moved and attracted these Oriental people more than the missionaries have done in as many centuries. They have now seventy-seven flourishing Theosophical societies. They are daily reaping from the unsettled Hindu mind a harvest where the missionaries merely trampled down the grain, because it was not such as made their own bread.

It has touched the Hindu imagination and heart. In Ceylon, Theosophy has given a distinct check to the missionary successes reported in recent years. Mr. Sinnett and other English Theosophists have said a good deal about "sacrifices" made by Colonel Olcott and Mme. Blavatsky in leaving their country (for Mme. Blavatsky is a naturalized American) to devote themselves to work of this kind. It is difficult to see the appropriateness of that plea, for the lives of the innovators have fallen in pleasant places. The Theosophists have given them gratuitous use of the fine mansion and park here at Adyar, with a hundred acres of cultured land.

14D. BHAVANI SHANKAR
JANUARY 1884, JUBBULPORE, INDIA

[Theosophical Society 1885, 79–80]

In the month of January 1884, I was at Jubbulpore with Brother Nivaran Chandra Mookerjee, who was then the Secretary of [the local branch of] the Theosophical Society. One night, while I was with him, I was [talking] to some twenty-seven members of that Branch and they were listening to me with great attention. On a sudden, there was deathlike silence for some time. I then felt the influence of Madame Blavatsky's Venerated Master [Morya], and it was so strong that I could not bear it. The current of electricity generated by an electromagnetic battery is nothing when compared with that current generated by the trained will of an Adept. When a Mahatma means to show himself to a chela, he sends off a current of electricity to the chela indicating his approach. It was this influence which I felt at that time. A few minutes after, the Mahatma [Morya] was actually present in the room where the meeting of the members was held and was seen by me and Bro. Nivaran while some of the members only felt the influence. All the members would have seen him much more vividly, had it not been for the fact that he did not materialize himself much more objectively. I have seen the same Mahatma, several times in his [astral] double during my travels in the North [of India]. Not only have I seen Madame B.'s Master in his double but also my venerated Guru Deva "K.H." I have also seen Master [K.H.] in HIS PHYSICAL BODY.

14E. FRANZ HARTMANN
DECEMBER 1883 – FEBRUARY 1884,
ADYAR, MADRAS, INDIA, AND BOMBAY, INDIA

[Hartmann 1884, Report 11–2, 13–5, 28–30,
and Hartmann 1884, "Phenomenal"]

On the evening of December 4, 1883, I arrived at Madras and was kindly received by Mr. G. Muttuswami Chettyar, who conducted me to his carriage, and away we went towards Adyar, situated in a suburb of the city of Madras, about six miles from the landing place of the steamer.

It was dark when we arrived, and the object of my dreams, who was said to possess the key that was to open before me the sanctuary of Occultism, was sitting in the lighted entrance hall, surrounded by a few friends. Poor and yet envied Madame Blavatsky, the sphinx of the nineteenth century, at once a sage and a woman. She upon whose brow shines the serene tranquility of a god, and who a minute afterwards will fly into a stew because the coffee is too hot. Her appearance neither surprised nor disappointed me. A stately figure, dressed in a loose flowing robe, she might as well have sat for the picture of one of the saints, and her kind and cordial manner at once gained my confidence.

Before retiring to rest, I expressed a desire to see the pictures of the Mahatmas, these mysterious beings, superior to man, of whom I had heard so much, and I was taken upstairs, to see the "shrine" in which those pictures were kept. The pictures represented two men with oriental features and in corresponding dress. The expression of their faces was mild and yet serene.

A week or two after my arrival at Adyar, seeing that several others, strangers as well as members of our Society, occasionally received letters from the Masters either by having them dropped from the air, thrust at them through solid walls, or sent to them through the "Shrine," I concluded to try whether I might not be equally fortunate.

Accordingly I wrote the following lines—

"*Reverend Master!* The undersigned offers you his services. He desires that you would kindly examine his mental capacity and if desirable give him further instructions. Respectfully yours, etc."

I copy this letter verbatim, so that the reader may not think me so silly as to trouble the "Adepts" of the Himalayas with my little private affairs. I am in the habit of keeping my own counsel, and there was not one in India or outside of San Francisco that knew anything about [my] affairs. I gave my letter to Col. Olcott and he put it into the Shrine.

A couple of days afterwards, I reasoned with myself about this matter, and thought that, if the Masters should find it worth the while to say anything to me, they would undoubtedly do so without my asking, and I therefore begged Colonel Olcott to return me my letter. Colonel Olcott would have done so, but my letter had disappeared in a mysterious manner. In its place I received another, the contents of which showed not only a complete knowledge of some of the events of my past life, but it also went into details about very private business. It will be perceived, that this letter was not given as a "test"—although it was a "test" to me—but to give me some information and advice (which afterwards proved very useful to me).

[Later] I [saw] Mahatma [Morya] in his astral form. He appeared to me, accompanied by the astral forms of two chelas. His presence left an exhilarating and elevating influence, which did not fade away until several days after.

The impaired health of Madame Blavatsky had rendered it desirable that she should have a change of air, and the physicians which were consulted, advised her to go to Europe, where Col. Olcott was called on account of some official business. Madame Blavatsky therefore resolved to accompany Col. Olcott, and having received an urgent invitation to visit the Thakore Sahib of Wadhwan and our friend Hurrisinghjee, she made up her mind to visit them before embarking at Bombay.

Two days before Madame Blavatsky left, February 5th, 1884, I went unasked up to her room to speak with her in regard to Society matters.

After this conversation, the thought came in my mind to ask her opinion in regard to a certain subject of which I had been thinking. Madame Blavatsky advised me to apply to the [Master Morya] himself, to ask him mentally, and that the Master himself would answer my question. A few seconds later she said she felt his presence, and that she saw him writing. I must say that I too felt his influence and seemed to see his face, but of course this circumstance will carry conviction to no one but myself.

Just then another lady came in, to my great annoyance, and expressed her wish to have a pair of pincers, which was needed for some purpose, and remembering that I had such a pair of pincers in the drawer of my writing desk, I went downstairs into my room to get them. I opened the drawer, saw the pincers and a few other things in there, but no vestige of any letter, as I had removed my papers the day before to another place. I took the pincers and was about to close the drawer, when—there lay *in the drawer* a great envelope, addressed to me in the well-known handwriting of the Master and with the seal bearing his initials in Tibetan characters. On opening it, I found a long, very kind letter treating of the identical questions about which I had just been talking with Madame Blavatsky, besides giving a detailed and satisfactory answer to the very question which had so perplexed my mind, and a satisfactory explanation of certain matters, which for some time had been foremost in my mind, but of which I had said nothing at all.

Moreover, there was in the same envelope a photograph, cabinet-size, of the Master's face, with a dedication to me at the back.

Now, if I know anything at all, I know that my drawer contained no such letter, when I opened it, and that there was nobody visible in my room at that time. The letter, giving a detailed answer to my question, must have been written, sealed and put into the drawer in less than four minutes, while it took exactly forty minutes to copy it the next day; and finally, it treated a very difficult problem in such an elaborate and yet concise manner, that only an intelligence of the highest order could have done the same.

On the seventh of February, Madame Blavatsky, Mohini Chatterji, and myself in company of Madame Coulomb left Adyar [for Bombay]. On the way we stopped at the residence of the Thakore Sahib of Wadhwan.

I left Wadhwan on the 15th of February in company with Madame Blavatsky and Mohini. We were on our way to Bombay. A few hours before we started, Madame Blavatsky had read [an] article [of mine], corrected a few words and returned it to me. I read it carefully to see what corrections she had made, and whether I might not myself make some changes. I only found a few words corrected, folded the paper, put it in my pocketbook, deposited the pocketbook in my satchel, locked the same, entered the car [of the train] and put the satchel on my seat, where it never left me and never was out of my sight, until the event which I am about to describe occurred. We traveled on, Madame Blavatsky being in the same car. Towards evening Madame Blavatsky requested me to let her see the article again. I took it out of my satchel, unfolding the paper before handing it to her, and as I did so, imagine my surprise to find on it four long lines written on a space which was blank before, in the well-known handwriting of our Master, and in a different kind of ink than that used by Madame Blavatsky. How that writing could have been done in my satchel and during the shaking of the car, I do not pretend to explain.

Another incident occurred [at Bombay] when I was alone by myself. On the morning of the 20th of February, I received a curious Tibetan medal from our Master through Madame Blavatsky. I then accompanied her on board the steamer on which she was to sail for Europe. On my return to the shore I went into a native jewelry shop and bought a locket to deposit my medal, but could not find a chain long enough for my purpose. I then returned to my room, and paced the floor, studying what to do in regard to the chain. I finally came to the conclusion that I would buy a rose-colored silk ribbon. But where to get it, being a stranger in Bombay, that was the question. My pacing the floor brought me again in front of the open window, and there right before me on the floor lay exactly the very silk ribbon, brand new, and just the one I wanted.

Archibald Keightley in his early years

Chapter 15

FRANCE AND ENGLAND

1884

H. P. BLAVATSKY went from India to France, where she was to remain while Olcott traveled to England to try to mediate in a dispute about the direction and leadership of the London Lodge. However, she received "orders" to attend the Lodge meeting, and the excitement caused by her presence there defused a potentially difficult situation. She returned to France for several months before going back to London as the houseguest of Francesca Arundale. However, there and elsewhere, HPB was not so much a houseguest as a house-master. Wherever she went, she attracted the curious as well as those desiring to come into contact with the Mahatmas, and she responded to them in her own uninhibited and unpredictable manner.

15A. WILLIAM Q. JUDGE
MARCH–APRIL 1884, PARIS

[Judge 1912, 17–9, 22]

I have been here now since the 25th [of March], and HPB arrived on the 28th. Crowds of people have been here constantly, and, therefore, I have not been able to have any long private conversations with her. I have had some talks with her.

I am ordered by the Masters to stop here and help Madame in writing the *Secret Doctrine*.

After the first hurry was over here, I said I had to go to India at once. Olcott thought I had better stay with HPB, and so did she. But I said that all the orders I had were to go to India, and without further ones I was going, and so she said I was probably right; and then it was decided that I would wait here until [Olcott] could get me a steamer in London. All was thus arranged definitely. But the next morning, as I was sitting in the bedroom with Mohini, in which he and I slept, and after we had been there about an hour after coffee, Olcott came from his room, which was at the other end of the hall, and called me out, and told me privately that the Master [Morya] had been then to his room and had told him that I was not to go yet to India, but to stay and help HPB on the *Secret Doctrine*.

So then, here I am for how long or short I do not know, and I am to make suggestions and write upon the work.

[One day] for about an hour the Masters sent messages through HPB in the parlor, questions to me to try her. Each message made a distinct effect upon my skin before she repeated it.

On the fifth [of April] Olcott and Mohini left for London leaving Madame and me here, as she had been ordered not to go to London. We went through the day and in the evening were sitting together in the parlor alone, talking very seriously of old times.

As we sat there I felt the old signal of a message from the Master and saw that she was listening. She said: "Judge, the

Master asks me to try and guess what would be the most extraordinary thing he could order now?" I said, "That Mrs [Anna Kingsford] should be the President of the London Lodge." Try again. "That HPB should be ordered to go to London." That was right and he ordered her to take the 7:45 express, giving the exact hours it would arrive at the different stations and in London—all of which was correct, and we had no timetable in the house. She disliked the order awfully, and I can tell you, knowing her ill health and present unwieldy size, it was an awful journey. But last night I took her to the station and saw her go off in the train with a little handbag. There is some peculiar object in this, as she might have gone with Olcott.

All the time she confessed her inability to see why she was ordered, as the Londoners will think it done for effect after her refusal to go then, and Olcott, when he sees her, will certainly feel like swearing. But the London situation is serious, and maybe they intend to work some phenomena there for some good end. So I am left here alone in this house.

[Mrs. Anna Bonus Kingsford (1846–1888), English mystical writer and doctor of medicine, was the author (in collaboration with Edward Maitland) of *The Perfect Way; or, The Finding of Christ* (1882), an esoteric interpretation of Christianity. —DHC]

15B. A. P. SINNETT
APRIL 7, 1884, LONDON

[Sinnett 1922, 54–6]

In the beginning of April 1884, Colonel Olcott arrived in London, Madame Blavatsky remaining behind at Nice and Paris. Colonel Olcott was accompanied by a young Indian Theosophist, Mohini, who became for a time a very conspicuous person in

Theosophical activities. He was introduced to us as a chela of the Master KH and was made cordially welcome.

The 7th [of April] was the occasion of the important meeting of the [London Lodge of the Theosophical Society]. It was held at Mr. Finch's Chambers in Lincoln's Inn, and its purpose was the election of a new President. Many of the members wished me to become President, but I shrank from allowing a personal rivalry between Mrs. [Anna] Kingsford and myself in regard to the Presidency. So I had arranged to nominate Mr. Finch for the office.

I duly proposed Mr. Finch and I think that Mr. Maitland went through the form of proposing Mrs. Kingsford. Anyhow, when the show of hands was taken (Colonel Olcott being in the chair) the vote was practically unanimous in favor of Mr. Finch.

The excitements of the meeting on the 7th were by no means confined to the circumstances of the election. After this was over I was in the midst of an address to the meeting when a disturbance at the door interrupted me and in a moment the whole room was aware that Madame Blavatsky had arrived. I broke off and went to meet her. A little crowd collected around her [and she] was formally introduced to the meeting.

The minutes relating to this go on as follows: She "intimated that if any members would communicate to her any inquiries they might like to make in regard to the meaning of obscure passages in *Isis Unveiled* such inquiries would receive attention and would be made the subject of explanations in the new version of that book which under the title *The Secret Doctrine* she proposed to bring out.

"Mr. [F. W. H.] Myers inquired whether documentary evidence could be obtained from India for the service of the Psychic Research Society in reference to cases in which the astral apparitions of the Mahatmas had been seen at various times and places.

"Madame Blavatsky called on Mr. Mohini to give some information on the subject and Mr. Mohini described the recent appearance of the astral figure of one of the Mahatmas at the Headquarters of the Society at Madras."

After the meeting was over Madame Blavatsky returned with us to Ladbroke Gardens, where she stayed with us for a week and then returned to Paris.

[Frederic W. H. Myers (1843–1901) was an English essayist, minor poet, and psychical researcher. He joined the Theosophical Society in 1883. He was on the SPR committee to investigate Madame Blavatsky's psychic phenomena and her claim to be in contact with the Mahatmas. He became convinced that she was a fraud and resigned his membership in the TS. His major work was published in two volumes in 1903 under the title *Human Personality and Its Survival of Bodily Death.* —DHC]

15C. ARCHIBALD KEIGHTLEY
APRIL 7, 1884, LONDON

[Keightley 1910, 110]

The first time I ever saw Mme. Blavatsky was in 1884, shortly after I had joined the Theosophical Society. A meeting had been called and was being held in the chambers of a member in Lincoln's Inn. The reason for the meeting lay in differences of opinion between Mr. Sinnett on the one hand and Mrs. Kingsford and Mr. Maitland on the other. Colonel Olcott was in the chair and endeavored to adjust the differences of opinion, but without success. By him were seated the contending parties, Mohini M. Chatterji, and one or two others, facing a long narrow room which was nearly filled with members of the Society.

The dispute proceeded, waxing warm, and the room steadily filled, the seat next to me being occupied by a stout lady who had just arrived, very much out of breath. At the moment some one at the head of the room alluded to some action of Mme. Blavatsky's, to which the stout lady gave confirmation in the words "That's so." At this point the meeting broke up in confusion, everybody ran to the stout lady, while Mohini arrived at her feet on his knees. Finally she was taken up to the end of the room where the "high gods" had been enthroned, exclaiming and protesting in several tongues in the same sentence and the meeting tried to continue. However, it had to adjourn itself.

Next day I was presented to Mme. Blavatsky, who was my stout neighbor of the meeting. Her arrival was totally unexpected and her departure from Paris was, she told me long afterwards, only arranged "under orders" half an hour before she left. She arrived at Charing Cross [Railway Station] without knowing the place of meeting, only knowing she had to attend it. "I followed my occult nose," she told me, and by this means got from the station to Lincoln's Inn and found her way to the rooms on foot. Her arrival was singularly opportune, for it broke up a meeting which declined to be peaceful, in spite of all the oil which Colonel Olcott was pouring on its troubled waters.

15D. WILLIAM Q. JUDGE
MAY 1884, ENGHIEN, FRANCE

*[HPB: In Memory, 52–5;
reprinted in Judge 1980, 2:17–20]*

In the spring of 1884, HPB was staying in Rue Notre Dame des Champs, Paris. She was engaged daily with her writing, save for an occasional drive or visit. Many visitors from all classes were constantly calling, and among the rest came the Countess d'Adhemar, who at once professed a profound admiration for HPB and invited her to come to the Chateau owned by the Count at Enghien, just outside the city, including in her invitation myself and Mohini Chatterji. The invitation was accepted and we all went out to Enghien, where HPB was given two large rooms downstairs and the others slept in rooms on the upper floors. Every convenience was given to our beloved friend, and there she continued her writing.

A lake was at one side of the house and extensive grounds covered with fine timber hid the building from the road, part being a well-kept fruit and flower garden. Wide stairs led up to the hall; on one side, which we may call the road front, was the billiard room, the high window of which opened upon the leaden roof of the porch; the dining room looked out at the back over the edge of the lake, and the drawing room opened from it on the other side at right angles to the side of the billiard room. This drawing room had windows opening on three sides, so that both garden and lake could be seen from it. In it was the grand piano at the end and side opposite the dining room door, and between the two side windows was a marble slab holding ornaments; between the windows, at the end near the piano, was the fireplace, and at that corner was one of the windows giving a view of the lake.

Every evening it was the custom to spend some time in the drawing room in conversation, and there, as well as in the dining room, took place some phenomena which indeed were no more interesting than the words of HPB, whether those were witty, grave, or gay. Very often Countess d'Adhemar's sister played the piano in a manner to delight even HPB, who was no mean judge. I remember well one melody, just then brought out in the world of Paris, which pleased her immensely, so that she often asked for its repetition. It was one suggestive of high aspiration and grandiose conceptions of nature. Many lively discussions with the Count on one side and HPB on the other had taken place there, and often in the very midst of these she would suddenly turn to Mohini and myself, who were sitting listening, to repeat to us the very thoughts then passing in our brains.

One day at dinner, when there were present the Count and Countess, their son Raoul, HPB, Mohini, the Countess's sister, myself, and one other, the strong and never-to-be-forgotten perfume which intimate friends of HPB knew so well as often accompanying phenomena or coming of itself, floated round and round the table, plainly perceptible to several and not perceived either before or afterwards. Of course, many sceptics will see nothing in this, but the writer and others well know that this of itself is a phenomenon, and that the perfume has been sent for many miles through the air as a message from HPB or from those hidden persons who often aided in phenomena or in teachings.

At this dinner, or at some other during the visit, we had all just come in from the flower garden. I had plucked a small rose-bud and placed it upon the edge of the tumbler between myself and the Countess's sister, who was on my left, HPB being seated on my right. This lady began to talk of phenomena, wondering if HPB could do as related of the Indian yogis. I replied that she could if she would, but did not ask her, and added that she could make even that small rosebud bloom at once. Just then HPB stretched her hand out towards the rose, not touching it, and said nothing, continuing at once her conversation and the dinner. We watched the bud until the end of the meal and saw that it grew in that space of time much larger and bloomed out into a rose nearly full grown.

On another evening after we had been in the drawing room for some time, sitting without lights, the moon shining over the lake and all nature being hushed, HPB fell into a thoughtful state. Shortly she rose and stood at the corner window looking over the water, and in a moment a flash of soft light shot into the room and she quietly smiled.

[Concerning this evening] the Countess d'Adhemar writes, "HPB seemed wrapped in thought, when suddenly she rose from her chair, advanced to the open window, and raising her arm with a commanding gesture, faint music was heard in the distance, which advancing nearer and nearer broke into lovely strains and filled the drawing room where we were all sitting."

This astral music was very plain to us all, and the Count especially remarked upon its beauty and the faintness of it as it sank away into the unknown distance. The whole house was full of these bell sounds at night when I was awake very late and others had retired. They were like signals going and coming to

HPB's room downstairs. And on more than one occasion as we walked in the grounds under the magnificent trees, have they shot past us, sometimes audible to all and again only heard by one or two.

I took away with me a book which could not be finished there, and just before leaving France went out to Enghien to return it. There I met the Countess d'Adhemar, who said that the peculiar and unmistakable perfume of which I spoke above had come in the house after we had left. It was one evening about two days after HPB's departure and the d'Adhemars had some friends for dinner. After dinner they all went into the drawing room and soon noticed the perfume. It came, as they said to me, in rushes, and at once they began to hunt it out in the room, coming at last to the marble slab described, where, from one spot in the stone, they found the perfume rushing out in volumes. Such was the quantity of it that, as the Countess said to me, they were compelled to open the windows, since the odor was overpowering in large masses. In returning to Paris I told HPB of this, and she only said, "It sometimes happens."

15E. VERA P. DE ZHELIHOVSKY
MAY 1884, PARIS

[Sinnett 1886, 266–9]

We were four of us at *Rue Notre Dame des Champs*, 46— Mme. N. A. de Fadeyev, Mme. Blavatsky, the eminent Russian author, M. Solovyov, and I—having tea at the same table of the little drawing-room, about 11 pm. Mme. B. was asked to narrate something of her "Master," and how she had acquired from him her occult talents. While telling us many things, she offered us to see a portrait of his in a gold medallion she wore on a chain round her neck, and opened it. It is a perfectly flat locket, *made to contain but one miniature, and no more.* It passed from hand to hand, and we all saw the handsome Hindoo face in it, painted in India.

Suddenly our little party felt disturbed by something *very strange*, a sensation which it is hardly possible to describe. It was as though the air had suddenly changed, was rarefied—the atmosphere became positively oppressive, and we three could hardly breathe. HPB covered her eyes with her hand, and whispered: "I feel that something is going to happen. Some phenomenon. He is preparing to do it."

She meant by "He," her *guru-master*, whom she considers so powerful.

At that moment Mr. Solovyov fixed his eyes on a corner of the room, saying that he saw something like a ball of fire, of oval form, looking like a radiant golden and bluish egg. He had hardly pronounced these words when we heard, coming from the farthest end of the corridor, a long melodious harp—a melody far fuller and more definite than any of the musical sounds we had previously heard.

Once more the clear notes were repeated, and then died away. Silence reigned again in the rooms.

I left my seat and went into the passage hall, brightly lighted with a lamp. Useless to say that all was quiet, and that it was empty. When I returned to the drawing room I found H. P. Blavatsky sitting quietly as before at the table between Mme. de Fadeyev and Mr. Solovyov. At the same time, I saw as distinctly as can be, the figure of a man, grayish, yet quite clear form, standing near my sister, and who, upon my looking at him, receded from her, paled, and disappeared in the opposite wall. This man—or, perhaps, his astral form—was of a slight build, and of middle size, wrapped in a kind of mantle, and with a white turban on his head. The vision did not last more than a few seconds, but I had all the time to examine it, and to tell every one what I distinctly saw, though, as soon as it had disappeared, I felt terribly frightened and nervous. Hardly come back to our senses, we were startled with another wonder, this one palpable and objective. HPB suddenly opened her locket, and instead of one portrait of a Master, there were two—her own facing his!

Firmly set inside the other half of the *medallion*, under its oval glass, there was her own miniature likeness, which she had just casually mentioned.

The locket was once more carefully examined by the three witnesses, and passed from hand to hand.

This was not the finale. A quarter of an hour later the magical locket, *from which we three literally never took off our eyes for one second*, was opened at the desire of one of us—*her portrait was no more to be found in it*. It had disappeared.

15F. FRANCESCA ARUNDALE
JUNE 30 – AUGUST 16, 1884, LONDON

[HPB: In Memory, 69; and Arundale
1932, 29–37, 40–2]

HPB returned to London June [30th] taking up her abode with us at No. 77 Elgin Crescent, Notting Hill.

The few months of the summer of 1884 which she passed in our house in Elgin Crescent were marked by events of a curious and exceptional character, all alike bearing witness to the fact that the personality called Madame Blavatsky was different in most characteristics from those around, and crowds of visitors of all classes testified to the interest she invoked.

It was her custom while with us to devote the earlier part of the day to writing; she usually began at seven o'clock, but often earlier, and it was very rarely indeed that when I went into her room at about eight o'clock in the morning I did not find her already at her desk, at which she continued with a slight interval for lunch till about three or four o'clock in the afternoon. Then the reception time began, and from early afternoon to late evening, one constant succession of visitors arrived. The old lady sitting in her armchair in the same drawing room, which was barely large enough for the influx of guests, would be the center of an inquiring circle. Many, of course, drawn by the fame of her great powers, merely came from curiosity.

Mohini M. Chatterji accompanied Madame Blavatsky, and Colonel Olcott was with us from time to time as his tours allowed. There was also a very important member of the Indian contingent, namely Babula, HPB's servant; in his picturesque turban and white dress, he created quite a little sensation; and on the afternoons when tea was served and HPB's Russian samovar glistened and shone on the table, and Babula bore cups of tea and sweet cakes to the visitors, we were certainly a unique house in suburban London. The house was always full of visitors, and as HPB often liked to invite friends to stay, I never knew whether I should have one person or twenty to lunch or dinner as the case might be.

The house was not large, but there were two good rooms with folding doors between, and it was a sight to see HPB seated in a big armchair surrounded by learned as well as fashionable people. A brilliant conversationalist, she kept young and old entranced, and at the same time her graceful fingers were constantly diving into the Nubian basket of tobacco that was ever by her side, and twisting the little cigarettes that she was constantly smoking. That was her social aspect. Then very often Mohini Chatterji would answer questions on Indian philosophy. His lectures were much sought after, and we rarely closed our doors till one or two o'clock in the morning.

During this time, the little George Arundale was sent to a day school quite near, but he was not entirely out of it all, and I remember one afternoon a party was made up to go to the Zoological Gardens. We all went there in carriages and the child with us. Then a bath chair was procured for HPB and we proceeded to visit the animals. There were no occult phenomena on that visit, but there was the manifestation of a trait that showed forth the kindly nature of HPB. The child was running about as children will and, running near HPB's chair, suddenly missed his footing and fell to the ground. HPB, in spite of the fact that she moved with difficulty, almost sprang out of the chair, throwing her umbrella on one side, and tried to help the child up. It was but a little thing, it is true, but it showed the kindly disregard of self.

A curious happening which has never been effaced from my memory took place in the early part of HPB's stay with us. Many people at that time wished to get into communication with the Masters through HPB, and would sometimes bring letters asking that they should be forwarded to the Masters. HPB always said, "It is not for me to forward the letters; the Masters will take them if They wish," and the letters were put into a certain drawer in her room. Sometimes the writers received a message through HPB, very often they did not; but the drawer was kept open. One day Mr. Sinnett had something he wished to ask of Master K.H., and that letter also was placed in the drawer. More than a week passed and there was no answer, and I was grieved, for we all desired that the questions should be answered. Day after day I looked into the drawer, but the letter was still there.

One morning at about 7:30 I went in to HPB (I always went to her room the first thing); I found her at her table, writing as usual, and I said to her, "How much I wish that letter could be taken." She looked very straight at me and said, "Bring me the letter," in rather a severe tone. I gave the letter into her hand. There was a candle on the table and "Light the candle," she said; then giving me the letter, she said, "Burn the letter." I felt rather sorry to burn Mr. Sinnett's letter but, of course, did as she said. "Now go to your room and meditate." I went up to my room, which I had only left a short time before. My room was at the top of the house, in what we call an attic, for all the lower rooms were being used by our visitors, and I and the little boy slept upstairs. I went to the window, which looked on to a beautiful garden with lovely trees. Before the window there was a box, covered with a pink cloth, and I stood there for a minute or two wondering what HPB meant [and] what I was to meditate on.

In a few minutes I cast my eyes down on the pink cloth, and in the middle of the cloth there was a letter which either I had not

noticed before or which had not been there. I took up the envelope and looked at it, and found there was no address on it; it was
quite blank, but it contained a thickness of paper and I concluded it was a letter. I held it in my hand and looked at it once or
twice, and still finding the envelope without name or address, I
felt sure it must be something occult and wondered for whom it
could be. At length I decided to take the letter to HPB, and looking at it once again saw, in the clear writing of the Master K.H.,
Mr. Sinnett's name. That the name had not been on it at the
beginning I am sure, nor during the many times when I looked at
it most carefully. The letter was an answer to the one I had burnt,
and it gave me much joy to be the recipient in the curious way in
which it was sent.

There were several instances of the same kind. Once, when
the letter I wanted answered was very private to myself, instead of
putting it in the usual drawer I carried it in my pocket unknown
to HPB or to anyone else. But one night when I was sitting with
her just before going up to my room, she handed me a letter in the
well-known handwriting [of Master K.H.].

It was a time of continual excitement; many people of note
came to see HPB. Among them I remember well Mr. Frederick W.
H. Myers of Psychic Research fame. HPB happened to be alone
that afternoon, and she and her visitor began talking about
the phenomena in which Mr. Myers was so interested. "I wish
you would show me a proof of your occult power," said he, "will
you not do something that will prove that there are these occult
forces of which you speak?" "What would be the good?" said
Madame Blavatsky. "Even if you saw and heard, you would not
be convinced." "Try me," he said.

She looked at him for a moment or so in that strange,
penetrating manner she had, and turning to me said, "Bring me a
finger bowl and some water in it." They were sitting in the full
light of a summer's afternoon; she was to the right of Mr. Myers,
who was seated in a small chair about three feet away. I brought
the glass bowl of water and she told me to place it on a stool just
in front of Mr. Myers and a fairly long distance from her, which I

did. We sat for a few moments in quiet expectation, and then from the glass there seemed to come four or five notes, such as we have called the "astral bells."

It was evident that Mr. Myers was astonished; he looked at HPB and her folded hands in her lap, and then again at the glass bowl; there was no visible connection between the two. Again the notes of the astral bell sounded, clear and silvery, and no movement on the part of Madame Blavatsky. He turned to me, and one could see that he was quite confused as to how the sounds could have been produced. HPB smiled, and said, "Nothing very wonderful, only a little knowledge of how to direct some of the forces of nature." As Mr. Myers left he turned to me and said, "Miss Arundale, I shall *never* doubt again."

But alas for the fickle, doubting mind; before a fortnight had passed he wrote to say he was not convinced, and that the sounds might have been produced in this way or that. HPB was not one whit disturbed, in fact she said, "I knew it, but I thought I would give him what he asked for." This incident goes to show that conviction is rarely gained through phenomena; they arouse the attention, and if the mind is receptive and willing to investigate and not declare that that which is not understood cannot be, then there is a possibility that new facts and laws may be discovered.

I see her of an early morning in her room writing at her table, the floor strewn with burnt matches which were my despair, careful housekeeper as I was, for coverlets, tablecovers, and carpets might well get burned, and even the house itself might have received considerable damage, for HPB was accustomed to throw her lighted match away without any consideration as to where it might fall. I have also lively remembrances of some of the difficult times involved by HPB's absolute disregard of all conventionality. People would come long distances to see her, and it was generally understood that visitors might come between four and six in the afternoon. Sometimes, however, for no reason that we could see, she would decline to come from her room.

I remember well one afternoon there was quite a distinguished set waiting to meet her, and when I went up to inform her that visitors had come to see her, I found her in a state of undress incompatible with a visit to the drawing room. When I told her who was there, a little strong language was used and she said that Mr. and Mrs. X might come up. I gently remonstrated that neither her room nor her person was quite in a suitable condition for visitors; she told me I might go somewhere, but if she came down she should come down as she was, and if she saw anyone she would see them as she was, and that I was to send her food as soon as possible for she was hungry. The visitors had to leave and I made what excuses I could.

The most pleasant time I had was always in the early morning; she always seemed more get-at-able then, her mouth settled in pleasant curves, her eyes kind and brilliant, and she always seemed to understand and sympathize not only with what one said but also with what one did not say. I never felt afraid of HPB in spite of the very strong language she sometimes used. One always somehow felt it was *surface* strong language.

15G. LAURA C. HOLLOWAY
JULY 1884, LONDON

[Langford 1912, 204–6]

Mr. [Hermann] Schmiechen, a young German artist, [was] residing in London [and] a number of Theosophists gathered at his studio. Chief among Mr. Schmiechen's guests was HPB, who occupied a seat facing a platform on which was [Schmiechen's] easel. Near him on the platform sat several persons, all of them women, with one exception. About the room were grouped a number of well-known people, all equally interested in the attempt to be made by Mr. Schmiechen.

The most clearly defined memory of that gathering, always in the mind of the writer, is the picture of Madame Blavatsky placidly smoking cigarettes in her easy chair and two women on the platform who were smoking also. She had "ordered" one of these women [Laura Holloway herself] to make a cigarette and smoke it, and the order was obeyed though with great hesitation, for it was a first attempt and even the mild Egyptian tobacco used was expected to produce nausea. HPB promised that no such result would follow, and encouraged by Mrs. Sinnett, who was also smoking, the cigarette was lighted. The result was a curious quieting of the nerves, and soon all interest was lost in the group of people about the room, and only the easel and the hand of the artist absorbed her attention.

Strange to relate that though the amateur smoker considered herself an onlooker it was her voice which uttered the words "begin it," and the artist quickly began to outline a head. Soon the eyes of every one present were upon him as he worked with extreme rapidity. While quiet reigned in the studio and all were eagerly interested in Mr. Schmiechen's work, the amateur smoker on the platform saw the figure of a man outline itself beside the easel and, while the artist with head bent over his work continued his outlining, it stood by him without a sign or motion. She leaned over to her friend and whispered, "It is the Master KH; he is being sketched. He is standing near Mr. Schmiechen."

"Describe his looks and dress," called out HPB. And while those in the room were wondering over Madame Blavatsky's exclamation, the woman addressed said: "He is about Mohini's height; slight of build, wonderful face full of light and animation; flowing curly black hair, over which is worn a soft cap. He is a symphony in greys and blues. His dress is that of a Hindu—though it is far finer and richer than any I have ever seen before— and there is fur trimming about his costume. It is his picture that is being made."

HPB's heavy voice arose to admonish the artist, one of her remarks remaining distinctly in memory. It was this "Be careful, Schmiechen; do not make the face too round; lengthen the outline, and take note of the long distance between the nose and the ears." She sat where *she could not see the easel nor know what was on it.*

How many of the number of those in the studio on that first occasion recognized the Master's presence was not known. There were psychics in the room, several of them, and the artist, Mr. Schmiechen, was a psychic, or he could not have worked out so successfully the picture that was outlined by him on that eventful day.

Henry Sidgwick in 1895

15H. HENRY SIDGWICK
AUGUST 9–10, 1884, CAMBRIDGE, ENGLAND

[Sidgwick 1906, 384–5]

[On August 8th] we went back to Cambridge. [The next day] after dinner we [went] to a meeting of the Cambridge Branch of the SPR [Society for Psychical Research], where Madame

Blavatsky, Mohini, and other Theosophists are to show off. The meeting is in Oscar Browning's spacious rooms, which are crowded to overflowing—all the members of the Branch, and more than as many outsiders. There must have been over seventy; I should not have thought that such a crowd could have been got together in the Long [summer] Vacation. [F. W. H.] Myers and I had the task of "drawing" Mme. B. by questions, Mohini taking a share of the answers. We kept it up better than I expected for a couple of hours; the interest of the miscellaneous throng—half of whom, I suppose, came with the very vaguest notions of Theosophy—being apparently fairly well sustained. On the whole I was favorably impressed with Mme. B. No doubt the *stuff* of her answers resembled [her book] *Isis Unveiled* in some of its worst characteristics; but her manner was certainly frank and straightforward—it was hard to imagine her the elaborate impostor that she must be if the whole thing is a trick. [On August 10] we all went to a Theosophical lunch with Myers. Our favorable impression of Mme. B. was sustained; if personal sensibilities can be trusted, she is a genuine being, with a vigorous nature, intellectual as well as emotional, and a real desire for the good of mankind. This impression is all the more noteworthy as she is externally unattractive—with her flounces full of cigarette ashes—and not prepossessing in manner. Certainly we like her, both Nora [Mrs. Sidgwick] and I. If she is a humbug, she is a consummate one: as her remarks have the air not only of spontaneity and randomness but sometimes of an amusing indiscretion. Thus in the midst of an account of the Mahatmas in Tibet, intended to give us an elevated view of these personages, she blurted out her candid impression that the chief Mahatma of all was the most utter dried-up old mummy that she ever saw.

[Henry Sidgwick, first president of the Society for Psychical Research, was on the special committee that investigated Madame Blavatsky and her claims. In the end Sidgwick came to believe that HPB was a fraud and that her Mahatmas did not exist. —DHC]

261

Isabel Cooper-Oakley

Chapter 16

GERMANY AND
RETURN TO INDIA
1884–1885

*B*LAVATSKY, after having stayed almost five months in
Paris and London, visited the Gebhard family in
Elberfeld, Germany, during the late summer and early
fall of 1884, when she was busily engaged in working on her
second book, *The Secret Doctrine.*

Meanwhile, a vicious attack on Blavatsky by two of her staff
members at Adyar, Alexis and Emma Coulomb, was rapidly building up. She returned to Adyar on December 21, 1884, to learn the
details of the situation. She wished to sue the couple, already dismissed from Adyar for their gross libel concerning her supposedly
fraudulent production of psychic phenomena. HPB was, however,
overruled by a Committee of leading Theosophical Society members, and in disgust resigned as Corresponding Secretary of the
Society. On March 31, 1885, she left for Europe, never to return
to Indian soil.

The Coulomb attack, as was later evident, had no solid foundation whatsoever. It was based on forged and partially forged letters, purporting to have been written by H. P. Blavatsky, with instructions to arrange fraudulent psychic phenomena of various kinds. A Christian missionary magazine in Madras published the most incriminating portions of these letters.

Meanwhile, the Society for Psychical Research (London) had appointed a special committee to investigate Madame Blavatsky's claims. In December 1884, Richard Hodgson, a member of this SPR committee, arrived in India to inquire into and report on the Coulombs' allegations. Based upon Hodgson's findings, the SPR committee in its final report of December 1885, branded Madame Blavatsky as "one of the most accomplished, ingenious and interesting impostors in history." Mr. Hodgson also accused Madame Blavatsky of being a Russian spy. This Hodgson Report to the SPR has been the basis for most subsequent attacks on H. P. Blavatsky, alleging dishonesty, the nonexistence of her Masters, and the worthlessness of Theosophy.

In 1963, Adlai Waterman (pseudonym of Walter A. Carrithers, Jr.), in his definitive work entitled *Obituary: The "Hodgson Report" on Madame Blavatsky*, analyzed and refuted Hodgson's contentions against Madame Blavatsky. A copy of Waterman's book can be purchased for $6.50 (including postage and handling) from the Blavatsky Foundation, P.O. Box 1844, Tucson, AZ 85702. Another refutation of some of Hodgson's charges against HPB is Vernon Harrison's article entitled "J'Accuse: An Examination of the Hodgson Report of 1885," published in *The Journal of the Society for Psychical Research*, London, April 1986, pp. 286–310, and expanded in his book *H. P. Blavatsky and the SPR: An Examination of the Hodgson Report of 1885* (Pasadena, CA: Theosophical University Press, 1997). Both books are available on the Web, at the following URLs:

Waterman: http://www.azstarnet.com/~blafoun/obituary.htm

Harrison: http://www.theosociety.org/pasadena/hpb-spr/hpb-spr-h.htm

16a. Francesca Arundale
August 1884,
Elberfeld, Germany

[Arundale 1932, 44–6]

In the summer of 1884 we received an invitation from a kind friend at Elberfeld, Herr Gustav Gebhard, to come and spend a few weeks at his home. Not only did he invite Colonel Olcott and Madame Blavatsky and Mr. Mohini, but he invited a large party to accompany them—my mother, myself, and my little George, Bertram Keightley, and some others, and many joined the party later.

The drawing-room at Elberfeld was a large, high room with very high doors. We used to sit in this room before going down to dinner, which was on a lower floor. It often happened that HPB did not go down and something was served to her upstairs. On the evening I am speaking of, she decided to remain upstairs and settled her bulky figure comfortably in a large armchair while all the rest of us went down, her host asking her what she would like sent up. After dinner the party returned to the drawing room and found HPB quietly ensconced in her chair, as if she had never left it. A party gathered round her as usual and talk was being carried on, when somebody said, "What is that white thing on the top of the portal of the door?" A high chair was brought, and the "white thing" proved to be an envelope [containing a letter from Mahatma K.H.] addressed to me as Treasurer of the London Lodge. I fully realized that there seemed to be no special reason why the missive should have been given in that peculiar manner. It may have been intended to show that HPB had no connection with it, for it would have been almost impossible for HPB to have mounted on a chair and placed a letter at that height.

CHAPTER 16

16B. RUDOLPH GEBHARD
AUGUST 25–26, 1884,
ELBERFELD, GERMANY

[Sinnett 1886, 279–86]

I have always taken a great interest in conjuring tricks. When in London, I had an opportunity of taking lessons from Professor Field, a most skillful sleight-of-hand conjuror, who very soon made me quite proficient in his art. From that time forward I have given performances wherever I went (as an amateur, of course), and made the acquaintance of nearly all our renowned "wizards," with whom I exchanged tricks. As every conjuror has some favorite sleight in which he excels, I was bound to be very careful in watching them, in order to make myself perfect in all the different lines of card or coin conjuring, or the famous mediumistic feats. This of course made me in good time a pretty close observer, as far as tricks are concerned; and I feel justified in giving here an opinion on the phenomena which came under my observation.

Two of them occurred in our house in Elberfeld, during the stay in it of Mme. Blavatsky, Colonel Olcott, and a small party of friends and Theosophists.

The first one was a letter from Mahatma KH to my father, and took place one evening in the presence of a number of witnesses. It was about nine pm. We were sitting in the drawing room discussing different topics, when Mme. Blavatsky's attention was suddenly attracted by something unusual taking place in the room. After a while she said that she felt the presence of the "Masters." That they had, perhaps, the intention of doing something for us, and so she asked us to think of what we should like to occur. Then a little discussion took place as to what would be the best thing, and finally it was unanimously resolved that a letter should be asked for, addressed to my father, Mr. G. Gebhard, on a subject on which he should mentally decide himself.

Now my father had, at the time being, great anxiety about a

son in America, my elder brother, and was very eager to get advice from the Master concerning him.

Meanwhile, Mme. B., who, on account of her recent illness, was resting on a sofa, and had been looking around the room, suddenly exclaimed that there was something going on with a large oil painting hanging over the piano in the same room, she having seen like a ray of light shooting in the direction of the picture. This statement was immediately corroborated by Mrs. [Holloway], and then by my mother also, who, sitting opposite a looking glass and turning her back to the picture, had also observed in the mirror, like a faint light going towards the painting. Mme. B. then required Mrs. [Holloway] to see, and say what was going on, when Mrs. [Holloway] said that she saw something forming over the picture, but could not distinctly make out what it was.

Everybody's attention was now fixed in the direction of the wall high above and under the ceiling, where so many saw bright lights. But, I must confess, that for my part, not being clairvoyant, I could neither see lights, nor any other thing except what I had always seen on that wall. And when Madame Blavatsky said she now felt absolutely sure that there was something going on, I got up (we had kept our seats all this while) and climbing on the piano lifted the picture right off the wall, but not off the hook, shook it well and looked behind it—nothing! The room was well lit up, and there was not an inch of the picture which I could not see. I dropped the frame, saying that I could see nothing; but Madame Blavatsky told me that she felt sure that there must be something, so on I climbed once more and tried again.

The picture in question was a large oil painting, suspended from the wall by a hook and a rope, which made it hang over at the top, so that when the lower part of the frame was lifted off the wall, there was a space of fully six inches between the wall and the back of the picture, the latter being virtually entirely off the wall. There being a wall gas bracket fixed on each side of the painting, the space between the latter and the wall was well lit up. But the second time, no better than the first, was I able to detect anything, though I looked very close. It was in order to make perfectly sure that I got up on the piano, and passed my hand twice very carefully along the frame, which is about three inches thick, up and down—nothing.

Letting the picture drop back, I then turned round to Madame Blavatsky to ask her what was to be done further, when she exclaimed, "I see the letter; there it is!" I turned quickly back to the picture, and saw at that moment a letter dropping from behind it on the piano. I picked it up. It was addressed to "Herr Consul G. Gebhard," and contained the information he had just asked for. I must have made rather a perplexed face, for the company laughed merrily at the "family juggler."

Now for me this is a most completely demonstrated phenomenon. Nobody had handled the picture but myself; I was careful to examine it very closely, and as I was searching for a letter, such a thing could not have escaped my attention, as perhaps would have been the case if I had been looking for some other object; as then I might not have paid any attention to a slip of paper. The letter was fully four by two inches, so by no means a small object.

Let us consider this phenomenon from a sleight-of-hand point of view.

Suppose several letters had been prepared beforehand, addressed to different persons, treating of different subjects. Is it possible to get a letter to an appointed place by a sleight-of-hand trick? Quite possible; it only depends what place it is, and if our attention is drawn beforehand to such a place or not. To get that letter behind that picture would have been very difficult, but might have been managed if our attention had for a moment been directed to another place, the letter being thrown behind the picture in the meantime. What is sleight-of-hand? Nothing else but the execution of a movement more or less swift, in a moment when you are not observed. I draw your attention for a short while to a certain spot, say for instance my left hand, my right is then free to make certain movements unobserved; as to "the quickness of the hand deceives the eye" theory, it is entirely erroneous. You cannot make a movement with your hand so quickly that the eye would not follow and detect it; the only thing you can do is either to conceal the necessary movement by another one which has nothing to do with what you are about, or to draw the attention of the looker-on to another point, and then quickly do what is required.

Now, in this instance all our attention had been drawn to the picture, before ever the question was put as to what we should like to have, and was kept there all the while; it would have been impossible for anyone to throw a letter without being observed. As for the letter having been concealed behind the picture beforehand, this is out of the question altogether, it could not have escaped my attention while I repeatedly searched for it. Suppose the letter had been placed on the top of the frame, and my hand had disturbed it passing along without my knowing it, this would have caused the letter to drop down instantly, whereas, about thirty seconds passed before it put in an appearance. Taking all circumstances together, it seems to me an impossibility to have worked this phenomenon by a trick.

The day after this had occurred, I went into Madame's room about noon; but seeing that she was engaged I retired to the drawing room, where we had been sitting the night before, and just then the idea struck me to try that picture again, in order to make perfectly sure that the letter could not have been concealed somewhere behind it, without being detected. I was alone in the room, and during my examination of the painting, nobody entered it; I fully satisfied myself that a letter could not have escaped my attention, had it been concealed behind the picture. I then went back to Madame's room, where I found her still engaged with the same woman. In the evening we were again sitting together.

"The Masters watched you today, and were highly amused with your experiments. How you did try to find out if that letter could not have been concealed behind the picture."

Now I am positively certain, first, that nobody was in the room at the time I tried the picture; and secondly, that I had told no one in the house of my experiment. It is impossible for me to explain how Madame could have found out my movements, except through clairvoyance.

16C. VSEVOLOD S. SOLOVYOV
AUGUST 26–27, 1884, BRUSSELS, BELGIUM,
AND THEN LATER AT ELBERFELD, GERMANY

[Hastings 1943–4, 27–9]

Having received a letter from my countrywoman, Madame Helena Blavatsky, in which she informed me of her bad health and begged me to go to see her at Elberfeld, I decided to take the journey. But as the state of my own health obliged me to be careful, I preferred to stop at Brussels, which town I had never seen, to rest, the heat being unbearable.

I left Paris on the 24th of August. Next morning, at the Grand Hotel in Brussels, where I was staying, I met Mlle. [Justine de Glinka] (daughter of [a] Russian ambassador and maid of honour to the Empress of Russia). Hearing that I was going to Elberfeld to see Mme. Blavatsky, whom she knew and for whom she had much respect, she decided to come with me. We spent the day together expecting to leave in the morning by the nine o'clock train.

At eight o'clock, being quite ready to depart, I go to Miss [de Glinka's] room and find her in a great state of perplexity. All her keys, which she always kept about her person in a little bag and that she had in this bag on going to bed, had disappeared during the night, although the door was locked. Thus, as all her baggage was locked, she could not put away the things she had just been using and wearing. We were obliged to postpone our departure to the one o'clock train and called a locksmith to open the largest trunk. When it was opened, all the keys were found in the bottom of the trunk, *including the key of this trunk itself, attached as usual to the rest.* Having all the morning to spare, we agreed to take a walk, but suddenly I was overcome by weakness and felt an irresistible desire to sleep. I begged Miss [de Glinka] to excuse me and went to my room, and threw myself on the bed. But I could not sleep and lay with my eyes shut, but awake, when suddenly I saw before my closed eyes a series of views of unknown places that my memory took in to the finest detail. When this vision ceased, I felt no more weakness and went to Miss [de Glinka], to whom I related all that had happened to me and described to her in detail the views I had seen.

We left by the one o'clock train and lo! after about half an hour's journey, Miss [de Glinka], who was looking out of the window, said to me, "Look, here is one of your landscapes!" I recognized it at once, and all that day until evening, I saw, with open eyes, all that I had seen in the morning with closed eyes. I was pleased that I had described to Miss [de Glinka] all my vision in detail. The route between Brussels and Elberfeld is completely unknown to me, for it was the first time in my life that I had visited Belgium and this part of Germany.

On arriving at Elberfeld in the evening, we took rooms in a hotel and then hurried off to see Madame Blavatsky at Mr. Gebhard's house. The same evening, the members of the Theosophical Society who were there with Mme. Blavatsky showed us two superb oil paintings of the Mahatmas [Morya] and Koot Hoomi [painted by Mr. Schmiechen]. The portrait of M especially produced on us an extraordinary impression, and it is not surprising that on the way back to the hotel, we talked on about him and had him before our eyes. Miss [de Glinka] may be left to relate her own experience during that night. [Miss de Glinka's experience was similar to Solovyov's. —DHC]

But this is what happened to me:

Tired by the journey, I lay peacefully sleeping when suddenly I was awakened by the sensation of a warm penetrating breath. I open my eyes and in this feeble light that entered the room through the three windows, I see before me a tall figure of a man, dressed in a long white floating garment. At the same time I heard or felt a voice that told me, in I know not what language, although I understood perfectly, to light the candle. I should explain that, far from being afraid, I remained quite tranquil, only I felt my heart beat rapidly. I lit the candle, and in lighting it, saw by my watch that it was two o'clock. The vision did not disappear. There was a living man in front of me. And I recognized instantly the beautiful original of the portrait we had seen during the evening before. He sat down near me on a chair and began to speak. He talked for a long time. Among other things, he told me that in order to be fit to see him in *his astral body* I had had to undergo much preparation, and that the last lesson had been given me that morning when I saw, with closed eyes, the landscapes that I was to see in reality the same day. Then he said that I possess great magnetic power, now being developed. I asked him what I ought to do with this force. But without answering, he vanished.

I was alone, the door of my room locked. I thought I had had a hallucination and even told myself with fright that I was beginning to lose my mind. Hardly had this idea arisen when once again I saw the superb man in white robes. He shook his head and, smiling, said to me, "Be sure that I am no hallucination and that your reason is not quitting you. Blavatsky will prove to you tomorrow before everyone that my visit is real." Then he disappeared. I saw by my watch that it was three o'clock. I put out the candle and immediately went into a deep sleep.

Next morning, on going with Miss [de Glinka] to Madame Blavatsky, the first thing she said to us with an enigmatical smile was "Well! How have you passed the night?" "Very well," I replied and I added, "Haven't you anything to tell me?" "No," she replied, "I only know that the Master was with you with one of his pupils."

That same evening, Mr. Olcott found in his pocket a little note, that all the Theosophists said was in the handwriting of M: "Certainly I was there, but who can open the eyes of him who will not see."

This was the reply to my doubts, because all the day I had been trying to persuade myself that it was only a hallucination, and this made Madame Blavatsky angry.

I should say that on my return to Paris, where I am now, my hallucinations and the strange happenings that surrounded me have completely stopped.

16D. LAURA C. HOLLOWAY
AUGUST–OCTOBER 1884, ELBERFELD, GERMANY

[Holloway 1889]

Mme. Blavatsky could produce a sound like the chime of bells, low and sweet, but perfectly clear, and these were heard by us all under various conditions. She would know what was going on in other parts of the building, and one day reproached one of the party for something that was said in the park, fully a mile away from the castle. Her hostess said that Mme. B. had not left her room all the afternoon. I remember an occasion when I excused myself to go to my room to write. In the evening when we all assembled in the drawing room, I was astonished to have her say to me, "You have not written today. I saw you idling the time away." It was true that I had sat at the large window the entire afternoon, looking out upon the hills, watching the clouds and pondering over many things. Mme. Blavatsky had been much in my thoughts, as I considered the question—a grave one to me— of remaining longer with the party or of returning to England. She knew by some means what had been agitating my mind, and said to me as we passed down the stairs, "You will go back with me." I said to myself that I would not, but events so shaped themselves that I did travel back to London in her company.

She seemed to divine the future in many ways, and sometimes when she made prophecies, it was dreadful to hear her voice, she would be so excited and vehement. Curious study she was; curious things she did. Her powers were phenomenal and were exhibited without premeditation. With no ambition, no home, no home ties, no strong attachments, she seemed alone in the world, and was in many respects the most indifferent person I ever knew. Reckless in statement, defiant in action, she made enemies without thought and pained those who loved her with apparent indifference. Sometimes it would be my confidential opinion that she mesmerized those about her when she desired, but never could prove it. Her heart was not such a hard one, but she cared very little for manifestations of affection. She was alone in some sphere of her own, and none could know her intimately. I have been in the room with her when I felt her real self to be far away, and have seen her look at strangers once and talk of them as though their past lives were all before her.

She sat at the desk writing one day when I entered her room without invitation, and, putting on a bold front, walked directly to her with a sealed letter in my hand, which I had written to the guru, or teacher, who had sent me letters through her. "I want an answer to this letter, and I have come to ask you to send it, Madam." She railed at me, flew into a rage, demanded to know by what right I intruded upon her and ordered her to send letters to the Mahatmas. When she had concluded I quietly asked her to send it, adding that it was important. "Nothing that concerns the emotions of people is important," she retorted. "You all think that if you make a prayer it must have an immediate personal response from Jehovah. I am tired of nonsense." I coolly laid the letter on the table, sat down near to and facing her, and looked at my letter. She opened a drawer of the desk, which I saw was empty, and told me to put it there, I pushed the letter from the table into it and closed it myself. She leaned back in her chair, looked with some interest at me, and remarked that my will was developing. I told her that I had staked much in writing the letter, and its reply would influence my future course. Impelled by a sudden feeling I asked her if the letter had not gone, and not waiting for her to reply, I pulled open the drawer and it was not there. I looked for it carefully everywhere. Days after I met Mme. Blavatsky in the hall as she was going out to drive with one of the guests, and she put out her hand for me to assist her down the step. As I took her hand, I smilingly said, "Where's my letter?" She looked at me steadily for a moment, and it suddenly occurred to me, but why I do not know, that it was answered. I ran my hand into the pocket of my dress and there was a letter folded and sealed in a Chinese envelope.

The world has abused her more than almost any other woman of her day. She is an object of suspicion not only to individuals, but to governments, and she is defended by those who would count it a privilege to die for her. To a person who once asked her who she was, she said, with much simplicity of matter, "I am an old Buddhist pilgrim, wandering about the world to teach the only true religion, which is truth."

16E. C. W. LEADBEATER
OCTOBER 31, 1884, LONDON

[Leadbeater 1948, 57, 59–62]

I had addressed [a letter] to the Master Koot Hoomi. I received a reply eventually. [But] I knew of no way to send [another letter] to the Master but to take it to Madame Blavatsky, and as she was to leave England on the following day for India, I hastened up to London to see her.

It was with difficulty that I induced her to read the letter [from Master K.H.], as she said very decidedly that such communications were intended only for the recipient. I was obliged to insist, however, and at last she read it and asked me what I wished to say in reply. I answered and asked her how this information could be conveyed to the Master. She replied that he knew it already, referring of course to the exceedingly close relation in which she stood with him.

She then told me to wait by her, and not to leave her on any account. She adhered absolutely to this condition, even making me accompany her into her bedroom when she went to put on her hat and, when a cab was required, declining to allow me to leave the room and go to the door to whistle for it. I could not at all understand the purpose of this at the time, but afterwards I realized that she wished me to be able to say that she had never been out of my sight for a moment between the time when she read my letter from the Master and my receipt of the reply to it. I remember as vividly as if it were yesterday how I rode with her in that hansom cab, and the bashful embarrassment that I felt, caused partly by the honor of doing so, and partly by my fear that I must be inconveniencing her horribly, for I was crushed side ways into a tiny corner of the seat, while her huge bulk weighed down her side of the vehicle, so that the springs were grinding all through the journey. Mr. and Mrs. Cooper-Oakley were to accompany her on the voyage to India, and it was to their house that I went with her very late that night.

Even at that hour a number of devoted friends were gathered in Mrs. Oakley's drawing room to say farewell to Madame Blavatsky, who seated herself in an easy chair by the fireside. She was talking brilliantly to those who were present, and rolling one of her eternal cigarettes, when suddenly her right hand was jerked out towards the fire in a very peculiar fashion, and lay palm upwards. She looked down at it in surprise, as I did myself, for I was standing close to her, leaning with an elbow on the mantelpiece; and several of us saw quite clearly a sort of whitish mist form in the palm of her hand and then condense into a piece of folded paper, which she at once handed to me, saying "There is your answer." Every one in the room crowded round, of course, but she sent me away outside to read it, saying that I must not let anyone see its contents. It was a very short note.

16F. ISABEL COOPER-OAKLEY
NOVEMBER 1884, EGYPT

[HPB: In Memory, 14–5]

HPB [joined] Mr. Oakley and myself [during the middle of October] and remained with us until we started for India with her. The house party [in London] consisted of HPB, my sister [Laura Cooper], Dr. [Archibald] Keightley, Mr. Oakley, and myself. It was early in November 1884 that we left Liverpool for Port Said en route for Madras. It had been arranged that we were to go first to Cairo in order to get some definite information about the antecedents of the Coulombs, who were well known there, as the news of their treachery [against HPB] had already reached us some months before. We reached Port Said on the 17th of November 1884 and there remained some few days for Mr. Leadbeater to join us; on his arrival we took the mail boat down the Suez Canal to Ismailia, and then went by train to Cairo. HPB was a most interesting fellow traveler, her varied information about every part of Egypt was both extensive and extraordinary. Would that I had space to go into the details of that time in Cairo, the drives through the quaint and picturesque bazaars, and her descriptions of the people and their ways. Especially interesting was one long afternoon spent at the Boulak Museum on the borders of the Nile, where HPB astonished [Gaston] Maspero, the well-known Egyptologist, with her knowledge, and as we went through the museum she pointed out to him the grades of the Initiate kings and how they were to be known from the esoteric side. On leaving Cairo, HPB and I went straight to Suez. Mr. Oakley remained at Cairo to get documents from the police about the Coulombs; Mr. Leadbeater joined us at Suez.

16G. C. W. LEADBEATER
NOVEMBER 1884, EGYPT

[Leadbeater 1948, 68, 71, 73–7]

In those days there was no railway running from Port Said, and the only way in which we could reach Cairo was by traveling down the Suez Canal as far as Ismailia, whence we could take train to the capital. The journey down the canal was performed in a tiny little steamer somewhat like a tugboat. Every night it left

Port Said at midnight and reached Ismailia in the early morning.

In the pale gold of the Egyptian morning we moored beside the wharf at Ismailia. There was an interval of some hours before our train started, so it seemed reasonable to go to a hotel and have some breakfast. So in due course we took our places in the train.

As the journey continued Madame Blavatsky favored us with the most gloomy prognostications of our future fate.

"Ah! you Europeans," she said, "you think you are going to enter upon the path of occultism and pass triumphantly through all its troubles; you little know what is before you; you have not counted the wrecks by the wayside as I have. The Indians know what to expect, and they have already passed through tests and trials such as have never entered into your wildest dreams, but you, poor feeble things, what can you do?"

She continued these Cassandra-like prophecies with a maddening monotony, but her audience was far too reverential to try to change the subject. We sat in the four corners of the compartment, Madame Blavatsky facing the engine, Mr. Oakley sitting opposite to her with the resigned expression of an early Christian martyr; while Mrs. Oakley, weeping profusely, and with a face of ever-increasing horror, sat opposite to me.

In those days trains were usually lit by smoky oil lamps, and in the center of the roof of each compartment there was a large round hole into which porters inserted these lamps as they ran along the roofs of the carriages. This being a day train, however, there was no lamp, and one could see the blue sky through the hole. It happened that Mr. Oakley and I were both leaning back in our respective corners, so that we both saw a kind of ball of whitish mist forming in that hole, and a moment later it had condensed into a piece of folded paper, which fell to the floor of our compartment. I started forward, picked it up, and handed it at once to Madame Blavatsky, taking it for granted that any communication of this nature must be intended for her. She at once unfolded it and read it, and I saw a red flush appear upon her face.

"Umph," she said, "that's what I get for trying to warn you people of the troubles that lie before you," and she threw the paper to me.

"May I read it?" I said, and her only reply was, "Why do you think I gave it to you?"

I read it and found it to be a note signed by the Master Koot Hoomi, suggesting very gently but quite decidedly that it was perhaps a pity, when she had with her some earnest and enthusiastic candidates, to give them so very gloomy a view of a path which, however difficult it might be, was destined eventually to lead them to joy unspeakable. And then the message concluded with a few words of kindly commendation addressed to each of us by name.

I need hardly say that we were all much comforted and uplifted and filled with gratitude; but, though no rebuke could possibly have been more gently worded, it was evident that Madame Blavatsky did not altogether appreciate it. Before our conversation began she had been reading some book which she wished to review for the *Theosophist*, and she was still sitting with the book open upon her knee and the paperknife in her hand. She now resumed her reading, stroking the dust of the desert (which came pouring in at the open window) off the pages of the book with her paper-knife as she read. When an especially vicious puff came in, Mr. Oakley started forward and made a motion as if to close the window; but Madame Blavatsky looked up at him balefully, and said with unmeasured scorn, "You don't mind a little dust, do you?" Poor Mr. Oakley shrank back into his corner like a snail into its shell, and not another word did our leader utter until we steamed into the station at Cairo. The dust certainly was rather trying, but after that one remark we thought it best to suffer it in silence.

16H. ISABEL COOPER-OAKLEY
DECEMBER 1884 – MARCH 1885, ADYAR, MADRAS, INDIA

[HPB: In Memory, 15–7]

On leaving Cairo, HPB and I went straight to Suez. After waiting two days for the steamer we started for Madras. Col.

Olcott and some members met us at Colombo [Ceylon], and we stayed there nearly two days, paying some deeply interesting visits to the old Buddhist Temples, and one especially charming visit to Sumangala, the High Priest, who evidently had a very high respect for HPB. We then proceeded to Madras. Never shall I forget the quaint picturesqueness of our arrival [at Madras on December 21st]. A deputation, accompanied by a brass band, came off in boats to meet us; but the sound of the music was somewhat marred by the fact that the drop between the waves is so great that sometimes our band was on the top of a high roller, and sometimes almost engulfed between two big waves. On landing at the pier head, there were hundreds to meet HPB, and we were literally towed by enthusiastic members down the pier in a truck, wildly decorated with paper roses, etc., and then surrounded by masses of smiling dark faces. She was driven off to Pachiappah Hall, where we had garlands of pink roses festooned round us and were sprinkled somewhat copiously with rose water. Then HPB and I were conducted by a Rajah to his carriage and driven off to Adyar. Here the warmest welcome awaited her. Members were assembling from all parts of India for the approaching [Theosophical Society] Convention; we went into the large hall and at once began discussing the all-absorbing Coulomb case.

Col. Olcott then informed us that the Society of Psychical Research [London] was sending out a member to investigate the matter, and accordingly a few days after, the notorious [Richard] Hodgson arrived fresh from Cambridge. Mr. Hodgson was an Australian by birth. I am quite confident that if an older man had come, one with more experience and a maturer judgment, the Coulomb affair would have been presented to the world in a very different way. Mr. Hodgson's investigations were not conducted with an unbiased mind, and from hearing everyone say Madame Blavatsky was an impostor he began to believe it: after a few interviews with Madame Coulomb and the missionaries, we saw that his views were turning against the minority.

Now his report was not by any means accurate, for he omitted some very valuable evidence of phenomena given to him by

Mr. Oakley and myself. Mr. Hodgson was treated with the greatest courtesy and friendliness by HPB and Col. Olcott, and every opportunity was afforded him for investigating every hole and corner at Adyar; and yet he preferred, and gave more credence to, the testimony of a discharged servant, whose bad character was by that time universally known, than to that of HPB and her friends, who had no monetary interest in giving their evidence.

The trap doors and sliding panels had all been made by [Alexis] Coulomb, in HPB's absence, and his wife sold the character of [HPB] who had saved her from starvation to the missionaries and forged the letters she showed to them. Any person of ordinary intellect and common sense could see that the trap doors and sliding panels were quite new, so new as to be immovable, *the grooves being quite fresh and unmarked by any* usage whatever, as Mr. Oakley and I found when we tried to move the largest sliding door. If we could not do so with our combined efforts, surely it is ridiculous to think Madame Blavatsky could have used them for conjuring tricks; the arrangements were so bad that any trick would have been inevitably discovered. However Mr. Hodgson was so bent on being a "success" that these simple commonsense facts were disregarded by him.

Immediately after the convention was over he left [Adyar] Headquarters, and went to live in Madras, until his investigations were ended.

The effect of all this worry was that [HPB] became seriously ill. Col. Olcott had started for Burma, Mr. Oakley and I were comparatively alone with her. Very anxious were the hours and days of nursing that I went through those three weeks, as she grew worse and worse and was finally given up in a state of coma by the doctors. It proves how wonderful was the protective influence of HPB, ill or well; for though I was completely isolated with her near the roof of the house, an open staircase leading up, hardly a soul within call, yet night after night have I wandered up and down the flat roof, to get a breath of fresh air between 3 and 4 a.m., and wondered as I watched the daylight break over the Bay of Bengal, why I felt so fearless even with her lying apparently at the point of death; I never could imagine a sense of fear coming near HPB.

Finally came the anxious night when the doctors gave her up, and said that nothing could be done, it was impossible. She was then in a state of coma and had been so for some hours. The doctors said that she would pass away in that condition, and I know, humanly speaking, that night's watch must be the last. I cannot here go into what happened, an experience I can never forget; but towards 8 a.m. HPB suddenly opened her eyes and asked for her breakfast, the first time she had spoken naturally for two days. I went to meet the doctor, whose amazement at the change was very great. HPB said, "Ah! doctor, you do not believe in our great Masters." From that time she steadily improved. The doctor insisted on her being sent to Europe as soon as possible.

161. RICHARD HODGSON
DECEMBER 1884 – MARCH 1885,
MADRAS, INDIA

*[Hodgson 1885, 3:207–9, 261–2, 249–50,
241, 239, 245–6, 313–4, 317]*

In November [1884] I proceeded to India for the purpose of investigating on the spot the evidence of the phenomena connected with the Theosophical Society. [Monsieur] and Madame Coulomb, who had been attached to the Theosophical Society for several years in positions of trust, had charged Madame Blavatsky with fraud and had adduced in support of their charge various letters and other documents alleged by them to have been written by Madame Blavatsky.

From these Blavatsky-Coulomb documents, it appears that Mahatma letters were prepared and sent by Madame Blavatsky;

that Koot Hoomi is a fictitious personage; that supposed "astral forms" of the Mahatmas were confederates of Madame Blavatsky in disguise—generally the Coulombs; that alleged [occult] phenomena—some of them in connection with the so-called Shrine at Adyar—were ingenious trickeries carried out by Madame Blavatsky with the assistance chiefly of the Coulombs.

Other apparently important phenomena had come before us which were not directly discredited by the Blavatsky-Coulomb letters. We may take the "raps" which Mr. [A. P.] Sinnett seems to regard as constituting important test phenomena. The raps occurring when Madame Blavatsky places her hands upon the patient's head, I have experienced, though as Madame Blavatsky sat behind me and placed her hands upon the back of my head, I was unable to watch her fingers. She had not informed me what she intended doing, and I conjectured that she was attempting to "mesmerize" me; the so-called shocks which I felt impressed me simply as movements of impatience on the part of Madame Blavatsky. My attention being then drawn to them as "phenomena," they were repeated, but I found them not at all like the "shocks" experienced when taking off sparks from the conductor of an electrical machine, as Mr. Sinnett describes them. The sharp thrilling or tingling feeling was quite absent. Unfortunately, I am unable to gently crack any of the joints of my fingers, I can but clumsily and undisguisedly crack one of the joints of my thumbs, yet I find that the *quality* of the feeling produced when I thus crack my thumb joint against my head exactly resembles that which I perceived under the supple hands of Madame Blavatsky.

I [also] called upon the Coulombs, who are living at the house of Mrs. Dyer. I conversed a short time with [Monsieur Alexis] Coulomb before Madame [Emma] Coulomb appeared. In the course of the conversation that followed I remarked, concerning certain cases of premonition, that I had no satisfactory theory at present to account for them. At this moment something white appeared, touching my hair, and fell on the floor. It was a letter. I picked it up. It was addressed to myself. M. and Madame Coulomb were sitting near me and in front of me. I had observed no motion on their part which could account for the appearance of the letter. Examining the ceiling as I stood I could detect no flaw; it appeared intact. On opening the letter, I found it referred to the conversation which had just taken place. I transcribe the words:

Because the existing cause of today foretells the effect of tomorrow— a bud assures us beforehand the full-blown rose of tomorrow; on seeing a fine field of corn in which are buried eggs of locusts, we are to foresee that that corn will never enter the granary; by the appearance of consumptive father and scrofulous mother a sickly child can be foretold. Now all these causes, which bring to us these effects, have in their turn their effects themselves, and so, *ad infinitum*; and as nothing is lost in Nature, but remains impressed in the *akasa*, so the acute perception of the seer beginning at the source arrives at the result with exactitude.

THE NEW ADEPT, COLUMBUS.

[Monsieur] Coulomb then described the origin of the letter. A large beam supported the ceiling, and resting on this, at right angles to it, was a series of small beams with spaces between them. These spaces were filled with blocks of wood, with mortar to keep them in place. Part of this mortar had been scraped out on the top of the large beam and between two smaller ones, so that a letter could be inserted and lie flat on the top of the large beam. Round the letter was twice passed a piece of thread of the same color as the ceiling. One end of the thread remained loose on the letter, the other end was in the hand of the person outside the room. The thread ran from the letter, close to the ceiling, passed outside and hung down. I was sitting under the main beam. The subject of conversation was led up to, and at the given signal (a call to the dog) the confederate in the verandah beyond pulled the thread and the letter fell. The confederate drew the thread entirely away and left the spot. The crevice for the letter might, in a few moments, have been stopped up and covered with dust, so that no aperture whatever appeared in the neighborhood of the ceiling.

The ceiling of Madame Blavatsky's sitting room was constructed in the same way as the one here described, and would, therefore, be suited for the occurrence of similar phenomena.

I [also] was left without any doubt that the [astral] appearances [of the Mahatmas] might have been well produced by [Monsieur] Coulomb in disguise. I have seen [Monsieur] Coulomb disguised as a Mahatma, and can understand that the figure may have been very impressive. A dummy head (with shoulders), like that of a Hindu, with beard, &c. and fehta [turban], is worn on the top of the head of the person disguised. A long flowing muslin garment falls down in front, and by holding the folds very slightly apart, the wearer is enabled to see, and to speak also, if necessary. I do not think it in the least degree likely that any of the witnesses would have penetrated this disguise had the figure been even much nearer than it was, and the light much better.

I cannot regard Colonel Olcott's testimony as of any scientific value. In particular, his testimony to the alleged "astral" appearance [of the Mahatma Morya] in New York proves, in my opinion, no more than that he saw someone in his room, who may have been an ordinary Hindu, or some other person, disguised as a Mahatma for the purpose, and acting for Madame Blavatsky. And the same may be said of all his testimony to apparitions of Mahatmas.

I need not here say much on the other alleged appearances of Mahatmas, in either their ordinary physical or their "astral" bodies. A confederate in disguise is generally an easy and sufficient explanation of them. There is no real difficulty in applying this explanation even to the case of Mr. Ramaswamier, whose account of his experience has made so much impression on Mr. Sinnett.

The question which will now inevitably arise is—what has induced Madame Blavatsky to live so many laborious days in such a fantastic work of imposture? I must confess that the problem of her motives, when I found myself being forced to the conclusion that her claims and her phenomena were fraudulent, caused me no little perplexity.

At last a casual conversation opened my eyes. I had put aside as unworthy of consideration the idea that the objects of the Theosophical Society were political and that Madame Blavatsky was a "Russian spy." But a conversation with Madame Blavatsky, which arose out of her sudden and curious excitement at the news of the recent Russian movement upon the Afghan frontier, compelled me to ask myself seriously whether it was not possible that the task which she had set herself to perform in India was to foster and foment as widely as possible among the natives a disaffection towards British rule.

I cannot profess myself, after my personal experiences of Madame Blavatsky, to feel much doubt that her real object has been the furtherance of Russian interests. But although I have felt bound to refer to my own view on this point, I suggest it here only as a supposition which appears best to cover the known incidents of her career during the past 13 or 14 years.

That she is a remarkably able woman will scarcely be questioned by any. It would be no venturesome prognostication to say that, in spite of recent exposures, she will still retain a goodly gathering of disciples on whom she may continue to inculcate the ethics of profound obedience to the behests of imaginary Mahatmas. The resources of Madame Blavatsky are great; and by the means of forged letters, fraudulent statements of chelas, and other false evidence, she may yet do much in the future for the benefit of human credulity. But acting in accordance with the principles upon which our Society [for Psychical Research] has proceeded, I must express my unqualified opinion that no genuine psychical phenomena whatever will be found among the pseudo-mysteries of the Russian lady alias Koot Hoomi Lal Sing alias Mahatma Morya alias Madame Blavatsky.

16J. HENRY S. OLCOTT
FEBRUARY 7–8, 1885, ADYAR, MADRAS, INDIA

[Olcott 1932, 732–4]

Again has our Master [Morya] snatched HPB from the jaws of death. A few days ago she was dying and I was recalled from Burma by telegraph, with little or no prospect of seeing her again. But, when three physicians were expecting her to sink into coma and so pass senseless out of life, *He* came, laid his hand upon her, and the whole aspect of the case changed.

The day before yesterday things looked so bad that Subba Row and Damodar lost heart and got quite panicky and said the T.S. would go to the dogs. Well, yesterday came here a certain Indian yogi, dressed in the usual saffron robes, and accompanied by a female ascetic—his supposed disciple. I was called, came and sat down, and we stared at each other in silence. Then he closed his eyes, concentrated himself, and gave me psychically his message. He had been sent by the Mahatma [Narayana] at Tirivellum (the one who dictated to HPB the "Replies to an English F.T.S.") to assure me that I should *not* be left alone. He recalled to me my conversation of the 7th with [Damodar] and [Subba Row]. And he asked me (mentally) if I could for a moment have believed that he, who had always been so true to me, would leave me to go on without help. Then he and his Maya of a she-chela went up to HPB's sick-chamber, and she—contrary to every Hindu usage for females of the sort—went straight at the [Old Lady] and made passes over her, and at the Guru's command began to recite mantrams. Then the Guru took from beneath his robe a ball, the size of an orange, of the *nirukti* or sacred ashes used in Hindu temples for external application after the bath, and told the disciple to put it in a small cupboard that hangs over the head of HPB's bed. He told the latter that when she needed him she should simply think of him *in his present visible form* and mentally repeat his name thrice. Then there was some conversation all around, and they went away.

Vera and Charles Johnston with Henry Olcott standing behind
HPB and her sister, Vera de Zhelihovsky, London, 1888

Chapter 17

FROM INDIA TO
ITALY AND GERMANY
1885–1886

ICHARD HODGSON gave a preliminary report on his
investigation into HPB's phenomena at two meetings
of the Society for Psychical Research (SPR) held on
May 29 and June 26, 1885, when Charles Johnston was present
(selection 17a). The vicious attack on H. P. Blavatsky by the
Coulombs having affected her health, she left India for Europe,
settling first in Italy. In late July 1885, HPB left Italy and after
stopping briefly in St. Cergues, Switzerland, arrived in Würzburg,
Germany, toward the middle of August. There she was visited by
a number of friends, including the Sinnetts (selection 17b), before
she settled down to work on *The Secret Doctrine*.

In late 1885, while writing *The Secret Doctrine*, HPB was
joined by the Countess Wachtmeister, who became her companion and assistant. Their quiet, productive life was interrupted,
however, by the arrival on the last day of the year of a copy of the

SPR report. After the initial shock of the report, HPB resumed work on the new book, and the Countess reported a number of unusual techniques in the process of composition (selection 17d). At the same time, HPB received a number of visitors, including Emily Kislingbury and Mary and Gustav Gebhard. In early May 1886, Countess Wachtmeister left Würzburg with Mary Gebhard to visit Franz Hartmann in Austria; at the same time HPB left Würzburg with Miss Kislingbury to spend the summer in Ostend, Belgium. However, Gustav Gebhard persuaded HPB to stop for a visit with him at Elberfeld (a German town in the Ruhr Valley, now incorporated into the city of Wuppertal). HPB was visited there by her sister, Vera Zhelihovsky, and niece, Vera, who was later to marry Charles Johnston (selection 17e).

17A. CHARLES JOHNSTON
JUNE 1885, LONDON

[Johnston 1907, 17–8]

During 1884, the "Society for Psychical Research" had become deeply interested in the phenomena described in *The Occult World* and in Mme. Blavatsky's magazine, *The Theosophist*, and had appointed a Committee to investigate these phenomena. A very favorable preliminary report had been issued.* It was decided to supplement this preliminary work by further investigation in India, and a young student of psychic phenomena, Mr. Richard Hodgson, was asked to go to India to carry this out.

During this period, events had been happening at Adyar, near Madras, the headquarters of the Theosophical Society. While Mme. Blavatsky and Colonel Olcott were absent in Europe, two members of the Society, [Alexis] and [Emma] Coulomb, who had for years been sheltered at the headquarters at Bombay and Madras, were asked to withdraw. There were charges of misappropriation of funds, evil speaking and trickery, which made it inexpedient for them to remain at the central office of the Society in a position of trust.

These two persons presently retaliated by making an attack on Mme. Blavatsky, to which publicity was given by a Madras [Christian] missionary organ, and in which it was asserted that the phenomena described in *The Occult World* and elsewhere were tricks, and that many of them had been produced by these two members [the Coulombs], who now repented of their misdeeds. Letters were published by them, which they said had been written by Mme. Blavatsky, and which gave color to the charge of fraud; but the originals of these letters were never available for impartial examination, and the alleged copies were full of mistakes, vulgarity and puerility, and bore little resemblance to the genuine letters of the great Theosophical writer.

Mr. Richard Hodgson arrived in India shortly after this attack was made. He found something congenial in the thought and methods of these two retired members who accused themselves of fraud, and he practically adopted their views and pretensions as to the whole of the phenomena he had been sent to investigate. He spent a short time in India, and returned to England early in 1885. Toward the end of June 1885, he read a part of his Report on the phenomena before a meeting of the Society for Psychical Research.

That meeting made an epoch in the attitude of public opinion toward the Theosophical Movement. Never sympathetic, public opinion thereafter became frankly hostile and incredulous. Mme. Blavatsky was treated as an imposter, and her friends as fools. The public accepted Mr. Hodgson's view without question or examination.

With others, I was present at that fateful meeting. After Mr. Hodgson had read his Report, members of the Committee went among the audience to discuss it. Mr. F. W. H. Myers was one of these. When he asked what impression the meeting had made on me, I remember replying that the whole thing was so scandalously unfair that, had I not been a member of the Theosophical

Society, I should have joined it forthwith, on the strength of Mr. Hodgson's performance.

*[The "very favorable preliminary report" of 130 pages was printed by the Society for Psychical Research in 1884 as *First Report of the Committee of the Society for Psychical Research, Appointed to Investigate the Evidence for Marvellous Phenomena offered by Certain Members of the Theosophical Society*. Although now very rare in its original edition, this report is available on the Web at the following URL:http://sites.netscape.net/dhcblainfo/sprrpcontents.htm. —DHC]

17 B. A. P. SINNETT
APRIL–OCTOBER 1885,
WÜRZBURG, GERMANY

[Collated from Sinnett 1922, 79, 83;
and Sinnett 1886, 302–3]

[Leaving India, Madame Blavatsky] arrived in Naples [Italy] some time in April 1885, and went to a hotel at Torre del Greco, near by. Madame Blavatsky only stayed a few months at Torre del Greco and then went on to Würzburg [Germany]. My wife and I went to see her at Würzburg in the course of our autumn tour in 1885. She was staying at 6 Ludwigstrasse.

The "Secret Doctrine" was still untouched in September 1885, when my wife and I saw her. We found her settled in an economical way, but in comfort and quietude, cheered just then by the companionship of her aunt, Mme. de Fadeyev. She was naturally seething with indignation at the wrongs she had suffered at the hands of the S.P.R. committee. On the whole, however, she seemed in better health and spirits than we expected, and some premonitory symptoms indicated that the preparation of the "Secret Doctrine" might shortly be set on foot.

A month or so after our return to London in October I received a note from Mme. Blavatsky, in the course of which she wrote:

I am very busy on 'Secret D.' The thing at New York [meaning the circumstances under which *Isis Unveiled* was written] is repeated—only far clearer and better. I begin to think it shall vindicate us. Such pictures, panoramas, scenes, antediluvian dramas, with all that! Never saw or heard better.

Countess Constance Wachtmeister

17 c. Countess Constance Wachtmeister October–December 1885, Würzburg, Germany

[Wachtmeister 1893, 16–21, 22–3, 25–6, 32]

In the autumn of 1885, I was making preparations to leave my home in Sweden to spend the winter with some friends in

Italy, and incidentally, *en route* to pay Madame Gebhard a promised visit at her residence in Elberfeld [Germany].

It was while I was engaged in putting my affairs in order, in view of my long absence, that an incident occurred, not indeed singular in my experience, but out of the normal. I was arranging and laying aside the articles I intended to take with me to Italy when I heard a voice saying, "Take that book, it will be useful to you on your journey." I may as well say at once that I have the faculties of clairvoyance and clairaudience rather strongly developed. I turned my eyes on a manuscript volume I had placed among the heap of things to be locked away until my return. Certainly it seemed a singular inappropriate *vade mecum* for a holiday, being a collection of notes on the Tarot and passages in the Kabbalah that had been compiled for me by a friend. However, I decided to take it with me, and laid the book in the bottom of one of my traveling trunks.

At last the day came for me to leave Sweden, in October 1885, and I arrived at Elberfeld, where I met with a cordial and affectionate greeting from Madame Gebhard. However, the time was drawing near for me to pass on into Italy. My friends never ceased pressing me to join them there, and at last the date of my departure was fixed.

When I told Madame Gebhard that I must leave her in a few days, she spoke to me of a letter she had received from HPB. She was ill in body and depressed in mind. Her sole companions were her servant and an Indian gentleman. "Go to her," said Madame Gebhard, "she needs sympathy, and you can cheer her up."

I thought the matter over. Madame Gebhard was genuinely pleased when I made known my decision to her and showed her a letter I had written to "the old lady" in Würzburg suggesting that if she cared to receive me I would spend a few weeks with her. The letter was dispatched, and we waited eagerly for the reply. When at last it lay upon the breakfast table, there was much excitement in regard to its contents, but anticipation soon turned into consternation on Madame Gebhard's part and disappointment on mine, when we found nothing more nor less than a polite refusal.

Madame Blavatsky was sorry, but she had no room for me; besides, she was so occupied in writing her *Secret Doctrine* that she had no time to entertain visitors, but hoped we might meet on my return from Italy. After the first natural disappointment, I set my eyes hopefully southward.

My luggage was soon ready, and a cab was actually waiting for me at the door when a telegram was put into my hands containing these words, "Come to Würzburg at once, wanted immediately—Blavatsky."

It may easily be imagined that this message took me by surprise. There was no resisting and instead of taking my ticket to Rome I took one to Würzburg.

It was evening when I reached Madame Blavatsky's lodgings, and as I mounted the stairs my pulse was a little hurried while I speculated upon the reception which awaited me.

Madame Blavatsky's welcome was a warm one, and after the first few words of greeting, she remarked, "I have to apologize to you for behaving so strangely. I will tell you the truth, which is, that I did not want you. I have only one bedroom here, and I thought that you might be a fine lady and not care to share it with me. My ways are probably not your ways. If you came to me I knew that you would have to put up with many things that might seem to you intolerable discomforts. That is why I decided to decline your offer, and I wrote to you in that sense; but after my letter was posted Master spoke to me and said that I was to tell you to come. I never disobey a word from Master, and I telegraphed at once. Since then I have been trying to make the bedroom more habitable. I have bought a large screen which will divide the room, so that you can have one side and I, the other, and I hope you will not be too uncomfortable."

I replied that whatever the surroundings to which I had been accustomed might have been, I would willingly relinquish them all for the pleasure of her companionship.

I remember very well that it was then, on going into the dining room together to take some tea, that she said to me abruptly, as of something that had been dwelling on her mind.

"Master says you have a book for me of which I am much in need."

"No, indeed," I replied, "I have no books with me."

"Think again," she said, "Master says you were told in Sweden to bring a book on the Tarot and the Kabbalah."

Then I recollected the circumstances that I have related before. From the time I had placed the volume in the bottom of my box it had been out of my sight and out of my mind. Now, when I hurried to the bedroom, unlocked the trunk, and dived to the bottom, I found it in the same corner I had left it when packing in Sweden, undisturbed from that moment to this. But this was not all. When I returned to the dining room with it in my hand, Madame Blavatsky made a gesture and cried, "Stay, do not open it yet. Now turn to page ten and on the sixth line you will find the words . . . ." And she quoted a passage.

I opened the book which, let it be remembered, was no printed volume of which there might be a copy in HPB's possession, but a manuscript album in which had been written notes and excerpts by a friend of mine for my own use; yet, on the page and at the line she had indicated, I found the very words she had uttered.

When I handed her the book I ventured to ask her why she wanted it.

"Oh," she replied, "for *The Secret Doctrine*. That is my new work that I am so busily engaged in writing. Master is collecting material for me. He knew you had the book and told you to bring it that it might be at hand for reference."

No work was done that first evening, but the next day I began to realize what the course of HPB's life was, and what mine was likely to be while I stayed with her.

The description of a single day will serve to give an idea of the routine of her life at this time.

At six o'clock I was awakened by the servant coming with a cup of coffee for Madame Blavatsky, who, after this slight refreshment rose and dressed, and by seven o'clock was at her desk in the sitting room.

She told me that this was her invariable habit, and that breakfast would be served at eight. After breakfast she settled herself at her writing desk and the day's work began in earnest. At one o'clock dinner was served, whereupon I rang a small hand bell to call HPB. Sometimes she would come in at once; at other times her door would remain closed hour after hour, until our Swiss maid would come to me, almost with tears in her eyes, to ask what was to be done with Madame's dinner, which was either getting cold, or dried up, burnt, and utterly spoiled. At last, HPB would come in weary with so many hours of exhausting labor and fasting; then another dinner would be cooked, or I would send to the Hotel to get her some nourishing food.

At seven o'clock she laid aside her writing, and after tea we would spend a pleasant evening together.

Comfortably seated in her big armchair, HPB used to arrange her cards for a game of Patience, as she said, to rest her mind. It seems as if the mechanical process of laying her cards enabled her mind to free itself from the pressure of concentrated labor during the day's work. She never cared to talk of Theosophy in the evenings. The mental tension during the day was so severe that she needed above all things rest, and so I procured as many journals and magazines as I could, and from these I would read the articles and passages that I thought most likely to interest and amuse her. At nine o'clock she went to bed, where she would surround herself with her Russian newspapers and read them until a late hour.

It was thus our days passed in the same routine; the only change worth noticing being that sometimes she would leave the door open between her writing room and the dining room where I sat, and then from time to time we would converse together, or I would write letters for her, or discuss the contents of those we had received.

The quiet, studious life continued for some little time, and the work progressed steadily, until, one morning, a thunderbolt descended upon us. Without a word of warning, HPB received a copy of the well-known *Report of the Society for Psychical Research.* I shall never forget that day nor the look of blank and stony despair that she cast on me when I entered her sitting room and found her with the book open in her hands.

"This," she cried, "is the karma of the Theosophical Society, and it falls upon me. I am the scapegoat. I am made to bear all the sins of the Society, and now that I am dubbed the greatest impostor of the age, and a Russian spy into the bargain, who will listen to me or read *The Secret Doctrine*? How can I carry on Master's work? O cursed phenomena, which I only produced to please private friends and instruct those around me. What an awful karma to bear! How shall I live through it? If I die Master's work will be wasted, and the Society will be ruined!"

In the intensity of her passion at first she would not listen to reason, but turned against me, saying, "Why don't you go? Why don't you leave me? You are a Countess, you cannot stop here with a ruined woman, with one held up to scorn before the whole world, one who will be pointed at everywhere as a trickster and an impostor. Go before you are defiled by my shame."

"HPB," I said, as my eyes met hers with a steady gaze, "you know that Master lives and that he is your Master, and that the Theosophical Society was founded by him. How, then, can it perish? And since I know this as well as you, since for me, now, the truth has been placed beyond the possibility of doubt, how can you for one moment suppose that I could desert you and the cause we both are pledged to serve? Why, if every member of the Theosophical Society should prove traitor to that cause you and I would remain, and would wait and work until the good times come again."

It is little to be wondered at that the progress of *The Secret Doctrine* was brought to a standstill during these stormy days, and that when at last the work was resumed, the necessary detachment and tranquility of mind were found hard of attainment.

17D. COUNTESS CONSTANCE WACHTMEISTER
JANUARY–MAY 1886,
WÜRZBURG, GERMANY

[Wachtmeister 1893, 32–3,
43–5, 49–50, 55–56, 59–61]

One day at this time, when I walked into HPB's writing room, I found the floor strewn with sheets of discarded manuscript. I asked the meaning of this scene of confusion, and she replied, "Yes, I have tried twelve times to write this one page correctly, and each time Master says it is wrong. I think I shall go mad, writing it so often; but leave me alone, I will not pause until I have conquered it, even if I have to go on all night."

I brought a cup of coffee to refresh and sustain her, and then left her to prosecute her weary task. An hour later I heard her voice calling me, and on entering found that, at last, the passage was completed to satisfaction, but the labor had been terrible, and the results were often at this time small and uncertain.

As she leant back enjoying her cigarette and the sense of relief from arduous effort, I rested on the arm of her great chair and asked her how it was she could make mistakes in setting down what was given to her. She said: "Well, you see, what I do is this. I make what I can only describe as a sort of vacuum in the air before me, and fix my sight and my will upon it, and soon scene after scene passes before me like the successive pictures of a diorama, or, if I need a reference or information from some book, I fix my mind intently, and the astral counterpart of the book appears, and from it I take what I need. The more perfectly my mind is freed from distractions and mortifications, the more energy and intentness it possesses, the more easily I can do this; but today, after all the vexations I have undergone, I could not concentrate properly, and each time I tried I got the quotations all wrong. Master says it is right now, so let us go in and have some tea."

Living in such close and familiar intercourse with HPB as I did at this time, it naturally happened that I was a witness of many of the phenomena which took place in her vicinity.

There was one occurrence, continuously repeated over a long period, which impressed me very strongly with the conviction that she was watched and cared for by unseen guardians. From the first night that I passed in her room, until the last that preceded our departure from Würzburg, I heard a regularly intermittent series of raps on the table by her bedside. They would begin at ten o'clock each evening, and would continue, at intervals of ten minutes, until six o'clock in the morning. They were sharp, clear raps, such as I never heard at any other time. Sometimes I held my watch in my hand for an hour at a stretch, and always as the minute interval ticked itself out, the rap would come with the most regularity. Whether HPB was awake or asleep mattered nothing to the occurrence of the phenomenon, nor to its uniformity.

When I asked her for an explanation of these raps I was told that it was an effect of what might be called a sort of psychic tele-graph which placed her in communication with her Teachers, and that the chelas might watch her body while her astral left it.

Another incident proved to me that there were agencies at work in her neighborhood whose nature and action were inex-plicable on generally accepted theories of the constitution and laws of matter.

As I have already remarked, HPB was accustomed to read her Russian newspapers at night after retiring, and it was rarely that she extinguished her lamp before midnight. There was a screen between my bed and this lamp, but, nevertheless, its powerful rays, reflected from the ceiling and the walls, often disturbed my sleep. One night this lamp was burning after the clock had struck one. I could not sleep, and, as I heard by HPB's regular breathing that she slept, I rose, gently walked round to the lamp, and turned it out. There was always a dim light pervading the bedroom, which came from a nightlight burning in the study, the door between that room and the bedroom being kept open. I had extin-guished the lamp, and was going back, when it flamed up again, and the room was brightly illuminated. I thought to myself—what a strange lamp, I suppose the spring does not act, so I put my hand again on the spring, and watched until every vestige of flame was extinct, and, even then, held down the spring for a minute. Then I released it and stood for a moment longer watching, when, to my surprise, the flame reappeared and the lamp was burning as brightly as ever. This puzzled me considerably, and I determined to stand there by that lamp and put it out all through the night, if necessary, until I discovered the why and wherefore of its eccentricities. For the third time I pressed the spring and turned it down until the lamp was quite out, and then released it, watching eagerly to see what would take place. For the third time the lamp burned up, and this time I saw a brown hand slowly and gently turning the knob of the lamp. Familiar as I was with the action of astral forces and astral entities on the physical plane, I had no difficulty in coming to the conclusion that it was the hand of a chela, and, surmising that there was some reason why the lamp should remain alight, I returned to my couch. But a spirit of perversity and curiosity dwelt within me that night. I wanted to know more, so I called out, "Madame Blavatsky!" then, louder, "Madame Blavatsky!" and again "Madame Blavatsky!" Suddenly I heard an answering cry: "Oh, my heart! my heart! Countess, you have nearly killed me"; and then again, "My heart! my heart!" I flew to HPB's bedside. "I was with Master," she murmured, "why did you call me back?" I was thoroughly alarmed, for her heart fluttered under my hand with wild palpitation.

I gave her a dose of digitalis, and sat beside her until the symptoms had abated and she had become calmer. Then she told me how Colonel Olcott had once nearly killed her in the same way, by calling her back suddenly when her astral form was absent from her body. She made me promise that I would never try experiments with her again, and this promise I readily gave, out of the fullness of my grief and contrition for having caused her such suffering.

We had a small, but very comfortable, apartment in Würzburg; the rooms were of a good size, lofty, and on the ground floor so as to enable HPB to move in and out in comfort. But during all the time that I was with her I could only persuade her to take fresh air three times. She seemed to enjoy these drives, but the trouble and exertion of preparing for them wearied her, and she esteemed them mere loss of time. I was in the habit of going out daily for half an hour, as I felt that both air and exercise were necessary for my health, and I recall a curious incident which happened to me in connection with one of these walks. As I passed a perfumer's shop, I saw some soap in a glass bowl in the display window. Remembering that I required some, I walked into the shop and chose a piece from the bowl. I saw the shop man wrap paper around it, took the parcel from his hand, put it in my pocket, and continued my walk. When I returned to my apartment I went straight to my room, without first going to see HPB, and took off my hat and cloak. Taking the parcel out of my pocket, I began to unfasten the string and pull off the wrappings, and, as I did so, I perceived a small sheet of folded paper inside. I could not help thinking, how fond people are of advertisements, they even stick them on a cake of soap! But then I suddenly remembered that I had seen the man fasten up the parcel, and that he assuredly had not inserted any. This struck me as strange, and, as the paper had fallen to the ground, I stooped down and picked it up, opened it, and there found a few remarks addressed to me from HPB's Master in his handwriting, which I had often seen before. They were an explanation of events which had been puzzling me for some days past, and gave me some directions as to my future course of action. This phenomenon was peculiarly interesting to me as having taken place without HPB's knowledge, and independently of her, for she was writing quite unconcernedly at her table in her writing room at the time.

I have been lingering on many points which have nothing directly to do with the writing of *The Secret Doctrine*; but it seems to me that by showing some of the details of HPB's life at that time, one gains a better comprehension of the woman who wrote that stupendous work. Day after day she would sit there writing through all the long hours, and nothing could be more monotonous and wearisome than her life regarded from an outside point of view. But, I suppose, at that time she lived much in the inner world, and there saw sights and visions which compensated for the dreariness of her daily life. She had, however, a distraction of rather a peculiar nature. In front of her writing table, attached to the wall, was a cuckoo clock, and this used to behave in a very extraordinary manner. Sometimes it would strike like a loud gong, then sigh and groan as if possessed, cuckooing in the most unexpected way. Our maid, Louise was very much afraid of it, and told us solemnly one day that she thought the devil was in it. "Not that I believe in the devil," she said, "but this cuckoo almost speaks to me at times." And so it did. One evening I went into the room and saw what appeared to me like streams of electric light coming out of the clock in all directions. On telling HPB she replied, "Oh, it is only the spiritual telegraph, they are laying it on stronger tonight on account of tomorrow's work." Living in this atmosphere and coming into contact so continually with these, usually unseen, forces, this all seemed the true reality to me, and the outer world was that which appeared vague and unsatisfactory.

But the winter sped by, and the spring came on, and one morning HPB received a letter from a friend of several years' standing, Miss [Emily] Kislingbury, who wrote that she would come and pay us a visit. At this time, too, we received a visit from Mr. and Madame Gebhard. As we were now in full spring it was time to think of our summer plans, and HPB decided to spend the ensuing summer months at Ostend with her sister and niece.

Madame Gebhard was anxious to make a short stay in Austria and persuaded me to accompany her to Kempten. We made our plans, and began the arduous task of packing. In a few days all HPB's boxes were corded and locked and the eventful journey was about to begin. Miss Kislingbury was returning to London, and kindly promised to accompany HPB as far as Ostend.

It was always a formidable thing for HPB to travel, and I looked in dismay at the nine packages which were to be placed inside her railway carriage. We started very early to go to the station, and there we seated HPB, surrounded by her numerous belongings, while we tried to make arrangements with the conductor to let her be alone in the compartment with Miss Kislingbury and her maid, Louise. Then began the serious task of piling up all the baggage, consisting of pillows, coverlets, handbags, and the precious box containing the manuscript of *The Secret Doctrine*. Well, poor HPB, who had not been out of her room for weeks, had to walk all along the platform, and this was performed with difficulty. We got her comfortably settled, and were just rejoicing to think that the onerous task was satisfactorily completed, when one of the officials came to the door and began to remonstrate violently against the carriage being crowded with packages. He talked in German, HPB answered in French, and I began to wonder how it would all end, when, fortunately, the whistle was heard and the train began to move out of the station.

17E. Vera Johnston (HPB's niece) June 1886, Elberfeld, Germany

[Wachtmeister 1893, 107–8]

In June 1886, I stayed with my aunt in Elberfeld. It was her habit to read out in the afternoon what she had written of *The Secret Doctrine* in the preceding night.

Generally on coming down in the morning from the bedroom I occupied in the house of Madame Gebhard together with my mother, I found my aunt deep in her work. One day I saw evident traces of perplexity written on her face. Not wishing to disturb her I sat down quietly and waited for her to speak. She remained silent a long time with her eyes fixed on some point on the wall, and with a cigarette between her fingers, as was her custom. At last she called out to me:

"Vera," she said, "do you think you could tell me what is a pi?"

Rather astonished at such a question, I said I thought a pie was some kind of an English dish.

"Please don't make a fool of yourself," she said rather impatiently, "don't you understand I address you in your capacity of a mathematical pundit. Come and see this."

I looked at the page that lay before her on the table, and saw it was covered with figures and calculations, and soon became aware that the formula $\pi = 3.14159$ was put down wrongly throughout them all. It was written $\pi = 31.4159$. With great joy and triumph I hastened to inform her of her mistake.

"That's it." she exclaimed. "This confounded [decimal point] bothered me all the morning. I was rather in a hurry yesterday to put down what I saw, and today at the first glance at the page I intensely but vaguely felt there was something wrong, and do what I could I could not remember where the [decimal point] actually was when I saw this number."

Knowing very little of Theosophy in general and my aunt's ways of writing in particular at that time, I of course was greatly struck with her not being able to correct such a slight mistake in the very intricate calculations she had written down with her own hand.

"You are very green," she said, "if you think that I actually know and understand all the things I write. How many times am I to repeat to you and your mother that the things I write are dictated to me, that sometimes I see manuscripts, numbers, and words before my eyes of which I never knew anything."

H. P. Blavatsky, portrait by Hermann Schmiechen, 1885

Chapter 18

BELGIUM AND ENGLAND: WRITING *THE SECRET DOCTRINE* 1886–1887

*B*LAVATSKY relocated to Ostend, Belgium, in July 1886 and continued writing *The Secret Doctrine*. In early 1887, several English Theosophists urged HPB to come to London to be the center for Theosophical work there. In early March, however, HPB became seriously ill with a kidney infection. Doctors, both Belgian and English, gave her only a short time to live; she drew up a will and made provision for her body. Yet spontaneously overnight she regained her health—having been offered by her Master, she reported, the options of dying or living on to complete *The Secret Doctrine*. Assisted by Bertram and Archibald Keightley, she moved to London. When she arrived there on May 1, 1887, she first settled in Mabel Collins's house, called "Maycot," where she stayed for a little more than four months. It almost immediately became a center of activity.

HPB continued steadily to write her great work, which was finally completed and published in two large volumes in October-December, 1888. Her indefatigable helpers in the transcription and editing of the manuscript were Bertram Keightley and Archibald Keightley, whose financial backing was also of immense assistance. *The Secret Doctrine* was the crowning achievement of H. P. Blavatsky's literary career. Volume 1 is concerned mainly with the evolution of the universe. The skeleton of this volume is formed by seven stanzas, translated from the Book of Dzyan, with commentary and explanations by HPB. Also in this volume is an extended elucidation of the fundamental symbols contained in the great religions and mythologies of the world. Volume 2 contains a further series of stanzas from the Book of Dzyan, which describe the evolution of humanity.

18A. COUNTESS CONSTANCE WACHTMEISTER
OCTOBER 1886 – APRIL 1887, OSTEND, BELGIUM

[Collated from HPB: In Memory, 20,
and Wachtmeister 1893, 71–6]

In October, 1886, I [rejoined] HPB in Ostend, and found her settled in comfortable enough quarters; she welcomed me with all the warmth of her genial nature. We recommenced our monotonous but interesting life, the thread being taken up from where it was last broken, and I watched with delight how the piles of manuscript for the *SD* were increasing. Our near vicinity to England caused people once more to come buzzing round HPB, and we received several visitors.

Towards the end of the winter [March 1887] HPB became very ill.

To my great distress, I now began to notice that [HPB] became drowsy and heavy in the middle of the day, and often was unable to work for an hour together. This increased rapidly, and as the doctor who attended her pronounced it to be an affection of the kidneys, I became alarmed, and sent a telegram to Madame Gebhard to tell her of my apprehensions, and to beg her to come and help me. I was thankful when I received a cordial response to my telegram and knew that in a few hours I should see Madame Gebhard.

When she came, I felt as if a great burden had been lifted off my shoulders. In the meanwhile HPB was getting worse, and the Belgian doctor, who was kindness itself, tried one remedy after another, but with no good result. I began to get seriously alarmed and anxious as to what course I should adopt. HPB was in a heavy, lethargic state, she seemed to be unconscious for hours together, and nothing could rouse or interest her. Finally, a bright inspiration came to me. In the London [Theosophical] group I knew there was a Doctor Ashton Ellis, so I telegraphed to him, described the state that HPB was in, and entreated him to come without delay.

I sat by HPB's bed that night listening to every sound as I anxiously watched the hours go by, till at last, at 3 a.m., the joyful sound of a bell was heard. I flew to the door, opened it, and the doctor walked in. I eagerly told him all her symptoms, and described the remedies that had been applied, whereupon he went to her and made her drink some medicine that he had brought with him.

The next day there was a consultation between the two doctors. The Belgian doctor said that he had never known a case of a person with the kidneys attacked as HPB's were, living as long as she had done, and that he was convinced that nothing could save her. Mr. Ellis replied that it was exceedingly rare for anyone to survive so long in such a state. He further told us that he had consulted a specialist before coming to Ostend, who was of the same opinion, but advised that, in addition to the prescribed medicine, he should try massage, so as to stimulate the paralyzed organs.

The night passed quietly, and several times the following day Mr. Ellis [massaged] her until he was quite exhausted; but she got no better, and to my horror I began to detect that peculiar faint odor of death which sometimes precedes dissolution. I hardly dared hope that she would live through the night, and while I was sitting alone by her bedside she opened her eyes and told me how glad she was to die, and that she thought the Master would let her be free at last. Still she was very anxious about her *Secret Doctrine*. I must be most careful of her manuscripts and hand all over to Col. Olcott with directions to have them printed. She had hoped that she would have been able to give more to the world, but the Master knew best. And so she talked on at intervals, telling me many things. At last she dropped off into a state of unconsciousness, and I wondered how it would all end.

It seemed to me impossible that she should die and leave her work unfinished; and then, again, the Theosophical Society . . . what would become of it? How could it be that the Master who was at the head of that Society would allow it to crumble away? The thought came to me that the Master had told HPB that she was to form a circle of students around her and that she was to teach them. How could she do that if she were to die? And then I opened my eyes and glanced at her and thought, was it possible that she who had slaved, suffered, and striven so hard should be allowed to die in the middle of her work?

None of those who knew her really understood her. Even to me, who had been alone with her for so many months, she was an enigma, with her strange powers, her marvelous knowledge, her extraordinary insight into human nature, and her mysterious life, spent in regions unknown to ordinary mortals, so that though her body might be near, her soul was often away in commune with others.

Such were the thoughts which passed through my mind, as I sat hour after hour that anxious night, watching her as she seemed to be getting weaker and weaker. A wave of blank despondency came over me, as I felt how truly I loved this noble woman, and I realized how empty life would be without her. My whole soul rose in rebellion at the thought of losing her. I gave a bitter cry and knew no more.

When I opened my eyes, the early morning light was stealing in, and a dire apprehension came over me that I had slept, and that perhaps HPB had died during my sleep—died whilst I was untrue to my vigil. I turned round towards the bed in horror, and there I saw HPB looking at me calmly with her clear gray eyes, as she said, "Countess, come here."

I flew to her side. "What has happened, HPB—you look so different to what you did last night."

She replied, "Yes, Master has been here; he gave me my choice, that I might die and be free if I would, or I might live and finish *The Secret Doctrine*. He told me how great would be my sufferings and what a terrible time I would have before me in England (for I am to go there); but when I thought of those students to whom I shall be permitted to teach a few things, and of the Theosophical Society in general, to which I have already given my heart's blood, I accepted the sacrifice, and now to make it complete, fetch me some coffee and something to eat, and give me my tobacco box."

I flew off to do her errands and ran to tell Madame Gebhard the good news.

18B. ARCHIBALD KEIGHTLEY
FEBRUARY–APRIL 1887, OSTEND, BELGIUM

[Keightley 1892]

In the early months of 1887 there were some few members of the TS in London who felt that if Theosophy did not receive some vital impulse, the center there would be confined to a few individuals only who were pursuing and would continue to pursue their studies. There were many anxious discussions as to how a vital interest could be awakened in the truths of Theosophy, and how attention should be restored to the ethical philosophy. We all felt that we were working in the dark and that we were ignorant of the real basis upon which the philosophy rested.

Obviously we required a leader who might intelligently direct our efforts. We then determined each separately to write to H. P. Blavatsky, who was then in Ostend, laying before the Founder of the TS and the messenger of the Masters the position as each of us saw it. We asked her to reply in a collective letter giving us advice as to what to do. She replied, however, to each individual, writing letters of eight to twelve pages. The result of this was that we all wrote and asked her to come over and direct our efforts. She had told us that she was writing *The Secret Doctrine* and must finish that before undertaking other work.

Nevertheless we wrote to her that there was, we believed, urgent need of her directing presence, and that she could finish *The Secret Doctrine* in London as well as or better than in Ostend. After receiving her reply, which urged objections, Mr. Bertram Keightley went over to Ostend during the latter part of February or beginning of March and talked matters over with her. She agreed to come to London at the end of April provided we would find a house for her somewhere a little out of London in which she could work in peace. Soon after he returned I went over to Ostend rather unexpectedly to myself. I naturally went to call after leaving my luggage at the hotel. Madame Blavatsky received me with the greatest kindness, although previously to that occasion I was almost unknown to her. She insisted that I should transfer my things to her house and stay with her while in Ostend. At that time she was occupying the first floor of the house, with a Swiss maid to wait on her and Countess Wachtmeister to keep her company. I was at once introduced to *The Secret Doctrine* with a request to read, correct, and excise, a privilege I naturally did not avail myself of.

Madame Blavatsky at that time had never ventured out of her rooms since the previous November, and never came from her writing and bedroom into the dining room until the windows had been closed and the room well warmed. Several attacks of inflammation of the kidneys had warned her that the slightest chill was dangerous to the completion of her work.

At the close of my visit I returned to England with renewed assurances of her arrival on May 1st, and under pledge to return and assist Madame Blavatsky on her journey to London. I had not been in London many hours when one of our members, Dr. Ashton Ellis, received a telegram from Countess Wachtmeister saying, as I recall its tenor, that Madame Blavatsky had had another inflammatory attack on the kidneys, that she was comatose, and that her life was in the utmost danger. Dr. Ellis went over to Ostend and attended her. He told me that he was extremely surprised, and so were the others who know her serious condition, to find her recovering in a few days. Her state then was so critical that she began arranging her affairs before the comatose attack came, burning up papers and having a will drawn up so as to be ready for the end. Later on she told me herself that her life was saved by the direct intervention of her Master. Her endurance manifested itself even at this point, for as soon as she could leave her bed she was at work on *The Secret Doctrine*.

In the middle of April, Mr. [Bertram] Keightley again went over, and I followed him about the 25th or 26th. We were rather in consternation because Madame Blavatsky said she could not possibly leave in such weather as then prevailed, especially on account of her late serious illness. Her landlord said she must leave, for the rooms were let. Countess Wachtmeister had previously left for Sweden to attend to urgent business affairs there under promise to rejoin Madame Blavatsky in London. Staying in the house with us was a friend of Dr. Ellis who assisted in the removal.

The fated day came, and in place of being bright but cold, as had been the case two days before, the morning proved to be cold and foggy, with a steady drizzling rain falling and penetrating all it touched, the thermometer being about 40 degrees. We fully expected Madame Blavatsky would decline to move, and thought her justified in doing so. Nevertheless she appeared that morning in full marching order, the trunks were packed, and all was ready.

The carriage arrived and Madame Blavatsky was assisted into it, and off it drove to the wharf. It must be remembered that she had not had a window open in her room while she was in it (and would not scarcely allow it open while she was out) for six months. She kept her room at a temperature of over 70 deg., believing that anything under that would kill her. Moreover, she was almost crippled with rheumatism and could hardly walk, and was a constant martyr to sciatica. On getting to the wharf we found the tide low, and in consequence there was only a narrow gangway leading at a very steep incline to the steamer's deck. Imagine our dismay. Madame Blavatsky, however, said nothing, but simply grasping the rails walked slowly and without assistance to the deck. We then took her to a cabin on deck, where she sank on the sofa and only then betrayed the pain and exhaustion caused by her effort. The journey was uneventful so far as Dover, save that for the first time in her life Mme. Blavatsky knew what the preliminary qualms of seasickness meant and was much puzzled.

At Dover the tide was still lower, and as a result four very stalwart piermen had to carry her to the top. Then came the greatest difficulty, for the platform is low and the English railway carriage steps were high. It required the united efforts of all the party (and the piermen as well) to assist Madame Blavatsky in her crippled state into the carriage. The journey to London was uneventful, and with the help of an invalid chair and a carriage she was safely lodged in the house we had secured for her. Secretly I was afraid the journey would have serious results, but, whatever was the reason, she seemed to enjoy better health for some time after her arrival in England then she had for months previously.

The day after her arrival she was at work on *The Secret Doctrine* at 7 a.m.

18c. JULIA W. KEIGHTLEY
(WIFE OF ARCHIBALD KEIGHTLEY)
1886–1891, PENNSYLVANIA

[Wachtmeister 1893, 121–5; this article was signed
"R.S." but the author was Julia W. Keightley]

Living some thousand miles from England, I never met Madame Blavatsky in person. Like others of my acquaintance, I first heard of [HPB] by coming across the S.P.R. pamphlet denouncing her as an impostor and asserting the Hodgson-Coulomb slander as a true fact.

Soon, however, I began to realize, through my own experience, that she was not what she seemed to be. The evidence I had caused me to ask HPB to teach me; and that fact that I fully trusted in and believed her is precisely what gained for me the fulfillment of my wish. The mental attitude of belief sets up, in our aura and in our inner bodies, magnetic and attractive conditions, very different to those of contraction and densification, which exist where doubt or criticism fill the mind. A literal quickening of my aura and inner body took place. The contraction in which men and women enfold themselves is too little understood. To be known, faith and devotion must first be had.

After HPB accepted me as a pupil, no rules were laid down, no plans formulated. I continued my daily routine, and at night, after I fell into a deep sleep, the new life began. On waking in the morning from a sleep so profound that the attitude of the previous night was still retained, I would vividly remember that I had gone, as it were, to HPB. I had been received in rooms which I could and did describe to those who lived with her—described, even to the worn places or holes in the carpet. On the first occasion of this kind she signified to me her acceptance of me as a pupil. After that, she would receive me in varying fashion, showing me pictures which passed like panoramas across the walls of the room.

At other times, times more rare, I would awake to find her standing at the foot of my bed, and as I leaned upon my elbow, her sign language would begin, the harmonies of Nature would fill the moonlit room, while the wondrous living pictures passed across the wall. All this was perfectly objective to me. I was fully awake to all the surroundings, to all the natural sounds of the night, and I have taken my pet dog into my arms because it shivered and whimpered at sight of her. All the expressions of HPB's face became familiar to me. I can see her now, her old bedgown—what dingy old gown was ever so cherished?—folded about her, as she opened out space before me, and then, too, expanded into her own real being.

I have hardly more than half a dozen letters from her, and these contain no teaching; they bore upon external Theosophic affairs and have this peculiarity. At night she would tell me to advise certain persons of certain things. I would obey, giving her as my authority, and a few days afterwards, but never long enough for the full voyage, would come her letter giving in writing the instructions previously heard at night. Thus I was enabled to prove that I really heard her wish over seas, for always the request concerned some sudden emergency which had just arisen a day, two days at most, before. I was able to check off my experience in this way, as I was also able to speak at times before an event occurred.

18D. BERTRAM KEIGHTLEY
MAY 1887 – OCTOBER 1888, LONDON

[*Wachtmeister 1893, 90–5*]

A day or two after our arrival at Maycot, HPB placed the whole of the so-far completed MS [of *The Secret Doctrine*] in the hands of Dr. [Archibald] Keightley and myself, instructing us to read, punctuate, correct the English, alter, and generally treat it as if it were our own—which we naturally did *not* do, having far too high an opinion of her knowledge to take any liberties with so important a work.

But we both read the whole mass of MS—a pile over three feet high—most carefully through, correcting the English and punctuation where absolutely indispensable, and then, after prolonged consultation, faced the author in her den—in my case with sore trembling, I remember—with the solemn opinion that the whole of the matter must be rearranged on some definite plan, since as it stood the book was another *Isis Unveiled* only far worse, so far as absence of plan and consecutiveness were concerned.

After some talk, HPB told us to go to Tophet and do what we liked. She had had more than enough of the blessed thing, had given it over to us, washed her hands of it entirely, and we might get out of it as best we could.

We retired and consulted. Finally, we laid before her a plan suggested by the character of the matter itself, viz., to make the work consist of four volumes. Further, instead of making the first volume to consist, as she had intended, of the history of some great Occultists, we advised her to follow the natural order of exposition, and begin with the Evolution of Cosmos, to pass from that to the Evolution of Man, then to deal with the historical part in a third volume treating of the lives of some great Occultists; and finally, to speak of Practical Occultism in a fourth volume, should she ever be able to write it.

This plan we laid before HPB, and it was duly sanctioned by her.

The next step was to read the MS through again and make a general rearrangement of the matter pertaining to the subjects coming under the heading of Cosmogony and Anthropology, which were to form the first two volumes of the work. When this had been completed, and HPB duly consulted, and her approval of what had been done obtained, the whole of the MS so arranged was typewritten out by professional hands, then reread, corrected, [and] compared with the original MS.

It then appeared that the whole of the Commentary on the Stanzas [of Dzyan] did not amount to more than some twenty pages of the present work. So we seriously interviewed her, and suggested that she should write a proper commentary, as in her opening words she had promised her readers to do. Her reply was characteristic, "What on earth am I to say? What *do* you want to know? Why it's all as plain as the nose on your face!!!" We could not see it; she didn't—or made out she didn't—so we retired to reflect.

The solution was this: Each sloka [verse] of the stanzas was written (or cut out from the typewritten copy) and pasted at the head of a sheet of paper, and then on a loose sheet pinned thereto were written all the questions we could find time to devise upon that sloka. HPB struck out large numbers of them, made us write fuller explanations, or our own ideas—such as they were—of what her readers expected her to say, wrote more herself, incorporated the little she had already written on that particular sloka, and so the work was done.

But when we came to sending the MS to the printers, the result was found to be such that the most experienced compositor would tear his hair in blank dismay. Therefore, Dr. Keightley and myself set to work with a typewriter, and alternately dictating and writing, made a clean copy of the first parts of volumes I and II.

Then work was continued till parts II and III of each volume were in a fairly advanced condition, and we could think of sending the work to press.

Of the further history of *The Secret Doctrine* there is not much more to say—though there were months of hard work before us. HPB read and corrected two sets of galley proofs, then a page proof, correcting, adding, and altering up to the very last moment.

Of phenomena in connection with *The Secret Doctrine*, quotations with full references, from books which were never in the house—quotations verified after hours of search, sometimes, at the British Museum for a rare book—of such, I saw and verified not a few.

H. P. Blavatsky at "Maycot," London, 1887

In verifying them I found occasionally the curious fact that the numerical references were reversed, e.g., p. 321 for p. 123, illustrating the reversal of objects when seen in the astral light.

Of the value of the work, posterity must judge finally. Personally, I can only place on record my profound conviction that when studied thoroughly but not treated as a revelation, when understood and assimilated but not made a text for dogma, HPB's *Secret Doctrine* will be found of incalculable value, and will furnish suggestions, clues, and threads of guidance, for the study of Nature and Man, such as no other existing work can supply.

18E. CHARLES JOHNSTON
SPRING 1887, LONDON

[Johnston 1900]

I first met dear old "HPB," as she made all her friends call her, in the spring of 1887. Some of her disciples had taken a pretty house in Norwood, where the huge glass nave and twin towers of the Crystal Palace glint about a labyrinth of streets and terraces. London was at its grimy best. The squares and gardens were scented with grape clusters of lilac, and yellow rain of laburnums under soft green leaves. The eternal smoke pall was thinned to a gray veil shining in the afternoon sun, with the great Westminster Towers and a thousand spires and chimneys piercing through. Every house had its smoke wreath, trailing away to the east.

HPB was just finishing her day's work, so I passed a half hour upstairs with her volunteer secretary, a disciple who served her with boundless devotion. I had known him two years before. So we talked of old times, and of HPB's great book, *The Secret Doctrine*, and he read me resonant stanzas [of Dzyan] about Universal Cosmic Night, when Time was not; about the Luminous Sons of Manvantaric Dawn; and the Armies of the Voice; about the Water Men Terrible and Bad, and the Black Magicians of Lost Atlantis; about the Sons of Will and Yoga and the Ring Pass-Not; about the Great Day Be-with-Us, when all shall be perfected into one, reuniting "thyself and others, myself and thee."

So the half hour passed, and I went downstairs to see the Old Lady. She was in her writing room, just rising from her desk, and clad in one of those dark blue dressing gowns she loved. My first impression was of her rippled hair as she turned, then her marvelously potent eyes, as she welcomed me: "My dear fellow! I am so glad to see you! Come in and talk! You are just in time to have some tea!" And a hearty handshake.

Then a piercing call for "Louise," and her Swiss maid appeared, to receive a voluble torrent of directions in French, and HPB settled herself snugly into an armchair, comfortably near her tobacco box, and began to make me a cigarette. The cuffs of a Jaeger suit showed round her wrists, only setting off the perfect shape and delicacy of her hands, as her deft fingers, deeply stained with nicotine, rolled the white rice paper around Turkish tobacco.

HPB with a quizzically humorous smile [asked]: "Of course you have read the SPR Report?—The Spookical Research Society—and know that I am a Russian spy, and the champion impostor of the age?"

"Yes, I read the Report. But I knew its contents already. I was at the meeting when it was first read, two years ago."

"Well," said HPB, again smiling with infinite humor, "and what impression did the frisky lambkin from Australia [Richard Hodgson] make upon your susceptible heart?"

"A very deep one. I decided that he must be a very good young man, who always came home to tea; and that the Lord had given him a very good conceit of himself. If he got an opinion into his head, he would plow away blandly, and contrary facts would be quite invisible. And all that Mr. Sinnett says in the *Occult World* seems to me absolutely unshaken by the whole Report."

"I am glad you think so, my dear," she answered in her courtly way, "for now I can offer you some tea with a good conscience." Louise had laid a white cloth on the corner table, brought in a tray, and lit a lamp. The secretary soon joined us, receiving a tart little sermon on being unpunctual, which he was not. Then we came back to the Psychical Researchers.

"They will never do much," said HPB "They go too much on

material lines, and they are far too timid. They were afraid of raising a storm if they said our phenomena were true. Fancy what it would have meant! Why it would practically have committed Modern Science to our Mahatmas and all I have taught about the inhabitants of the occult world and their tremendous powers. They shrank at the thought of it, and so they made a scapegoat of this poor orphan and exile." And her eyes were full of humorous pity for herself.

"It must have been something like that," I answered, "for there is simply no backbone in the Report itself. It is the weakest thing of the kind I have ever read. There is not a shred of real evidence in it from beginning to end."

"Do you really think so? That's right!" cried HPB; and then she turned on her secretary, and poured in a broadside of censure, telling him he was greedy, idle, untidy, unmethodical, and generally worthless. When he ventured an uneasy defense, she flared up and declared that he "was born a flapdoodle, lived a flapdoodle, and would die a flapdoodle." He lost his grip, and not unnaturally made a yellow streak of egg across her white tablecloth.

"There!" cried HPB, glaring at him with withering scorn, and then turning to me for sympathy in her afflictions. That was her way, to rate her disciples in the presence of perfect strangers. It speaks volumes for her, that they loved her still.

"There is one thing about the SPR Report I want you to explain. What about the writing in the occult letters [of the Masters]?"

"Well, what about it?" asked HPB, immediately interested.

"They say that you wrote them yourself, and that they bear evident marks of your handwriting and style. What do you say to that?"

"Let me explain it this way," she answered, after a long gaze at the end of her cigarette. "Have you ever made experiments in thought-transference? If you have, you must have noticed that the person who received the mental picture very often colors it, or often changes it slightly, with his own thought, and this where perfectly genuine transference of thought takes place. Well, it is something like that with the precipitated letters. One of our

Masters, who perhaps does not know English, and of course has no English handwriting, wishes to precipitate a letter in answer to a question sent mentally to him. Let us say he is in Tibet, while I am in Madras or London. He has the answering thought in his mind, but not in English words. He has first to impress that thought on my brain, or on the brain of someone else who knows English, and then to take the word forms that rise up in that other brain to answer the thought. Then he must form a clear mind picture of the words in writing, also drawing on my brain, or the brain of whoever it is, for the shapes. Then either through me or some chela with whom he is magnetically connected, he has to precipitate these word shapes on paper, first sending the shapes into the chela's mind, and then driving them into the paper, using the magnetic force of the chela to do the printing, and collecting the material, black or blue or red, as the case may be, from the astral light. As all things dissolve into the astral light, the will of the magician can draw them forth again. So he can draw forth colors of pigments to mark the figures in the letter, using the magnetic force of the chela to stamp them in, and guiding the whole by his own much greater magnetic force, a current of powerful will.

"That sounds quite reasonable," I answered. "Won't you show me how it is done?"

"You would have to be clairvoyant," she answered, in a perfectly direct and matter-of-fact way, "in order to see and guide the currents. But this is the point: Suppose the letter [is] precipitated through me; it would naturally show some traces of my expressions, and even of my writing; but all the same, it would be a perfectly genuine occult phenomenon, and a real message from that Mahatma. Besides, when all is said and done, they exaggerate the likeness of the writings. And the experts are not infallible. We have had experts who were just as positive that I could not possibly have written those letters, and just as good experts, too. But the Report says nothing about them. And then there are letters, in just the same handwriting, precipitated when I was thousands of miles away. Dr. Hartmann received more than one at Adyar, Madras, when I was in London; I could hardly have written them.

But you have seen some of the occult letters? What do you say?"

"Yes," I replied; "Mr. Sinnett showed me about a ream of them: the whole series that the *Occult World* and *Esoteric Buddhism* are based on. Some of them are in red, either ink or pencil, but far more are in blue. I thought it was pencil at first, and I tried to smudge it with my thumb; but it would not smudge."

"Of course not!" she smiled; "the color is driven into the surface of the paper. But what about the writings?"

"I am coming to that. There were two: the blue writing, and the red; they were totally different from each other, and both were quite unlike yours. I have spent a good deal of time studying the relation of handwriting to character, and the two characters were quite clearly marked. The blue was evidently a man of very gentle and even character, but of tremendously strong will; logical, easy-going, and taking endless pains to make his meaning clear. It was altogether the handwriting of a cultivated and very sympathetic man."

"Which I am not," said HPB, with a smile; "that is Mahatma Koot Hoomi; he is a Kashmiri Brahman by birth, you know, and has traveled a good deal in Europe. He is the author of the *Occult World* letters, and gave Mr. Sinnett most of the material of *Esoteric Buddhism*. But you have read all about it."

"Yes, I remember he says you shriek across space with a voice like Sarasvati's peacock. Hardly the sort of thing you would say of yourself."

"Of course not," she said; "I know I am a nightingale. But what about the other writing?"

"The red? Oh that is wholly different. It is fierce, impetuous, dominant, strong; it comes in volcanic outbursts, while the other is like Niagara Falls. One is fire, and the other is the ocean. They are wholly different, and both quite unlike yours. But the second has more resemblance to yours than the first."

"This is my Master," she said, "whom we call Mahatma Morya. I have his picture here."

And she showed me a small panel in oils. If ever I saw genuine awe and reverence in a human face, it was in hers, when she spoke of her Master. He was a Rajput by birth, she said, one of the old warrior race of the Indian desert, the finest and handsomest nation in the world. Her Master was a giant, six feet eight, and splendidly built, a superb type of manly beauty. Even in the picture, there is a marvelous power and fascination; the force, the fierceness even, of the face; the dark, glowing eyes, which stare you out of countenance; the clear-cut features of bronze, the raven hair and beard—all spoke of manhood strength. I asked her something about his age. She answered:

"My dear, I cannot tell you exactly, for I do not know. But this I will tell you. I met him first when I was twenty—in 1851. He was in the very prime of manhood then. I am an old woman now, but he has not aged a day. He is still in the prime of manhood. That is all I can say. You may draw you own conclusions."

Then she told me something about other Masters and adepts she had known. She had known adepts of many races, from Northern and Southern India, Tibet, Persia, China, Egypt; of various European nations, Greek, Hungarian, Italian, English; of certain races in South America, where she said there was a Lodge of adepts.

"And now, my dear, it is getting late, and I am getting sleepy. So I must bid you goodnight!" And the Old Lady dismissed me with that grand air of hers which never left her, because it was a part of herself. She was the most perfect aristocrat I have ever known.

There was something in her personality, her bearing, the light and power of her eyes, which spoke of a wider and deeper life. That was the greatest thing about her, and it was always there; this sense of a bigger world, of deeper power, of unseen might; to those in harmony with her potent genius, this came as a revelation and incentive to follow the path she pointed out. To those who could not see with her eyes, who could not raise themselves in some measure to her vision, this quality came as a challenge, an irritant, a discordant and subversive force, leading them at last to an attitude of fierce hostility and denunciation.

When the last word is said, she was greater than any of her works, more full of living power than even her marvelous writings.

H. P. Blavatsky in 1889

Chapter 19

LANSDOWNE ROAD, LONDON
1887–1888

*T*HE BLAVATSKY LODGE was organized within a few weeks of HPB's arrival in England and held meetings in which she was the central figure. Her time was occupied with writing, meetings, conversation, and her solitaire card games (often referred to by the British term "patience"). She also started a new magazine, *Lucifer*, so named partly to tease the conventional associations people had with that term.

In early September 1887, HPB moved to a house at 17 Lansdowne Road in the Holland Park area of London and continued with her many activities there. Shortly thereafter the first issue of *Lucifer* was published—a magazine intended to "bring to light the hidden things of darkness." About the same time the Theosophical Publishing Company was founded in London.

CHAPTER 19

19A. ARCHIBALD KEIGHTLEY
MAY 1887 – 1889,
LONDON

[Keightley 1910, 113–9]

It was no very long time before Mme. Blavatsky's presence began to be felt. People began to gather round her, and Maycot became the scene of the pilgrimage of a good many people. It was a remarkable experience to see those who came. Some had private interviews: others were received in company with us who lived in the house. And the method of treatment! At times argumentative, at others sarcastic, very rarely appealing for credence or justice, always the same driving energy which spared neither herself nor any other who might in any way further her Master's work.

The nominal day began for Mme. Blavatsky before 7 a.m. When it really began I do not know. The body had to have its sleep, for it could not be driven too hard. But I had reason to believe that many hours of the night were spent in writing, though this never interfered with her usual hour to get to her desk. She was invisible till she called for her midday meal. I say midday, but it was a very movable meal and might be called for at any hour between twelve and four, a proceeding which naturally disconcerted a cook. Woe betide any disturber of those hours of work, for the more quiet she was, the more seriously was she engaged.

Finally at 6:30, came for Mme. Blavatsky the evening meal, which was taken in company with the rest of us. The table cleared, came tobacco and talk, especially the former, though there was plenty of the latter. I wish I had the memory and the power to relate those talks. All things under the sun and some others, too, were discussed. Here was a mind stored with information gathered in very extensive travels, an experience of life and experience of things of an "unseen nature," and with it all an acuteness of perception which brought out the real and true.

Of one thing Mme. Blavatsky was intolerant—cant and sham—and of hypocrisy. For these she had no mercy; but for genuine effort, however mistaken, she would spare no trouble to give advice and readjustment. She was genuine in all her dealings, but I learned then and later that she at times had to remain silent in order that others might gain experience and knowledge, even if in gaining it they at times deceived themselves. I never knew her to state what was not true; but I knew she had sometimes to keep silence, because those who interrogated her had no right to the information. And in those cases, I afterwards learned that she was accused of deliberate untruth.

The evenings passed in such talks, and all the while she arranged her "patiences." Among other things which I learned was the fact that while Solitaire occupied the brain, HPB was engaged in very different work, and that Mme. Blavatsky could play Solitaire, take part in a conversation going on around her among us others, attend to what we used to call "upstairs," and also see what was going on in her own room and other places in the house and out of it, at one and the same time.

It was at one of these tobacco parliaments that Mme. Blavatsky stated her difficulty in getting her views expressed in the *Theosophist*. This was the magazine which she had started with Colonel Olcott in India. It was under his charge and he edited it in India and not unnaturally he conducted it on his own lines. But with the commencement of Mme. Blavatsky's work in England, a more immediate expression of *her* views became a matter of importance. So a new magazine was proposed and decided on and steps were taken to secure its publication. Oh, but there were discussions as to its title! "Truth," "Torch," and a variety of others were offered as suggestions and rejected. Then came the "Lightbringer" and finally "Lucifer," as an abbreviation. But this was most vehemently opposed by some as being too diabolical and too much opposed to *les convenances* [the proprieties]. Perish the word! This secured its instant acceptance.

The Blavatsky Lodge was originally started as a body of people who were prepared to follow HPB implicitly and a pledge embodying this was drawn up. We all took it and the meetings began. Every Thursday evening they were held in Mme. Blavatsky's room, which was thrown into one with the dining room. Members flocked in, so that the rooms were too small, the interest being in the questions which were propounded for Mme. Blavatsky to answer. Some of the results were printed in *Transactions of the Blavatsky Lodge*.

The procedure under such circumstances is worth recalling. You would, as I did, present your thesis or remarks. It would be received vehemently, be opposed with a variety of eloquence—an eloquence calculated to upset your balance, and the impression given that you were a most evilly designing person, aiming to upset some of Mme. Blavatsky's most cherished plans of work. But with your sincerity of purpose becoming plain, there would come a change in Mme. Blavatsky. Her manner would change, even the expression of her face. "Sound and fury" evaporated, she became very quiet, and even her face seemed to become larger, more massive and solid. Every point you raised was considered, and into her eyes—those wonderful eyes—came the look we learned to recognize. That look was one to be earned as a reward, for it meant that the heart had been searched and that guile was not found, also that HPB was in charge.

It must be remembered that during all this time of stress and effort Mme. Blavatsky was still a sick woman, always suffering pain and often hardly able to walk. But her inflexible will and devotion got her from her bed to her writing table and enabled her to persist in the carrying through the press of *The Secret Doctrine*, to edit *Lucifer*, to write her Russian articles and those for *Lucifer*, the *Theosophist*, the *Path*, to receive her visitors both in private and in public, and in addition to deal with an enormous private correspondence.

It was at this time I got a form of erysipelas with high fever, and had to stay in bed. It so happened that Mme. Blavatsky's physician was calling and he looked in on me. What was said I do not know, but as I lay in a kind of stupor I found that Mme. Blavatsky had made a progress up two flights of fairly steep stairs (she who never went up a step if it could be helped, on account of the pain so caused) and had arrived to judge for herself of her doctor's report of me. She sat and looked at me, and then she talked while she held a glass of water between her hands, and this water I afterwards drank; then she went downstairs again, bidding me to follow.

Down I went and was made to lie on the couch in her room and covered up. I lay there half asleep while she worked away at her writing, sitting at her table in her big chair, with her back towards me. How long I was there I do not know, but suddenly just past my head went a flash of deep crimson lightning. I started, not unnaturally, and was saluted through the back of the chair with "Lie down, what for do you take any notice?" I did so and went to sleep and, after I had been sent upstairs to bed, I again went to sleep and next morning was quite well, if a little shaky. This was the only time I saw the crimson light, though I have seen, and others saw, the pale blue light attached to some objects in the room and then flitting about. One of us rashly touched it one day when Mme. Blavatsky was in the next room. He got an electric shock and was also electrified by sounds of wrath from Mme. Blavatsky, greeting him by name and asking what on earth he meant by meddling with what he had no business to touch and by making an impertinently curious intrusion into matters with which he had no concern. I am sure he has not forgotten either the shock or rap to his knuckles or the rap to his curiosity. I know he remembered the shock to his arm for a long time.

The meetings of the Blavatsky Lodge were out of the ordinary. The discussions were informal and all sat round and asked questions of Mme. Blavatsky. All sorts and conditions of men and women were present, and one part of our delight was for Mme. Blavatsky to reply by the Socratic method—ask another question and seek information on her own account. It was a very effective method and frequently confounded the setter of the conundrum. If it was a genuine search for information which dictated the question, she would spare no pains to give all information in her power. But if the matter was put forward to annoy her or puzzle, the business resulted badly for the questioner. The meetings took up a lot of time, but Mme. Blavatsky enjoyed the contest of wits. All nations would be represented in those rooms on Thursday nights, and one could never tell who would be present. Sometimes there would be unseen visitors, seen by some but not by others of us. Results were curious.

Mme. Blavatsky felt the cold very much and her room was therefore kept very warm, so much so that at the meetings it was unpleasantly hot very often. One night before the meeting time, I came downstairs to find the room like an ice-house, though fire and lights were fully on. I called HPB's attention to this, but was greeted with a laugh and "Oh, I have had a friend of mine here to see me and he forgot to remove his atmosphere." Another time I remember that the rooms gradually filled until there was no vacant seat. On the sofa sat a distinguished Hindu, in full panoply of turban and dress. The discussion proceeded and apparently our distinguished guest was much interested, for he seemed to follow intelligently the remarks of each speaker. The President of the Lodge arrived that night very late, and coming in looked around for a seat. He walked up to the sofa and sat down—right in the middle of the distinguished Hindu, who promptly, and with some surprise, *fizzled and vanished!*

During this winter, affairs had been moving in America and there had been a gradually increasing interest in things Theosophical. I was called to Mme. Blavatsky's room and asked, "Arch, when can you start for America?" I was off in three days. The voyage was an odd experience for me, as I had never been on an ocean trip before or to such a distance. On board in my cabin, my attention was attracted to a number of little taps and cracks. These might naturally be due to the ship. But my attention was enforced to a series of little flashes of light, especially at night. The point to me was that these flashes and also these taps and cracks invariably associated themselves in my mind with the idea of HPB, and by this time I had begun to learn that most of these "happenings" meant something. Afterwards by letter and later when I returned, I found she could tell me accurately what I had been doing during my journey to and from and throughout my stay in America. I was told that these taps and cracks and flashes were the coming and going of elemental forms of force which took a snapshot of me and my proceedings.

19 B. WALTER R. OLD
SUMMER 1887, LONDON

[HPB: In Memory, 38–9]

During the year 1887 I was in daily correspondence with members of the Theosophical Society, and every day the fact of my not having seen [Madame Blavatsky], the chief mover in the occult renaissance of the 19th century, was growing more and more a source of annoyance to me. [Then] a letter from a London friend informed me that he had arranged for a few friends to meet at his house to discuss some of the problems in which we were mutually interested and that if I would go up to town that evening, he would take me round to see "HPB" on the morrow.

I went with the sole idea and purpose of seeing "HPB." That evening it seemed that time stood still for the special purpose of laughing at my impatience. At last, however, the morning dawned and grew into a fine summer day, and towards noon I found myself with my friend at the house, whence, he informed me, all the life of the Theosophical Society came. Entered, we were shown into the drawing room, at least I presumed that was its appellation, though I have never seen, nor ever expect to see, another room like it. No, I was mistaken, for a few seconds later, in response to a familiar greeting from my friend, HPB rose from her desk, where she had been hidden from view by an unusually large armchair, and came forward to receive us.

The largest and brightest blue eyes I have ever seen opened widely upon me as she took my hand and gave me welcome. All the confusion I had secretly predicted for myself fled from me on her first words. I felt at home and at ease with HPB at once. "No,

I will not be called 'Madame,' not by my best friend, there was nothing said of that when I was christened, and if you please I will be simply HPB. Have a seat there; you smoke of course; I'll make you a cigarette. E———, you flapdoodle (this to my friend), if you can find my tobacco box on the place there, I'll mistake you for a gentleman." Then amid some laughter, as playful and buoyant as that of a child, she explained to me that E——— and she were "old friends" and that she was very fond of him, but that he often "took advantage of her old age and innocence," and amid some repartee the tobacco was produced, and HPB made cigarettes for each of us. Then we settled down to more serious talk, HPB asking me about my studies in Theosophy and western occultism, and telling me of the success of the Theosophical movement, and how the people said this and that, and how the papers said much more, and that all were wrong because they did not understand, and had forgotten their history books, and could not see where the movement was going to. And then she asked me to tell her about myself, and gave me some practical advice, and soon afterwards I had taken leave of the most interesting person that I had ever seen.

I was most pleasurably impressed with all that I had heard and seen during my brief visit to the home of the Theosophists, and the impression I most vividly recollect of HPB herself, was of her surpassing kindliness of manner, her fearless candor, her remarkable vivacity, and above all the enthusiasm with which she spoke of the work which lay before the Theosophical Society. When, many months later, it was suggested that I should go to live at the London headquarters, then in Lansdowne Road, I was only too glad to do so.

19c. Alice L. Cleather
1887, London

[Cleather 1923, 2–4]

My husband and I, with our two children, were living at Eastbourne when HPB came over to England from Ostend in 1887. I had met Mr. Bertram Keightley shortly after I joined the Theosophical Society, and from him received help and encouragement that was invaluable—as from an older to a younger member. He knew my keen desire to meet HPB, and kindly undertook to arrange it, if possible, while they were at Maycot, Norwood (a London suburb). But he warned me that it might be a difficult matter as "our old Lady" was apt to be—well, a little uncertain and capricious at times. I did not care the proverbial two pins what she was in those respects, if only she would *see me*. I had a profound conviction that I was approaching a crisis in my inner life, and that everything depended upon getting into touch with her. See her, therefore, I must and would.

We were not well-off at this time, and a journey from Eastbourne to London and back was not easy to compass. I had a small sum at "the bottom of a stocking," put by against a rainy day. This I now determined to use for my little pilgrimage. Indeed, I felt like a pilgrim, to an unknown goal; and I set out for London with no small excitement, and very definite high hopes. A friend had lent me a room for a couple of days, so I was spared that expense. Maycot was a small villa occupied at that time by Mrs. Kenningale Cook (a well-known novelist) better known to Theosophists by her maiden name, Mabel Collins, as the scribe of *Light on the Path*.

I well remember Mr. Keightley telling me on our way out to Norwood that, in their frequent "arguments," she and HPB could be "heard halfway down the road"—when the windows were open! We walked from Western Norwood station and, sure enough, when we got within about a hundred yards of Maycot, I heard loud and apparently angry voices floating—or rather ricochetting—towards us down the road. I was rather aghast, and Mr.

Keightley's murmured remark that he was afraid "the old Lady" was in "one of her tempers" was not reassuring, particularly as he added that she would probably refuse to see me! *She did:* Nothing would induce her to, I could hear her saying so when Mr. Keightley went in (leaving me outside on the doorstep), and rating him soundly for bringing a total stranger to call at such an inopportune moment. In vain he reminded her that she herself had made the appointment, and that I had come up from the country on purpose to keep it. No, she was adamant, also angry (at least I thought so then). So I had to return sadly to London, and thence to Eastbourne, my "savings" gone, and my "high hopes" dashed to the ground. Truly I was greatly upset, as I imagined I must be "unworthy." All the same, I by no means abandoned my determination to see HPB in the end—worthy or unworthy.

Later in the same year, 1887, I at last attained my heart's desire, and once more Mr. Keightley was the *deus ex machina.* He obtained an invitation for me to 17 Lansdowne Road, and himself took me there late one afternoon. HPB had moved into the West End of London from Maycot, and we had left Eastbourne for Harrow, a northwestern suburb, so journeys were no longer a dif- ficulty. When we were ushered into the well-known double draw- ing room on the ground floor, my attention immediately became riveted on the figure of a stout, middle-aged woman seated with her back to the wall before a card table, apparently engaged in playing patience. She had the most arresting head and face I had ever seen, and when she lifted her eyes to mine, on Mr. Keightley presenting me, I experienced a distinct shock as her extraordinar- ily penetrating blue eyes literally "bored a hole" through my brain. She looked steadfastly at me for a few seconds (most uncomfort- able ones for me) then, turning to Mr. Keightley, remarked indig- nantly, "You never told me she was like this!"—absolutely ignor- ing his assertion that he had repeatedly done so. Exactly what "like this" indicated, I never subsequently discovered.

19 D. REGINALD W. MACHELL
FALL 1887 – 1888, LONDON

[Tingley 1921, 34–5]

It was in [1887] that I made the acquaintance of Madame Blavatsky in London and visited her at the house in Lansdowne Road, where she was then living. In 1888 I joined the Theosophical Society and attended the meetings of the Blavatsky Lodge, which met at the house of the foundress of the Society on Lansdowne Road, at that time. Madame Blavatsky was present on all the occasions of my weekly visits and took part in all the proceedings, answering questions as to the teachings of Theosophy and incidentally speaking on a great range of topics more or less connected with the main subject of study, Theosophy.

The thing that had compelled my attention to this subject was my intense conviction of the absolute sincerity of the foundress of the Society and of her power to expound the true teachings of Theosophy, as well as of her fitness to be a guide to one who aspired to lead a higher life. My conviction was based on my own personal observation and judgment of character, and not at all on anybody's evidence or opinions. So, when I heard stories of a kind that did not agree with my own observations and conclusions, I was not influenced by them, but found support for my faith in Madame Blavatsky as a spiritual teacher in the internal evidence supplied by her works.

The more I studied her works, the stronger grew my faith in the reality of Madame Blavatsky's mission and in her ability to transmit to the world the teachings entrusted to her for that purpose. It seemed to me that her devotion to the cause of Theosophy was absolute, and was wholly disinterested.

I saw that she suffered acutely from the slanders that were circulated about her former life, but I felt that no amount of calumny could turn her from the task which she had undertaken and which she was carrying out under conditions of ill health that seemed to make work of any kind impossible.

It was obvious that her self-sacrificing devotion to the cause of Theosophy could bring to herself no other reward than denunciation and vilification, on the one hand, and on the other the very doubtful support of those who were anxious to get from her some of the vast store of knowledge that was evidently at her command. While a few earnest followers honestly endeavored to lead the life and to follow the teacher, the majority of those who called themselves her followers were in reality seeking knowledge for their own gratification, rather than for the service of humanity. Some of these resented what they contemptuously called the "parrot cry of Brotherhood," which the "old lady" was constantly insisting upon as the foundation of Theosophy, and which they considered "MERE ethics."

In spite of the constant failure of her professed followers to understand her, and the unscrupulous misrepresentations of avowed enemies, she never lost faith in the cause nor wavered in her absolute devotion to the task she had undertaken. Suffering martyrdom both mentally and physically, she worked indefatigably, and her writing showed no trace of her physical condition, which was such as to make her life a wonder in itself and her literary achievement a marvel.

What need to refute attacks upon her character, when there remain such monuments to her nobility of soul and intellect as *The Secret Doctrine*, *The Voice of the Silence*, *Isis Unveiled*, and *The Key to Theosophy*?

19E. BERTRAM KEIGHTLEY
MAY–JUNE 1888, LONDON

[Keightley 1931, 21–3]

HPB always wrote the editorial [for *Lucifer*] herself, and also many other articles under more than one *nom de plume*, and she had a fancy for very often heading it with some quotation, and it used to be one of my troubles that she very seldom gave any reference for these, so that I had much work, and even visits to the British Museum Reading Room, in order to verify and check them, even when I did manage, with much entreaty, and after being most heartily "cussed," to extract some reference from her.

One day she handed me as usual the copy of her contribution, a story for the next issue, headed with a couple of four-line stanzas. I went and plagued her for a reference and would not be satisfied without one. She took the MS and when I came back for it, I found she had just written the name "Alfred Tennyson" under the verses. Seeing this, I was at a loss, for I knew my Tennyson pretty well and was certain that I had never read these lines in any poem of his, nor were they at all in his style. I hunted up my Tennyson, could not find them, consulted every one I could get at—also in vain. Then back I went to HPB and told her all this and said that I was sure these lines could not be Tennyson's, and I dared not print them with his name attached, unless I could give an exact reference. HPB just damned me and told me to get out and go to Hell. It happened that the *Lucifer* copy *must* go to the printers that same day. So I just told her that I should strike out Tennyson's name when I went, unless she gave me a reference *before* I started. Just on starting I went to her again, and she handed me a scrap of paper on which were written the words: *The Gem*—1831. "Well, HPB," I said, "this is worse than ever, for I am dead certain that Tennyson has never written any poem called "The Gem." All HPB said was just, "Get out and be off."

So I went to the British Museum Reading Room and consulted the folk there; but they could give me no help, and they one
and all agreed that the verses could not be, and were not,
Tennyson's. As a last resort, I asked to see Mr. Richard Garnett,
the famous Head of the Reading Room in those days, and was
taken to him. I explained to him the situation and he also agreed
in feeling sure the verses were not Tennyson's. But after thinking
quite a while, he asked me if I had consulted the Catalogue of
Periodical Publications. I said no, and asked where that came in.
"Well," said Mr. Garnett, "I have a dim recollection that there was
once a brief-lived magazine called the Gem. It might be worth
your looking it up." I did so, and in the volume for the year given
in HPB's note, I found a poem of a few stanzas signed "Alfred
Tennyson" and containing the two stanzas quoted by HPB
verbatim as she had written them down. And anyone can now
read them in the second volume of *Lucifer**: but I have never
found them even in the supposedly most complete and perfect edition of Tennyson's works.

*[The poem, "No More," written by A. Tennyson, Esq., when
he was 17 years old, is included in present-day editions of his
works:

> Oh sad *No More!* Oh sweet *No More!*
>   Oh strange *No More!*
> By a mossed brookbank on a stone
> I smelt a wildweed-flower alone;
> There was a ringing in my ears,
>   And both my eyes gushed out with tears.
> Surely all pleasant things had gone before.
> Lowburied fathomdeep beneath with thee, No More!

A facsimile reproduction of the relevant pages from the Gem of
1831 containing the poem is in *Collected Writings* 9:321–2. —DHC]

19F. WILLIAM KINGSLAND
JUNE 2, 1888, LONDON

[Kingsland 1928, collated from 18–9, 24, 258, 259, 261]

I had the good fortune to meet [Madame Blavatsky] for the first time on the 2nd June, 1888, when she was living at No. 17, Lansdowne Road, Notting Hill, and had gathered round her a considerable number of devoted workers. This visit was not, however, my first introduction to Theosophy, for I had for some two months previously been attending Mr. A. P. Sinnett's weekly gatherings at his own house; I had read his *Occult World* and *Esoteric Buddhism*, and the early numbers of *The Theosophist* published in India. This literature opened out for me a new world of thought and endeavor. Theosophy struck a chord to which my inmost nature immediately responded. Here was disclosed not merely the possibility of a positive knowledge where science and philosophy and religion were only making guesses, but the whole cosmology and anthropology of this "Ancient Wisdom" appeared to me to be the only rational explanation of what we actually do know scientifically and historically of the world we live in, of our own nature as human beings, and of the literary records which have come down to us from a remote past. Underneath all this appeal to my rational faculty was an indefinable feeling—which so very many others have also experienced—that I was not now contacting this knowledge for the first time, that I was only recovering in my outer consciousness what was already familiar to my inner self. It was, therefore, with mind already eager for further enlightenment that I sought to know the remarkable woman who was the great pioneer of this modern movement for the revival of the old occult teachings and traditions. It was, in fact, the *teachings* and not the woman that attracted me. I desired to go to the fountain source; but I held very much in reserve any opinion I might be inclined to form as to the personality of a woman at that time accused of being a fraud and a charlatan.

341

There was certainly in my case no emotional approach, and I held very largely in reserve any judgment I might feel inclined to pass as to her temperamental and most marked personal characteristics. I never asked her to perform, nor did I ever see her perform, any occult phenomena. These phenomena, upon which so many placed their whole reliance and which probably made for her more enemies than friends, always appeared to me to be of secondary importance to the teachings, though I might say that they appeared to me not merely to have been overwhelmingly vouched for, but also not inherently impossible in themselves. Psychical research has made great progress since that time, and it is hardly too much to say that their inherent possibility is now scientifically demonstrated.

The most that can be said for the remarkable powers which H. P. Blavatsky undoubtedly possessed from her childhood up, and which she undoubtedly did exhibit on many occasions, is that they demonstrate the fact that these powers can be possessed and intelligently used, not in any "mediumistic" manner, but by the proper use of the trained will. But there is nothing new in this; it is an age-long knowledge in the East under the name of *Yoga*.

I did not see how any of the phenomena she was reputed to have performed could be any evidence of the truth of the teachings, though they might possibly have gone to prove the existence of the Masters, as also the fact that every individual possesses unknown and undeveloped psychic faculties and powers. I did consider, however, in spite of the SPR report, that her phenomenal powers had been fully testified by a very large number of credible witnesses. I naturally held in reserve a great many conclusions when I first made her acquaintance; but I have never seen any reason to go back on my first favorable impressions; and I have since then made the philosophy which I learnt from her the basis of all my own literary work.

The H. P. Blavatsky whom I knew personally was certainly not the "accomplished impostor" presented to us in the SPR report. If such a personality as is presented ever existed, she must have utterly vanished by the time I came to know the author of *The Secret Doctrine*.

Nevertheless, the [SPR] report [is] even now sometimes quoted as having definitely *proved* that the psychic phenomena associated with Mme. Blavatsky were entirely fraudulent and also that the Masters or Mahatmas from whom she claimed to have received her teachings were her own invention, and do not, in fact, exist. The report does not *prove* by any evidence that would be accepted in a court of law either the one or other of these assumptions.

It is apparently thought by detractors that, if they only throw sufficient mud at the woman who gave the [Theosophical] teachings to the world, they are thereby amply discrediting the teachings themselves. [As regards] the great work which Mme. Blavatsky accomplished in the literature which she gave to the world in *Isis Unveiled*, *The Secret Doctrine*, *The Key to Theosophy*, and *The Voice of the Silence*—it is by that literature and its gradual acceptance as being a fresh inflow of spiritual teaching at a time when the world was drifting into materialism, and not by the report, that H. P. Blavatsky will be judged by posterity. The teachings and literary work which she gave to the world will most assuredly as time goes on place her name amongst those of the world's great light-bringers.

Alice Leighton Cleather

Chapter 20

LONDON:
THE ESOTERIC SCHOOL
AND LIFE WITH HPB
1888

OCTOBER 1888 was a significant month in Madame Blavatsky's life and the history of the Theosophical Society. First, HPB then assumed the complete editorship of *Lucifer*, which she had earlier been sharing with Mabel Collins. On October 9, Colonel Olcott, who was visiting England at the time, chartered the Esoteric Section (or School) for the deeper study of the esoteric philosophy by dedicated students, with HPB as its head. HPB eventually wrote three "ES Instructions" for its members. The British Section of the Theosophical Society was also organized and chartered by Colonel Olcott at that time, with the Blavatsky Lodge as its premier group. On October 20, the first volume of *The Secret Doctrine* was published in a printing of 500 copies, which had all been sold even before publication. The second volume of the book appeared later in the year. At the end of the year, William Quan Judge was in Ireland and in England, where he helped HPB with drafting the rules of the Esoteric Section.

20A. ALICE L. CLEATHER
OCTOBER–NOVEMBER 1888,
LONDON

[Cleather 1923, 15–6]

In *Lucifer* for October 1888, a notice had appeared to the effect that an "Esoteric Section of the Theosophical Society" was to be formed under HPB, and that those who wished to join and abide by its rules should send in their names. Mrs. Chowne and I, also Colonel Chowne, if I remember rightly, at once responded; but for some time we heard nothing. Then, one day, Mrs. Chowne came down to Harrow to see me—I was ill at the time—bringing the ES Pledge from HPB for me to write out and sign. She said that HPB had told her that, on our sending in our signed Pledges, each one would be "tested" (i.e., "examined for fitness") on inner planes, *by the Master*. Mrs. Chowne's exact words were, "taken out and tested." Our past lives would be called up, and upon what was there seen and known of our *real selves*, would depend whether or not we were accepted as candidates. She told me later that, when she handed our signed Pledges to HPB, she had looked very seriously—almost solemnly—at her, and said, "It is a great trust that you have given me."

So we waited; days, even weeks, passed, and nothing occurred. I had almost forgotten what Mrs. Chowne had warned me *might* happen, until, one Tuesday night, (it was full Moon, I remember) I had the most wonderful experience, save one, that had ever happened to me. I knew I was myself, lying half awake, half asleep, in my own room at home. Yet I was also in an Egyptian temple of extraordinary grandeur, and going through things quite unspeakable and most solemn. This experience began soon after 10 PM, and almost exactly as a neighboring church clock struck midnight, I lost consciousness in an overpowering and almost terrible blaze of light, which seemed completely to envelope me. The next morning I recorded all I could remember in my diary, and on Thursday went up to Lansdowne Road as usual for the Lodge meeting. I was a little early, but HPB at work in the inner room must have known who had arrived, for she called me in and, turning round, said most seriously: "Master told me *last night* that you are accepted." Nothing more; but I at once realized vividly that my experience the previous Tuesday night had indeed been my "testing." Thereupon I related the whole thing to HPB, who only nodded several times, but made no remark whatever about it.

Mrs. Chowne told me afterwards that she and her husband had had similar experiences, adding that only a few of the first applicants were so "tested"; that it did not, in fact, apply generally.

20B. WILLIAM Q. JUDGE
DECEMBER 1888,
LONDON

[Judge 1889]

Mme. Blavatsky is living with the Countess Wachtmeister in Holland Park, London, and is devoting herself to the most arduous labors in the cause of Theosophy. She scarcely ever leaves the house, and from 6:30 o'clock in the morning until evening is constantly engaged in writing articles for her magazine, *Lucifer* or other Theosophic publications, replying to correspondence, and preparing the matter for further forthcoming volumes of her gigantic work, *The Secret Doctrine*. In the evening she has many visitors of all sorts—inquirers, critics, skeptics, curiosity seekers, friends—and all are welcomed with such charming grace, friendliness, and simplicity that everyone is made to feel at home with her. By 10 o'clock generally all but intimate friends have retired, but they remain an hour or two later.

Notwithstanding that Mme. Blavatsky is beyond the vigor of middle age and for nearly three years past has been living in defiance of the leading London physicians, who gave her up long ago as hopelessly incurable of a deadly kidney disease that was liable to kill her at any moment, she never seems weary, but is the animated leader of conversation, speaking with equal ease in English, French, Italian, and Russian, or dropping into Sanskrit and Hindustani as occasion requires. Whether working or talking, she seems to be constantly rolling, lighting, and smoking cigarettes of Turkish tobacco. As for her personal appearance, she hardly seems changed at all from what she was when in [America] several years ago, except that she has grown somewhat stouter perhaps. The characteristics that are apparent in her countenance are, in equal blending, energy and great kindness.

Mme. Blavatsky now very seldom gives any manifestation of her occult powers, except to intimate friends; but I had, while over there, several evidences that she can do things quite inexplicable by any laws of "exact" science. Two years ago I lost, here in New York, a paper that was of considerable interest to me. I do not think anybody but myself knew that I had it, and I certainly mentioned to no one that I had lost it. One evening, a little over a fortnight ago, while I was sitting in Mme. Blavatsky's parlor with Mr. B. Keightley and several other persons, I happened to think of that paper. The Madame got up, went into the next room, and returning almost immediately, handed to me a sheet of paper. I opened it and found it an exact duplicate of the paper that I had lost two years before. It was actually a facsimile copy, as I recognized at once. I thanked her, and she said, "Well, I saw it in your head that you wanted it."

The silvery bell sounds in the astral current that were heard over her head by so many persons when she was here in New York still continue to follow her, and it is beyond question to those familiar with her life and work that she is in constant receipt of the most potent aid from the adepts, particularly her teacher, the Mahatma Morya, whose portrait hangs in her study and shows a dark and beautiful Indian face, full of sweetness, wisdom, and majesty. Of course it does not seem possible that he in Tibet instantaneously responds, either by a mental impression or a "precipitated" note to a mental interrogatory put by her in London, but it happens to be the fact that he does so all the same.

Her most intimate friends in London are the Countess Wachtmeister, the Keightleys, Mabel Collins, and Dr. Ashton Ellis. Mr. A. P. Sinnett drops in occasionally.

20c. ANONYMOUS
DECEMBER 1888, LONDON

["Theosophy and Theosophists" 1888]

It was as one from the outer darkness that I visited [Madame Blavatsky] a day or so ago. I had a delightfully humorous little note in my pocket, inviting me to tea and warning me that I should find the writer "as easy to interview as a sacred crocodile of old Nile." The envelope of this note bore a mystic symbol and the unimpeachable motto that there is no religion higher than truth.

I was led into a little snug room on the ground floor of a substantial house, where two lamps and a gas stove glowed like a triple star. I smelt Turkish tobacco strongly, and behind the red disk of a cigarette I saw the broad and impressive countenance of Madame Blavatsky. Short and redundant, and swathed rather than fitted in black silk, she is a very remarkable figure. The dark almost swarthy face looks a little heavy at first (my immediate impression was of a feminine reincarnation of Cagliostro), with its wide nostrils, large soft eyes, and full and weighty lips. But by and by it shows itself a mobile and expressive face, very sympathetic and very intellectual. And whilst on this gross subject of personal description (a liberty for which the interviewer should always apologize sincerely to the interviewed) let me note the delicate plumpness of the hands.

A circular box of carved wood at her elbow furnishes Madame Blavatsky with the tobacco for the cigarettes which she

HPB's drawing room at 17 Lansdowne Road, London

smokes incessantly, from six in the morning, when she commences work, until she puts out her lamp for the night. Besides the tobacco box, there is only one other notable object in her sanctum, the portrait of the Mahatma Morya (a descendant, she says, of the old dynasty of the Moryas), whom she calls her Master, a dark and beautiful Indian face, full of sweetness and wisdom. This seer Madame Blavatsky has seen, she says, at various times in the flesh: in England once, in India on many occasions, and some years ago she went to seek him in the fastnesses of Tibet, a romantic pilgrimage by no means free from peril, during which she penetrated some of the Buddhist monasteries or Lamaseries and had converse with the recluses there. But Madame Blavatsky's disciples have many stories to tell of the extraordinary way in which her Mahatma communicates with her. Letters that never paid postage, nor passed through St. Martin's-le-Grand, are seen to flutter down into her lap. Literary quotations that she is sometimes bothered to find are put into her hand written out upon strips of paper. The manuscript that she leaves on her desk overnight is often found by her in the morning with passages corrected, expunged, or rewritten, marginal notes inserted, and so on, in the handwriting of the Mahatma Morya.

Sufficiently surprising too are the powers with which her Theosophical associates credit Madame herself. Those who live with her in Lansdowne Road see wonders daily and have left off being surprised. Once accept the theory that the psychic faculties latent within us are capable, under certain conditions, of being developed to any extent, and magical doings of all sorts become easy of credence, and belief in what is called the astral is, I believe, a cardinal article of belief with the Theosophists. But these phenomena are not witnessed by everybody, and perhaps I need

HPB's residence at 17 Lansdowne Road, London

scarcely add that Madame Blavatsky (though freely offering me the contents of her tobacco box) declined to work a miracle for me. Doubtless her refusal was wise, for if I had seen one of these uncanny signs with my own eyes, which of you would have believed my report of it?

We talked of many things.

"What is Theosophy, Madame?" I asked. "Do you call it a religion?"

"Most distinctly not," she replied, "there are too many religions in the world already. I don't propose to add to the number."

"What, may I ask, is the Theosophical attitude towards these too numerous religions?"

Madame Blavatsky thereupon entered upon a long and interesting explanation on this subject, from which I gathered that Theosophy looks upon all religions as good in one sense, and all religions as bad in another sense. There are truths underlying all, and there are falsities overlying all. Most faiths are good at the core, all are more or less wrong in their external manifestations; and all the trappings of religions, all their shows and ceremonies, are entirely repudiated by the Theosophists. The conditions under which aspirants become members of the Theosophical Society are few and simple. Merely to join the Society, it is sufficient to profess oneself in sympathy with its objects, of which there are three in chief—the promotion of a universal brotherhood amongst men, the study of religions, and the development of the psychic faculties latent in man. The last-named object is for the attainment of advanced members, who have gained admittance to the esoteric section of the society.

Madame herself, in her vigorous intellectual way, is quite as dogmatic as the most dogmatic professor of what (under Theosophical favor) are called the exact sciences; and, indeed, dogmatism, both in affirmation and denial, seems the badge of all the Theosophical tribe.

It was seven o'clock before Madame Blavatsky had exhausted my interest, or I, as I hoped, her patience; and at seven the members of the household assembled for dinner.

The household consists of six or seven persons, including a young doctor of medicine, a student of law and a Frenchman, an American (the friend of Edison), and a Swedish Countess. The flourishing prospects of Madame's new work, *The Secret Doctrine*, the first edition of which is already disposed of, though the volumes are scarcely out of the printer's hands, were discussed during the meal. Madame's years—she is bordering on the sixties—and her occasional difficulties with the language—she is a Russian by birth—do not prevent her from being the most energetic and entertaining talker at her table.

It was the evening on which the Blavatsky Lodge holds its weekly meeting, and by half past eight the sanctum, whither we adjourned after dinner, was filled with a little gathering of both sexes. The subject for discussion was dreams. The circular tobacco box having been replenished by Madame's little maid, and the president in evening dress having taken his place by Madame's side, the secretary of the lodge began to ask questions from a paper.

20D. FRED J. DICK
DECEMBER 1888, LONDON

[Tingley 1921, 35–6]

Prior to meeting Madame H. P. Blavatsky in London in 1888 I had been admitted, along with others in Dublin, to membership in the Theosophical Society by William Q. Judge, then on a visit to Ireland. At that time I had already become familiar with the details of many infamous attacks which had been fulminated against the honor and integrity of HPB.

The pettiness and feebleness of all these stood out in clear-cut contrast with the spiritual nobility of her writings in *Isis Unveiled* and the magazines edited by her, and such accusations but served to strengthen one's enthusiasm for the great principles which underlie the idea of man's essential solidarity—to the philosophic rationale of which, demonstrated by her work and her references to the lore and knowledge of countless Teachers throughout the long ages, she had devoted her life energies and her very heart's blood.

Such attacks brought her unremitting suffering, as affecting the Cause she labored for; yet, for us beginners in the Science of Life, they showed well the inherent weaknesses of our complex nature, and enabled us better to realize the enormous import to the race of the message Theosophy holds out—a message delivered by H. P. Blavatsky in no uncertain terms, and in fact with a vigor, an eloquence, and an amplitude of historical and philosophic detail unrivaled in known history. While iconoclastically tearing to tatters most of the generally accepted beliefs and dogmas, scientific or otherwise, she stands revealed in her writings as a Master-builder possessed of a complete constructive philosophy of practical life and equally of cosmogenesis and anthropogenesis.

Her main purpose was to permeate the world with the ideas and teaching of the *ancient Wisdom-Religion*, primal source of all the world religions. It certainly was not to promulgate spiritualism, marvel seeking, or psychism of any kind. Let her writings attest.

She brought to both east and west the truths so long obscured regarding the great laws of karma, reincarnation, and the dual nature of man, together with a spiritual philosophy so exalted as to furnish the keynote for many successive lives of endeavor.

20E. BERTRAM KEIGHTLEY
1888, LONDON

[Keightley 1931, 25–7]

After a time, one learnt to realize that all [HPB's] storming, "cussing," and general raising Cain over the smallest trifles was just a "put-up job" and also an outlet and safety valve for the over-pressure of nervous energy which flowed in such an intense stream through her whole nature.

I well remember one incident that cut deep and taught me a lesson I never forgot. The work for some time had been heavy and anxious; in addition I had just then many personal worries and difficulties, so that my nerves got badly frayed. One day HPB sent upstairs for me before breakfast, and when I came to her, she just let loose and abused, scolded, and scarified me, hitting just every one of my weakest and tenderest spots, scarifying every weakness and fault, and "telling me off" till at last she "got my goat," and suddenly I felt a surge of real red-hot anger rise within me. I may remark that the whole matter, about which HPB was scolding and carrying on so angrily and almost viciously, was a matter with which I had nothing whatever to do, and of which even, I knew absolutely nothing. But I could not get in a word of denial or explanation, even edgeways. Well, I felt my temper go and my eyes flash. On the moment, HPB, who seemed almost raving with fury, stopped dead-silent and absolutely quiet. There was not even a quiver or vibration of anger *from* HPB in the air. She just looked me up and down and remarked coldly, "And you want to be an occultist." Then I saw and knew, and went off deeply ashamed, having learnt no small lesson.

20F. EDMUND RUSSELL
1888, LONDON

[Russell 1918, 262–4]

I knew [HPB] well in the last few years of her life and was often at her house in Lansdowne Road.

The whole world clamored for her likeness. I persuaded her to go with me to a photographer. What a day! Wind and rain and scurries of autumn leaves. She had no out-of-door clothes. Everything was given away as soon as brought to her.

I never could have accomplished it without the aid of Countess Wachtmeister. Appointment made, the cab was kept waiting for hours. Unaccustomed to go out, she would not move. "You want my death. I cannot step on the wet stones." Shawls, scarfs, fur were piled on. A sort of Russian turban tied over her head with a veil. Rugs spread from door to carriage. These were lifted and blown about by the storm so the Countess with the help of the coachman had to hold them down while I raised the umbrella over her head and helped her in. Afterwards the Countess told me that, when she first came to London, wife of an Ambassador from Sweden, two powdered footmen in livery followed wherever she went. "If my poor husband could know the day had come when I held carpets for another woman to tread upon, he would turn in his grave." This only smiling—she would have lain herself down for Madame to walk over.

Van der Weyde was a friend of mine. There disembarkation even more terrible! They don't unroll red carpets in Regent Street for nothing. "Come along, Your Majesty!" I said to keep up the illusion.

Once up the stairs, she flatly refused to [have her photograph] be taken. She was not an actress. What had I brought her to such a place for? Finally she was held, as I knew she would be, by the story of Van der Weyde's own experiments in the adaptation of electricity to photography.

"I will sit for you—only one—be quick—take me just as I am."

I bent over her and whispered, "Now let all the devil in you shine out of those eyes."

"Why, child, there is no devil in me."

She laughed, so the sitting was spoiled, but then all went well, and we got the famous likeness. She was pleased with it. I was not. She is there, but not all of her. I would have wished something at her writing table—taken by chance—in the long folds of her seamless garment—vibrations of light all around. She really enjoyed the adventure I think, for she told of being "bossed" and "carried as a bundle" for a long time, especially of the "Come along, your Majesty."

20G. VIOLET TWEEDALE
1888–1889, LONDON

[*Tweedale 1919, 51, 56–61*]

I shall never forget that first interview with a much maligned woman [Madame Blavatsky], whom I rapidly came to know intimately and love dearly. She was seated in a great armchair, with a table by her side on which lay tobacco and cigarette paper. Whilst she spoke, her exquisite taper fingers automatically rolled cigarettes. She was dressed in a loose black robe, and on her crinkly gray hair, she wore a black shawl. Her face was pure Kalmuck, and a network of fine wrinkles covered it. Her eyes, large and pale green, dominated the countenance—wonderful eyes in their arresting, dreamy mysticism.

I have often heard Blavatsky called a charlatan, and I am bound to say that her impish behavior often gave grounds for this description. She was foolishly intolerant of the many smart West End ladies who arrived in flocks, demanding to see spooks, masters, elementals, anything, in fact, in the way of phenomena.

Madame Blavatsky was a born conjuror. Her wonderful fingers were made for jugglers' tricks, and I have seen her often use them for that purpose. I well remember my amazement upon the first occasion on which she exhibited her occult powers, spurious and genuine.

I was sitting alone with her one afternoon, when the cards of Jessica, Lady Sykes, the late Duchess of Montrose and the Honorable Mrs. S——— (still living) were brought in to her. She said she would receive the ladies at once, and they were ushered in. They explained that they had heard of her new religion and her marvelous occult powers. They hoped she would afford them a little exhibition of what she could do.

Madame Blavatsky had not moved out of her chair. She was suavity itself, and whilst conversing, she rolled cigarettes for her visitors and invited them to smoke. She concluded that they were not particularly interested in the old faith which the young West called new; what they really were keen about was phenomena.

That was so, responded the ladies, and the burly Duchess inquired if Madame ever gave racing tips or lucky numbers for Monte Carlo?

Madame disclaimed having any such knowledge, but she was willing to afford them a few moments' amusement. Would one of the ladies suggest something she would like done?

Lady Sykes produced a pack of cards from her pocket and held them out to Madame Blavatsky, who shook her head.

"First remove the marked cards," she said.

Lady Sykes laughed and replied, "Which are they?"

Madame Blavatsky told her, without a second's hesitation. This charmed the ladies. It seemed a good beginning.

"Make that basket of tobacco jump about," suggested one of them.

The next moment the basket had vanished. I don't know where it went, I only know it disappeared by trickery, that the ladies looked for it everywhere, even under Madame Blavatsky's ample skirts, and that suddenly it reappeared upon its usual table. A little more jugglery followed and some psychometry, which was excellent, then the ladies departed, apparently well satisfied with the entertainment.

When I was once more alone with Madame Blavatsky, she turned to me with a wry smile and said, "Would you have me throw pearls before swine?"

I asked her if all she had done was pure trickery.

"Not all, but most of it," she unblushingly replied. "But now I will give you something lovely and real."

For a moment or two she was silent, covering her eyes with her hand, then a sound caught my ear. I can only describe what I heard as fairy music, exquisitely dainty and original. It seemed to proceed from somewhere just between the floor and the ceiling, and it moved about to different corners of the room. There was a crystal innocence in the music, which suggested the dance of joyous children at play.

"Now I will give you the music of life," said Madame Blavatsky.

For a moment or two there fell a trance-like silence. The twilight was creeping into the room and seemed to bring with it a tingling expectancy. Then it seemed to me that something entered from without and brought with it utterly new conditions, something incredible, unimagined, and beyond the bounds of reason.

Someone was singing, a distant melody was creeping nearer, yet I was aware it had never been distant, it was only becoming louder.

I suddenly felt afraid of myself. The air about me was ringing with vibrations of weird, unearthly music, seemingly as much around me as it was above and behind me. It had no whereabouts, it was unlocatable. As I listened my whole body quivered with wild elation and the sensation of the unforeseen.

There was rhythm in the music, yet it was unlike anything I had ever heard before. It sounded like a pastorale, and it held a call to which my whole being wildly responded.

Who was the player, and what was his instrument? He might have been a flautist, and he played with a catching lilt, a luxurious abandon that was an incarnation of Nature. It caught me suddenly away to green Sicilian hills, where the pipes of unseen players echo down the mountain sides, as the pipes of Pan once echoed through the rugged gorges and purple vales of Hellas and Thrace.

Alluring though the music was, and replete with the hot fever of life, it carried with it a thrill of dread. Its sweetness was cloying, its tenderness was sensuous. A balmy scent crept through the room, of wild thyme, of herbs, of asphodel and the muscadine of the wine press. It enwrapt me like an odorous vapor.

CHAPTER 20

The sounds began to take shape and gradually mold themselves into words. I knew I was being courted with subtlety and urged to fly out of my house of life.

My soul seemed to strain at the leash. Should I let go? Like a powerful opiate the allurement enfolded me, yet from out its thrall a small insistent voice whispered, "Caution! Where will you be led: Supposing you yield your will, would it ever be yours again?"

Now my brain was seized with a sense of panic and weakness. The music suddenly seemed replete with gay sinfulness and insolent conquest. It spoke the secrets which the nature myth so often murmurs to those who live amid great silences, of those dread mysteries of the spirit which yet invest it with such glory and wonderment.

With a violent reaction of fear, I rose suddenly, and as I did so, the whole scene was swept from out the range of my senses. I was back once more in Blavatsky's room with the creeping twilight and the far off hoarse roar of London stealing in at the open window. I glanced at Madame Blavatsky. She had sunk down in her chair, and she lay huddled up in deep trance. She had floated out with the music into a sea of earthly oblivion. Between her fingers she held a small Russian cross.

I knew that she had thrust me back to the world which still claimed me, and I went quietly out of the house into the streets of London.

On another occasion when I was alone with Madame Blavatsky, she suddenly broke off our conversation by lapsing into another language, which I supposed to be Hindustani. She appeared to be addressing some one else, and on looking over my shoulder I saw we were no longer alone. A man stood in the middle of the room. I was sure he had not entered by the door, window, or chimney, and as I looked at him in some astonishment, he salaamed to Madame Blavatsky and replied to her in the same language in which she had addressed him.

I rose at once to leave her, and as I bade her good-by she whispered to me, "Do not mention this." The man did not seem aware of my presence; he took no notice of me as I left the room.

He was dark in color and very sad looking, and his dress was a long, black cloak and a soft black hat, which he did not remove, pulled well over his eyes. I found out that evening that none of the general staff were aware of his arrival, and I saw him no more.

G. R. S. Mead

Chapter 21

London:
A Time of Fulfillment
1888–1889

*B*LAVATSKY'S YEARS in London were both remarkably productive in publications and notably influential in the response she evoked from those who met her. One of the most important of those responses was that of Annie Besant. William T. Stead, the social activist editor of the *Pall Mall Gazette*, who had received a review copy of *The Secret Doctrine*, enlisted Annie Besant to write that review (selection 21a). The result was Besant's admission as a Fellow of the Theosophical Society (selection 21b)—a revolutionary reversal of direction in her own life—followed by her rapid rise to prominence in the Society.

The year 1889 was one of completion for HPB. On May 10, Annie Besant joined the Theosophical Society. July saw the publication of *The Key to Theosophy*, a "clear Exposition, in the form of Question and Answer, of the Ethics, Science and Philosophy for the study of which the Theosophical Society has been founded." HPB took a vacation that same month at Fontainebleau, in France. There she wrote the major part of the devotional, mysti-

Annie Besant

cal work *The Voice of the Silence*, based on excerpts from an Eastern scripture, *The Book of the Golden Precepts*, which she had learned by heart during her training in the East. Later that month and early the next one, HPB was on the island of Jersey, to the south of Britain, where she called for G. R. S. Mead, who was serving as her secretary, to come to read critically the final part of *The Voice*, which was then published in September.

In August, Annie Besant put her property at 19 Avenue Road, in the St. John's Wood area of London, into trust as a headquarters for the British Section of the Theosophical Society. At the end of the year, HPB appointed Col. Olcott as her agent for the Esoteric Section of the Society in Asia.

21A. WILLIAM T. STEAD
1888, LONDON

[Collated from Stead 1909, 1:130–1, and Stead 1891]

It was in the year [1887] that Madame Blavatsky took up her abode in London. Madame [Olga] Novikov was charmed by her powerful intellect, which commanded her homage altogether apart from her pretension to have explored with steady foot the bewildering mazes of the occult world. She was, besides, a great Russian patriot.

Madame Novikov wrote to me one day: "I made Madame Blavatsky translate the enclosed letter for you, as I thought it so very interesting. Don't you think *so?* By the bye, she is dying to see you; so, unless you commit a murder, shall you not go there with me some afternoon?"

I did not respond to the appeal. My interest in occult studies, which had been stimulated by a curious prediction made at the first seance I ever attended, in 1881, had languished under the stress of mundane preoccupations. Madame Novikov repeated her invitation more insistently than before. Even then I do not think I should have consented to go had Madame Blavatsky not been a Russian. However, to make a long story short, I went. I was delighted with, and at the same time somewhat repelled by, Madame. Power was there, rude and massive, but she had the manners of a man, and a very unconventional man, rather than those of a lady. But we got on very well together, and Madame

Blavatsky gave me her portrait, certifying that I might call myself what I pleased, but that she knew I was a good theosophist.

The pleasant relations thus established with Madame Blavatsky had unexpected results. When the *Secret Doctrine* came in for review to the *Pall Mall* office I shrank dismayed from the task of mastering its contents. I took it down to Mrs. [Annie] Besant, who had been for some time past attending seances and interesting herself in the other world, and asked her if she would review it. She grappled with the task, was fascinated by its contents, and when she finished her review she asked me if I could introduce her to the author. I did so with pleasure.

There are those who imagine that because they can crack a joke about a teacup, they have disposed of Theosophy. Madame Blavatsky, they say, "was an impostor, a vulgar fraud. She was exposed by the Coulombs, shown up by the Psychical Research Society." They say all that, no doubt, but when all that is said and more besides, the problem of the personality of the woman remains full of interest, and even of wonder, to those who look below the surface of things.

Madame Blavatsky was a great woman. She was huge in body; and in her character, alike in its strength and weakness, there was something of the Rabelaisian gigantesque. But if she had all the nodosity of the oak, she was not without its strength; and if she had the contortions of the Sibyl, she possessed somewhat of her inspiration.

Of Madame Blavatsky the wonder-worker I knew nothing; I did not go to her seeking signs, and most assuredly no sign was given. She neither doubled a teacup in my presence nor did she even cause the familiar raps to be heard. All these manifestations seemed as the mere trivialities, the shavings, as it were, thrown off from the beam of cedar wood which she was fashioning as one of the pillars in the Temple of Truth. I do not remember ever referring to them in our conversation, and it is slightly incomprehensible to me how any one can gravely contend that they constitute her claim to respect.

What Madame Blavatsky did was an immeasurably greater thing than the doubling of teacups. She made it possible for some

of the most cultivated and skeptical men and women of this generation to believe—believe ardently, to an extent that made them
proof against ridicule and disdainful of persecution—that not only
does the invisible world that encompasses us contain Intelligences
vastly superior to our own in knowledge of the Truth, but that it
is possible for man to enter into communion with these hidden
and silent ones, and to be taught of them the Divine mysteries of
Time and of Eternity. Madame Blavatsky, a Russian, suspected of
being a spy, converted leading Anglo-Indians to a passionate
belief in her Theosophy mission.

Madame Blavatsky taught not merely that the Mahatmas
existed, but that they were able and willing to enter into direct
communication with men. Madame Blavatsky proclaimed herself as the directly commissioned messenger of the celestial
hierarchy, charged by them to reveal the Path by which any
one who was worthy and willing might enter into direct communion with these sublime Intelligences. I was but an outsider in
the court of the Gentiles, a curious observer, and never a disciple.
I cannot speak of these inner mysteries to which only the initiates
are admitted.

But I can say of my own knowledge that she was undoubtedly a very gifted and original woman to converse with, a fiery,
impulsive, passionate creature, full of failings, and personally the
very reverse of beautiful. There she was, a wonderful and powerful
personality, the like of which I have never met either in Russia or
in England. She was unique, but she was intensely human.

21 B. ANNIE BESANT
SPRING 1889, LONDON

[Besant 1893, 308–13]

Since 1886 there had been slowly growing up a conviction
that my philosophy was not sufficient, that life and mind were

other than, more than, I had dreamed. Psychology was advancing with rapid strides; hypnotic experiments were revealing unlooked-for complexities in human consciousness. I studied the obscurer sides of consciousness, dreams, hallucinations. The phenomena of clairvoyance, clairaudience, thought-reading were found to be real. I finally convinced myself that there was some hidden thing, some hidden power, and resolved to seek until I found, and by the early spring of 1889 I had grown desperately determined to find at all hazards what I sought. At last, sitting alone in deep thought as I had become accustomed to do after the sun had set, filled with an intense but nearly hopeless longing to solve the riddle of life and mind, I heard a Voice that was later to become to me the holiest sound on earth, bidding me take courage for the light was near. A fortnight passed, and then Mr. [W. T.] Stead gave into my hands two large volumes. "Can you review these? My young men all fight shy of them, but you are quite mad enough on these subjects to make something of them." I took the books; they were the two volumes of *The Secret Doctrine*, written by H. P. Blavatsky.

Home I carried my burden, and sat me down to read. As I turned over page after page, the interest became absorbing; but how familiar it seemed; how my mind leapt forward to presage the conclusions, how natural it was, how coherent, how subtle, and yet how intelligible. I was dazzled, blinded by the light in which disjointed facts were seen as parts of a mighty whole, and all my puzzles, riddles, problems, seemed to disappear.

I wrote the review, and asked Mr. Stead for an introduction to the writer, and then sent a note asking to be allowed to call. I received the most cordial of notes, bidding me come, and in the soft spring evening, Herbert Burrows and I—for his aspirations were as mine on this matter—walked from Notting Hill Station, wondering what we should meet, to the door of 17 Lansdowne Road. A pause, a swift passing through hall and outer room, through folding doors thrown back, a figure in a large chair before a table, a voice, vibrant, compelling. "My dear Mrs. Besant, I have so long wished to see you," and I was standing with my hand in her firm grip, and looking for the first time in this life straight into the eyes of HPB. I was conscious of a sudden leaping forth of my heart—was it recognition?—and then, I am ashamed to say, a fierce rebellion, a fierce withdrawal, as of some wild animal when it feels a mastering hand. I sat down, after some introductions that conveyed no ideas to me, and listened. She talked of travels, of various countries, easy brilliant talk, her eyes veiled, her exquisitely molded fingers rolling cigarettes incessantly. Nothing special to record, no word of occultism, nothing mysterious, a woman of the world chatting with her evening visitors. We rose to go, and for a moment the veil lifted, and two brilliant, piercing eyes met mine, and with a yearning throb in the voice: "Oh, my dear Mrs. Besant, if you would only come among us!" I felt a well-nigh uncontrollable desire to bend down and kiss her, under the compulsion of that yearning voice, those compelling eyes, but with a flash of the old unbending pride and an inward jeer at my own folly, I said a commonplace polite good-bye, and turned away with some inanely courteous and evasive remarks. "Child," she said to me long afterwards, "your pride is terrible; you are as proud as Lucifer himself."

Once again I went, and asked about the Theosophical Society, wishful to join, but fighting against it. For I saw, distinct and clear—with painful distinctness, indeed—what that joining would mean. I had largely conquered public prejudice against me by my work on the London School Board. Was I to plunge into a new vortex of strife, and make myself a mark for ridicule—worse than hatred—and fight again the weary fight for an unpopular truth? Must I turn against materialism, and face the shame of publicly confessing that I had been wrong, misled by intellect to ignore the Soul?—what would be the look in Charles Bradlaugh's eyes when I told him that I had become a Theosophist? The struggle was sharp and keen. And so it came to pass that I went again to Lansdowne Road to ask about the Theosophical Society. H. P. Blavatsky looked at me piercingly for a moment. "Have you read the report about me of the Society for Psychical Research?" "No, I never heard of it, so far as I know." "Go and read it, and if, after read-

369

ing it, you come back—well." And nothing more would she say on the subject, but branched off to her experiences in many lands.

I borrowed a copy of the report, read and reread it. Quickly I saw how slender was the foundation on which the imposing structure was built: the continual assumptions on which conclusions were based, the incredible character of the allegations, and—most damning fact of all—the foul source from which the evidence was derived. Everything turned on the veracity of the Coulombs, and they were self-stamped as partners in the alleged frauds. Could I put such against the frank, fearless nature that I had caught a glimpse of, against the proud fiery truthfulness that shone at me from the clear, blue eyes, honest and fearless as those of a noble child? Was the writer of *The Secret Doctrine* this miserable impostor, this accomplice of tricksters, this foul and loathsome deceiver, this conjuror with trapdoors and sliding panels? I laughed aloud at the absurdity and flung the report aside with the righteous scorn of an honest nature that knew its own kin when it met them, and shrank from the foulness and baseness of a lie. The next day saw me at the Theosophical Publishing Company's office at 7 Duke Street, Adelphi, where Countess Wachtmeister—one of the lealest of HPB's friends—was at work, and I signed an application to be admitted as fellow of the Theosophical Society.

On receiving my diploma, I betook myself to Lansdowne Road, where I found HPB alone. I went over to her, bent down, and kissed her, but said no word. "You have joined the Society?" "Yes," "You have read the report?" "Yes." "Well?" I knelt down before her and clasped her hands in mine, looking straight into her eyes. "My answer is, will you accept me as your pupil, and give me the honor of proclaiming you my teacher in the face of the world?" Her stern, set face softened, the unwonted gleam of tears sprang to her eyes; then, with a dignity more regal, she placed her hand upon my head. "You are a noble woman. May Master bless you."

21c. HERBERT BURROWS
SPRING 1889,
LONDON

[HPB: In Memory 1891, 36–7]

Beset with problems of life and mind that our materialism could not solve, dwelling intellectually on what are now to us the inhospitable shores of agnosticism, Annie Besant and I ever craved more light. We had read *The Occult World*, and in bygone years we had heard—who had not?—of the strange woman whose life seemed to be a contradiction of our most cherished theories, but as yet the philosophy of the book was to us but assertion, the life of the woman a career which we had no means of examining. Skeptical, critical, trained by long years of public controversy to demand the most rigid scientific proof of things which were outside our experience, Theosophy was to us an unknown, and, as it then seemed, an impossible land. And yet it fascinated, for it promised much, and with talking, with reading, the fascination grew. With the fascination also grew the desire to know, and so, on an ever-to-be remembered evening, with a letter of introduction from Mr. W. T. Stead, then editor of the *Pall Mall Gazette*, as our passport, we found ourselves face to face, in the drawing room of 17 Lansdowne Road, with the woman whom we afterwards learned to know and to love as the most wonderful woman of her time.

I was not foolish enough to look for miracles. I did not expect to see Madame Blavatsky float, nor did I crave for materialized teacups, but I did want to hear about Theosophy, and I did not hear much. She whom we were there to see was a stout, unwieldy lady, playing Russian "patience," and keeping up a stream of conversation on nearly every subject except the one which was just then nearest our minds. No attempt at proselytizing, no attempt to "fix" us (we were *not* hypnotised!), but all the while the wonderful eyes were flashing light, and, in spite of the bodily infirmity, which was even then painfully apparent, there was a reserve of power which gave the impression that we were seeing, not the real woman, but only the surface character of someone who had endured much and who knew much.

I tried to keep an open, impartial mind, and I believe I succeeded. I was genuinely anxious to learn, but I was critical and on the watch for the slightest attempt at hoodwinking. When I afterwards discovered something of HPB's extraordinary insight, I was not surprised to find that she had gauged accurately and unerringly my mental attitude on this my first visit, and it is an attitude which she never really discouraged. If those who talk so foolishly about her magnetizing people could but know how she continually impressed upon us the absolute duty of proving all things and holding fast only to that which is good!

To go once was to go again, and so it came that after a few visits I began to see light. I caught glimpses of a lofty morality, of a self-sacrificing zeal, of a coherent philosophy of life, of a clear and definite science of man and his relation to a spiritual universe. These it was which attracted me—not phenomena, for I saw none. For the first time in my mental history I had found a teacher who could pick up the loose threads of my thought and satisfactorily weave them together; and the unerring skill, the vast knowledge, the loving patience of the teacher grew on me hour by hour. Quickly I learned that the so-called charlatan and trickster was a noble soul, whose every day was spent in unselfish work, whose whole life was pure and simple as a child's, who counted never the cost of pain or toil if these could advance the great cause to which her every energy was consecrated. Open as the day to a certain point, she was the incarnation of kindness—silent as the grave if need be, she was sternness personified at the least sign of faithlessness to the work which was her life. Grateful, so grateful for every affectionate attention, careless, so careless of all that concerned herself, she bound us to her, not simply as wise teacher, but as loving friend. Once I was broken down through long bodily and mental strain and the wheels of my life ran so heavily that they nearly stopped. Through it all her solicitude was untiring, and one special proof of it that she gave, too personal to mention here, would have been thought of, perhaps, but by one in a million.

Perfect—no; faults—yes; the one thing she would hate most of all would be the indiscriminate praise of her personality. But when I have said that she was sometimes impetuous as a whirlwind, a very cyclone when she was really roused, I have told nearly all. And I have often thought it was more than possible that some of these outbursts were assumed for a special object. Lately they had almost vanished. Her enemies sometimes said she was rough and rude. We who knew her knew that a more unconventional woman, in the very realest sense of the word, never lived. Her absolute indifference to all outward forms was a true indifference based upon her inner spiritual knowledge of the verities of the universe. Sitting by her when strangers came, as they did come from every corner of the earth, I have often watched with the keenest amusement their wonder at seeing a woman who always said what she thought. Given a prince and she would probably shock him; given a poor man and he would have her last shilling and her kindliest word.

21D. ANNIE BESANT
JULY 1889,
FONTAINEBLEAU, FRANCE

*[Collated from Besant 1893, 321–3,
and Besant 1969, 32–3]*

I was called away to Paris to attend, with Herbert Burrows, the great Labor Congress held there from July 15th to July 20th, and spent a day or two at Fontainebleau with H. P. Blavatsky, who had gone abroad for a few weeks' rest. There I found her translating the wonderful fragments from "The Book of the Golden Precepts," now so widely known under the name of *The Voice of the Silence*. She wrote it swiftly, without any material copy before her. I sat in the room while she was writing it. I know that she did not write it referring to any books, but she wrote it down steadily, hour after hour, exactly as though she were writing either from memory or from reading it where no book was and in the evening made me read it aloud to see if the "English was decent." Herbert Burrows was there, and Mrs. Candler, a staunch American Theosophist, and we sat round HPB while I read. The translation was in perfect and beautiful English, flowing and musical; only a word or two could we find to alter, and she looked at us like a startled child, wondering at our praises—praise that any one with the literary sense would endorse if they read that exquisite prose poem.

A little earlier in the same day I had asked her as to the agencies at work in producing the taps so constantly heard at Spiritualistic seances. "You don't use spirits to produce taps," she said; "see here." She put her hand over my head, not touching it, and I heard and felt slight taps on the bone of my skull, each sending a little electric thrill down the spine. She then carefully explained how such taps were producible at any point desired by the operator and how interplay of the current to which they were due might be caused otherwise than by conscious human volition. It was in this fashion that she would illustrate her verbal teachings, proving by experiment the statements made as to the existence of subtle forces controllable by the trained mind. The phenomena all belonged to the scientific side of her teaching, and she never committed the folly of claiming authority for her philosophic doctrines on the ground that she was a wonder worker. And constantly she would remind us that there was no such thing as "miracle," that all the phenomena she had produced were worked by virtue of a knowledge of nature deeper than that of average people and by the force of a well-trained mind and will; some of them were what she would describe as "psychological tricks," the creation of images by force of imagination, and in pressing them on others as a "collective hallucination"; others, such as the moving of solid articles, either by an astral hand projected to draw them towards her, or by using an elemental; others by reading in the astral light, and so on.

21E. G. R. S. MEAD
AUGUST 1889 – 1891,
LONDON

[HPB: In Memory 1891, 31–4]

It was not until the beginning of August 1889 that I came to work permanently with HPB. She was away [from London] in Jersey [an island off the south coast of England]. A pressing telegram came from HPB, and I started for Jersey. What a warm greeting there was in the porch of that honeysuckle-covered house, and what a fuss to have everything comfortable for the new comer!

It has often been a surprise to me that the chief of the accusations and slanders brought against HPB have been those of fraud and concealment. According to my experience, she was ever overtrustful of others and quite prodigal in her frankness. As an instance, no sooner had I arrived than she gave me the run of all her papers and set me to work on a pile of correspondence that would otherwise have remained unanswered till doomsday; for if she detested anything, it was answering letters. I then was initiated into the mysteries of *Lucifer* and soon had my hands full with transmission of directions, alterations, and counterdirections to Bertram Keightley, who was then subeditor, for in those days HPB *would* not let one word go into *Lucifer* until she had seen and reseen it, and she added to and cut up the proofs until the last moment.

One day, shortly after my arrival, HPB came into my room unexpectedly with a manuscript and handed it to me, saying, "Read that, old man, and tell me what you think of it." It was the MS of the third part of the *Voice of the Silence*, and while I read she sat and smoked her cigarettes, tapping her foot on the floor, as was often her habit. I read on, forgetting her presence in the beauty and sublimity of the theme until she broke in upon my silence with, "Well?" I told her it was the grandest thing in all our Theosophical literature and tried, contrary to my habit, to convey in words some of the enthusiasm that I felt. But even then HPB was not content with her work and expressed the greatest apprehension that she had failed to do justice to the original in her translation and could hardly be persuaded that she had done well. This was one of her chief characteristics. Never was she confident of her own literary work and cheerfully listened to all criticisms, even from persons who should have remained silent. Strangely enough, she was always most timorous of her best articles and works and most confident of her polemical writings.

When we returned to Lansdowne Road, both Dr. Archibald Keightley and Bertram Keightley left for abroad, the former on a voyage round the world, the latter to lecture in the United States. And so their duties came mostly to me, and I gradually began to see a great deal of her alone at her work owing to the necessity of the case.

Let me see if I can give some idea of how the work was done.

To begin with there was *Lucifer*, of which she was then sole editor. In the first place HPB never read a MS, she required to see it in proof and then mostly "averaged" its contents. What she *was* particular about was the length of the copy, and she used to laboriously count the number of words in each paper, and would never be persuaded of the accuracy of my count when I in my turn "averaged" the length. If I suggested that mine was the most expeditious method, she would proceed to tell me some home truths about Oxford and Cambridge education, and I often thought she used to continue her primitive methods of arithmetical computation on purpose to cure me of my impatience and my confidence in my own superiority. Another great thing was the arranging of the different articles. In those days she would never entrust this to any other hand, and the measuring of everything was a painful operation.

Getting *Lucifer* through the press was invariably a rush, for she generally wrote her leader [editorial] the last thing and, having been used to it, considered the printers, if anybody, were to blame if it did not appear in time.

The first hour in the morning after breakfast will ever remain with me a pleasant recollection. Everything was so unconventional. I used to sit on the arm of her great armchair and obediently smoke the cigarette she offered, while she opened the letters, told me what she wanted done, and signed diplomas and certificates, the latter under great pressure, however, for she detested such mechanical work.

Though HPB left much of her correspondence to me, still it was not without a distinct supervision, for she would suddenly call for a reply that had not yet gone out or for the copy of an old letter, without any warning, and if there were any mistakes, the lecture I received was not reassuring to my discomfiture. One thing she was always impressing upon me, and this was to develop a sense of the "fitness of things," and she was merciless if this law of harmony were broken, leaving no loophole of escape, and listening to no excuse, with her overpowering reason and knowledge, which in spite of its apparently disconnected expression, always went home; although, indeed, the minute afterward, she was again the affectionate friend and elder brother, shall I even say, comrade, as she alone knew how to be.

21F. ANONYMOUS
SEPTEMBER 1889, LONDON

["Visit to Madame Blavatsky" 1889]

A few days ago it was the writer's good fortune to call upon Madame Blavatsky at her home in London. The day was rainy, as London days always are, and the drive from Charing Cross to

Holland Park in a two-wheeled cab would have been anything but agreeable, had not the mind for a time forgotten the body and busied itself with memories of the long years of patient waiting since first the desire to see her had taken possession of it. Pilgrims to Mecca, the devout who at length have audience with the Pope, the American who gains the privilege of a presentation at court, the tourist who sees Mont Blanc for the first time, all these sink into insignificance before the experience of emotions in which all these are blended, and a something added which mystery alone gives, as one wheels along the crowded London thoroughfares on a visit to Madame Blavatsky.

The rain increases every moment, and after twenty minutes' hard driving the cabman stops at No. 7 Lansdowne Road. It no longer rains, it pours, and the pilgrim dashes through the falling torrents to find that the number is not 7, but 17. With thanks for the information and the mental comment that the lady in question must be well known, another dash through the rain is made and the number is sought. Lansdowne Road is one of those wide, beautiful streets that are to be found in the neighborhood of Hyde Park, where every house is a home, and a home that might satisfy nobility. Well kept gardens or yards of green shrubbery add a charm to the substantial stone buildings that are here the fashion. "Oui, Madame, entrez, s'il vous plait," was the cordial response to the question, "Is Madame Blavatsky in, and can I see her?"

Ushered into the first room to the left, wherein a large table and furniture betoken use—perhaps as a dining room, perhaps as a reception room, and sometimes as a study, for upon the table were divers papers and writings—I waited for further orders. A few moments later the folding doors were thrown open and I stood face to face with a gentleman of grand physique, of genial face, of wonderful beard, a gentleman so unique in manner and appearance that I at once involuntarily exclaimed, "Colonel Olcott."

"The same, and you are my countrywoman. Be seated." He had only arrived in London from India a few days before, and the minutes flew as he spoke of the work, and was only interrupted by a door opening, announcing the entrance of Madame Blavatsky.

How shall I describe her? It would be impossible. A general impression of kindliness, of power, of wonderful gifts, is all that remains at this moment on my mind. She moved with difficulty, for she was suffering greatly from rheumatism, but she laughingly asserted, as she seated herself in an easy chair, "I have cheated the doctors and death so many times before, they say, that I hope to cheat this rheumatism also, but it is not so easy to manage."

"But you still write, Madame?"

"Of course, I write as much as ever"; and Colonel Olcott interrupted with, "What matters about a little rheumatism so long as it does not creep into her head or her writings?" And we all laughed. When I said, "*Lucifer* is quite at home in America," she replied with spirit, "They have boycotted it in London and will not allow it to be sold at the newsstands." I could scarcely comprehend this, and she laughed as she said, "There are people who believe I am the devil with horns and hoofs," and again we laughed.

We talked of Theosophy and its rapid spread. "Have you seen this work noticed, Madame?" and she laid in my hand the advanced sheets of her new book, *The Key to Theosophy*. I had not; and she said it would be issued very soon, also a smaller work she had just finished, *The Voice of the Silence*. When I expressed surprise at the amount of writing she had done, as well as the immense knowledge displayed, Colonel Olcott remarked: "I worked with Madame Blavatsky several years and know all about it. She is a steam engine at writing, and when I tell you that in writing *Isis Unveiled*, with its large number of extracts from ancient writings, she had access but to a small bookcase of ordinary books, you will believe me when I tell you that she reads as clearly in the Astral light as from the open pages."

All this time I was conscious of a pair of eyes that were reading my very thoughts, and a face opposite me that might become any moment as immovable as a sphinx, but was very kindly and animated at the present moment. I can imagine no personality so expressive of indomitable will power as that of Madame Blavatsky.

The room in which we sat was instinct with her individuality. It was full of everything that suggested thought, refinement, literary labor, an interest in friends, but there was no place for mere display of useless ornament. The table, with Colonel Olcott on one side and herself on the other, was loaded with papers and books. The walls were covered with photographs and here in the heart of the bustling city lives and works the founder of the Theosophical Society that now numbers in America alone more than thirty branches. All this has been accomplished in little over a decade.

As I rose to go, Madame Blavatsky took my hand warmly in her own and bade me adieu, with kind regards to her American friends. "America," she said, "is the best and the worst, the kindest and most abusive country in the world."

It was still pouring when Colonel Olcott escorted the stranger to the cab and with the words, "We hope Madame will soon be completely restored," the door closed, and another half hour over London pavements in a two-wheeled cab, in a pouring rain, only intensified the impressions made by the visit to the most wonderful woman of the age.

21G. JAMES BERNARD OLD
NOVEMBER 1889, LONDON

[Old 1941, 107–9]

My first recollection of HPB is in connection with my brother Walter ("Sepharial," astrological nom de plume). He was very much interested in Theosophy. Walter resigned his banking position and went to London to become a helper at the Theosophical headquarters. My mother was extremely anxious about his connection with the Theosophical Society, and naturally thought he had made a great mistake on leaving a very profitable bank employment for a nonpaid secretarial position. So I was sent to see what they were doing with him.

I have a description of [HPB's] personal appearance as she struck me on first meeting her at Lansdowne Road, [November] 1889. This is taken from a personal diary which I used to write up.

After arriving in London we went to Lansdowne Road, and my brother introduced Mme. H. P. Blavatsky. Imagine an elderly woman, stout and phlegmatic, in an unconventional armchair, draped in a loose black gown which hid her immense proportions. A large head almost leonine and masculine in its bold outlines. Imagine two gray eyes soft as a gazelle's, very prominent, and having a faraway vision. Further peculiarity in the personality of HPB were her hands, fingers long and tapering, soft and agile; turned outward at the ends, the nails were thin and beautifully shaped.

I told my mother when I got home from my first visit that Walter was all right. If he got nothing in the nature of a salary, he certainly was getting wisdom and happiness. He had full scope for the study of astrology in an excellent atmosphere and environment.

She was quite a character and a very remarkable one at that; she certainly had powers beyond the ordinary which she used on special occasions. Of one such occasion, I happened to be a silent witness, and on this occasion my brother Walter was the subject. He had been thinking about some astrological problem and came into the sitting room looking serious and harassed. HPB and I were having a chat; she evidently sensed something from my brother, so in a masterful way directed him to sit down on the sofa and rest himself. Then she turned to me and softly said, "Don't be alarmed, I am going to show him what he wants to know." She only touched his thumb with the ring she had upon her finger, and he instantly fell asleep as in a trance, just as one sees a sensitive go into a trance during a performance of hypnotism. In a very short time, he was awakened and she said to him, "Do you understand what you saw?" He said, "Yes, and it is the answer to my astrological problem in Hebrew letters of fire." "Yes," she said, "that is right. But at present you must not go over by yourself." Then she again turned to me and said that she had been away from her body three times during my brother's trance or sleep.

H. P. Blavatsky's last photograph

Chapter 22

AVENUE ROAD,
ST. JOHN'S WOOD:
CONCLUSION
1890–1891

A NNIE BESANT'S house at 19 Avenue Road, St. John's Wood, was inaugurated on July 3, 1890, as a new center of Theosophical work, serving as the European headquarters of the Theosophical Society and as HPB's residence. That house became also the meeting place of HPB's Inner Group, twelve of her students who were eager for more intense training than was feasible in a larger, more general gathering. HPB, being concerned for the continuance of the esoteric side of her work after her death, probably regarded the Inner Group as a training ground for a successor.

In February 1891, the British Section headquarters were moved to 17 Avenue Road, next door to Besant's house. In March or April a second edition of *The Key to Theosophy* was published, including a glossary by HPB. In April, Annie Besant brought the last letter from HPB to the American Theosophical Society convention, meeting that year in Boston. That same month an epidemic of influenza broke out in London, and most of the staff at Avenue Road contracted the disease, several critically so. HPB had a very high fever and difficulty breathing. On May 8, at 2:25 PM, she passed away peacefully in the company of several of her students. Olcott, who was on a lecture tour in Australia, had several premonitions of her death on that and the following day, before the news reached him by cable. HPB's body was cremated on May 11 at the Woking Crematorium in Surrey.

With the background of her writings and teachings, her life and character, her mission and inner powers, H. P. Blavatsky was the greatest esotericist in the history of Western civilization, and a link with the lore and adepts of the East.

22A. HENRY S. OLCOTT
JULY 1890, LONDON

[Olcott 1931, 4:254–6]

It was in [July] 1890 that HPB and her staff settled in the "Headquarters," 19 Avenue Road, St. John's Wood, London, and it was here that in the following year she died. It was a large house, standing in its own grounds, which formed a pleasant garden, with bits of lawn, shrubbery, and a few tall trees. Mounting the front steps, one entered a vestibule and short hall, from each side of which doors opened into rooms. The front one on the left was HPB's working room, and her small bedchamber adjoined it. From this inner room a short passage led into a rather spacious chamber, which was built for and occupied by the Esoteric Section. To the right of the hall on entering was an artistically furnished dining room, which was also used for the reception of visitors. Back of this was a small room, then used as a general workroom. A door cut through the north wall of the dining room gave access to the new hall of the Blavatsky Lodge; while one cut in the south wall of HPB's room led into the office of the General Secretary of the European Section [of the Theosophical Society]. The upper stories of the house were sleeping apartments. The meeting hall of the Blavatsky Lodge was of corrugated iron, the walls and ceiling sheathed with unpainted wood. Mr. R. Machell, the artist, had covered the two sloping halves of the ceiling with the symbolic representations of six great religions and of the zodiacal signs. At the south end was a low platform for the presiding officer and the lecturer of the evening. The hall had a seating capacity of about 200. On the opening night [July 3, 1890] the room was crammed, and many were unable to gain admission. The speakers were Mrs. Besant, Mr. Sinnett, a Mrs. Woolff (of America), and Mr. [Bertram] Keightley. HPB was present but said nothing, on account of the critical state of her health.

HPB's workroom was crammed with furniture, and on the walls hung a large number of photographs of her personal friends and of members of the Esoteric Section. Her large writing desk faced a window through which she could see the front grassplot and trees, while the view of the street was shut out by a high brick wall. Avenue Road was a veritable beehive of workers, with no place for drones, HPB herself setting the example of tireless literary drudgery, while her strong auric influence enwrapped and stimulated all about her.

22B. ALICE L. CLEATHER
JULY 1890 – MAY 1891, LONDON

[Cleather 1923, 21–4]

[In July, 1890] HPB and the Lansdowne Road household [moved] into Mrs. Besant's house in Avenue Road. A lecture hall had been added to [the] house (a large detached one, standing in a garden) for the meetings of the Blavatsky Lodge, both public and private. It was also used for the meetings of the ES [Esoteric Section]. This hall was at the side of the house furthest from HPB's quarters, and she did not appear as frequently, nor was she as accessible as was the case at Lansdowne Road. Failing health had much to say to this, but before she became almost entirely confined to her own rooms she would sometimes be present at the Lodge meetings. On such occasions her presence was both an inspiration and a "terror." Once, when Mrs. Besant was in the chair, and a rather lengthy and stupid paper was being read, the whole room could hear HPB's stage whisper of agonized appeal: "Oh stop her, Annie—*stop her!*"

To the ES meetings HPB rarely, if ever, came (in person, at least); and, on the formation of the Inner Group of the ES [in August 1890], she was seen even less often outside her own rooms, save in her bath chair, in the garden at the back of the house.

The twelve members of the Inner Group were six men and six women: Countess [Constance] Wachtmeister, Mrs. [Isabel] Cooper-Oakley, Miss Emily Kislingbury, Miss Laura Cooper, Mrs. [Annie] Besant, [Mrs. Alice Cleather herself], Dr. Archibald

H. P. Blavatsky in her bath chair with James Pryse and G. R. S. Mead

Keightley, Mr. Herbert Coryn, Mr. Claude Wright, [Mr. G. R. S.] Mead, Mr. [E. T.] Sturdy, [and] Mr. Walter Old.

The Inner Group was formed, and held its weekly meetings at 19 Avenue Road, in a room which had been specially built for it, leading out of HPB's bedroom; into it no one but herself and her twelve pupils ever entered. We had each our own place and our own chair; and HPB sat with her six men pupils on her right, and the six women on her left-hand side, in semi-circular formation, during our instructions.*

*[The complete and unabridged version of HPB's instructions to the Inner Group is now available under the title *The Inner Group Teachings of H. P. Blavatsky to Her Personal Pupils (1890-91)*, compiled and annotated by Henk J. Spierenburg, 2nd revised and enlarged edition (San Diego, CA: Point Loma Publications, 1995). —DHC]

22c. ESTHER WINDUST
JULY 1890 – MAY 1891,
LONDON

[Windust 1950, 1–2]

The first time that I saw [HPB] has made an ineffaceable impression on me. An acquaintance invited me to go with her to a meeting of members and associates to Avenue Road, London. It was a regular evening meeting. "One should see this woman," she said, "as there is told so much about her, good and bad, but most people look on her as a fraud."

So I went—without much enthusiasm—to see an interesting woman, and with a strong resolution to look well out of my eyes!

The hall was not full, and we sat more or less in the middle and could well see the podium, on which stood two easy chairs and at the side a stand for the speaker. Soon two ladies appeared, Mrs. Besant, who shortly before had become president of the Blavatsky Lodge, and another lady, not tall, but stout. "Look, that must be Mme. Blavatsky," whispered my cicerone. I could only say "Sh!" and pulled a little away.

I had seen many people in many lands, stars in their own fir-mament, art, theatre, politics, literature, etc.—but this—never! This small, simple woman with a shawl on her shoulders, who filled the big chair, looked smaller than she was because of her stout body. But at that moment I only saw her face with those clear, blue eyes, and the hands on the lap. I studied art at that time, and never in my life had I seen such perfect hands. But this was not even of so much importance. What overwhelmed me was the force and the impersonal love that surrounded her and radiated from her and which gave me the impression of moving, flimsy light in which faces and forms appeared and disappeared, and even scenes that came up and then disappeared again. Later, much later, I believe, I recognized many of those faces. I knew nothing then of auras, and sat looking, fascinated. I knew then that I sat in the presence of someone greater, enormously greater, than ever I had dreamt.

Scenes out of Egypt appeared and disappeared, and also from other Southern or Eastern countries, which I had never seen. I remember that I thought of her as a living Sphinx, in contact, conscious intimate contact, with the occult Mysteries of the olden time. The light remained, though the mysterious images of per-sons dissolving changed. I had never seen such a thing, and the impression was formidable. I heard little of the lecture. Walter Old gave a lecture about the Sun, and after the lecture one could put questions, and when the audience did not do it, the speaker himself put questions to HPB.

Later I attended many lectures, but that one remains for me a landmark. I joined the Theosophical Society and became a member of the Blavatsky Lodge, but my life was changed; it could not be the same. I had a look into another world. Had I not been so impossibly shy, I would have written to HPB and visited her to put questions. But I did not dare, and when I had to go to the continent some months later, I was very glad to get an invitation to come to Avenue Road that gave me the opportunity to take leave of her before my departure to France. But once in the room, I took a chair near the door. When HPB came in I was very glad, but could only sit and look, overwhelmed at the remembrance of what I had seen that first evening, and now by the feeling of the enormous majesty of that small figure, the Messenger sent out by the Great White Lodge to bring help to the suffering humanity of the West.

I believe that I would have remained sitting in that chair till the end of the evening, without saying a word to any one, if Countess Wachtmeister had not come to me and, with a soft urge, taken me with her to talk to HPB.

When at last I took leave, very much under the impression of her charm, she looked at me with kind eyes and said, after the good wishes for the journey, "Come to see us as soon as you get back!" I was delighted, and at the same time on the point of tears, for I knew at once that I would never see her again in that body.

22D. JAMES MORGAN PRYSE
AUGUST 1889, LOS ANGELES,
CALIFORNIA, AND 1890–91, LONDON

[Pryse 1935, 1–4]

As a personality, "the Old Lady," as we affectionately called her, was like a mother to me; but if my reminiscences were to be confined to that personality, dealing only with happenings and doings in the physical world, they would be of little interest and would convey an utterly false impression of the real HPB with whom I was acquainted. So I must tell this tale of two worlds, however strange and incredible it may seem to many.

During the most impressionable years of childhood, I lived in a Welsh community in Minnesota, among a people who believed in fairies, saw ghosts occasionally, and had other psychic experiences, of which they spoke freely. Being of the same race myself, I had similar experiences.

In those days, while yet but a small boy, I first came into mental contact, vaguely, with HPB. In my father's library there was an old "Dictionary of Biography," Goodrich's, if I remember correctly. It gave brief biographical sketches of ancient worthies and unworthies, and was illustrated with many small woodcut portraits. There was one of Paracelsus, the great Swiss occultist, and it fascinated me so that I gazed at it long and often. The text characterized him as a charlatan or impostor; but as I read it, I knew that it was false and that he was one of the best men that ever lived. This was not merely a psychometric impression such as I received from some of the other portraits in the book: it was a haunting sense of familiarity, a conviction that I had known him when he was on earth and would meet him again, incarnated. Years afterward, while doing newspaper work in Nebraska, I read a brief dispatch from New York, stating that Mdme. Blavatsky and Col. Olcott had started a society for the study of Oriental literature. Again came that haunting sense of familiarity, and I wanted to write to that Mdme. Blavatsky (whose name I then read for the first time); but the dispatch gave no address. Later, in Philadelphia, I met Mrs. Verplanck, ("Jasper Niemand"), who was closely associated with Mr. Judge in making the *Path* an intensely interesting and instructive magazine. She told me of the T.S. and set me to studying *Isis, Esoteric Buddhism,* and other Theosophical literature then obtainable. For years I corresponded constantly with her, and occasionally with Mr. Judge, with whom I came to be well acquainted "in the astral," after I had settled in Los Angles in 1886.

In those days many Theosophists were ambitious to become "chelas" or "lay chelas" by getting into communication with the Masters whom HPB represented. Having no doubt that the Masters were being pestered by so many applicants, I refrained from any attempt to reach HPB or her Master, or to attract their attention to my unimportant self. But my mind kept dwelling on Paracelsus, with a distinct impression that he was again incarnated; so I resolved to find him, if possible, and in my daily meditation concentrated my mind on him. One evening [in 1889] while I was thus meditating, the face of HPB flashed before me. I recognized it from her portrait in *Isis*, though it appeared much older. Thinking that the astral picture, as I took it to be, was due to some vagary of fancy, I tried to exclude it; but at that, the face showed a look of impatience, and instantly I was drawn out of my body and immediately was standing "in the astral" beside HPB in London. It was along toward morning there, but she was still seated at her writing desk. While she was speaking to me, very kindly, I could not help thinking how odd it was that an apparently fleshy old lady should be an Adept. I tried to put that impolite thought out of my mind, but she read it, and as if in answer to it her physical body became translucent, revealing a marvelous inner body that looked as if it were formed of molten gold. Then suddenly the Master M appeared before us in his mayavi rupa. To him I made profound obeisance, for he seemed to me more like a God than a man. Somehow I knew who he was, though this was the first time I had seen him. He spoke to me graciously and said, "I shall have work for you in six months." He walked to the further side of the room, waved his hand in farewell, and departed. Then HPB dismissed me with the parting words, "God bless you," and directly I saw the waves of the Atlantic beneath me; I floated down and dipped my feet in their crests. Then with a rush I crossed the continent till I saw the lights of Los Angles and returned to my body, seated in the chair where I had left it. Thus by looking for Paracelsus, while resolved not to intrude on HPB and the Master M, I found them all. For HPB simply was Paracelsus, and in my ignorance of that fact I had blundered, happily stumbling upon a triumphant outcome vastly beyond anything I had expected.*

Six months afterward the Master's promise was made good. My brother John and I, returning from a trip to South America, landed in New York City. We found Mr. Judge perplexed by a difficult problem: HPB had directed him to send her Instructions to all the American members of the E.S., but had sent him only one copy, and he had no facilities for making the many copies needed. We solved that problem for him by establishing the Aryan Press and printing the Instructions in book form. Then, in response to a cable from HPB, I went to London to do the same work there, and started the HPB Press. When I met HPB we did not need to "become acquainted." It was as if we had known each other always. She invited Dr. Keightley and myself to eat Christmas [1890] dinner with her; and after dinner we played whist, HPB taking the dummy.

One evening at the dinner table gloom was cast over the [London] Headquarters' staff by the announcement that HPB was so ill that the doctor did not expect her to live till morning. Pondering sadly on this when I had retired to my room, I decided to try a certain experiment. In years past I had made hundreds of mesmeric experiments, with different subjects, sometimes using my prana as a healing force. As HPB was dying for lack of this vital force, while I, a young man, had plenty of it, I determined to transfer, by a mesmeric process, half my prana to HPB. It is analogous psychically to the transfusion of blood physically. As soon as I began concentrating to make the transfer HPB called to me, psychically but audibly, "Don't do it; it's black magic." Undeterred, I called back to her, "Very well, Old Lady, black magic or not, I'm going to do it anyway"—and I did. Next morning I felt decidedly feeble; but that was a matter of no lasting consequence, as it took but a few days to renew my strength. At the breakfast table we had good news; HPB was recovering, having made a sudden remarkable improvement which nonplussed the doctor.

*[James Pryse wrote to William Q. Judge about his out-of-body experience and "vision" of HPB. Judge referred to these experiences in his reply to Pryse dated September 3, 1889:

My dear Pryse:

I have your letter, and fully appreciate your feelings as they resemble my own.

I do not think your position is so strange or remarkable as to be beyond our ken, nor do I look at your experiences as being solely mediumistic, nor at the dream or vision as unsolvable. You are now struggling with the personal self in the early stages, and can consider yourself fortunate that you have the chance to overcome in the initial battle.

1. You have a natural tendency—as everyone—to accentuate your own experience. Pray consider it first of all as worthless, and then you will be in position to understand it and not before.

2. Your vision that when you looked at HPB and saw no old woman but a God is correct. You were privileged to see the Truth—for the Being in that old body called H. P. Blavatsky is a mighty Adept working on his own plan in the world. And thus we do not need to go to Tibet or S. America to find the sort of Being so many wish to see. Yet having seen the reality, better keep silent and work with that in view. For even did you go and tell Him you knew He was there, he would smile while he waited for you to do something such as you could in your limited sphere. For flattery counts not, and professions are worse than useless. But it is a great thing to see as much as you have, and a greater thing it will be if you do not doubt, for you may never see it again.

William Quan Judge, *Practical Occultism: From the Private Letters of William Q. Judge* (Pasadena, CA: Theosophical University Press, 1951), pp. 162–3.]

22E. COUNTESS CONSTANCE WACHTMEISTER
MARCH–APRIL 1891, LONDON

[Wachtmeister 1929]

Things are going pretty well here [at 19 Avenue Road]. The Thursday evenings are continued, though HPB is seldom present; in fact, we rarely see her now. She shuts herself up for days together. She is having a room built out into the garden, leading from her own room; and then, I expect, she will shut herself away altogether. As she grows weaker, she finds it trying to have so many people buzzing around her.

HPB is certainly growing more and more feeble, and she feels that to be able to do any work at all she must be quite alone, so as to enable her to concentrate her energies. Her present sitting room is a passage room to the ES, and she cannot have that quiet and solitude that are necessary; and so the inner room, now being built, will be closed to all outsiders, relations included. She says that her body is now so broken and shattered that it is only by being much alone that she can keep it together; and I expect the day will come when she will shut herself up altogether, and only occasionally see those in the house. As it is, we never go near her except in the evening.

22 F. G. R. S. MEAD
APRIL 1891,
LONDON

[HPB: In Memory, 34]

One of the greatest proofs to me of HPB's extraordinary gifts and ability, if proof were needed in the face of the manifest sincerity of her lifework, was the way in which she wrote her articles and books. I knew every book she had in her small library, and yet day after day she would produce quantities of MS abounding in quotations, which were seldom inaccurate. I remember almost the last day she sat at her desk, going into her room to query two Greek words in a quotation, and telling her they were inaccurate. Now though HPB could in her early years speak modern Greek and had been taught ancient Greek by her grandmother, she had long forgotten it for all purposes of accuracy, and the correction of the words I objected to required precise scholarship. "Where did you get it from, HPB?" I asked. "I'm sure I don't know, my dear," was her somewhat discouraging rejoinder, "I saw it!" adding that she was certain that she was right, for now she remembered when she wrote the particular passage referred to. However, I persuaded her that there was some mistake, and finally she said, "Well, of course you are a great Greek pundit, I know, but you're not going to sit upon me always. I'll try if I can see it again, and now get out," meaning that she wanted to go on with her work, or at any rate had had enough of me. About two minutes afterwards, she called me in again and presented me with a scrap of paper on which she had written the two words quite correctly, saying, "Well, I suppose you'll be a greater pundit than ever after this!"

22G. LAURA M. COOPER
APRIL 21 – MAY 8, 1891,
LONDON

[HPB: In Memory, 3–7]

It was on Tuesday, the 21st of April, that I went to stay at Headquarters for the few days, which, owing to the unexpected events that followed, turned into a visit of some weeks. HPB seemed in her usual state of health, and on Thursday, the 23rd, attended the Lodge and remained chatting with the friends who surrounded her for some time after the proceedings of the evening were over; she then adjourned to her room where, according to their habit, members who live at Headquarters [at 19 Avenue Road] followed to sit with her while she took her coffee before retiring for the night. Saturday, she was very bright. My sister, Mrs. [Isabel] Cooper-Oakley, and I, with one or two others, remained talking with her until eleven o'clock, when she retired with a cheery "Good night all," apparently in her usual health.

The next morning, however, HPB's maid came early to my room to tell me she had passed a very restless night and had been seized with shivering attacks. The doctor was immediately sent for, and the day passed with HPB alternately in a heavy sleep, or in a state of restlessness. Late in the afternoon Dr. Mennell came, pronounced the illness to be influenza; the fever was very high, her temperature being 105. From that memorable Sunday night, April 26th, began the succession of misfortunes, the illness of one member of the household after another, which culminated in the passing away of our beloved HPB. Towards the end of Thursday the 30th, HPB began to suffer very much from her throat, and as the hours went by she had increasing difficulty in swallowing; her cough became very troublesome and her breathing very labored. On Friday morning she was no better, and when Dr. Mennell arrived he found a quinsy had formed in the right side of the throat; hot poultices were applied and some relief was gained. The morning of Sunday, May 3rd, found HPB very ill indeed, for the pain of swallowing made it very difficult for her to take the necessary amount of nourishment, and her weakness increased in consequence. How bravely she struggled against her illness only those who were with her can realize. On Wednesday, the 6th of May, she partially dressed and walked into the sitting room, remained there for her luncheon, resting for some time on the sofa; in the evening Dr. Mennell found her going on fairly well, all fever had entirely left her, but the great weakness and the difficulty in breathing caused him considerable anxiety. That Wednesday night was the turning point in her illness. On Thursday [May 7th] HPB rallied and about three in the afternoon dressed, and with very little assistance walked into the sitting room; when there she asked for her large armchair to be brought her. The chair was turned facing into the room and when HPB was sitting in it she had her card table with the cards drawn in front of her, and she tried to "make a patience"; notwithstanding all these brave efforts, it was quite apparent that she was suffering intensely. Dr. Mennell came shortly after 5 o'clock and was much surprised to find her sitting up, and he congratulated her and praised her courage; she said, "I do my best, Doctor"; her voice was hardly above a whisper and the effort to speak was exhausting, as her breath was very short. She handed Dr. Mennell a cigarette she had managed with difficulty to prepare for him; it was the last she ever made. The night that followed, her last with us, was a very suffering one; owing to the increased difficulty in breathing, HPB could not rest in any position; every remedy was tried without avail, and finally she was obliged to remain seated in her chair propped with pillows. About 4 AM HPB seemed easier. [But] about 11:30 [AM on May 8th] I was aroused by Mr. Wright, who told me to come at once as HPB had changed for the worse, and the nurse did not think she could live many hours; directly I entered her room I realized the critical condition she was in. She was sitting in her chair and I knelt in front of her and asked her to try and take the stimulant; though too weak to hold the glass herself she allowed me to hold it to her lips, and she managed to swallow the contents; but after that we could only give a little nourishment in a spoon. The nurse said HPB might linger some hours, but suddenly there was a further change, and when I tried to moisten her lips I saw the dear eyes were already becoming dim, though she retained full conscious-ness to the last. In life HPB had a habit of moving one foot when she was thinking intently, and she continued that movement almost to the moment she ceased to breathe. When all hope was over, the nurse left the room, leaving C. F. Wright, W. R. Old, and myself with our beloved HPB; the two former knelt in front, each holding one of her hands, and I at her side with one arm round her supported her head; thus we remained motionless for many minutes, and so quietly did HPB pass away that we hardly knew the second she ceased to breathe; a great sense of peace filled the room, and we knelt quietly there.

CHAPTER 22

22H. HENRY S. OLCOTT
MAY 9–10, 1891, SYDNEY, AUSTRALIA

[Olcott 1931, 4:300]

My first intimation of HPB's death was received by me "tele-pathically" from herself, and this was followed by a second similar message. The third I got from one of the reporters present at my closing lecture in Sydney, who told me, as I was about leaving the platform, that a press message had come from London announcing her decease. In my diary entry for 9th May, 1891, I say: "Had an uneasy foreboding of HPB's death." In that of the following day it is written: "This morning I feel that HPB is dead." The last entry for that day says "Cablegram, HPB dead." Only those who saw us together, and knew of the close mystical tie between us, can understand the sense of bereavement that came over me upon receipt of the direful news.

H. P. Blavatsky and H. S. Olcott in London, 1888

Julia Keightley

221. Julia Keightley
May 1891, Pennsylvania

[Wachtmeister 1893, 127]

A few days after Madame Blavatsky died, HPB awoke me at night. I raised myself, feeling no surprise, but only the sweet accustomed pleasure. She held my eyes with her leonine gaze. Then she grew thinner, taller, her shape became masculine; slowly then her features changed, until a man of height and rugged powers stood before me, the last vestige of her features melting into his, until the leonine gaze, the progressed radiance of her glance alone remained. The man lifted his head and said, "Bear witness!" He then walked from the room, laying his hand on the portrait of

HPB as he passed. Since then, he has come to me several times, with instructions, in broad daylight while I was busily working, and once he stepped out from a large portrait of HPB.

22J. ANONYMOUS
MAY 1891,
NEW YORK CITY

["Madame Blavatsky" 1891]

Few women in our time have been more persistently misrepresented, slandered, and defamed than Madame Blavatsky, but though malice and ignorance did their worst upon her, there are abundant indications that her lifework will vindicate itself, that it will endure, and that it will operate for good. She was the founder of the Theosophical Society, an organization now fully and firmly established, which has branches in many countries, East and West. For nearly twenty years she had devoted herself to the dissemination of doctrines the fundamental principles of which are of the loftiest ethical character.

Madame Blavatsky held that the regeneration of mankind must be based upon the development of altruism. In this she was at one with the greatest thinkers, not alone of the present day, but of all time.

In another direction, she did important work. No one in the present generation, it may be said, has done more towards reopening the long sealed treasures of Eastern thought, wisdom, and philosophy. No one certainly has done so much towards elucidating that profound wisdom-religion wrought out by the ever cogitating Orient, and bringing into the light those ancient literary works whose scope and depth have so astonished the Western world. Her own knowledge of Oriental philosophy and esotericism was comprehensive. No candid mind can doubt this after reading her two principal works. The tone and tendency of all her writings were healthful, bracing, and stimulating. The lesson which was constantly impressed by her was assuredly that which the world most needs, and has always needed, namely the necessity of subduing self and of working for others.

The work of Madame Blavatsky has already borne fruit, and is destined, apparently, to produce still more marked and salutary effects in the future. Thus Madame Blavatsky has made her mark upon the time, and thus, too, her works will follow her. Some day, if not at once, the loftiness and purity of her aims, the wisdom and scope of her teachings, will be recognized more fully, and her memory will be accorded the honor to which it is justly entitled.

Biographical Sketches

ARUNDALE, FRANCESCA (18??–1924), Englishwoman who converted to the Church of England and later to the Roman Catholic Church. After her growing skepticism finally made her leave orthodox religion, she investigated Spiritualism. Upon learning of Theosophy in 1881, she joined the British Theosophical Society and by 1884 was international Assistant Treasurer. [Arundale, *My Guest: H. P. Blavatsky.*]

BALLARD, ANNA, American journalist and lifelong member of the New York Press Club. No other biographical information is available.

BESANT, ANNIE (1847–1933), English social reformer, Theosophist, Indian independence leader, and one of the greatest orators of her day. Rejecting Christianity, Annie Besant joined the National Secular Society in 1874 and became an associate of Charles Bradlaugh, an atheist freethinker. In the 1880s she developed an interest in socialism and worked with George Bernard Shaw in the Fabian Society. In March 1889, she met Madame Blavatsky and joined the Theosophical Society. After HPB's death, Besant became joint outer head of HPB's Esoteric School along with W. Q. Judge. In 1893 she went to India, where in later years, she campaigned for Indian nationalism and founded the Indian Home Rule League (1916). Mrs. Besant was president of the Theosophical Society (Adyar) from 1907 until her death. She was the author of several hundred books including *The Ancient Wisdom* (1897) and *Esoteric Christianity* (1901). [Nethercot, *The First Five Lives of Annie Besant* and *The Last Four Lives of Annie Besant.*]

BROWN, WILLIAM TOURNAY (1857– ?), Scotsman with a law degree from the University of Glasgow. Brown became interested in Theosophy while living in London in 1883. After visiting India from September 1883 to January 1885, Brown settled in the United States in 1886. In the following year he converted to the Christian faith and came to believe that Madame Blavatsky had "sold herself . . . to the devil." He wrote two pamphlets on his Theosophical experiences: *Some Experiences in India* (1884) and *My Life* (1885). [Blavatsky, *Collected Writings* 6:31–2, 428–30.]

BURROWS, HERBERT (1845–1922), English civil servant. Son of a Methodist parson and educated at Cambridge University, Burrows was a vocal partisan of Secularism, Irish independence, and women's rights. A founding member of the Social Democratic Federation, Burrows was active with Annie Besant in leading the Match Girls' Strike of 1888. He was a Parliamentary candidate in 1908 and 1910.

CHETTY, GRANDHI SOOBIAH (1858–1946). Born in southern India, G. Soobiah Chetty held various positions in the Customs Department of the Madras government. He met Madame Blavatsky when she came to Madras on a visit in spring 1882 and became a life-long member of the Theosophical Society (Adyar). Chetty wrote a number of accounts of his experiences with Madame Blavatsky and the Mahatmas.

CLEATHER, ALICE LEIGHTON (1846–1938), English Theosophist, Buddhist, and musician. After joining the Theosophical Society in 1885, Alice Cleather became a member of the Inner Group of HPB's Esoteric School. In 1918, Cleather, with her son Graham Gordon Cleather and Basil Crump, went to India and in 1925 to Peking, China, where they met the Panchen Lama of Tibet. At the request of the Panchen Lama, Cleather and Crump republished HPB's *Voice of the Silence* (Peking, 1928). She founded the H.P.B. Library (now located at Toronto, Ontario, Canada) and was connected with the Blavatsky Association of London. Alice Cleather's published works include H. P. Blavatsky: Her Life and Work for Humanity (1922) and H. P. Blavatsky As I Knew Her (1923). [Blavatsky, Collected Writings 14:518–21.]

CONWAY, MONCURE DANIEL (1832–1907), American author, reformer and minister. Having attended Harvard Divinity School, he became a controversial Unitarian minister, questioning New Testament miracles and even the divinity of Jesus Christ. In 1863, Conway and his family moved to England, where he was minister of South Place Chapel, London, from 1864 to 1884. He was a prolific writer, publicizing Eastern and other world religions in English and American periodicals. His published works include an autobiography and My Pilgrimage to the Wise Men of the East (1906).

COOPER, LAURA MARY (18??–1924), the younger sister of Isabel Cooper-Oakley. Laura was a member of the Inner Group of HPB's Esoteric School. From her pen we have an eyewitness account of HPB's death: "How She Left Us." In 1899 she married G. R. S. Mead.

COOPER-OAKLEY, ISABEL (1854–1914), English Theosophist. Born at Amritsar, India, Isabel in 1881 entered Girton College, Cambridge, where she met her future husband Alfred J. Oakley. In March 1884 she joined the Theosophical Society, and in 1889 she joined the staff at Lansdowne Road and was also a member of the Inner Group of HPB's Esoteric School. Her published works include Mystical Traditions (1909) and The Comte de St. Germain (1912). [Blavatsky, Collected Writings 12:730–3.]

CORSON, EUGENE ROLLIN (1855–19??), medical doctor, son of Professor Hiram Corson. Eugene published HPB's letters to his father in Some Unpublished Letters of Helena Petrovna Blavatsky (1929).

CORSON, HIRAM (1828–1911), American educator and distinguished professor (1870–1903) of English Literature at Cornell University, Ithaca, New York. He was proficient in mathematics and in classical languages. As early as 1874, he avowed his faith in Spiritualism. Professor Corson's writings published in the 1880s include books on Robert Browning and William Shakespeare. [Blavatsky, *Collected Writings* 1:450–3.]

COULOMB, EMMA, an Englishwoman who first met HPB in Cairo, Egypt, in 1872. In mid 1879, HPB, then in Bombay, received a letter from Emma Coulomb in Ceylon. In March of the next year, Emma and her French husband, Alexis, arrived penniless at the Bombay Theosophical Headquarters. For the next four years, Emma served as housekeeper and Alexis as general handyman, carpenter, and mechanic for the Theosophical Headquarters. In May 1884, the Coulomb couple were expelled from the Theosophical Society for theft, attempted extortion, and slander. "Certain crude, unworkable and newly made trapdoors and sliding panels," writes Theosophical historian, Walter Carrithers, Jr., "were found in H.P.B's private quarters then exclusively under the care of the Coulomb couple. After a lapse of months, Emma Coulomb contracted to supply the local Christian missionaries with several dozen letters ostensibly in H.P.B's handwriting. *If genuine*, some few letters and parts of others clearly implicated her in a conspiracy with the Coulombs to produce fraudulent 'occult phenomena.'" [Gomes, "The Coulomb Case, 1884–1984"; Hastings, *Defence of Madame Blavatsky*; Waterman, *Obituary: The "Hodgson Report" on Madame Blavatsky.*]

DHARMAPALA, ANAGARIKA (1864–1933), Buddhist reformer, born in Colombo, Ceylon. In December 1884, he accompanied HPB and Olcott to Adyar. HPB encouraged him to study the Buddhist Pali writings. In May 1891 he founded the Maha Bodhi Society in Calcutta, India. In 1893, Dharmapala spoke at the World Parliament of Religions in Chicago. The remainder of his life was spent in promoting Buddhism and working on behalf of the Maha Bodhi Society. [Fields, *How the Swans Came to the Lake*.]

DICK, FREDERICK J. (1856–1927), civil engineer and Theosophist. Fred Dick was Head of the Harbors and Lighthouse Board for Ireland. He joined the Theosophical Society in Dublin, Ireland, in December 1888. In 1905, he went to Point Loma, San Diego, California, where he served as professor of mathematics and astronomy at the School of Antiquity. [Blavatsky, *Collected Writings* 11:571–2.]

EGLINTON, WILLIAM (1857–1933), English medium. Eglinton was noted for his materialization and slate-writing performances. In late 1881 and early 1882, Eglinton visited Calcutta, India, where he was the guest of J. G. Meugens, a wealthy Indian merchant. He also stayed with Col. William and Alice Gordon of Howrah, Calcutta. In later life, Eglinton became the editor of the magazine *New Age* and was a director of a firm of British exporters. [Melton, *Encyclopedia of Occultism & Parapsychology* 1:388–91.]

FADEYEV, NADYEZHDA ANDREYEVNA DE (1829–1919), HPB's favorite aunt, her mother's sister. Nadyezhda was only two years older than her niece. Her correspondence with HPB in the 1870s and 1880s is preserved in the archives of the Theosophical Society (Adyar). She died in Prague, Czechoslovakia.

GEBHARD, RUDOLF ERNST (1857–1935), German Theosophist, son of Gustav and Mary Gebhard. He was the fourth of six sons and one daughter. Rudolf went with Col. Olcott to India in October 1884 and was present at the Theosophical Convention in Adyar, December 1884. Madame Blavatsky twice stayed at the Gebhard home in Elberfeld.

GORDON, ALICE, English Spiritualist, Theosophist, and wife of Major General William Gordon (1831–1909) of the Indian

Army. A resident of Howrah, India, Alice Gordon went in December 1879 to A. P. Sinnett's house in Allahabad to meet Madame Blavatsky and Colonel Olcott. In 1890, she gave a talk in London on HPB and her occult phenomena. [Gordon, "Some Experiences of the Occult."]

HARTMANN, FRANZ (1838–1912), German physician, Theosophist, and author. He came to live in the United States in 1865. After reading *The Occult World* (1881) by A. P. Sinnett, Hartmann became interested in Theosophy. His books include *Magic, White and Black* (1886), *The Life of Paracelsus* (1887), and *Occult Science in Medicine* (1893). [Blavatsky, *Collected Writings* 8:439–57.]

HODGSON, RICHARD (1855–1905), Australian psychical researcher. He joined the Society for Psychical Research in 1882. Known for his "exposés" of Madame Blavatsky and the Italian medium Eusapia Palladino, Hodgson also investigated the mediumship of Leonora Piper of Boston and became convinced not only that she had genuine psychic powers but that deceased persons communicated through her. [Berger, *Lives and Letters in American Parapsychology*, 11–33; Waterman, *Obituary: The "Hodgson Report" on Madame Blavatsky*.]

HOLLOWAY, LAURA CARTER (1848–1930), American author and journalist. Her first book, *Ladies of the White House* (1870), sold more than 100,000 copies. Laura Holloway was an associate editor (1870–1884) of the *Brooklyn Daily Eagle*. In spring 1884, she met Madame Blavatsky in Paris.

HOLT, ELIZABETH G. K. No biographical information is available.

JOHNSTON, CHARLES (1867–1931), Irish Theosophist, Sanskritist, and Orientalist. In 1885, Johnston joined the Theosophical Society. In autumn 1888 he married HPB's niece, Vera V. de Zhelihovsky. In 1896, the Johnstons moved permanently to the United States. In later life, Johnston was one of the editors of the *Encyclopedia Britannica*. He translated several

Indian scriptures into English, including *The Bhagavad-Gita* (1908), *The Yoga Sutras of Patanjali* (1912), and *The Great Upanishads* (1927). [Blavatsky, *Collected Writings* 9:422–6.]

JOHNSTON, VERA VLADIMIROVNA (1864–1923), daughter of HPB's sister Vera Petrovna de Zhelihovsky. In the autumn of 1888, Vera married Charles Johnston.

JUDGE, WILLIAM QUAN (1851–1896), attorney and Theosophist. Born in Dublin, Judge and his family emigrated to Brooklyn, New York, in 1864. He studied law and was admitted to the bar in 1872. Judge was one of the founders of the Theosophical Society. In 1886, he started publishing *The Path*, a Theosophical monthly that he edited till his death. Also in 1886, Judge was elected General Secretary of the American Section of the Theosophical Society. In 1888, he assisted H. P. Blavatsky in establishing her Esoteric School. After HPB's death, Judge became joint outer head of the Esoteric School along with Annie Besant. His writings include *The Ocean of Theosophy* (1893) and *Echoes of the Orient* (3 volumes; 1975–87). [Eek and de Zirkoff, *William Quan Judge.*]

KEIGHTLEY, ARCHIBALD (1859–1930), English physician, Theosophist, and one of HPB's most faithful friends. In spring 1884, he joined the Theosophical Society. In 1887–8, Archibald organized (with the help of his uncle, Bertram Keightley, and Countess Wachtmeister) HPB's household in London. During this same period, Archibald and Bertram prepared HPB's manuscript of *The Secret Doctrine* for publication. In 1891, Archibald married Julia ver Planck of Pennsylvania. [Blavatsky, *Collected Writings* 9:427–32.]

KEIGHTLEY, BERTRAM (1860–1945), English Theosophist and close supporter of HPB. Cambridge-educated, Bertram Keightley became interested in Theosophy in 1883. In spring 1884, Colonel Olcott admitted Bertram and his nephew Archibald Keightley into the Theosophical Society. In 1887 Bertram joined forces with Archibald and the Countess Wachtmeister in forming HPB's household in London. Both Keightleys worked with HPB in preparing the manuscript of *The Secret Doctrine* for publication. [Keightley, *Reminiscences of H.P.B.*; Blavatsky, *Collected Writings* 9:432–5.]

KEIGHTLEY, JULIA CAMPBELL VER PLANCK, pen name Jasper Niemand (185?–1915), American Theosophical writer. Daughter of a prominent lawyer and congressman, Julia's first writings were published in *Harper's Magazine* and *Galaxy*. In 1886, she joined the Theosophical Society and soon became a frequent contributor to W. Q. Judge's magazine, *The Path*. In 1891, she married Archibald Keightley. [Blavatsky, *Collected Writings* 9:435–8.]

KINGSLAND, WILLIAM (1855–1936), English electrical engineer and Theosophical writer. In 1923, Kingsland and Alice Cleather helped to form the Blavatsky Association to perpetuate and defend HPB's name and work. His writings include *The Real H. P. Blavatsky* (1928) and *The Gnosis or Ancient Wisdom in the Christian Scriptures* (1937). [Blavatsky, *Collected Writings* 10:419–24.]

KISLINGBURY, EMILY, English teacher, Spiritualist, and Theosophist. Kislingbury became a spiritualist in 1870 and served later as Secretary of the British National Association of Spiritualists. In June 1878, she was elected the first secretary of the British Theosophical Society. In 1890, she became a member of the Inner Group of HPB's Esoteric School.

LEADBEATER, CHARLES WEBSTER (1854–1934), English clergyman and Theosophical author. C. W. Leadbeater joined the Theosophical Society in 1883. He became a Theosophical lecturer and writer, collaborating with Annie Besant on several clairvoyant studies (*Thought Forms*, 1901, and *Occult Chemistry*, 1908). His writings include *Man, Visible and Invisible* (1902) and *The Chakras* (1927). [Shearman, *Charles*

Webster Leadbeater; Tillett, *The Elder Brother*; Michel, *Charles W. Leadbeater*.]

MACHELL, REGINALD WILLOUGHBY (1854–1927), English painter, illustrator, and Theosophist. Reginald Machell is famous for mystical paintings such as *The Path* at the Theosophical Society, Pasadena. In 1893, he was elected a member of the Royal Society of British Artists. In 1900, Machell left England to reside at and work for the Point Loma Theosophical Society. [Blavatsky, *Collected Writings* 12:755–7.]

MAITLAND, PELHAM JAMES (1847–1935), English military officer. In 1880–1, Captain Maitland was Deputy Assistant Quarter Master General (English Intelligence Branch) at Simla. He was Military Secretary (1896–1901) to the Government of India. His writings include *Modern Military Organizations and the British Army* (1906).

MASSEY, CHARLES CARLETON (1838–1905), English attorney, metaphysician, Spiritualist, and Theosophist. In 1878 Massey was elected first president of the British Theosophical Society. In 1882, he became one of the founders of the Society for Psychical Research (London). He resigned from the Theosophical Society in 1884. [Blavatsky, *Collected Writings* 1:497–9.]

MAVALANKAR, DAMODAR K. (1857– ?), Hindu member of the Theosophical Society and disciple of Mahatma KH. Born into a wealthy family of the Brahmin caste, Damodar joined the Theosophical Society in 1879. Becoming a member of the Theosophical headquarters staff, Damodar became business manager of the Society's publications department and assisted in the publication of the *Theosophist*. In spring 1885, Damodor left India for Tibet. [Mavalankar, *Damodar and the Pioneers of the Theosophical Movement*.]

MEAD, GEORGE ROBERT STOWE (1863–1933), Cambridge-educated Theosophist and scholar of Gnosticism and early Christianity. In 1884, Mead joined the Theosophical Society.

He first met HPB in 1887 and became her private secretary during the last few years of her life. His writings include *Pistis Sophia: A Gnostic Gospel* (1896, 1921) and *Fragments of a Faith Forgotten* (1909). [Blavatsky, *Collected Writings* 13:393–7.]

NAGNATH, MARTANDRAO BABAJI, a Hindu Brahmin and member of the Theosophical Society. Nagnath was a clerk in the Examiner's Office of Public Accounts, Bombay, India. In the early 1880s, he was Treasurer of the local Bombay Theosophical Society.

OLCOTT, HENRY STEEL (1832–1907), American journalist, editor, attorney, co-founder and first president of the Theosophical Society. Olcott was associate agricultural editor (1859–1861) of the *New York Tribune*. He served in the Civil War as Special Commissioner (1862–6) in the War and Navy Departments to investigate corruption and fraud in military arsenals and navy yards. Colonel Olcott practiced law in New York City from 1868 to 1878. In 1875 he was elected President of the Theosophical Society, an office he held for the rest of his life. He worked tirelessly on behalf of the Theosophical Society, traveling throughout India, southern Asia, Australia, Europe, and elsewhere. Olcott also worked for the renewal of Buddhism in Ceylon, helping to establish three colleges and 250 schools. His writings include *People from the Other World* (1875), *The Buddhist Catechism* (1881), and *Old Diary Leaves* (1895–1935), a six-volume history of the Theosophical Society. [Murphet, *Yankee Beacon of Buddhist Light*; Prothero, *The White Buddhist*.]

OLD, JAMES BERNARD (1866–?), brother of Walter Old and a clergyman. No other biographical information is available.

OLD, WALTER RICHARD (1864–1929), English author and professional astrologer. Old wrote under the name "Walter Gorn Old" and the pseudonym "Sepharial." A student of medicine and the Kabbalah, he became a member of the Inner Group of HPB's Esoteric School. His writings include *Second Sight* (1911) and *The Kabala of Numbers* (1913).

PADSHAH, SORAB J., a Parsi poet, journalist, and member of the Theosophical Society. A graduate of Bombay University, he was Assistant Recording Secretary to the Theosophical Society in 1880–1. In the early 1880s, Padshah was the editor of the *Indian Spectator*, a weekly publication.

PASHKOV, COUNTESS LYDIA ALEXANDROVNA DE, Russian author and traveler. A member of the Geographical Society of France, Countess Pashkov was an author of several books on travel, including *En Orient, Drames et Paysages* (1879). In April 1878, on a trip to New York City, Countess Pashkov visited her old friend Madame Blavatsky. [Blavatsky, *Collected Writings* 1:521–2.]

PILLAI, R. CASAVA, Hindu police officer and inspector at Nellore, India. In 1881, Pillai joined the Theosophical Society. The following year he was the Secretary of the local Theosophical Branch in Nellore. [Theosophical Society, *Report of the Result of an Investigation into the Charges against Madame Blavatsky*, 87–91.]

PRYSE, JAMES MORGAN (1859–1942), American Theosophist, writer, and printer. Joining the Theosophical Society in 1886, Pryse met W. Q. Judge in New York in late 1889. With his printing skills, he helped Judge found the Aryan Press the same year. In 1890, Pryse went to the London Theosophical headquarters and started the H.P.B. Press, on which HPB's *Esoteric Instructions* were printed in early 1891. In his later years, he moved to Los Angeles, California. His books include *Reincarnation in the New Testament* (1900), *The Apocalypse Unsealed* (1910), and *The Restored New Testament* (1916). [Blavatsky, *Collected Writings* 12:761–5.]

RACOWITZA, PRINCESS HELENE VON (1844–19??), German princess. She was born Helene von Donniges. In 1864,

Ferdinand Lassalle, the German Socialist, fought a duel over her and lost his life. Her *Autobiography* was published in 1910.

RAJAMIENGAR, T. C. Richard Hodgson described Rajamiengar as a "native doctor." No other biographical information is available.

RAMASWAMIER, S. (18??–1893), a Brahmin who worked in the English Government service as a District Registrar of Assurances at Tinnevelly, India. Ramaswamier joined the Theosophical Society in 1881. [Barborka, *The Mahatmas and Their Letters*, 320–32.]

ROY, PARBATI CHURN (1840– ?), a Western-educated Hindu. Roy first met Blavatsky in 1882 in Darjeeling, India, and saw her again in London in spring 1888. In 1896, he described himself as follows: "I was born a Hindu, but subsequently became a Brahmo, an Agnostic and a Sceptic. I am now a Hindu again" (*From Hinduism to Hinduism*, preface).

RUSSELL, EDMUND, a widely traveled American artist who resided in Paris for many years. No other biographical information is available.

SAXON, ELIZABETH LYLE (1832–1915), American writer and woman's suffrage advocate. Saxon was a writer of poems and short stories. She was also a social activist and was involved in both the suffrage movement for women and the Women's Christian Temperance Union. She had an interest in various aspects of religion and investigated the Adventists, Mormons, Shakers, Quakers, and other religious groups. She was interested in Spiritualism and had some psychic ability of her own.

SEN, NORENDRO NATH (1843– ?), proprietor and editor of the *Indian Mirror*, a daily newspaper published in Calcutta, India. According to Boris de Zirkoff, the paper under Sen's editorship "became the leading paper in India voicing the opinions of Indians on political matters." [Blavatsky, *Collected Writings* 6:257.]

SHANKAR, BHAVANI (1859–1936), a Canarese Brahmin and disciple of Master KH. Bhavani Shankar met HPB soon after she landed in Bombay in 1879. He worked for the Theosophical Society for many years. In the early 1930s, Shankar gave a series of talks on *The Bhagavad-Gita* under the auspices of the United Lodge of Theosophists (Bombay). His book *The Doctrine of the Bhagavad-Gita* was published in 1966.

SIDGWICK, HENRY (1838–1900), English philosopher and psychical researcher. He was professor of moral philosophy at Cambridge University (1883–1900). Sidgwick was a founding member and the first president (1882–1885) of the Society for Psychical Research (London). His writings include *The Methods of Ethics* (1874). [Gauld, *The Founders of Psychical Research.*]

SINNETT, ALFRED PERCY (1840–1921), English journalist, editor of the *Pioneer* (Allahabad, India), and Theosophical writer. A. P. Sinnett achieved fame as the recipient of letters from two adepts, later published as *The Mahatma Letters*. Sinnett's *Occult World* (1881) and *Esoteric Buddhism* (1883) popularized Theosophy. [Linton and Hanson, *Readers' Guide to The Mahatma Letters to A. P. Sinnett*, 349–56; Hanson, *Masters and Men: The Human Story in The Mahatma Letters.*]

SMITH, JOHN (1821–1885), Scottish-born professor of chemistry and experimental physics. Smith taught at the University of Sydney, Australia, from 1852 until his death. In his later years, he devoted much time to civic affairs and the promotion of education. He joined the Theosophical Society in 1882. [*Australian Dictionary of Biography* 6:148–50.]

SOLOVYOV, VSEVOLOD SERGUEYEVICH (1849–1903), Russian novelist and brother of the Russian philosopher Vladimir Solovyov. Vsevolod Solovyov met HPB in Paris in spring 1884. At first, relations between the two were friendly, but Solovyov turned against HPB and wrote a book, *A Modern Priestess of Isis* (Russian ed., 1893; abridged English ed., 1895), in which he attempted to portray HPB as a fraud. [Blavatsky, *Collected Writings* 6:446; Hasting, *Solovyoff's Fraud*.]

STEAD, WILLIAM THOMAS (1849–1912), English journalist, editor, and Spiritualist. In 1883, Stead became editor of the London *Pall Mall Gazette*. In 1890, he started publishing the prestigious monthly *Review of Reviews*. Becoming interested in Spiritualism, psychical research, and Theosophy, W. T. Stead founded *Borderland* (1893–1897), a periodical specially devoted to these subjects. Bound for New York, Stead lost his life on the liner *Titanic*.

TWEEDALE, VIOLET (1862–1936), English novelist. Violet Tweedale, a psychic herself who could see auras, became interested in Spiritualism and attended seances with Lord Richard Haldane (1856–1928), English statesman, and William E. Gladstone (1809–1898), prime minister of England. She wrote nearly thirty books, including *Ghosts I Have Seen* (1919) and *The Cosmic Christ* (1930).

WACHTMEISTER, CONSTANCE (1838–1910), Theosophist and widow of the Swedish Count Karl Wachtmeister (1823–1871). Investigating Spiritualism in the late 1870s, the Countess Wachtmeister became interested in Theosophy and joined the Society in 1880. She first met HPB in April 1884 on a visit to London. Her book *Reminiscences of H. P. Blavatsky and "The Secret Doctrine"* (1893) gives an account of HPB's sojourn in Wurzburg, Germany, and Ostend, Belgium (1885–1887). [Blavatsky, *Collected Writings* 6:448.]

WIGGIN, JAMES HENRY (1836–1900), American Unitarian clergyman and editor. A Bostonian by birth, Wiggin moved to New York in 1875 to edit the *Liberal Christian* but returned to Boston the following year. By 1881 he had become an agnostic and left the ministry. From 1885 to 1891, Wiggin assisted Mary Baker Eddy (founder of Christian Science) with the preparation of several of her works.

WILDER, ALEXANDER (1823–1908), American physician, author, editor, and Platonic scholar. Wilder received a medical degree in 1850. He was on the editorial staff of several newspapers and was the editor of various medical and philosophical journals. He also held teaching positions at a number of medical colleges. Wilder wrote many scholarly essays on religious, metaphysical, and Platonic subjects. His published works include *New Platonism and Alchemy* (1869) and *History of Medicine* (1901). [Blavatsky, *Collected Writings* 1:531–3.]

WINDUST, ESTHER. No biographical information is available.

WOLFF, HANNAH M., wife of John B. Wolff, president of the First Spiritual Society of Washington, DC. No other biographical information is available.

WYLD, GEORGE (1821–1906), Scottish physician, Spiritualist, and Theosophist. Having received his MD degree in 1851, Wyld took up the study of homeopathy, mesmerism, and Spiritualism. In 1879, he joined the Theosophical Society but resigned in 1882. He was one of the original founders of the Society for Psychical Research (London) in 1882. His writings include *Clairvoyance* (1883) and *Theosophy, or Spiritual Dynamics and the Divine and Miraculous Man* (1894). [Blavatsky, *Collected Writings* 3:538–9.]

ZHELIHOVSKY, VERA PETROVNA DE (1835–1896), HPB's younger sister. Vera was married twice and had six children. She was a writer of children's stories and a contributor to various Russian magazines. Her writings on HPB's life include *When I Was Small* (2nd ed., 1894), *My Adolescence* (1893), "The Truth about Helena Petrovna Blavatsky," *Rebus* [St. Petersburg] (1883), and "Helena Petrovna Blavatsky," *Lucifer* [London] (Nov., 1894 – April, 1895). Vera traveled several times to western Europe in the 1880s to visit HPB. [Blavatsky, *Collected Writings* 1:534–7.]

Suggested Readings

Algeo, John. *Getting Acquainted with The Secret Doctrine: A Study Course.* Revised Edition. Wheaton, IL: Department of Education, Theosophical Society in America, 1990. 66 pp.

Barborka, Geoffrey A. *The Divine Plan: Written in the Form of a Commentary on H. P. Blavatsky's Secret Doctrine.* Adyar, Madras, India: Theosophical Publishing House, 1964. xxvii + 564 pp.

———. *H. P. Blavatsky, Tibet and Tulku.* Adyar, Madras, India: Theosophical Publishing House, 1966. xxii + 476 pp.

———. *The Mahatmas and Their Letters.* Adyar, Madras, India: Theosophical Publishing House, 1973. xix + 422 pp.

Blavatsky, Helena P. *An Abridgement of The Secret Doctrine.* Ed. Elizabeth Preston and Christmas Humphreys. Wheaton, IL: Theosophical Publishing House, 1967. xxxii + 260 pp.

———. *Collected Writings.* 15 volumes. Ed. Boris de Zirkoff. Wheaton, IL: Theosophical Publishing House, 1966–91. Vol. 15 is a Cumulative Index. The most complete, definitive collection of HPB's articles and miscellaneous writings; arranged in chronological order covering the years 1874 through 1891.

———. *Dynamics of the Psychic World: Comments by H. P. Blavatsky on Magic, Mediumship, Psychism, and the Powers of the Spirit.* Comp. Lina Psaltis. Wheaton, IL: Theosophical Publishing House, 1972. xviii + 132 pp.

———. *Foundations of Esoteric Philosophy: From the Writings of H. P. Blavatsky.* Ed. Ianthe H. Hoskins. London: Theosophical Publishing House, 1980. 68 pp.

———. *H.P.B. Speaks.* 2 vols. Ed. C. Jinarajadasa. Adyar, Madras, India: Theosophical Publishing House, 1950–1. viii + 248 pp, xvi + 181 pp.

————. *H.P.B. Teaches: An Anthology.* Comp. Michael Gomes. Adyar, Madras, India: Theosophical Publishing House, 1992. 579 pp.

————. *H. P. Blavatsky to the American Conventions, 1888–1891.* With a Historical Perspective by Kirby Van Mater. Pasadena, CA: Theosophical University Press, 1979. x + 74 pp.

————. *The Inner Group Teachings of H. P. Blavatsky to Her Personal Pupils (1890–1).* Ed. H. J. Spierenburg. 2nd rev. and enl. ed. San Diego, CA: Point Loma Publications, 1995. xxxvi + 254 pp.

————. *Isis Unveiled: A Master-Key to the Mysteries of Ancient and Modern Science and Theology.* 2 vols. in 1. Los Angeles, CA: Theosophy Company, 1982. Photographic facsimile of the original edition. xiv + 628 pp., iv + 708 pp. (1st ed., 1877)

————. *Isis Unveiled: A Master-Key to the Mysteries of Ancient and Modern Science and Theology.* 2 vols. Collected Writings Edition, ed. Boris de Zirkoff. Wheaton, IL: Theosophical Publishing House, 1972. [63] + xlv + 657 pp., iv + 848 pp. Includes a historical introduction, index, and bibliography. (1st ed., 1877)

————. *Isis Unveiled: Secrets of the Ancient Wisdom Tradition. Madame Blavatsky's First Work: A New Abridgment for Today.* Ed. Michael Gomes. Wheaton, IL: Theosophical Publishing House, 1997. xvii + 274 pp.

————. *The Key to Theosophy, Being a Clear Exposition, in the Form of Question and Answer, of the Ethics, Science, and Philosophy for the Study of Which the Theosophical Society Has Been Founded.* Pasadena, CA: Theosophical University Press, 1987. Verbatim reprint of the original edition, including the glossary of the 2nd ed., and index. xii + 373 + 53 pp. (1st ed., 1889)

————. *The Key to Theosophy: An Abridgement.* Ed. Joy Mills. Wheaton, IL: Theosophical Publishing House, 1981. xv + 176 pp.

————. *The Letters of H. P. Blavatsky to A. P. Sinnett and Other Miscellaneous Letters.* Ed. A. T. Barker. Pasadena, CA: Theosophical University Press, 1973. xv + 404 pp. (1st ed., 1925)

————. *Madame Blavatsky on How to Study Theosophy*. Notes made by Robert Bowen. Adyar, Madras, India: Theosophical Publishing House, 1979. 17 pp.

————. *The Secret Doctrine: The Synthesis of Science, Religion and Philosophy*. 2 vols. Pasadena, CA: Theosophical University Press, 1988. Photographic facsimile of the original edition. xlvii + 676 pp., xiv + 798 + xxxi pp. (1st ed., 1888)

————. *The Secret Doctrine: The Synthesis of Science, Religion and Philosophy*. 3 vols. Collected Writings Edition with a historical introduction, general index and bibliography, ed. Boris de Zirkoff. Wheaton, IL: Theosophical Publishing House, 1993. [84] + xlvii + 696 pp., v + xx + 817 pp., vii + 520 pp. (1st ed., 1888)

————. *Secret Doctrine Commentary / Stanzas I–IV: Transactions of the Blavatsky Lodge with a Section on Dreams*. Photographic facsimile ed. Pasadena, CA: Theosophical University Press, 1994. 64 + 51 pp. (1st ed. issued in two parts, 1890 and 1891)

————. *The Voice of the Silence: Being Chosen Fragments from the "Book of the Golden Precepts" for the Daily Use of Lanoos (Disciples)*. Translated and annotated by "H.P.B." Historical introduction by Boris de Zirkoff and index. Wheaton, IL: Theosophical Publishing House, 1992. xi + 122 pp. (1st ed., 1889)

Caldwell, Daniel H. K. *Paul Johnson's House of Cards? A Critical Examination of Johnson's Thesis on the Theosophical Masters Morya and Koot Hoomi*. Tucson, AZ: D. H. Caldwell, 1996. 43 pp.

Campbell, Bruce F. *Ancient Wisdom Revived: A History of the Theosophical Movement*. Berkeley: University of California Press, 1980. x + 249 pp.

Cranston, Sylvia. *HPB: The Extraordinary Life and Influence of Helena Blavatsky, Founder of the Modern Theosophical Movement*. 3rd rev. ed. Santa Barbara, CA: Path Publishing House, 1998. xxiv + 660 pp.

Endersby, Victor *The Hall of Magic Mirrors*. New York: Carlton Press, 1969. 351 pp.

Farthing, Geoffrey A. *Deity, Cosmos and Man: An Outline of Esoteric Science*. San Diego, CA: Point Loma Publications, 1993. xxvi + 253 pp.

————. *Exploring the Great Beyond: A Survey of the Field of the Extraordinary*. Wheaton, IL: Theosophical Publishing House, 1978. xi + 214 pp.

————. *When We Die: A Description of the After-Death States and Processes*. San Diego, CA: Point Loma Publications, 1994. xv + 116 pp. Compiled from *The Mahatma Letters to A. P. Sinnett* with commentary and notes.

Fuller, Jean Overton. *Blavatsky and Her Teachers: An Investigative Biography*. London: East-West Publications, 1988. 270 pp.

Godwin, Joscelyn. *The Theosophical Enlightenment*. Albany: State University of New York Press, 1994. xiii + 448 pp.

Gomes, Michael. *The Dawning of the Theosophical Movement*. Wheaton, IL: Theosophical Publishing House, 1987. x + 248 pp.

Hanson, Virginia, ed. *H. P. Blavatsky and The Secret Doctrine*. 2nd ed. Wheaton, IL: Theosophical Publishing House, 1988. xvii + 240 pp.

————. *Masters and Men: The Human Story in The Mahatma Letters*. Wheaton, IL: Theosophical Publishing House, 1980. xx + 323 pp.

Harrison, Vernon. *H. P. Blavatsky and the SPR : An Examination of the Hodgson Report of 1885*. Pasadena, California: Theosophical University Press, 1997. xii + 78 pp.

Johnson, K. Paul. *The Masters Revealed: Madame Blavatsky and the Myth of the Great White Lodge*. Albany: State University of New York Press, 1994. xxii + 288 pp.

Kingsland, William. *The Real H. P. Blavatsky: A Study in Theosophy, and a Memoir of a Great Soul*. London: Theosophical Publishing House, 1985. xiv + 322 pp. (1st ed., London: J. M. Watkins, 1928)

————. *Was She a Charlatan? A Critical Analysis of the 1885 Report of the Society for Psychical Research on the Phenomena Connected with Mme. H. P. Blavatsky*. London: Blavatsky Association, 1927. Reprint in *The Real H. P. Blavatsky*, by William Kingsland, 255–312.

Kuhn, Alvin Boyd. *Theosophy: A Modern Revival of Ancient Wisdom*. Kila, MT: Kessinger, 1992. viii + 381 pp. (1st ed., 1930)

Lancri, Salomon. *Selected Studies in The Secret Doctrine.* Translated by Ianthe H. Hoskins. London: Theosophical Publishing House, 1977. 86 pp.

Letters from the Masters of the Wisdom: 1870–1900. First Series. Ed. C. Jinarajadasa. Adyar, Madras, India: Theosophical Publishing House, 1988. 124 pp. (1st ed., 1919)

Letters from the Masters of Wisdom. Second Series. Ed. C. Jinarajadasa. Adyar, Madras, India: Theosophical Publishing House, 1977. 189 pp. (1st ed., 1925)

Linton, George E., and Virginia Hanson, eds. *Readers' Guide to The Mahatma Letters to A. P. Sinnett.* 2nd ed. Adyar, Madras, India: Theosophical Publishing House, 1988. xviii + 430 pp.

The Mahatma Letters to A. P. Sinnett from the Mahatmas M. & K.H. Transcribed by A. T. Barker. 4th (chronological) ed. Ed. Vicente Hao Chin, Jr. Adyar, Chennai, India: Theosophical Publishing House, 1998. xxv + 600 pp. (1st ed., 1923)

Maroney, Tim. *The Book of Dzyan: Being a Manuscript Curiously Received by Helena Petrovna Blavatsky with Diverse and Rare Texts of Related Interest.* Ed. Tim Maroney. Oakland, CA: Chaosium, 2000. 270 pp.

McDavid, William Doss. *An Introduction to Esoteric Principles.* 2nd ed. Wheaton, IL: Department of Education, Theosophical Society in America, 1990. ix + 91 pp.

Meade, Marion. *Madame Blavatsky: The Woman behind the Myth.* New York: Putnam's, 1980. 528 pp.

Murphet, Howard. *When Daylight Comes: A Biography of Helena Petrovna Blavatsky.* Wheaton, IL: Theosophical Publishing House, 1975. xxxi + 277 pp.

———. *Yankee Beacon of Buddhist Light: Life of Col. Henry S. Olcott.* Wheaton, IL: Theosophical Publishing House, 1988. xii + 345 pp. (Orig. pub. as *Hammer on the Mountain,* 1972.)

Nicholson, Shirley. *Ancient Wisdom—Modern Insight.* Wheaton, IL: Theosophical Publishing House, 1985. xvii + 198 pp.

Ransom, Josephine. *A Short History of the Theosophical Society.* Adyar, Madras, India: Theosophical Publishing House, 1989. xii + 591 pp. (1st ed., 1938)

Reigle, David, and Nancy Reigle. *Blavatsky's Secret Books: Twenty Years' Research.* San Diego, CA: Wizards Bookshelf, 1999. 181 pp.

Ryan, Charles J. *H. P. Blavatsky and the Theosophical Movement: A Brief Historical Sketch.* 2nd ed. Ed. Grace F. Knoche. Pasadena, CA: Theosophical University Press, 1975. xviii + 358 pp. (1st ed., 1937)

Sinnett, Alfred P. *Esoteric Buddhism.* Reprint of the 5th (1885) ed. San Diego, CA: Wizards Bookshelf, 1981. xxvii + 244 pp.

Taimni, I. K. *Man, God and the Universe.* Wheaton, IL: Theosophical Publishing House, 1974. xliii + 447 pp.

The Theosophical Movement, 1875–1950. Los Angeles, CA: Cunningham, 1951. xiii + 351 pp.

Van Pelt, Gertrude W. *Archaic History of the Human Race: As Recorded in The Secret Doctrine by H. P. Blavatsky.* San Diego, CA: Point Loma Publications, 1979. 52 pp.

Warcup, Adam. *Cyclic Evolution: A Theosophical View.* London: Theosophical Publishing House, 1986. viii + 144 pp.

Waterman, Adlai E. *Obituary: The "Hodgson Report" on Madame Blavatsky, 1885–1960: Re-examination Discredits the Major Charges against H. P. Blavatsky.* Adyar, Madras, India: Theosophical Publishing House, 1963. xx + 92 pp.

References

Arundale, Francesca. 1932. *My Guest: H. P. Blavatsky*. Adyar, Madras, India: Theosophical Publishing House. Selections 15f, 16a.

Australian Dictionary of Biography. 1966. 14 vols. Melbourne: Melbourne University Press.

Barborka, Geoffrey. 1973. *The Mahatmas and Their Letters*. Adyar, Madras, India: Theosophical Publishing House.

Berger, Arthur S. 1988. *Lives and Letters in American Parapsychology: A Biographical History, 1850–1987*. Jefferson, NC: McFarland.

Besant, Annie. 1893. *Annie Besant: An Autobiography*. London: T. Fisher Unwin. Selections 21b, 21d.

———. 1969. *The Masters*. 3d ed. Adyar, Madras, India: Theosophical Publishing House. 1st ed. 1912. Selection 21d.

Besterman, Theodore. 1934. *Mrs. Annie Besant: A Modern Prophet*. London: Kegan Paul, Trench, Trubner. Selection 7b.

Blavatsky, H. P. 1966–1991. *Collected Writings*. 15 vols. Ed. Boris de Zirkoff. Wheaton, IL: Theosophical Publishing House.

Brown, William T. 1884. *Some Experiences in India*. London: London Lodge of the Theosophical Society. Selection 13h.

Chetty, G. Soobiah. 1928. "Master M.'s Visit to Madras in 1874." *Adyar Notes and News* 1 (October 25): 2. Selection 13c.

Cleather, Alice Leighton. 1923. *H. P. Blavatsky As I Knew Her*. Calcutta: Thacker, Spink. Selections 19c, 20a, 22b.

"A Coming Buddhist Book. 'The Veil of Isis' and the Lady Who Is Writing It—A Double Attack upon Science and Dogmatic Theology." 1877. *World* (New York) 17 (January 23): 5. Selection 7a.

Conway, Moncure D. 1884. "The Theosophists." *Religio-Philosophical Journal* (Chicago, IL), May 10, p. 1. Selection 14c.

Corson, Eugene Rollin, ed. 1929. *Some Unpublished Letters of Helena Petrovna Blavatsky*. London: Rider & Co. Selection 5c.

Coulomb, Emma. 1884. *Some Account of My Intercourse with Madame Blavatsky from 1872 to 1884, with Additional Letters and a Full Explanation of the Most Marvellous Theosophical Phenomena*. Madras, India: Higginbotham and Co.; reprint London: Published for the Proprietors of the "Madras Christian College Magazine" by Elliot Stock, 1885. Selections 3c, 13d.

Dharmapala, Anagarika. 1927. "On the Eightfold Path: Memories of an Interpreter of Buddhism to the Present-Day World." *Asia* (New York), September 1927, pp. 720–7, 769–70. Selection 9d.

Eek, Sven, and Boris de Zirkoff. 1969. *William Quan Judge, 1851–1896: The Life of a Theosophical Pioneer and Some of His Outstanding Articles*. Wheaton, IL: Theosophical Publishing House.

Eglinton, William. 1882. "Spiritualism and Theosophy." *Light* (London) 2 (June 24): 301–2. Selection 11e.

———. 1886. "Mr. Eglinton and 'Koot Hoomi.'" Letter to the Editor. *Light* (London) 6 (January 30): 50–1. Selection 11e.

Fields, Rick. 1981. *How the Swans Came to the Lake: A Narrative History of Buddhism in America*. Boulder, CO: Shambhala.

Gauld, Alan. 1968. *The Founders of Psychical Research*. New York: Schocken Books.

Gomes, Michael. 1984–5. "The Coulomb Case, 1884–1984" *Theosophist* (Adyar, Madras, India) 106 (Dec. 1984, Jan. 1985, Feb. 1985): 95–102, 138–47, 178–86.

Gordon, Alice. 1882. "Instantaneous Transmission of Another Letter." *Psychic Notes* (Calcutta, India) 1 (March 30): 60–1. Selection 11f.

———. 1890. "Some Experiences of the Occult." *Light* (London) 10 (November 29): 575–7. Selection 10e.

Hanson, Virginia. 1980. *Masters and Men: The Human Story in The Mahatma Letters*. Wheaton, IL: Theosophical Publishing House.

Hartmann, Franz. 1884. "Phenomenal." Supplement to *Theosophist* 5 (April): 65. Selection 14e.

———. 1884. *Report of Observations Made during a Nine Months' Stay at the HeadQuarters of the Theosophical Society at Adyar (Madras), India.* Madras, India: Printed at the Scottish Press by Graves, Cookson, and Co. Selection 14e.

Hastings, Beatrice. 1934. *Defence of Madame Blavatsky.* Vol. 2: *The "Coulomb Pamphlet."* Worthing, England: Beatrice Hastings.

———. 1943–4. *Solovyoff's Fraud.* Reprint Edmonton, Alberta, Canada: Edmonton Lodge of the Theosophical Society in Canada, 1988. Orig. pub. serially. Selection 16c.

Hodgson, Richard. 1885. "Account of Personal Investigations in India, and Discussion of the Authorship of the 'Koot Hoomi' Letters." *Proceedings of the Society for Psychical Research* (London) 3:207–380. Selection 16i.

Holloway, Laura C. 1889. "Blavatsky's Mesmerism." *Current Literature* (New York) 1 (March): 243–4. Selection 16d.

Holt, Elizabeth G. K. 1931. "A Reminiscence of H. P. Blavatsky in 1873." *Theosophist* 53 (December): 257–66. Selection 4b.

"H. P. Blavatsky's Adieux: The Ci-Devant Countess Ready to Depart for the East." 1878. *Daily Graphic* (New York), December 10, p. 266. Selection 7g.

HPB: In Memory of Helena Petrovna Blavatsky. 1891. By some of her pupils. London: Theosophical Publishing Society. Selections 7d, 15f, 16f, 16h, 18a, 19b, 21c, 21e, 22f, 22g.

Hume, A. O. 1882. *Hints on Esoteric Theosophy, No. 1: Is Theosophy a Delusion? Do the Brothers Exist?* 2d ed. Calcutta, India: Calcutta Central Press. Selections 8d, 11a, 11d.

Jinarajadasa, C., ed. 1977. *Letters from The Masters of the Wisdom, Second Series.* Adyar, Madras, India: Theosophical Publishing House. Selection 3a.

Johnston, Charles. 1900. "Helena Petrovna Blavatsky." *Theosophical Forum* (New York) 5–6 (Apr.–Jul.). Reprint in Blavatsky, *Collected Writings* 8:392–409. Selection 18e.

———. 1907. "The Theosophical Movement." *Theosophical Quarterly* (New York) 5 (July): 16–26. Selection 17a.

Judge, William Q. 1889. "Blavatsky Still Lives and Theosophy Is in a Flourishing Condition." *New York Times*, January 6, p. 10. Reprint in Judge, *Echoes of the Orient: The Writings of William Quan Judge*, comp. Dara Eklund, 3:138–43. Selection 20b.

———. 1890. "The Headquarters at Adyar." *Path* (New York) 5 (April): 8. Reprint in Judge, *Echoes of the Orient: The Writings of William Quan Judge*, comp. Dara Eklund, 1:131. Selection 13b.

———. 1892. "Habitations of H.P.B." *Path* (New York) 7 (June): 71–75. Reprint in Judge, *Echoes of the Orient: The Writings of William Quan Judge*, comp. Dara Eklund, 1:245–9. Selection 13b.

———. 1912. "Extracts from Letters Written by William Q. Judge from Paris to a Long-time Friend." *Word* (New York) 15 (April): 17–24. Selection 15a.

———. 1975, 1980, 1987, 1993. *Echoes of the Orient: The Writings of William Quan Judge*. Comp. Dara Eklund. 4 vols. San Diego, CA: Point Loma Publications. Selections 13b, 15a, 15d, 20b.

Keightley, Archibald. 1892. "From Ostende to London." *Path* (New York) 7 (November): 245–8. Selection 18b.

———. 1910. "Reminiscences of H. P. Blavatsky." *Theosophical Quarterly* (New York) 8 (October): 109–22. Selections 15c, 19a.

Keightley, Bertram. 1931. *Reminiscences of H.P.B.* Adyar, Madras, India: Theosophical Publishing House. Selection 19e, 20e.

Kingsland, William. 1928. *The Real H. P. Blavatsky: A Study in Theosophy, and a Memoir of a Great Soul*. London: John M. Watkins. Selection 19f.

Kislingbury, Emily. 1877. "Spiritualism in America." *Spiritualist Newspaper* (London) 11 (December 14): 277–9. Selection 7d.

Langford, Laura C. 1912. "The Mahatmas and Their Instruments." *Word* (New York) 15 (July): 200–6. Selection 15g.

Lazenby, Charles. 1910. "Isis Unveiled." *Path* (Hale, England) 1 (July): 9. Selection 5d.

Leadbeater, C. W. 1948. *How Theosophy Came to Me*. Adyar, Madras, India: Theosophical Publishing House. 1st ed. 1930. Selections 16e, 16g.

Linton, George E., and Virginia Hanson, eds. 1988. *Readers' Guide to the Mahatma Letters to A. P. Sinnett*. 2nd ed. Adyar, Madras, India: Theosophical Publishing House.

"Madame Blavatsky." 1891. *Tribune* (New York) May 10, p. 6. Selection 22j.

The Mahatma Letters to A. P. Sinnett from the Mahatmas M. & K. H. 1962. Transcribed and compiled by A. T. Barker. 3rd ed. by Christmas Humphreys and Elsie Benjamin. Adyar, Madras, India: Theosophical Publishing House.

Massey, Charles C. 1884. Quoted in "Mr. C. Reimers, Mrs. Hollis-Billing, and Madame Blavatsky." *Light* (London) 4 (August 30): 360. Selection 8a.

Mavalankar, Damodar K. 1883–4. "A Great Riddle Solved." *Theosophist* 5 (December-January): 61–2. Reprint in Mavalankar, *Damodar and the Pioneers of the Theosophical Movement*, comp. Sven Eek, 332–7. Adyar, Madras, India: Theosophical Publishing House, 1965. Selection 14b.

———. 1907. "Echoes from the Past." *Theosophist* 28 (May): 633–4. Reprint in Mavalankar, *Damodar and the Pioneers of the Theosophical Movement*, comp. Sven Eek, 307–9. Adyar, Madras, India: Theosophical Publishing House, 1965. Selection 13e.

———. 1965. *Damodar and the Pioneers of the Theosophical Movement*, comp. Sven Eek. Adyar, Madras, India: Theosophical Publishing House. Selections 9e, 9g, 13e, 14b.

Melton, J. Gordon, ed. 1996. *Encyclopedia of Occultism & Parapsychology*, 4th ed. 2 vols. Detroit, MI: Gale.

Michel, Peter. 1998. *Charles W. Leadbeater: Mit den Augen des Geistes*. Grafing, Germany: Aquamarin Verlag.

Murphet, Howard. 1988. *Yankee Beacon of Buddhist Light: Life of Col. Henry S. Olcott*. Wheaton, IL: Theosophical Publishing House. 1st ed. as *Hammer on the Mountain*, 1972.

Nethercot, Arthur H. 1960. *The First Five Lives of Annie Besant*. Chicago: University of Chicago Press.

———. 1963. *The Last Four Lives of Annie Besant.* Chicago: University of Chicago Press.

Olcott, Henry Steel. 1876. Letter to Stainton Moses and C. C. Massey, transcribed in the Francis G. Irwin and Herbert Irwin manuscript commonplace book, *Rosicrucian Miscellany* (1878), 68–79, United Grand Lodge of England Library, Freemason's Hall, London. Selection 6b.

———. 1890. "The First Leaf of T. S. History." *Theosophist* 12 (November): 65–70. Selection 6a.

———. 1895. *Old Diary Leaves: The True Story of the Theosophical Society.* Vol. 1 (1874–1878). New York: G. P. Putnam's Sons. Selections 4a, 4d, 4e, 6c, 7c.

———. 1896. *A Historical Retrospect—1875–1896—of the Theosophical Society.* Adyar, Madras, India: Theosophical Society. Selection 6a.

———. 1900. *Old Diary Leaves: The Only Authentic History of the Theosophical Society.* Vol. 2 (1878–1883). London: Theosophical Publishing Society. Selections 8b, 8d, 9b, 9c, 9f, 12a, 13f.

———. 1929. *Old Diary Leaves: The Only Authentic History of the Theosophical Society.* Vol. 3 (1883–1887). Adyar, Madras, India: Theosophical Publishing House. Selections 13f, 14a.

———. 1931. *Old Diary Leaves: The Only Authentic History of the Theosophical Society.* Vol. 4 (1887–1892). Adyar, Madras, India: Theosophical Publishing House. Selections 22a, 22h.

———. 1932. "Letters of H. S. Olcott to Francesca Arundale." *Theosophist* 53 (September): 727–35. Selection 16j.

Old, James Bernard. 1941. "Memories of H.P.B.—Over 50 Years Ago." *Theosophist* 63 (November): 107–10. Selection 21g.

Pashkov, Lydia A. de. 1878. Quoted in "Ghost Stories Galore: A Night of Many Wonders at Second Hand in the Eighth Avenue Lamasery." *World* (New York), April 21, p. 9. Selection 3d.

Pillai, R. Casava. 1885. "How a Hindu of Madras Interviewed a Mahatma at Sikkim." *Indian Mirror* (Calcutta) 25 (March 3): 2 and (March 7): 2. Selection 12b.

Prothero, Stephen. 1996. *The White Buddhist: The Asian Odyssey of Henry Steel Olcott.* Bloomington: Indiana University Press.

Pryse, James Morgan. 1935. "Memorabilia of H.P.B." *Canadian Theosophist* 16 (March 15): 1–5. Selection 22d.

Racowitza, Helene von. 1902. [Selected extracts translated into English from Racowitza's *Wie ich mein selbst fand* (1901).] *Theosophical Review* (London) 29 (January): 386–8. Selection 7f.

Rajamiengar, T. C. 1884. "Theosophy." *Indian Mirror* (Calcutta) 24 (September 30): 2. Selection 13g.

Ramaswamier, S. 1882. "How a 'Chela' Found His Guru." *Theosophist* 4 (December): 67–9. Selection 12d.

Roy, Parbati Churn. 1896. *From Hinduism to Hinduism*. Calcutta, India: Printed by W. Newman. Selection 12c.

Russell, Edmund. 1918. "Isis Unveiled: Personal Recollections of Madame Blavatsky." *Occult Review* (London) November, pp. 260–9. Selection 20f.

Saxon, Elizabeth L. 1877. "Madam Blavatsky: Her Opinions and Her Book." *Daily Picayune*, (New Orleans, Louisiana), November 4, p. 2. Selection 7e.

Sen, Norendra Nath. 1882. "Theosophy in Calcutta." *Indian Mirror* (Calcutta) 22 (April 14): 2. Selection 11g.

Shearman, Hugh. 1980. *Charles Webster Leadbeater: A Biography*. London: St. Alban.

Sidgwick, Arthur, and Eleanor M. Sidgwick. 1906. *Henry Sidgwick: A Memoir*. By A.S. and E.M.S. London: Macmillan. Selection 15h.

"Silence in the Lamasery: Madame Blavatsky and the Hierophant Off for India." 1878. *Sun* (New York), December 19, p. 1. Selection 7h.

Sinnett, A. P. 1881. *The Occult World*. London: Trubner. Selections 8f, 10a, 10b, 10c, 10d.

———., ed. 1886. *Incidents in the Life of Madame Blavatsky, Compiled from Information Supplied by her Relatives and Friends*. London: George Redway. Reprint New York: Arno Press, 1976. Selections 1a, 1b, 1c, 1d, 2b, 2c, 2d, 3b, 5a, 8f, 11c, 13a, 15e, 16b, 17b.

———. 1922. *The Early Days of Theosophy in Europe*. London: Theosophical Publishing House. Selections 15b, 17b.

Stead, William T., 1891. "Madame Blavatsky." *Review of Reviews* (London) 3 (June): 548–50. Selection 21a.

———., ed. 1909. *The M. P. for Russia: Reminiscences and Correspondence of Madame Olga Novikoff.* London: Andrew Melrose. Selection 21a.

Theosophical Society. 1885. *Report of the Result of an Investigation into the Charges against Madame Blavatsky Brought by the Missionaries of the Scottish Free Church of Madras, and Examined by a Committee Appointed for that Purpose by the General Council of the Theosophical Society.* Madras, India: Theosophical Society, 1885. Selections 3a, 11b, 14d.

"Theosophic Thaumaturgy—A Startling Story (Communicated)." 1879. *Bombay Gazette*, March 31, p. 3. Selection 8e.

"Theosophy and Theosophists: An Interview with Madame Blavatsky and an Evening with the Brethren." 1888. *Star* (London) December 18, p. 7. Selection 20c.

Tillett, Gregory. 1982. *The Elder Brother: A Biography of Charles Webster Leadbeater.* London: Routledge & Kegan Paul.

Tingley, Katherine, ed. 1921. *Helena Petrovna Blavatsky: Foundress of the Original Theosophical Society in New York, 1875.* Point Loma, CA: The Woman's International Theosophical League. Selections 19d, 20d.

Tweedale, Violet. 1919. *Ghosts I Have Seen and Other Psychic Experiences.* New York: Frederick A. Stokes. Selection 20g.

"A Visit to Madame Blavatsky." 1889. *Commercial Gazette* (Cincinnati, Ohio) October 13, p. 3. Selection 21f.

"Voyage with Mme. Blavatsky: The Summary Manner in Which She Silenced a Skeptical First Officer." 1891. *Philadelphia Inquirer*, May 11, p. 5. Reprint in *Canadian Theosophist* 70 (January-February 1990): 121–3. Selection 9a.

Wachtmeister, Constance. 1893. *Reminiscences of H. P. Blavatsky and the Secret Doctrine.* London: Theosophical Publishing Society. 2nd ed., Wheaton, IL: Theosophical Publishing House, 1976. Selections 2a, 17c, 17d, 17e, 18a, 18c, 18d, 22i.

————. 1929. "Extracts from Countess Wachtmeister's Letters as to H.P.B.'s Last Days." *Theosophist* 50 (May): 124–5. Selection 22e.

Waterman, Adlai E. 1963. *Obituary: The "Hodgson Report" on Madame Blavatsky, 1885–1960.* Adyar, Madras, India: Theosophical Publishing House.

Wiggin, James H. 1875. "Rosicrucianism in New York," *Liberal Christian* (New York) 30 (September 4): 4. Selection 5b.

Wilder, Alexander. 1908. "How *Isis Unveiled* Was Written." *Word* 7 (May): 77–87. Selection 6d.

Windust, Esther. 1950. "Personal Reminiscences of H.P.B." *Eirenicon* (Hyde, Cheshire, England), no. 97 (Winter Solstice): 1–3. Reprint in *Canadian Theosophist* 32 (May 15, 1951): 33–5. (The *Canadian Theosophist* indicated this article was "written for . . . *Theosofische Beweging*, Rotterdam, in 1938.") Selection 22c.

Wolff, Hannah M. 1891. "Madame Blavatsky." *Two Worlds* (Manchester, England) 4 (December 11): 671–2. Selection 4c.

Wyld, George. 1903. *Notes of My Life.* London: Kegan, Paul, Trench, Trubner. Selection 8c.

Zhelihovsky, Vera P. de. 1894–5. "Helena Petrovna Blavatsky." *Lucifer* (London) 15–16 (November–April): 202–8, 273–9, 361–4, 469–77, 44–50, 99–108. Selections 1b, 2b, 3b.

Index

NOTE: Within an entry for the author of a selection, subentries are ordered as follows:
biographical note,
photograph, portrait, or sketch,
narratives (selections written by the author) ordered chronologically,
subjects ordered alphabetically.

A

𝒩

QUEST BOOKS

are published by

The Theosophical Society in America

Wheaton Illinois 60189–0270

a branch of a world fellowship,

a membership organization

dedicated to the promotion of the unity

of humanity and the encouragement of the study

of religion, philosophy, and science, to the end that

we may better understand ourselves and our place

in the universe. The Society stands for complete

freedom of individual search and belief.

For further information about its activities,

write, call 1–800–669–1571,

e-mail olcott@theosophia.org,

or consult its Web page:

http://www.theosophia.org

The Theosophical Publishing House
is aided by the generous support of
THE KERN FOUNDATION,
a trust established by Herbert A. Kern
and dedicated to Theosophical education.